After the Spring

After the Spring

Probation, Justice Reform, and Democratization from the Baltics to Beirut

Johannes Wheeldon

eleven
international publishing

Published, sold and distributed by Eleven International Publishing
P.O. Box 85576
2508 CG The Hague
The Netherlands
Tel.: +31 70 33 070 33
Fax: +31 70 33 070 30
e-mail: sales@budh.nl
www.elevenpub.com

Sold and distributed in USA and Canada
International Specialized Book Services
920 NE 58th Avenue, Suite 300
Portland, OR 97213-3786, USA
Tel.: 1-800-944-6190 (toll-free)
Fax: +1 503 280-8832
orders@isbs.com
www.isbs.com

Eleven International Publishing is an imprint of Boom uitgevers Den Haag.

ISBN: 978-94-90947-59-0

Printed in The Netherlands

Dedication

I would like to thank my friends and colleagues in Latvia and Canada without whom this work would be incomplete. I would also like to acknowledge my dearest Liz who continues to offer edits, ideas, and constant support even as I retreat, once again, into the office to write and try to make sense of the world around me.

Finally, I would like to dedicate this work to the late Dr. Elizabeth Elliott who encouraged me to do a PhD and to try to live up to the values I espouse. This book is also dedicated to our new addition, Ms. Margaret Elizabeth. May the lessons so carefully considered in these pages be more than words – I truly hope your Papa can practice what he preaches.

Acknowledgments

This work has been shaped by a number of colleagues at Dalhousie University, University of Durham, Simon Fraser University, George Mason University, and Washington State University. I would like to specifically thank my dissertation committee at Simon Fraser University whose advice, assistance, and calm assurances allowed me to keep my focus and produce what I hope is an original and useful contribution to the scholarship of law, development, and criminology.

I have been extremely lucky to meet and work with three very special people during my academic career to date. First, I would like to acknowledge Mr. Florian Bail, who has influenced my work since our first meeting more than fifteen years ago. His kindness, insight, and constant support has led me to where I am today. I would also like to extend a special thanks to Dr. Simon Verdun-Jones, who worked with me throughout my time at Simon Fraser University and offered sage advice and wise counsel. Finally, I would like to acknowledge Dr. Otto Marenin who has supported me to continue my research at Washington State University and whose international contributions on justice reform and democratization continue to inspire.

Few books are merely the result of the efforts of its author. In my case, John Zucchi and Maria Los offered early and integral support on this project. I am also in debt to Selma Hoedt and Mariska Duindam at Eleven International Publishing who assisted me to bring this project from a rough manuscript to a completed book. My work has also benefitted from the insights of Robert Canton, Ian Lankshear, Robert Lutes, Walid Madhoun, Mike Nellis, David Perry, Elizabeth Suiter, Robert Watts, Caleb Wheeldon, and my mother Linda Wheeldon. I would also like to thank two editors who helped me manage the creative destruction that often accompanies academic writing. My sincere thanks to David Antrobus and Julie Sutherland for making my prose read better than it would have otherwise and for insisting on the Oxford comma! Any errors remain my own. Finally, I would like to thank Henrik Ibsen for his reminder that:

> To live is to war with trolls in heart and soul.
> To write is to sit in judgment on oneself.

Glossary

ABA	American Bar Association
AUCC	Association of Universities and Colleges of Canada
CLCP	Canada Lithuania Corrections Project
CEE	Central and Eastern Europe
CIDA	Canadian International Development Agency
CIDA-INC	Canadian International Development Agency Industrial Cooperation Program
CSC	Correctional Services of Canada
DAC	Development Assistance Committee
DFAIT	Department of Foreign Affairs and International Trade
ECHR	European Convention on Human Rights
EU	European Union
FSU	Former Soviet Union
IDRC	International Development Research Council
IMF	International Monetary Fund
INTERPOL	International Criminal Police Organization
IRO	International Refugee Organization
LCJRP	Latvian Criminal Justice Reform Project
LIAPO	Lithuanian Social Rehabilitation Organization
LLRP	Latvian Legal Reform Program
LRCP	Legal Reform Capacity Project
MDG	Millennium Development Goals
MENA	Middle East and North Africa
NATO	North Atlantic Treaty Organization
NGO	Non Governmental Organization
ODA	Overseas Development Assistance
OECD	Organization for Economic Cooperation and Development
OSI	Open Society Institute
RBM	Results Based Management
ROL	Rule of Law
SIDA	Swedish International Development Agency
SPS	Latvian State Probation Service
UK	United Kingdom
UN	United Nations
UNDOC	United Nations Office for Drugs and Crime

UNDP	United Nations Development Program
UNICEF	United Nations Children's Fund
USSR	Union of Socialist Soviet Republics
VAK	Latvian Environmental Protection Club
VBTAC	State Agency for the Protection of Children
WTO	World Trade Organization

Foreword

I remember the smell ...

My consultant had stopped on the stairs and was trying to back out. "Keep going," I urged, quietly. It was too late to turn back now. I tried to control my irritation and contain the anger that threatened to erupt. I had not wanted to organize this tour. Based on previous experience, I knew that even the 'best prison in Latvia,' was not a place I wanted to spend any time. I had tried to put it off, made excuses, and hoped that my request would be forgotten or lost within the Ministry of Justice until it was too late. The consultant was adamant, though, and here we were.

The women prisoners were gaunt and pale. The cells were crowded and not everyone could stand when we entered. Those that did try kept their heads bent. Sad eyes peered over the bunks. I felt horrible – like a child touring a dilapidated zoo. The animals, though dirty and desperate, were made to present themselves. Our guide later identified the rusted bucket that hung on a nail as an emergency toilet. Judging from the smell, it was often the only option.

When we came out of the prison, it was raining. Relief washed over me and I tried to reconnect with the consultant who mere minutes ago I had been silently cursing. We were both quiet now – lost in our thoughts – as the van wound its way back to the city center.

There were days I was sure the project I was working on would offer real and meaningful alternatives to the kind of incarceration we had just witnessed. More often, though, I wondered what in the world I was doing here. I had no idea how to assist criminal justice reform or how to confront a system that seemed so reliant on punishment.

Ten years later, there is a question that still troubles me: Can reform be accomplished without imposing one set of beliefs and assumptions about justice on others?

Preface

Looking back, the confluence of events that brought me to the Baltics seems unlikely. It is useful to remember how events like these can influence and shape the direction of our lives. I arrived in Latvia on July 29, 2001 late on the evening of the Riga 800 celebration, the famous Latvian Song Festival that includes massive choirs and a huge outdoor concert. As I left customs, loaded down with the possessions I had managed to squeeze into my suitcases and hockey bags, Riga's remarkably modern airport was empty. I had taken my driver, Rolands, away from the celebrations and we passed the short trip to the city center in polite, but rather basic, English. I would find out later that Rolands, like many others in Latvia, spoke much better English after a drink or two. Driving by the large concrete apartment buildings, I had no idea what to make of my surroundings.

I was to serve as an Intern through the Canadian Department of Foreign Affairs and International Trade's Young International Internship Program, now known as the International Youth Internship Program. I had just finished my Masters in International Law at Durham University in the United Kingdom and was full to the brim with European history, international human rights law, and the promise of the European community. I had turned down an internship in the European Parliament after travelling to Brussels and realizing my basic bilingualism was no match for the European *stagiaires* who spoke 4 and 5 languages easily. Brussels was too much for me at the time – the dusty streets were full of other tourists, but I could not shake the sense that I was out of my league. The chance to return to Nova Scotia and do my training at Acadia University, mere minutes from my home, was too tempting to resist.

Through the program I had originally been scheduled to travel to Suriname. When on short notice officials there refused to host an intern, I somewhat dejectedly traded my sandals and sunscreen for boots and scarves. Within days, the program coordinator, Marsh Conley, informed me that I was the only intern heading to Europe and gave me a large package of documents to read before departing. He coaxed me with Latvian folk songs and told me tales of the USSR occupation and the challenges of independence. I had no idea of the opportunities I would have there. One rarely does. Once in Latvia, I was to stay on the fifth floor of an old building near the center of the city. The building had inconsistent heating, no hot water, and lacked a kitchen. In the apartment next door, devout nuns rested from their daily duties at a nearby hospice. Over the next few months whenever I passed them, I would be encouraged to come with them on Sunday to pray. I would politely make my excuses while thanking them for their kindness. Of course, I was as ignorant of this as I was of everything else that would take place as I walked my suitcases, guitar, and assorted baggage up the long and winding wooden staircase that first night. What I do recall is a strong sense of entitlement.

> *Five floors and no elevator? Sleep in this tiny room? What was that smell? Surely they didn't expect me to stay here. Didn't they know how educated, experienced, and important I was?*

No one knew of course – and moreover no one cared. Thank goodness. I humbly suggest: take the opportunity to leave your comfort zone, adjust to new and strange surroundings, and challenge yourself in a foreign country at least one time in your life. Whatever I do and wherever I end up, I hope I can work to support young people to travel. It is important to recognize that most of the world thinks very differently from those of us who have grown up firmly ensconced in our Western cocoon. It took me a few years to understand that my way of seeing the world is but one of many. I hope others can learn this before age and obligation rob them of the elasticity of youth.

The *Valsts Bērna tiesību aizsardzības centrs* or State Center for Children's Rights in Riga, Latvia had agreed to sponsor my internship. They gave me duties, found me accommodation, and provided me with office space and a computer. After a nearly sleepless first night in Latvia, I awoke early to a cold shower, and dressed for my first day at the office. The office manager Aldis came to meet me and we walked to a shop for a short, strong coffee and a sweet pastry. Aldis paid with a silver coin out of a small change purse. I recall thinking that this coffee experience was mostly for me – a gesture that I recognized as kind, but one whose significance I could not quite understand. I later learned that few Latvians, at least at that time, paid for coffee in a shop. *Why would you waste money on fancy filtered coffee when one could simply pour hot water over coffee grounds at the office?* While frugal, Latvians were not ungenerous. Gritty cowboy coffee was a feature of many meetings, workshops, and visits in Latvia. The only time during my years in Latvia in which coffee and cookies were not available during a meeting, the host apologized so many times, I began to feel bad that I had caused this embarrassment by showing up unannounced.

Aldis and I walked the 2 miles to the office along crowded streets. He pointed to the tram that for 20 centimes (50 cents), I could take anywhere in the city. On that day, the Latvians I saw walked quickly with their heads down with little interaction or even acknowledgment of those around them. We arrived at the office to great fanfare. I met the Director, a strong character I came to find out alternated between fits of rage and often more terrifying bouts of generosity. On that day, I was introduced around the office, desk by desk, until I had been introduced to the staff of 12. Everyone nodded politely and tried their English out on me – a few seemed to be stifling giggles and laughs. I was ecstatic – I was a hit. I was informed that one of my duties would be to start an English language course in the office. I nodded politely and was relieved when I was shown to my office and learned how to log in to my computer. As I sat down, I noticed my zipper was down. My face flushed as I put the giggles in context.

I soon discovered that I shared my office with another Canadian. Tawnia Sanford was not only from Nova Scotia, but had grown up in New Minas near my hometown. She preferred Russian techno pop to the BBC World Service, and overruled my news addiction whenever she was in the office – which luckily was not often. Tawnia had an amazing ability to bring people together and involve them in whatever she was working on – she was the first to teach me that with a cell phone and a computer I could work anywhere. She would share tidbits over conspiratorial coffees and was incredibly generous to me; she opened doors that would have otherwise remained closed. Within weeks I began to assist her while working on my internship duties, and thus began my international development education.

At that time, Tawnia was running the Legal Reform Capacity Project (LRCP) in Latvia. Funded by the Canadian International Development Agency (CIDA) and implemented by the Association of Universities and Colleges of Canada (AUCC), the project built on past reform efforts. That project, I learned, had offered funding and technical assistance for the development of various pilot projects for young offenders by modelling a range of alternatives in communities throughout Latvia. It had been an unqualified success. By 2001, these pilots were being presented to the Ministry of Justice as models for a national justice reform initiative. Over the next few months, I absorbed as much as I could, asked a million dumb questions, and watched how Tawnia interacted with partner agencies, local participants, and international trainers. In one of her most impressive feats, she brought together the three major development players in Latvia and through her efforts AUCC, UNDP, and the Soros Foundation began working together more cooperatively, co-funding activities, and sharing information. Some months later, it was she who encouraged me to consider staying on in Latvia to take over her role on the project when my internship ended. She was very persuasive.

Soon I was caught up in the strange world of international development, with its complications and confusions. I could not shake the sense that we were doing something that mattered but that no one understood – least of all the funder to whom one must report. It was the sum of my experiences with project participants, local experts, and international trainers that made my time bearable. I am in debt to the many consultants from Canada, the United States, and the United Kingdom who spent time with me over coffee and a beer or two. People with decades of experience in the field were fascinated by what was happening. I was just happy to have a front row seat. By discussing what they saw, what they thought, and what it meant, I soon discovered the project was on the cusp of success – and appeared to be fueling a national conversation about how best to institute these reforms. At the time, it seemed to me the goals were overly optimistic, and the monies provided through the project made possible meetings that would not have otherwise occurred. While during this period I began to see both the promise and the challenges of international development, looking back it was a blessing to be so wide-eyed, guileless, and curious.

In March of 2002 I was promoted. I wrapped up the LRCP as best I could and drafted a more detailed two-year extension. This third project was designed to build on past successes and support the Latvian Ministry of Justice to develop the State Probation Service (SPS). Within a year I had written a new project proposal to build on the successes of the past, been hired by AUCC, and was on my way to Ottawa to finalize the contract with CIDA.

I think we often overlook the power of the young and the eager. In Latvia it was clear a new generation was emerging and I was happy to be among many younger adults, learning alongside them. Although not Latvian myself, I tried to learn the language, to play Latvian folks songs on the guitar, and understand the social protocol of 'name days' and the role of flowers and gifts. My time in Latvia allowed me to meet an experienced group of international researchers, authors, and justice experts, and dedicated local community leaders. Working with each allowed me to frame my role in this endeavor in a way that gave me a sense of purpose, and my time there shaped me in ways I cannot easily untangle – although this book is one attempt. As an old Latvian proverb states: "as long as you live, you learn." This book is an attempt to understand what I learned in Latvia, and what it might mean for the Middle East and North Africa.

Table of Contents

Introduction

It is perhaps simplistic to compare the Arab uprisings in 2011 with the end of the Cold War in 1989. Yet similarities do exist. The economic hopelessness that often results from the arbitrary rule of autocratic regimes, and the repeated failure of political institutions to defend and promote basic human liberties are relevant in both cases. In 1989 in the Baltic States it was tens of thousands who linked arms from Lithuania to Estonia that led to the fall of the USSR. In 2011 those in the streets were spurred by the social media revolution through thousands of online networks. In both, committed activists were able to outmaneuver dictators who once seemed invincible. Today many are struggling to mimic the early successes in Tunisia, Egypt, and Libya as part of the "Arab Spring." Even where these uprisings have been initially successful, it is clear that there are many challenges to overcome if realities on the ground are ever to live up to the promise of freedom and democracy.

One such challenge will be related to the institutions of social control, and specifically the criminal justice system. It is this system that must balance the competing duties in a democracy to defend individual liberty and at the same time protect the collective safety of its citizens. It is also this system that has the potential everywhere in the world to become highly politicized and reliant upon practices that can too easily result in treatment that is cruel, degrading, and abhorrent. It does appear there is a new region of the world that is beginning the often slow, frustrating, and sometimes – successful expansion of the human rights project. This is a region that cannot be ignored. Yet on what basis might new sorts of interactions be promoted?

Law and development focuses on the relationship between law as an instrument and the promotion of economic development, democracy and human rights. In the past, scholars have focused perhaps too much on how laws can be used to advance economic stability and development in a country. Of growing interest is how the law and legal institutions can promote, support, and sustain human security through good governance. Comprising the traditions, institutions and processes that determine how power is exercised, governance is an important way to understand the connection between rulers, citizens and institutions. In a 2008 report by the United Nations Development Agency (UNDP) more than 4 billion people around the world were reported to live under dysfunctional governance regimes (UNDP, 2008).

Despite this recognition, it is easy to be cynical about international development of any sort. Accounts of systemic abuse and corruption have resulted in serious doubts about the role and utility of developmental in general, and in recent years public opinion has shifted away from supporting development initiatives. Critical scholars accuse development of amounting to international imperialism, driven either by craven national economic interests or naïve global impulses. This book presents a more optimistic account. While the assumptions of the past must always be critically evaluated, a fundamental assumption that informs my work is that multiple paths to reform exist. As such development is perhaps best seen as a process of constructive and collaborative interactions. It cannot succeed when it is externally planned, and proscriptively delivered. In this book, I argue that to be sustainable, it must be voluntary, truly participatory, and above all else pragmatic in its delivery. Instead of relying upon outdated solutions such as simply changing old laws or drafting new ones, legal technical assistance must find ways to support the development of formal tools while increasingly focus on building the human capacity required to utilize and adapt those tools.

States that lack effective, transparent and accountable institutions have several options to bring about structural reform in line with international norms and standards. They may seek to implement reforms themselves through international financial aid or may have norms, standards and administrative structures imposed on them by occupation or through external pressure. Of particular interest, however, is a third 'collaborative' approach to governance reform through international legal technical assistance projects and programs. Since the late 1980s the Canadian International Development Agency (CIDA) has pursued international programming focusing on the justice systems of developing nations. While these systems are important in the determination of whether people will be denied life or liberty, they also mediate between the competing interests of individual rights and collective public safety. As such, it is often through the mechanisms of justice that people define their relationship with the state and other communities. In Canada, as in other donor countries, legal technical assistance initiatives have been used to support the promotion of human rights, democracy and good governance.

The Latvian Legal Reform Program (LLRP) is an example of a 'collaborative' governance project that CIDA funded in the Baltic States. Initial programming in 1999 was designed to assist in reforming appellate courts and the prosecution system. By 2000 it was refocused on juvenile justice reform in response to the high incarceration rates of Latvian youth in conflict with the law. Encouraged by Canada's Latvian diaspora, the project grew first to support a series of pilot projects intended to develop community-based alternative programs for youth. Its success at the local level resulted in a one-year extension in 2001. During this period, guided by the experience of past pilot project directors, the Ministry of Justice formed the Probation working group and passed a series of legislative amendments that would enshrine Probation in law (AUCC, 2005). Based on these new developments, CIDA funded a final two-year extension to coincide with the "graduation" of its Baltic program. Between 2002 and 2004, this extension offered targeted legislative support, institutional capacity development and human resources training to the Latvian Ministry of Justice as it developed Latvia's first Probation service.

Programming included technical assistance through study visits to Canada, job shadowing in Canada and training seminars and capacity development activities in Latvia. These were provided by probation officers, probation trainers, and senior Canadian officials from both Provincial and Federal justice agencies. For less than a million dollars over five (5) years, the LLRP succeeded where so many justice reform projects have failed. It is identified as an example of successful Canadian programming in the region, based on the establishment of the State Probation Service (SPS) in 2003. Probation was successful in Latvia in part because it offered a means to reduce incarceration rates while retaining a state role in the control of offenders. Through the supervisory role played by probation officers throughout Latvia, offenders are out of internationally condemned jails and increasingly involved in a variety of community-based rehabilitation programs. By identifying reform leaders in local communities, supporting their efforts to develop local services, and promoting new forms of local and regional participation, this project offers an important exemplar of how collaborative justice reform initiatives can be designed and delivered.

After two decades of focusing on justice reform in the Former Soviet Union (FSU), it is essential that lessons are learned and models of international collaboration be proposed, investigated, revised, and improved. At issue are the past failures to properly account for the multitude of ways in which political culture, legal traditions, and societal attitudes create contextual impediments to reform. This cannot be limited to simply exporting one nation's approach to probation to another. Instead, international justice projects can facilitate dialogue, debate, and deliberation among host country participants about the role and proper mix of punitive and rehabilitative approaches to criminal justice. While the success of the Latvian project is important, the lessons and challenges encountered through this process may offer valuable insight for future initiatives far beyond the FSU.

It is through the mechanisms of justice that people often define their relationship with the state and other communities, all of which incur local contextual, organizational, and individual complications and constraints. Only by considering how these elements, separately and together, impact a project can the development community get a better sense of what works. Based on the proposed three-tier model of international interactions, this book tells three stories. The first considers the contextual challenges inherent in any justice reform endeavor. This may include the challenge faced by international donors in a time of economic austerity and growing doubts about the role and utility of international development. In Canada, international commitments, inter-departmental strife, and reduced public support for development have constrained strategic and evidence-based approaches to aid. These are challenges faced by a number of donor countries and too often undermine the important potential for development assistance to spur broader international interactions. Of course, contextual challenges also exist within countries seeking to reform their institutions. In Latvia, and other countries of the FSU, a politicized history of occupation and state surveillance hampered reform efforts and resulted in a number of additional organizational challenges and individual impediments. In the countries of the Middle East and North Africa (MENA), it may be the role of rehabilitation within traditional and more modern approaches to Islam that presents the most difficult challenge for future justice reform initiatives.

The second story is about how Latvia overcame some of the legacies of occupation including the organizational challenges that resulted from the upheaval following independence. One challenge was the impact of broad social disorganization on the development of community-based intermediate sanctions and volunteer-based rehabilitative programs. In Latvia, reform can be traced to the efforts of a small group of individuals based in eight Latvian communities who partnered with international justice practitioners to offer alternatives for youth in conflict with the law. Over two years, the success of these pilot projects formed the basis for a series of systemic reforms that resulted in new laws and polices throughout Latvia. Since the establishment of the SPS, the service has expanded in both personnel and programs. It has also created a new means of social control, reducing incarceration rates and promoting community based services including prevention programs, social rehabilitation treatment and post prison release. This 'trial and error' approach offers a means to involve more people in the development and delivery of justice at the community-level, and potentially democratize public policy in practical ways. For countries emerging from autocratic regimes in MENA and beyond, it is how local and participatory processes are supported that may be a precursor to meaningful democratic reform.

The third story revolves around the process by which those involved in the project interacted. It concerns the process of engagement and the attempts to overcome and mitigate the individual impediments to reform that result from the contextual constraints and organizational challenges. While justice reform projects have historically focused on formal top-down and hierarchical approaches, the results of this project suggest that to fully engage with the criminal justice system in transition countries, one must consider how the norms, values, and assumptions that inform these societies impact efforts to reach the individuals who will ultimately sustain justice reform over the long term. In Latvia, legal technical assistance served as a means to explore new power relations and model more inclusive and participatory approaches to training and education environments. This involved interactive training and experiential learning processes and had to contend with individuals who were educated using an authoritative learning style that focused on memorization over extrapolation. The role of education practices modeled through international development initiatives should not be underestimated.

Based on these stories, this book argues that these approaches have significant import for other countries emerging from undemocratic, centralized, and top-down command and control style regimes. By supporting community-based models and pilot projects based on locally identified needs, country relevant reform can emerge. In the place of arrogant and hierarchical training models that focus on rote memorization instead of critical thinking, more interactive and experiential models can provide a means to establish personal relationships and integrate individual experiences. In this way democracy can be encouraged through broad-based discussions, disagreement, and authentic dialogue on issues of common and very practical concern.

Beyond the traditional narrative reporting and critical analysis that is the hallmark of many other scholarly attempts, this book relies upon three additional techniques or perhaps conceits. The first is the use of concept maps and mind maps to visually present additional information throughout the book. This visual presentation of data offers another means to "see" how the project operated and how various challenges were identified and in some cases overcome. In chapter 3, visual maps are presented as an innovative means to collect data in international settings because they offer a means to gather unique user-generated reflections to guide subsequent traditional data collection through interviews and focus groups. In the first intermission, the maps also serve to showcase how Canadian trainers and Latvian participants viewed the project on their own terms and in their own words.

Another technique employed is the use of personal reflections in the preface, two intermissions, and the epilogue. While perhaps not to every readers taste, these reflections are a reminder of the many roles the author played through this project. Although some may try valiantly to separate their academic endeavors from their personal beliefs, in some cases this is impossible. These reflections are an attempt to embrace reflexivity, and acknowledge how the project shaped and was shaped by the author's own participation.

The final mechanism employed through this book is inspired by the critical, skeptical, and even cynical views of many who work in development and who write about reform in the Former Soviet Union (FSU). While this book presents a more optimistic account of development than is often the case, chapters 4, 5, and 6 include recent and more critical accounts that have emerged regarding the Latvian project. Some suggest Probation in Latvia is a product of just the latest "occupation" of Latvia by the European Union (EU) based on the power imbalances that resulted from regional and international pressures. Others charge that probation is an euphemistic attempt to expand covert state control, and view the local Latvian adaptation of international models as merely the insecure adoption of an approach that few understand, by a country desperate for regional respect and recognition. By acknowledging the strongest criticism and concerns, the book seeks a detailed examination and resists simplistic conclusions.

Despite the inclusion of more critical voices and views, overall this book argues that probation projects may be an especially valuable tool to engage in the cross-national exchange of experience. Existing on a wide continuum and in different forms, probation offers governments a means to adhere to international standards, while providing new roles for community-based alternatives to prison within the existing justice system. In this way probation may offer the most practical way to support community based rehabilitation efforts and democratize social control in developing and transition countries. At the very least, through the kinds of interactions international development affords, these projects can serve as a unique site for debate and deliberation about the role of law and society. By giving a voice to those who actually participate in international projects, this book presents narrative accounts as a complementary approach to empirical data gathering.

Finally, and of perhaps most value, is the presentation of the three-tier model of project analysis to outline how contextual, organizational, and individual challenges operate separately and together to influence a project's success. This model may serve as a means to expand discussions of what an evidence-based development policy would require, and how it ought to be challenged, contested, revised, and reformed. While the lessons of this book have been applied with some success to other countries of the Former Soviet Union (FSU), of perhaps more interest is how the model can be applied to other post authoritarian countries and regions and can guide the future provision of technical assistance in more meaningful ways.

Of specific interest in Chapter 7 are the countries of the Middle East and North Africa. While simplistic comparisons between 1989 and 2011 must be resisted, all justice systems are shaped both by the laws and administrative practices and the people and personalities who make these abstract concepts concrete. Better research designs and models, and accurate instruments to collect data can assist international efforts to advance justice reform in meaningful and country specific ways. The promise of probation from the Baltics to Beirut does not argue that probation represents a panacea for all the ills faced by countries with dysfunctional justice systems. Instead, it represents a practical place to start and a pragmatic pretext to begin a dialogue about where each country seeking justice reform should draw the line on the continuum between care and control. Perhaps the most important question is: who should get invited to that discussion?

1 Governance, Criminal Justice Reform, and Legal Technical Assistance

The importance of good governance for development and human security is not controversial and few doubt its importance as a way to understand how power is exercised within a state. Yet challenges exist when deciding how best to focus development dollars to reform dysfunctional governance structures. This chapter argues that governance can be usefully associated with the institutions of the criminal justice system. Indeed, a number of development initiatives have sought to influence these institutions through the provision of legal technical assistance. While the nature of this assistance has and will continue to change, this chapter argues these projects will remain a part of international development programming and serve as a useful platform from which to explore in more depth the formal and informal impediments to justice reform.

To do so, this chapter introduces the history of international development generally, and Canada's role more specifically. Globally, development agencies are often trapped between significant cross pressures and contradictory motives as they struggle to articulate a clear mission with stable and coherent policy priorities. Nevertheless, as this chapter will demonstrate Canadian programming in the Baltics represents a rare if incomplete success. For a fraction of the cost of many multi-million dollar development projects, project activities between 1999 and 2004 resulted in the establishment of the probation service in Latvia by the Ministry of Justice. Latvian-Canadian cooperation played a central role and these interactions may offer a counterpoint to simplistic charges that justice reform represents Western legal imperialism. Whatever the emergent interest in justice reform as a means to facilitate a dialogue about the role of law in society, justice reform must also serve more immediate goals. Probation offers a unique means with which to engage a variety of government, community, and justice sector actors. Development, however, has proved to be a complex endeavor, easily manipulated by those in both host and donor countries. The potential for probation within the existing aid architecture cannot be understood in a vacuum.

1.1 Development Assistance: History, Architecture, and Agendas

The Development Assistance Committee (DAC) of the Organization for Economic Cooperation and Development (OECD) defines Overseas Development Assistance (ODA) as resources to eligible recipients or multilateral institutions that are administered with the promotion of the economic development and welfare of developing countries as its main objective. Today, as part of an array of international institutions – the United Nations, the World Bank, the International Monetary Fund, among others – international aid remains tied to assumptions from the Enlightenment that rational initiatives can be used to achieve progress and can be applied universally (Rist, 2008). While development activities of one kind or another had long been funded by colonial powers in their overseas territories, the importance of assistance from rich, industrialized countries to poorer, developing countries took on a new meaning following the end of WWII. Based on the failure of the League of Nations to avert aggression leading up to WWI, the more robust construction of the 1945 UN Charter explicitly provided for assistance, cooperation, and coordination.

In the post-WWII era, this initially resulted in reconstruction and large-scale support for economic stability organized bi-laterally. It also led to the establishment of the Breton Woods system, and through additional institutions and programs for economic co-operation created under the United Nations (Führer, 1996). The approach that later emerged to economically assist countries on the periphery of the Communist Bloc was influenced by the past success of the Marshall Plan. Guided by the excessive optimism about the prospects for helping others through external assistance, differences in circumstances, histories, and socio-political context were largely ignored. The formal embrace of development as a world vision can be traced to a famous speech that President Truman gave at his inauguration in 1949. He proposed that the United States

> ...embark on a bold new program for making the benefits of our scientific advances and industrial progress available for the improvement and growth of underdeveloped areas. More than half the people of the world are living in conditions approaching misery. Their food is inadequate. They are victims of disease. Their economic life is primitive and stagnant. Their poverty is a handicap and a threat both to them and to more prosperous areas. For the first time in history, humanity possesses the knowledge and skill to relieve the suffering of these people.

Truman cast this project as a high-minded endeavor, and he argued for a program of development based on the concepts of "democratic fair-dealing." Pointing to the many positive outcomes resulting from channeling US resources to war-torn Europe, many Western leaders became convinced that this model, if applied elsewhere, would lead in turn to rapid development in other countries, too. Yet overcoming the complexity of colonization in Africa, Asia, and Latin America proved more difficult. Instead of meaningful development, many have argued development priorities were too closely tied to economic interests and served as either a means to economic neo-colonialism or as a bad case of tax-dollar waste premised on utopian ideals (McDonald, 1995).

As a part of the new mode of development that followed World War II, the new discourse made imperialism and market colonization based on western models a natural, universal, and profoundly enlightened way of perceiving the world (Rist, 2008). Through the lens of 'development,' the idea that economic improvement and the national interest were inextricably linked became conventional wisdom. Economic liberalization might be usefully seen in the context of the Cold War, in which the competition for markets and countries were a proxy for traditional military combat. Indeed, it is this feature of development in the post-Cold War era that may not be properly understood; economic advantage was not only a means to benefit important industries in donor countries, but expansion was a patriotic duty, tethered to what was presented as an existential battle for freedom and liberty. Figure 1.1 outlines the major eras of overseas development assistance as reported by the International Development Association (2007, p. 27).

Figure 1.1 Development Eras and Aid Architecture

In the post-Cold War era, the focus on economic development has been retained, even as aid practices continue to be criticized for failing to meet the real needs on the ground. Responding to these observations, the *Paris Declaration* represented the culmination of ten years of donor discussion on ways to improve aid effectiveness. An integral first step was the adoption of the United Nations Millennium Development Goals (MDGs) at the Millennium Summit in September 2000. A key tool in monitoring the implementation of the MGDs is the Poverty Reduction Strategy Papers (PRSPs), prepared by governments in low-income countries. These papers are prepared through participatory processes involving domestic stakeholders and external development partners, including the IMF and the World Bank. A PRSP describes the macroeconomic, structural, and social policies and development programs that a country will pursue over several years to promote broad-based growth and reduce poverty.

First initiated by the IMF and the World Bank in late 1999, this approach is an attempt to provide a comprehensive country-based strategy for poverty reduction. It aims to provide the crucial link between national public actions, donor support, and the development outcomes needed to meet the United Nations Millennium Development Goals (MDGs) – centered on halving poverty between 1990 and 2015. The *Paris Declaration* was signed in February 2005 by 91 donor and recipient countries, International Financial Institutions (IFIs), multilateral organizations, and civil society organizations; and was subsequently adopted by 22 donor countries at the Development Assistance Committee (DAC) of the Organization for Economic Cooperation and Development (OECD) in March 2005. As a mechanism designed to improve aid effectiveness and align development with the UN Millennium Development Goals, all donors have agreed to be evaluated against the commitments in the Declaration and the indicators of progress. Consequently, the Declaration will have a decisive influence on how international donors organize in the future. The EU, OECD, multilateral financing institutions, UN agencies, Canada, US, and several non-OECD countries, including Russia, India and China, alongside aid recipient countries, are signatories. The *Paris Declaration* reforms focus on five areas outlined in Figure 1.2.

Figure 1.2 Reforms Areas Outlined by Paris Declaration

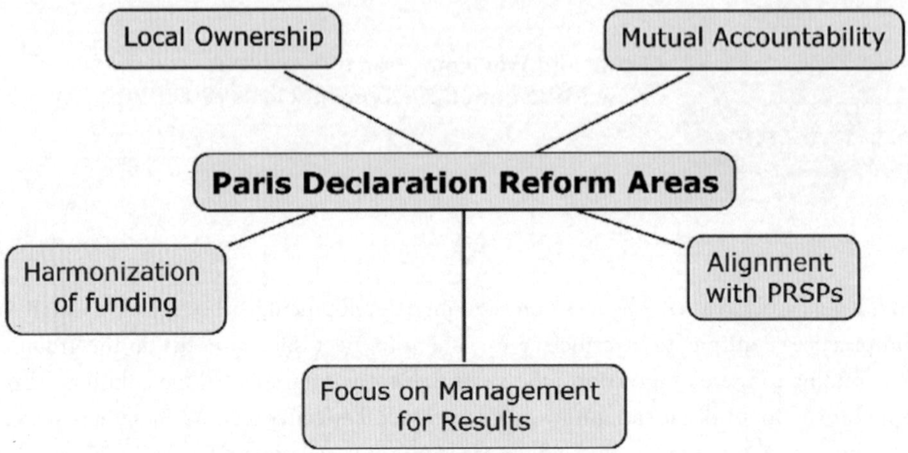

Immediate aims include: improving the understanding of complexity and the use of holistic approaches such as Program Based Approaches (PBA); increasing peer pressure of donors to untie aid and move towards a concerted approach led by recipient countries; and increased attention to aid effectiveness. To achieve this, the *Paris Declaration* calls for reducing tied aid by increasing the flow of funds directly to recipient countries to ensure development priorities are determined locally, and not by donors. It is argued that this must involve improvements in ownership, better alignment, increased harmonization, and a focus on managing for results by implementing the action plans previously developed (Wheeldon, 2006).

Despite the potential benefits of such worthy goals, critiques remain. The use of key terms such as participatory, ownership, locally relevant, and poverty reduction is part of what Rist (2008) suggests is the historic attempt to make development assistance appear more socially constructive. Whatever rhetorical flourishes are employed, the underlying assumptions of assistance remain tied to principles of "mainstream" economics and the acceptance that rabid individualism is the only valid conception of social relations. Too often, the reliance in economics is on what Rist (2008, p. 248) calls the "...vocabulary of mechanistic physics such as force, flux, equilibrium, balance, mass, elasticity... [to establish] ...laws comparable to those of nature." By seeking to naturalize social phenomena, they also might be said to normalize the notion of economic neo-colonialism, and rationalize the continued exploitation of 'developing' countries as ultimately being in their best long-term interests.

While many continue to hold the view that development is guided by neo-colonialist imperatives, others suggest the West suffers from naïve globalist impulses. On this view, the justification for international aid is based not on self-interest but on more altruistic motives which, incidentally, are no more likely to be achieved. Despite rampant cynicism, moving beyond assumptions that development is simply code for the internationalization of western models of capitalism allows other more intricate stories to be told. Smaller countries that seek to explicitly balance economic freedoms with social welfare internally often promote the idea that development assistance is a duty. While this idea forms part of nearly all development agencies and programs, it has perhaps been most evident in the Nordic countries of Sweden, Norway, and Finland, among others. Of immediate interest is the role of the Canadian International Development Association (CIDA).

1.1.1 A Brief History of Canadian Development

CIDA's mandate is to "support sustainable development in developing countries, in order to reduce poverty and to contribute to a more secure, equitable, and prosperous world" through Overseas Development Assistance (ODA).[1] Canada's first foray into foreign aid in 1950 was designed to prevent the expansion of Soviet influence in South Asia. As the

1 Retrieved from <www.acdi-cida.gc.ca/CIDAWEB/acdicida.nsf/En/NIC-5493749-HZK> on June 14, 2008.

Cold War became a geopolitical reality, development assistance provided a useful avenue for western involvement around the world. The *Colombo Plan for Cooperation and Economic Development* (1950) was established specifically to target South East Asia. While there was a general assumption that aid would be temporary, the Development Assistance Committee (DAC) was formed in 1960 as a small external aid office in the Department of External Affairs.

During the next two decades, Canada's program grew steadily, ebbing and flowing based on the personalities of the various men and women who have headed CIDA (Morrison, 1998). Morrison's "monumental work" of political science (Therien, 1999) serves as the lynchpin in understanding the complex and confused history of development assistance in Canada. Historically in Canada, as he points out, foreign aid has been an all-encompassing term. While appearing to suggest "philanthropic generosity" (Head, 1991) over the years, it has included everything from military weapons and massive public works projects to humanitarian relief and university scholarships (Morrison, 1998, p. 4).

Between 1950 and 1998, CIDA allocated more than 50 billion in development dollars, and Canada's commitment to human rights, democratic development, and good governance comprised 10% of Canadian development assistance (Cameron, 2006). Beginning in the early 1990s, CIDA faced a host of new challenges. The fall of the Berlin Wall, the end of South African apartheid, and a broader recognition of the stark challenges faced by developing countries suggested more Canadian development assistance was required. Yet during this period of fiscal austerity in Canada, CIDA was forced to cut programs and downsize significantly. In addition, CIDA became far more politicized as the independent role for the President of CIDA was reduced. While in the past, policies had been determined largely by the personalities at CIDA and senior policy makers (Morrison, 1998, p. 436), during this period CIDA was reconstituted and rebuilt based on priorities identified by the Liberal government of the day. Aid was shifted away from infrastructure and food and commodity aid, toward sustainability and private sector development (Black & Thiessen, 2007).

To respond to the developments in Eastern Europe, human rights, democracy, good governance, and peace building were prioritized. In 2004 – perhaps the high water mark – more than 2,000 Canadian experts worked overseas on technical assistance contracts providing training and advisory services to various government agencies in developing and transition countries.[2] This focus was justified through policy documents suggesting aid must support democratic development. Historically, the use of policy documents to influence aid policy in Canada has some pedigree. In 1970, Prime Minister Lester B.

2 In 2003/04, governance programming comprised 18% of CIDA's total Oversea Development Assistance (ODA) budget, or approximately $349 million. See <www.tbs-sct.gc.ca/est-pre/20032004/CIDA-ACDI/CIDA-ACDIr34_e.aspsann> retrieved April 22, 2007.

Pearson headed an international commission to examine the results of twenty years of development assistance and to propose policies for improvement. The final report, entitled *Partners in Development,* called for donor countries to each provide foreign aid equal to 0.7% of their Gross Domestic Product (GDP). Although Canada accepted this target in 1970, and has repeatedly reaffirmed this commitment, it has never met it. While personalities played a significant role in aid policy during CIDA's early years, policy documents since the early 1990s – especially those related to human rights and democratic development – have arguably had more influence.

In 1992, the *Challenge of Democratic Development: Sustaining Democratization in Developing Societies* argued for ODA to target democratic institution building and the promotion of political participation. Within CIDA, this shift was evident by the embrace of human rights prioritization in Canadian foreign policy. Development assistance was targeted at projects and programs that could build the essential components of a democratic regime, and the publication in 1995 of *Canada in the World* formally and specifically added the promotion of "human rights, democracy, and good governance "to CIDA's mandate (Cameron, 2006). Although never formally adopted by CIDA, *Canada Making a Difference in the World: A Policy Statement on Strengthening Aid Effectiveness* (2002) hinted at a new pressure on CIDA requiring more attention to sustainability in international development. Canada committed, along with other donors, to increase the cost-effectiveness of assistance by allowing developing countries to use development funds to buy programs and project services themselves.

Since that time and building on the international commitment to aid effectiveness through international donor cooperation in the *Paris Declaration* (2005), principles such as local ownership, greater partnership, donor harmonization, policy coherence, and aid outcomes have been prioritized (Brown, 2008). Canada's *International Policy Statement* (2005) also appears to promote domestic policy integration as well. As Cameron (2006) notes, this "whole-of-government" approach emphasizes the policy integration of the various departments involved in the international arena. Early incarnations of this policy were initially presented as the "3D approach" (diplomacy, defense and development) and then "3D+T" (three Ds plus trade). On one view, this integration has strengthened the role of economic interests through the Department of Foreign Affairs and International Trade's (DFAIT) renewed primacy in international policy at the expense of other development actors (Brown, 2008).

1.1.2 Motives, Interests and Doubts

While Canada's development priorities may have arisen as a result of broader East-West security concerns during the Cold War (Morrison, 1998, pp. 1-3), and been rooted in the "humane internationalism" promoted by Prime Minister Pearson, more recently, Canadian programming has been influenced by the Global War on Terror (Dandurand, 2006). A number of theories have been advanced to explain Canada's changing role in international development. Dominant class theory draws on Marxism and dependency theories to suggest that foreign aid fundamentally benefits the privileged classes in the North and South. This view suggests that development simply seeks to "…entrench western dominance by using development assistance to identify and secure raw materials, new markets and investment opportunities" (Carty & Smith, 1981, pp. 38-41). Laura McDonald (1995, p. 124), citing the influential Edward Said, argues Canada has learned from the UK a paternalistic view of the developing world, and suggests early development aid was being promoted with the fervor of early Christian missionaries, substituting the religion of free markets for the salvation of Christ.

Another view suggests development policy is best seen through a Statist analysis, in which the outcome is the result of the influence of competing actors within States. In this view, the State is not a unitary entity with a singular interest, but is instead comprised of a host of individualized interests that it mediates, exerting its influence only where a conflict exists. For Nossal (1998), State interests can be discerned through the trinity of prestige, organizational maintenance, and limited expenditure – in his words: "…the least Canada can do to maintain its international standing while maximizing prestige and spending as little as possible" (Nossal, 1989, p. 56). As Morrison points out, this theory does not provide much assistance in understanding the content or delivery modes of Canadian development (1998, p. 438). As an explanatory model, however, it is very useful in understanding the 1990 cuts in aid budgets (Black & Smith, 1993), the new focus on aid effectiveness, the continued maintenance of such a large headquarters staff despite decades of criticism, and the reorganization of Canadian development aid to target only twenty five countries.[3]

A recent and useful means with which to frame development assistance in Canada has been advanced by David Black and Rebecca Thiessen (2007), who argue CIDA is beset by significant "cross pressures" based on transnational, governmental, and state-societal interests. At the transnational level, this model provides a basis for critics to suggest that Canada, and the international community more generally, is promoting an institutional and state-based approach to development and undermining civil-society-development actors. By formalizing aid policies that are at best unproven and at worst of dubious value (Pratt, 2005), it is argued that the desire to reduce the transactional costs traditionally involved with international development has trumped the need for empirical study to

3 By 2010, Canada will direct two-thirds of aid toward 25 development partners. These include: Benin, Burkina Faso, Cameroon, Ethiopia, Ghana, Kenya, Malawi, Mali, Mozambique, Niger, Rwanda, Senegal, Tanzania, Zambia, Bolivia, Guyana, Honduras, Nicaragua, Bangladesh, Cambodia, Indonesia, Pakistan, Sri Lanka, Vietnam and Ukraine. See CIDA report <www.acdi-cida.gc.ca/CIDAWEB/acdicida.nsf/En/JER-324115437-MU7> retrieved June 27, 2008.

establish the utility of direct monetary transfers and budget support over more complex technical assistance packages (Pratt *et al.* 2006). Indeed, it may be that, without significant monitoring, direct monetary transfers may suffer from the very corruption development aid is meant to address.[4]

At the governmental level, others view the "whole of government approach" as the latest in a long-running turf war between CIDA and DFAIT (Brown, 2008). As Morrison has noted:

> ...every effort to enhance CIDA's autonomy... provoked a strong reaction, aimed at putting the Agency under the thumb of External/Foreign Affairs and harnessing aid more fully to commercial and foreign policy priorities (Morrison, 1998, p. 401).

With a fundamentally different philosophical approach to foreign aid, sustainable development priorities within CIDA may be forgone and replaced by DFAIT's mandate of "...advanc[ing] Canada's national interests... and...achiev[ing] increased economic opportunity and enhanced security for Canada and for Canadians" (Brown, 2008, p. 3).

Though appearing to retain elements of the 2005 *International Policy Statement,* Stephen Harper's Conservative government has provided, as yet, very little policy direction of its own on foreign aid – although there has been the suggestion that Harper's new mandate will refocus Canadian development policy to create more opportunities for the private sector. While this sector has long had a role in Canadian development initiatives through the Canadian International Development Assistance-Industrial Co-operation Program (CIDA-INC),[5] in recent years the Harper government has actively sought to provide a more robust role for private enterprise in the planning and delivery of international assistance (Berthiaume, 2008).

At the state societal level, Black and Thiessen (2007) focus on the role of civil society partnerships which have been traditionally important as part of cooperative development approaches. The importance of this role, however, may have been undermined by the *Paris Declaratio (2005)* that failed to explicitly include a specific role for civil society within the new framework of developmental consolidation. In addition to these pressures, another societal pressure originates from the Canadian public at large. Historically, the prevailing

4 For a broader discussion of the challenges represented by corruption, see Transparency International's 2005 Report retrieved August 14, 2006 from: <www.transparency.ca/Reports/CPI%202005%20PressKITfinal111005.pdf>.

5 CIDA-INC a cost-sharing program that provides a financial incentive to Canadian companies to start a business or provide training in developing countries or countries in transition to a market economy. See <www.acdi-cida.gc.ca/cidaweb/acdicida.nsf/En/JUD-1129121142-N6V> retrieved August 10, 2008. Reports of the Harper government's new drive toward private sector improvement in international development are based on interviews and private communication with former colleagues at CIDA and beyond.

motivation for Canadian foreign aid, as revealed in public-opinion surveys and in the statements of political leaders, is a humanitarian concern for the many millions of people who are obviously far poorer than most Canadians. Yet recent surveys suggest a "softening" in public opinion, due at least in part to a lack of information (Black & Thiessen, 2007, p. 189) or perhaps too much negative coverage.

While the explanatory "cross pressure" model reframes the challenges faced by CIDA, it might be said that many development agencies and international actors operate with mixed motives, combining both self-interest and altruism. On one view, development assistance is a tool of self-interest, designed to further donors' own political, commercial, and security interests as a "...weapon in the political armoury of the nation" (Morgenthau, 1962, p. 309). Another is that aid is an expression of international solidarity, and many believe it should be provided out of ethical concern and compassion (Morrison, 1998). Cranford Pratt (2000) characterizes these two visions as *international realism* and *humane internationalism*. Of course, it is not difficult to find examples of development initiatives that benefited the 'development jet set' or resulted in collusion among international elites at the expense of meaningful reform (Wedel, 1998). In Canada, among those who are committed to a humanitarian justification for foreign aid (Pratt, 2003), many view aid as too often serving corporate interests and the Canadian business community (Morrison, 1998). This view fails to account for programs and policies that do not result in beneficial trade deals, nor does it properly consider the aspects of development programming that have assisted hundreds of millions of people in developing countries to escape the abject poverty associated with living on less than $1.25 per day.

Perhaps the question is not whether development is a good or a bad thing in and of itself, but to what extent cross-national collaborations serve the interests of the many and not the few. Scholars might better ask who has benefited from development assistance in the past, how it can be refocused today to support average citizens instead of privileged elites. In short: how can the development community learn from past successes and failures and integrate this knowledge to guide future actions? Of specific interest to this book is the role of legal technical assistance to result in pragmatic and locally relevant outcomes, while creating the space required for governments, civil society, and communities to consider the role of law, justice, and punishment in their own societies.

1.2 From Law and Development to the Rule of Law

The law and development movement emerged as part of the United States' Cold War-inspired foreign aid programs. Yet it was based on historic precedent. From about 1880 to the Second World War, the United States sought to extend its political and economic influence through legal reform in China, the Philippines, Thailand, and elsewhere in Asia

(Goodnow, 1915). These attempts included efforts to remake and restructure constitutional law, criminal law, and even judicial processes. The Nuremberg trials in post-war Europe solidified the idea that western notions of justice could be employed to fill legal gaps, most notably the lack of legal remedies for the atrocities of Nazi Germany (Schnitzer, 2010). While debates continue about whether Nuremberg's legacy was of a civilizing influence or legalized vengeance (Blumenthal & McCormack, 2008), the exportation of western legal models continued the consolidation of Allied power in the new structures being built in war-torn Japan, and in other parts of Asia (Pound, 1942).

These legal models helped to bolster new constitutional orders, sought to reduce the absolute power of executive leaders, and in Europe appeared to promote democratic rights and stability. According to Karstedt (2005, p. 13):

> None of the contemporaries who witnessed the end of World War Two, and saw the sheer scale of European calamity, would have dared to predict that only a decade later Western European economies would be thriving, and a union amongst the former enemies would have been forged in the Western parts of the continent. If anything else, this unique European experience demonstrates that peace and reconciliation are possible, even after the most horrific atrocities and unspeakable injustices, and even after two wars that had cost the lives of millions of European citizens within the lifetime of one generation, leaving nearly no family unaffected.

The perceived successes of the Marshall plan in post-war Europe provided additional economic incentives for aid. Law was an important part of the financial reconstruction process in Europe, and many believed these successes could be easily reproduced elsewhere. The law and development movement that emerged in the 1960s first grew out of the interest of a small group of lawyers working within the international development assistance community (Trubeck, 2003). To spur economic growth, they advocated strengthening legal reform to address weak law enforcement and insufficient regulation, and engaged in a series of legal education, research projects, and scholarly writing on law in Africa, Asia, and Latin America during the 1960s and early 1970s (Mclnerney, 2004).

With hindsight, it is clear the early days of the movement embodied the ethnocentric, ahistoric assumption that the "modernization" of underdeveloped countries would approximate the pattern of American capitalist development. On this view, idealized forms of law were tacitly presumed to be central to all other forms of development (Gardner, 1980). Consequently, it encouraged underdeveloped countries to adopt ideas about law and to establish legal institutions and systems of legal education similar to those in the United States (Trubeck & Santos, 2006). Building sustainable enforcement mechanisms was difficult, of course, because the practices promoted by Western lawyers were often inappropriate to specific national contexts.

In addition, the focus on simply changing the rules also failed to consider various administrative deficiencies and the problem of corruption within developing countries (Carothers, 2003). Too often, the law on the books bore no resemblance to the law on the ground and new models sought to transform legal culture and institutions through educational reform and more rigorously selected models of governance within institutions. This view held that the most important thing to do was to create a new instrumental legal culture and promote the reform of legal education and the development of a new generation of lawyers (Trubeck, 2003).

While the focus on critical thinking and analytic problem solving offered a new means with which to engage those in developing countries, this approach was never properly investigated, and by the 1970s, the potential of development through legal reform was in doubt. New partnerships between donors, legal experts, and law schools sought to implement the lessons of the past just as support for projects focused on democracy building through social justice and human rights waned (Kennedy, 2003). Instead, the programs that did remain returned to a focus on making the legal system more effective and efficient in order to spur economic growth. In developing countries, as in the West, this period was marked by a widespread belief that economic growth would invariably lead to individual rights and democratic institutions (Fiss, 2001; Rittich, 2001).

Since the 1990s, law and development has made something of a comeback, albeit as a result of a different but related set of assumptions (Fukuyama, 1992). The fall of the Soviet Union led to a remarkable resurgence of law and development work involving a wide range of donor actors such as governments, multilateral and bilateral agencies, private funders, and NGOs, among others (Leys, 1996). Once again development assistance through ROL projects focused on the exporting laws at the root of the popular neo-liberal economic agenda. Through an over focus on the development of an open global economy with minimal state involvement, economic indicators have been prioritized at the expense of law's other functions (McInerney, 2004). This approach has been shown to be problematic, particularly in Eastern Europe (Wedel, 1998).

1.2.1 Governance and the Rule of Law

The focus on economic outputs belies a central assumption that informs questions surrounding governance. Various authors and organizations have produced a wide array of governance definitions. Some are broad, such as the definition offered by the World Bank in 2002: "rules, enforcement mechanisms, and organizations", while others are more specific. Kaufmann, Kraay, and Zoido-Lobatõn (1999, p. 1) suggest it comprises "the traditions and institutions by which authority in a country is exercised." This may include how governments are selected and/or replaced and how the government formulates and implements policies. CIDA, for example, defines governance as "...encompass[ing] the values, rules, institutions, and processes through which people and organizations attempt to work towards common objectives, make decisions, generate authority and legitimacy, and exercise power."[6]

A recent and related debate within development circles pits optimistic views about the role of foreign aid in providing a means to jump start economic development (Sachs, 2006) against more pessimistic accounts of waste and corruption that cost donor nations trillions (Easterly, 2006). In Sachs' view, economic development is a precursor to the sorts of institutions required for political stability and order. Thus, democratic institutions, instruments to protect minority rights, an independent judiciary, the free press, and transparent, accountable, and responsible governance structures all arise from economic development, not the other way round. Easterly, by contrast, contends that while development dollars can be useful, too often assumptions are made about how the money should be spent and the ability of institutions in developing countries to effectively manage these sums. Thus, without investing in governing institutions, subsequent investments may be simply throwing good development dollars after bad. Figure 1.3 explores some of these questions.

Figure 1.3 Rule of Law and Governance Priorities

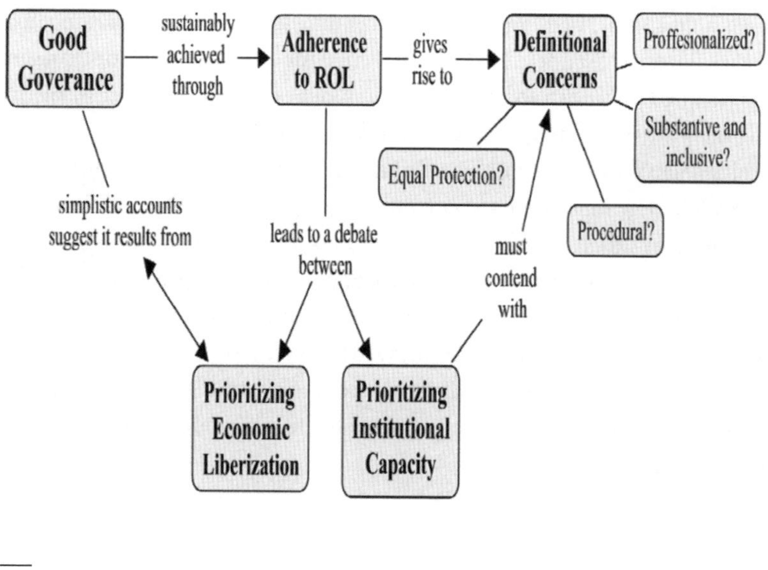

6 See CIDA <www.acdi-cida.gc.ca/CIDAWEB/acdicida.nsf/En/JUD-121132928-PPH> retrieved June 24, 2008.

Most definitions of "good" governance include an assumption that a state should be capable and democratically accountable, and should operate under the ROL. This focus, while useful in some ways, is conceptually difficult in others (Kaufman *et al.* 2005). A major aspect of modern governance (Sundstrom, 2005) and the basis for economic development, democracy, human rights, and international stability, the term 'rule of law' means many things to many people (Sklar, 1987). Tamanaha (2004) has identified three very different themes that have evolved from Ancient Greece to the present day. These might be usefully reframed as protective, procedural, and professional. The first can be traced to antiquity and is based on equality under the law for citizens and officials. In a broad sense, this means that all governments must abide by the laws and are restrained on how they make new laws or amend existent ones. Whether formally presented in a written constitution or informally outlined by customary law, this view of the rule of law *protects* against governmental tyranny, upholds the primacy of individual liberty, and is based on the notion that government exists for and is made up of the people.

The second theme is related to *procedural* developments in law developed in the 19th century. They include that laws be known in advance and have characteristics of generality, equality, and certainty. This view of law emphasizes stability and predictability and rejects personalized or politicized approaches to justice. Provided an individual has not been harmed, this view restricts the state from deciding what is and what is not consistent with living a 'good' life. This rejection of a strict moral basis for the rule of law represents a departure from ancient conceptions of politics articulated by Plato and Aristotle, who viewed the role of the state as cultivating virtuous citizens of good character and sentiment. While it has a substantial pedigree – from left-leaning liberals to right-leaning libertarians – it remains contested (Sandel, 2009). A challenge for cross-cultural comparisons is that if law is concerned only with formal legality, countries that do not necessarily have laws protecting individual rights may still claim to adhere to the ROL.

The third theme, more recently developed in the 20th century, attempts to make the application of the law more *professional* and less arbitrary. Relying on trained specialists who act as guardians of the law, this aspect involves the careful selection of impartial and independent experts who believe in a government of laws, the stability inherent in upholding general principles, and recognition of the responsibility inherent in attempting to balance individual liberty and community safety. While this view rejects personalized or politicized approaches to justice, it is also connected to the idea that the amount of discretion used by legal actors to interpret or apply the law should be reduced (Tamanaha, 2004). Figure 1.4 presents these themes.

Figure 1.4 Rule of Law Variants and Variance

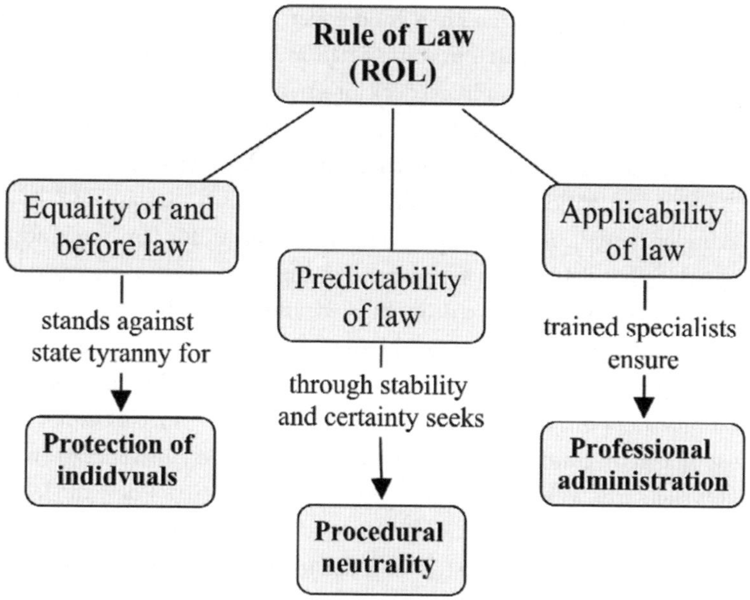

While historically useful, these themes fail to consider developments within legal systems that see law as an agent of social change. During the last few decades in the West, the law has undergone a shift away from a sole focus on formal rights protection into substantive rights promotion and social justice. While important, the protection of individuals against governmental excesses has evolved in recent years into the protection of minority rights against majority rule, especially through human and civil rights instruments (Roach, 1999). It might be said to include efforts to "...include rather than to exclude, to accept rather than to censor, to respect rather than to stigmatize, and to welcome rather than reject" (Wolfe, 2009, p. 19). At its core, this approach is open to change and sees the law as not fixed but the product of properly facilitated attempts at dialogue and deliberation. On this view, law is both a product and a cause of social change, and can provide a means for the resolution of competing value claims, and that through compromise, people can progress, improve, and advance. It is a social phenomenon.

> The wording, purpose and usage of law are, in this respect as in others, indistinguishable. Law is not the fount from which social acts spring, but is itself a social product, and by no means necessarily the most influential (Harris & Timms, 1993, p. 21).

Ironically, as Western societies increasingly professionalize and specialize within the justice system, thus reducing the number of actors involved, it is exactly the opposite that may offer the best opportunity to strengthen good governance abroad. This is an irony that cannot be ignored, and is revisited in some detail in Chapter 7. What is clear is that, as calls for greater participation in political decision-making increase, debates about the rule of law from its ancient roots re-emerge. From the writings of Plato and Aristotle and through the more detailed theoretical foundations established by Locke and Rousseau, questions about participation in the process of law and governance remain relevant today. One way to understand the role of law in society is based on a "thin" or "thick" formulation. The thin conception is deliberately narrow and means that government, in all its actions, is bound by formal rules that are fixed, announced, and predictable. A thicker conception includes more substantive components like equal protection, an independent judiciary, and due process protections, among others (Tamanaha, 2004). This definitional disparity allows for a broad endorsement of the concept from a wide range of donor agencies to government officials in countries not normally known for their adherence to even minimal human rights standards. While the ROL is a product of Western political and legal thought, the conceptual confusion that surrounds it is a result of tensions within the concept itself (Trebilcock & Daniels, 2008, pp. 12-13). This tension is presented in figure 1.5.

Figure 1.5 Rule of Law: Formal and Substantive Considerations

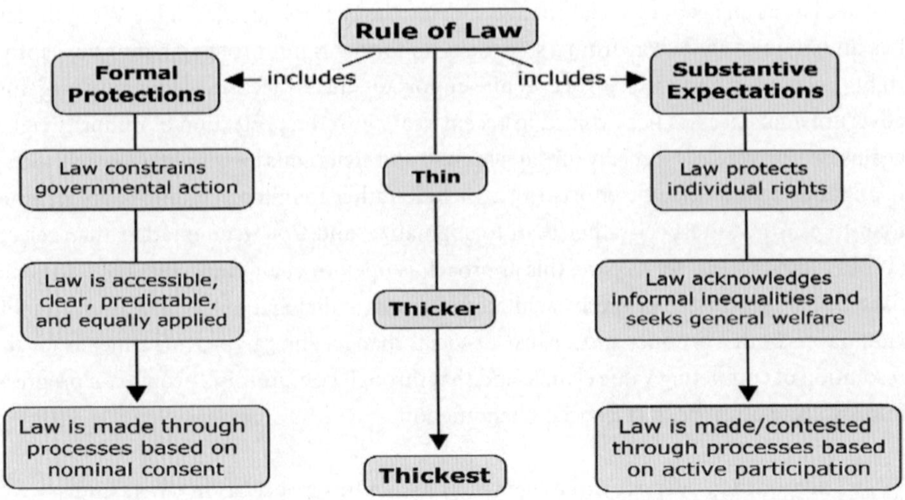

1.2.2 *The Challenge of Criminal Justice Reform*

If the expansion of actors participating in a dialogue about the role of law in society is an important trend in the promotion of human security and economic stability, where and how might this discussion occur? There may be no better place to start than development projects as the sites of interaction, and particularly those associated with building, rebuilding, and reforming national justice systems. This approach is both principled in its defense and promotion of human rights, and pragmatic given the different sorts of country-specific challenges about which Sachs and Easterly disagree. Whichever view of development one adheres to, there is a growing recognition that abusive police, corrupt officials, and inefficient legal systems undermine other kinds of developmental investments (Power, 2009).

Focusing on justice programming has additional benefits. The first is based on the belated recognition that a state's ability to maintain law and order is a precondition for economic advancement (Fukuyama, 2004). As the World Bank (2002, pp. 17-18) has reflectively noted, practical experience has suggested that reform efforts designed to simply shrink the state and liberalize and privatize the economies were misguided. Without paying sufficient attention to institutions generally, and the role of legal institutions specifically, economic development and poverty reduction is much more difficult to achieve. The second benefit is that it is through the justice system that tangible and sustainable results can be achieved that secure the protection of rights and promote social inclusion (Canton, 2009). By supporting social autonomy for marginalized regions, countries, and peoples, and by engaging the State on the processes required to accept new and existing forms of self-organization, people can begin to become involved in decisions that impact them (Rist, 2008). This requires new models and approaches to development that can better consider local, political, and cultural variance and facilitate new sorts of arrangements between individuals, communities, and the state (Chodosh, 2005).

Questions remain about how best to engage institutions within the justice system and how best to conceptualize the relationship between "law" and "development". The reliance on the formal structures of state has in the past resulted in enacting new laws, and while legislative reform may be integral to broader sustainable reform initiatives, few would argue that real reform is simply a matter of drafting and enacting new rules (Hendley, 1996). Indeed, new laws imported from elsewhere undermine sustainable solutions because they formalize rules about which there is no general agreement (Seidman & Seidman, 1996). An underexplored way to conceive of this challenge is to view justice reform projects as a means to develop democratic mechanisms that involve a greater segment of the population in decision-making about crime, law, and justice. It is this character of justice reform projects that may be of most interest. They offer a window into how decision-making about crime, law, and justice occurs in the developing and transition countries, and offer a way to identify and understand more ingrained challenges within these societies. These include public perceptions of crime, lack of civil liberties, racial or ethnic inequalities, poverty, and emergent concerns around justice and security (Karstedt, 2001; Seidman & Seidman, 1996).

1.2.3 Policy Transfer, Legal Technical Assistance, and the Promise of Probation

Whatever the potential for democratic discourse, engaging the justice system needs to meet practical and pragmatic local goals. The increasing professionalism and specialization of western justice, both real and as portrayed in popular culture, creates a market for 'developed' justice models. As discussed in Chapter 2, so too does the promise of the risk/needs responsivity (RNR) supervision model, which seeks to bring scientific precision and empirically validated approaches to the management of offenders. Borrowing ideas has a long and venerable history (Rose, 2005), and past research has located policy transfer as a conscious, goal oriented process and investigated the conditions under which policies are "transferable" from one state to another through a:

> ...process in which knowledge about policies, administrative arrangements, institutions, etc. in one time and/or place is used in the development of policies, administrative arrangements and institutions in another time or place (Dolowitz & Marsh, 1996, p. 344).

Legal technical assistance is a specific type of policy transfer, and may range from policy advice to assistance in drafting legislation to introducing, implementing, and enforcing new laws and regulations. It often includes devising procedures and developing or otherwise supporting institutions to carry out new laws and functions by working with the staff of those institutions to provide training and to build capacity and competence (Linn, 1999). As discussed above, the way one defines the ROL leads to the type of legal assistance offered. For Carothers (1998, pp. 97-98), whether projects focus on constitutional drafting, anti-corruption programs, or the promotion of judicial independence and accountability, or on more targeted institutional capacity-building to agencies of the justice system, this assistance must always consider governmental legitimacy and incorporate moral criteria in the form of the explicit and implicit inclusion of human rights.

The focus on the justice system might be justified on two grounds. Philosophically, justice systems must contemplate the complexity inherent in balancing individual rights, on the one hand, and collective public safety on the other. In more practical terms, without institutions with a stable and predicable track record, investments – economic or otherwise – are at an increased risk of being trapped by the institutional dysfunction that characterizes many developing and transition countries (UNDP, 2008). Within legal technical assistance, a variety of training tools and capacity development activities have been identified. They may include: manuals, handbooks, assessments and report templates, performance indicators and evaluation (Dandurand *et al.* 2008, pp. 56-65).

While formal organizational tools and training *products* are often a general feature of many legal technical assistance projects (UNODC, 2004), project success is also related to more individual elements such as the role of intercultural competence and relationship-building within development (Kealey *et al.* 2005). Based on emergent views within organizational and international development literature (Chodosh, 2005; Rogers, 2005), other "soft skills" include the development of procedures and training *processes* related to interview skills, client interaction, conflict resolution, facilitating community participation, inter-agency networking, and collective problem solving. While broader conceptions of the role of legal technical assistance have been articulated (Dandurand *et al.* 2008; Kaufman, 2003), few studies exist to guide the provision of legal technical assistance and the relationship between sharing tools versus developing processes (Wheeldon, 2011). Figure 1.6 explores this distinction.

Figure 1.6 Tools and Processes

As discussed above, of particular interest is whether legal technical assistance should target formal structures and existing state institutions (Kleinfeld, 2003; Steinmo *et al.* 1992; Thelen, 2003), pursue judicial reform (Hammergren, 2007), or focus on bottom-up approaches, local adaptation, and a broader engagement with communities (Chodosh,

2003; Jacoby, 2006). Probation may offer a means to engage all of the above. Operating at the intersection of a number of justice actors, probation often combines an institutional presence with connections and cooperation between and with communities. As discussed below, it combines aspects of both control and care. As an entry point to international justice reform, probation represents a means to tackle the formal processes of the state, and the informal processes of those who work within it. While common in many countries, it operates differently based on the histories, cultures, and legal systems in which it is located. Probation provides an institutional framework to support the twin goals of state supervision and offender reintegration. These services are usually understood as existing on a continuum between care and control and this dualism means that:

> Probation is an act of kindness offered as an opportunity for reformation, but containing in its fabric the possibility of overt punishment in the event of infraction (Harris, 1995, p. 8)

While probation practices vary, in general terms, probation involves the selection of suitable offenders who are supervised in the community based on the conditional suspension of a custodial punishment. Traditionally, the role of the probation officer has been to advise, assist, and befriend its clients. It should always be recalled that probation was established in strict opposition to the brutally punitive criminal justice system that preceded it (Whitehead & Statham, 2007). At that time, based on the old idiom 'love the sinner, hate the sin' (Morgan, 2007), probation operated under the assumption that offenders could be supported to live an offence-free lifestyle through rehabilitation and treatment.

Outlined in Chapter 2, from around the 1820s to the present day, probation officers have tried in various ways to reform, remake, and restructure the lives of offenders into good, honest, law-abiding citizens. It was only after the Second World War, however, that probation developed into the kind of service and structure that exists in many countries today. During this period, probation involved a variety of techniques commonly associated with social work. These included group work, community work, task-centered work, family therapy, behaviourial contracts, transactional analysis, reality therapy, behavior modification and social skills, to name a few. By the 1960s, this progressive approach to penal practice meant that probation:

> ...was the exemplar, the paradigm of the welfarist approach to dealing with crime and offenders. It emphasized rehabilitation, resettlement, individualized social case-work, re-integration – a social welfare approach to social problems. The problem of crime was understood as a problem of individuals and families in need of help and support, of communities that were disorganized and disadvantaged. The focus of attention was not the crime itself – the instant offence

> being a matter of mostly legal concern – but instead the personal and social problems that underlay criminal behavior. Crime was a presenting symptom, a trigger for intervention, rather than the focal point for the probation officer's action (Garland, 1997, p. 3).

Since the 1970s, probation has faced significant pressures. In the US, UK, and Canada, as the public mood shifted toward neo-conservative and punitive approaches to social problems, justice agencies increased their use of capture, monitor, and detect technologies (Haggerty, 2004). This compromised the notion that probation officers should try to keep individuals out of the criminal justice system and away from the damaging effects of prison. Instead, while public knowledge about crime and offenders has remained fairly limited, attitudes have hardened. Demands to "do something" about offenders who commit crimes of violence have led to mandatory consecutive sentences and mandatory minimum sentences (Campbell, 2000).

Part of the challenge faced by probation in the 1980s was also a function of probation practices that failed to meaningfully supervise clients. As caseloads grew and funding decreased, supervision increasingly was reduced to meetings by phone. In the 1990s, new technological developments have made drug testing a useful proxy for monitoring conditional sentences, and few programs existed or were used in such a way to meaningfully meet the needs of offenders (Dean-Myrda & Cullen, 1998). As the rehabilitative ideal has faded, probation has been forced to respond to a new era of 'public punitiveness' (Bottoms, 1995). Now focused on ensuring offender compliance through supervision and monitoring, control rather than care is favored, often at the expense of client welfare (Whitehead & Statham, 2007). Recent criminal justice policies are far more concerned with the administration and management of crime rather than in finding ways to diminish it (Schicor, 2000). Today, many probation services rely on risk-frameworks that attempt to categorize offenders, and design supervision strategies to manage them (Hacking, 1990). Where once relationships based on mutual respect were at the core of successful interventions through rehabilitation, some view these interactions as compulsory, non-negotiable forms of punishment (Morgan, 2007).

Despite these concerns, the potential for probation services and their increased importance in many justice systems has brought about new interest in best practices and dynamic innovations (Kalmthout & Durnescu, 2008). In Europe for example, the Council of Europe and the European Union are working toward a means to establish a common framework regarding conditional and suspended sentences, alternative sanctions, and probation measures (Canton, 2009). In the world of academia, there is more and more interest in the effectiveness of probation methods, including restorative principles, and investigating the underlying processes that lead to successful client outcomes (Hedderman & Hough, 2004; Vanstone & Priestley, 2008). Probation emerged in the 19th century based on philanthropy and was consolidated in the 20th century. The shift in focus from the offence and punishment to the offender and rehabilitation of the individual remains relevant as a part of broader justice reform projects. Of specific interest is the development of the State Probation Service (SPS) in Latvia. The culmination of five years of project activities, it represents Canada's most tangible and concrete result in the justice sector of the Former Soviet Union (FSU).

1.3 Latvian-Canadian Cooperation and Justice Reform Successes

Since 1991, Canada's involvement in the FSU has underscored a broader recognition of the challenges faced by transition and the process of societal restructuring. In many countries of the FSU, there was a need to reform the justice system in line with international standards, reduce crime, and meet public demands for safety and security (Joutsen, 1996). These challenges have been augmented by the history of Soviet occupation. A common feature in these countries was the reorganization of society through the state apparatus (Los, 2003), and the use of the justice system to enforce conformity with socialist ideology (Shelley, 1996). Discussed in more detail in Chapter 4, this history has impacted public confidence in the institutions of the state (Gestautaite, 2001), and created a widespread punishment-based mentality (Lauristin, 1997). As the social upheavals of transition resulted in higher crime rates, the lack of effective alternatives to imprisonment resulted in long periods of pre-trial detention periods, especially in cases involving juveniles (Asquith, 2002). In the 1990s, Latvia had one of the highest rates of per capita incarceration rates in Europe and housed inmates in crowded facilities, routinely identified as unsanitary, inhumane, and degrading.[7]

The recognition of the severity of the situation facing countries of the FSU re-invigorated ROL programming in the 1990s, and a number of governance projects were funded. While in financial terms, Canada's contribution to the FSU has been modest, in the past it relied upon partnerships with Canadian universities and scholars who often looked to academic literature to propose development models and acknowledge regional constraints. This scholarship, reviewed in some detail in Chapter 3, suggests that in the FSU, external actors can assist to expand the circle of interested reformers and deter opponents of reform but need to focus on developing local solutions before attempting national reforms (Jacoby, 2006). Important critiques remain. In a seminal study reviewing Western aid to Eastern Europe in the 1990s, Janine Wedel (2001) highlights the political character of aid and cynically presents Western aid as an essentially useless waste of money, with few tangible outcomes. Others argue projects of this kind too often serve the economic, political and

7 See Latvian Centre of Human Rights Report retrieved from <www.ihf-hr.org/viewbinary/viewhtml.php?doc_id=4392> on March 18, 2009.

social interests of the donor countries involved (Cohen, 1985; Gardner, 1980; Igbinovia, 1989).

While the mistakes of the past ought not to be overlooked or ignored, there is a tendency to focus on failures and to present development initiatives in simplistic terms. This often fails to acknowledge that the role of sharing expertise is not based on a simplistic dichotomy between expert and learner. Indeed, the view that personnel in developing and transition countries as empty vessels, easily programmed using western models is perhaps just as pejorative – albeit in a different way. It also fails to account for the day-to-day practices that may affect issues of legal regulation through the existence of and interactions between different sorts of 'hybrid knowledges' (Valverde, 2003). Arguably, it is the lack of this on-the-ground understanding that has stymied reform efforts of the past (Carothers, 2003). Perhaps more attention ought to be paid to the opinions of those that actually provided, received, and participated in these projects. These views can guide new sorts of participation, deliberation, and experimentation in development assistance (Wheeldon, 2010).

Since 1991, Canada-funded projects – worth a combined $54.9 million – numbered more than 250 in the Baltic states of Estonia, Latvia, and Lithuania. Although without a distinct country program-development framework during the early years of the program, CIDA produced its first policy document relating specifically to this region in 1996. It outlined three broad objectives: to promote democratic development, support the transition to a market-based economy, and increase Canadian trade and investment links with the region. The program encompassed a wide variety of initiatives. These included establishing sound and effective public administration through a restructured public service, supporting the financial system through community credit unions and micro lending practices, and developing language immersion programs to support the integration of linguistic minorities, most notably Latvia's Russian-speaking population (CIDA, 2004). Some projects in the Baltic states of Estonia, Latvia and Lithuania were designed to support the transition to a market-based economy, increase Canadian trade and investment links with the region, and to promote democratic development.

The Baltic Economic Management Training Program (BEMTP) was a project to support young, mid-level "high achievers" who were likely to make significant impacts in future macroeconomic and public procurement policy. Through special instruction in fields such as business skills, market economics, and language training, the MBA Faculty Development Program was designed in cooperation with the University of Ottawa, the State University of New York, and the Riga Business School (RBS). Other projects supported credit unions in Latvia and Lithuania by improving access to financial services in rural areas for farmers and small business owners. In addition, several CIDA-funded projects concentrated on social integration for linguistic minorities to provide more opportunities for their participation in the economy, political structures, and society in general (CIDA, 2004). Other Canadian projects during this period focused on governance and democratization and on the development of institutions able to support democratic practices. This included reforming criminal and penal codes, training and technical assistance, and broader capacity development to transition the old 'command and control' style of the Soviets to one more in line with international norms and standards (CIDA, 2004).

As discussed throughout the book, the Latvia project represented something of a shift in program design. Based on the Canadian experience in Lithuania, there was a recognition that sustainable criminal justice reform could not occur without local partnerships, municipal adaptation, and a broader engagement with communities. Baltic programming also highlighted the need for flexibility. Both projects, while initially designed around programming for youth, soon expanded to probation programming in Latvia and prison programming in Lithuania. Since Baltic programming has been concluded, CIDA has funded two additional youth justice reform programs. In Ukraine, the CIDA-funded Juvenile Justice Reform Project in Ukraine (2010-2015) is designed to support the development of a national legislative and policy framework and to train judges and other stakeholders involved in the delivery of the juvenile justice system.

Another example is the Canadian-Russian Youth at Risk project. Designed to assist Russian authorities and social service workers to revamp youth justice in the country, the overall goal of the $3.5 million four-year project (2004-2009) was to support democracy and good governance in the Russian Federation. While discussed in more detail in Chapter 3, project activities appear to have been based on the Latvian experience, and include many of the programmatic elements, staff, and approaches employed in the Baltics. As yet, these projects have not been subject to detailed and independent reviews or scholarly analysis. As such, important questions remain about to what extent the lessons of the Latvian projects are relevant for these larger and perhaps politically more complex countries. For now, it may be useful to focus on Latvian-Canadian cooperation and justice reform.

1.3.1 Latvian-Canadian Cooperation and Justice Reform: Projects, Goals, and Successes

In 1995, CIDA took on the responsibility of administering Canada's official assistance programs in Central and Eastern Europe (CEE), and the Former Soviet Union (FSU) by supporting democratic development and economic liberalization. The 1995 *Policy on Human Rights, Democratization and Good Governance* presented 'responsive' and 'flexible' programming, a focus that continued throughout the 1990s (Cameron, 2006). In 1999, Canada began working in Latvia through the CIDA-funded *Latvian Criminal Justice Reform Project* (LCJRP). Through the project (1999-2001) there was an initial focus on workshops and seminars between Latvian Canadians and senior members of the Latvian justice sector, including representatives from the Ministry of Education, Ministry of Justice, and Prison

Administration. Although they did not result in tangible project results, these activities resulted in the development of key relationships, informational exchanges, and a better understanding of the relevant issues.

In 2000, the project shifted to local municipalities in which young professionals working in the justice sector had indicated an interest in both alternative programs and in local governmental support. Initial meetings were held to present details on a pilot project competition held in a number of local municipalities. A study tour to Canada was organized with a variety of community members and Ministry of Justice officials. Discussed in more detail later, study tours to Canada had a profound effect on building relationships between Latvians and Canadians and local reformers in Riga and local municipalities. Following the tour, training was offered to those who expressed interest in developing a proposal in line with CIDA funding requirements. Projects were funded that relied upon cooperation with a local municipal agency such as police, school, or prison, and could demonstrate cost-sharing between citizens, local business, and local governments (Wheeldon & Sanford, 2002).

As a result, a number of local models of alternative youth-centric programs were developed and a significant base of local expertise was established. Early programs included a Youth Crime Prevention Program in Broceni and Saldus that offered early intervention programs for youth at risk and operated a youth center. The youth center also partnered with local schools to offer peer-mentoring programs and workshops on life skills, health care, and drug prevention. Other programs were offered in partnership with the Youth and Adult Detention facilities in Cesis and Valmiera to model cognitive behaviourial models, youth wilderness therapy programming, and after-care for adults returning to the community (Wheeldon & Sanford, 2007).

Two additional programs developed through the pilot project competition are of specific interest. Youth probation services in Tukums and Cēsis were funded to address the lack of resources for youth in conflict with the law. In Cēsis, a municipal social worker and the police inspector responsible for youth collaborated to develop the proposal, and the service began in 2001 serving more than 100 clients by 2002 (Bell *et al.* 2002). While initial reactions within the community were dismissive of the project, police soon became supportive based on the success of the program, the positive changes observed in the youth, and the fact that it freed police to focus on other crimes. These services were the first in Latvia to adapt a Canadian Risk Needs Assessment model from the Ontario Ministry of Community and Social Services, and received in-depth training from Ms. Gail Steeds, who has gone on to work on a number of probation projects in the FSU. Those associated with these early probation programs would become central in future Canadian-funded projects (Wheeldon & Sanford, 2007).

Between 2001 and 2002, CIDA extended this funding through the *Legal Reform Capacity Project* (LRCP) that relied upon the LCJRP's pilot project experience to promote the transfer of community expertise in the field of justice to National institutions. The LRCP has supported activities in four key areas: pilot projects, the Latvian Youth Justice Strategy, the Latvian Probation Service, and a variety of public education and awareness campaigns. The LRCP supported municipal pilot projects and matched Canadian expertise and Latvian experience. The project focused in more detail on promoting a co-operative approach between communities and national governmental bodies. In addition, the project supported two national working groups tasked with developing and implementing strategies that built on the pilot project successes to date. The first was the Latvian National Youth Justice Working Group, established by the Ministry of Education and the National Centre for the Rights of the Child. The project funded workshops, document translation, and the formation and subsequent activities of the working group as it finalized the Youth Justice Strategy. The strategy was divided into four areas of concern, including: Prevention Programs, Alternative Measures in the court system, Youth Corrections, Rehabilitation and re-entering society after incarceration. The second was the National Probation Working Group, established by the Ministry of Justice. While the concept of probation developed in Latvia was broader than other probation programs, it resembled the Canadian system in that probation officers would act as the case managers for all offenders from the time of arrest through to incarceration and post-release care.

National developments and progress on probation initially slowed until the combination of project-funded activities, external pressures, and internal events sparked renewed interest in 2001. Based on commitments by the Ministry of Justice, and the development of a Probation Concept document and Probation law, the Latvian Legal Reform Program (LLRP) was funded by CIDA and implemented by the Association and Universities of Colleges of Canada (AUCC). Planned functions of the probation service identified in 2002 were: the assessment of an offender and recommendations made to the court concerning sentencing; the supervision of alternative sentences, such as community service, probation, conditional sentencing; the continued management of the case if the offender is incarcerated; and the development of a release plan for the offender.

As discussed in Chapter 6, the project supported the Latvian Ministry of Justice to establish the State Probation Service (SPS) and provided training, technical assistance, and capacity development to ensure the probation service was based in law and would conform to and uphold international standards of human rights and justice. The LLRP responded to and further supported a number of additional developments within the field of criminal justice, including bail supervision, victim-offender mediation, and alternative dispute resolution (AUCC, 2005). The project assisted with establishing the SPS by developing new laws, amending existing laws, training staff, assisting in policy development, developing resource materials, and providing support to leading officials within the Latvian Ministry of Justice. Chapter 2 suggests that the SPS has emerged as a central institution in the Latvian justice system and has presided over an unprecedented reduction in the prison population, alongside the expansion of community-based crime prevention programs since 2004.

1.3.2 *Understanding this Book's Contribution in Context*

It is widely recognized that too few empirical studies explore internationalized efforts at criminal justice policymaking and little is known about how changes to crime control occur, or what role policy transfer plays in that process (Carothers, 2003; Chodosh, 2005; Jones & Newbury, 2005). This is certainly the case in post-communist and transition countries, where while the need for alternatives to incarceration have long been recognized, the question of how to best support sustainable reform efforts remains challenging (Jacoby, 2006; Joutsen, 1996). This book presents probation services as offering a unique *kind* of alternative to incarceration. It retains a role for the state by applying conditions set by the court, but allows for the supervision of a convicted individual by a probation officer in the community. Although probation is of growing interest in Europe and around the world (Kalmthout & Durnescu, 2008), it remains largely unexplored in comparative terms, and perhaps more importantly, as part of collaborative, cross-cultural justice reform projects (Harris *et al.* 1995). In functional, operational, and administrative terms, the establishment of the SPS in Latvia represents an important exemplar.

Latvian-Canadian cooperation may also be seen as a model by which transnational juridical norms were tested, revised, and ultimately legitimized in Latvia, and among project stakeholders (Dezalay & Garth, 2010). Although this book has emerged from exploratory research using novel methods, its findings provide an empirical basis for views that have emerged from other literature. The model that is presented through this book may usefully serve future studies and the subsequent design and delivery of justice reform programming. For less than a million dollars, itself a pittance when compared to many development initiatives, the project has succeeded where so many others have failed (Caldwell, 2005; Lukensaite, 2005; Morrison, 1998). By working together, Latvians and Canadians have shared experiences, discussed alternatives, argued, respectfully disagreed, and ultimately worked together toward the development of the State Probation Service (SPS). Judging the project might be based solely on the achievement of CIDA-designed project outputs and outcomes as reported by AUCC (2005) and mapped in figure 1.7.

Figure 1.7 LLRP Outcomes and Impacts (AUCC, 2005)

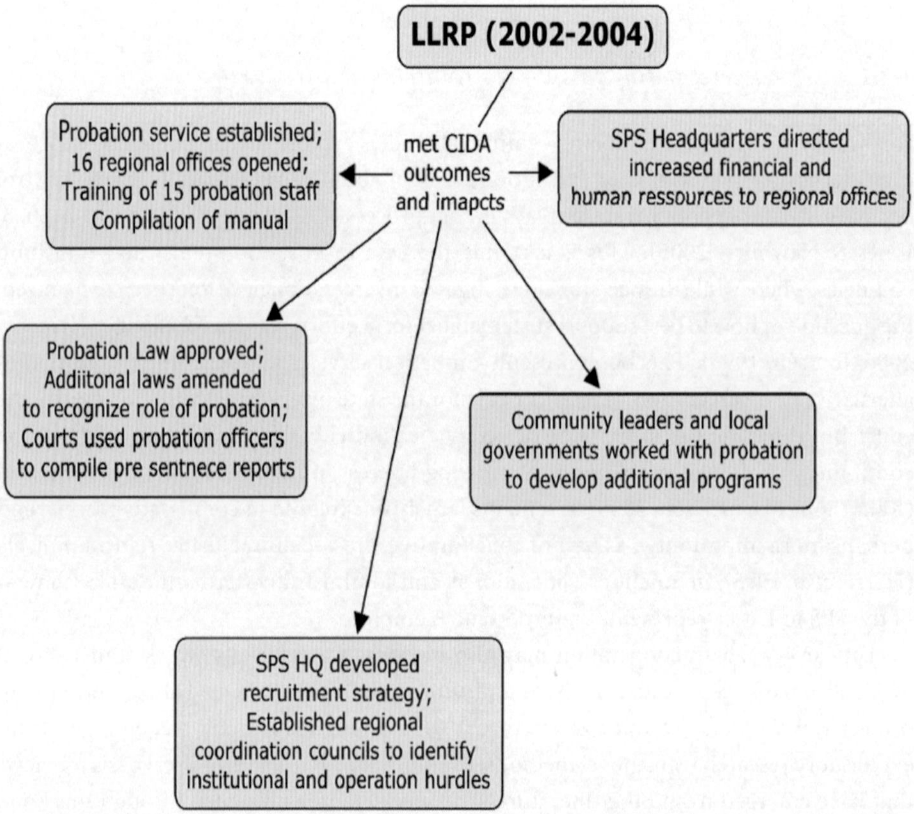

However, although the official project outcomes and impacts presented above are important, these formal outcomes were the result of a variety of informal encounters over a number of years. For the Canadians, this process involved a willingness to present, discuss, and consider the values these international norms presume, while remaining humble when comparing these assumptions with the prevailing views within Latvia. For the Latvians, it was the informal way Canadian programming provided the means for participants' themselves to debate the role of law within society. This approach may have allowed the function of probation and probation officers to be based on the experience of Latvian communities.

1.4 Concluding Remarks

This history of modern international development and its complex architecture cannot be divorced from the socio-political times in which it emerged. Often and justifiably criticized for its economic focus, aid has nonetheless emerged as valuable in some cases. Yet the assumptions inherent in the dichotomy between expert and learner, developed and developing, can result in even good intentions backfiring. Since 1990, the importance of human rights, good governance, and democracy development emerged as thematic watchwords in the post-Cold War era, but once again assumptions about the relationship between law and society led to proscriptive rather than constructive engagement.

The criminal justice system consistently emerges as a key institution in understanding and assessing governance. This chapter has argued that an unexplored means by which to consider how institutions operate in developing and transition countries is justice reform projects themselves. For most of the world's population, the state is not a guarantor of individual liberty and economic fair play, but an oppressive and easily corrupted structure of control. It is this corruption and the broader failure of institutions that led to the instability that gave rise to the so-called Arab Spring. It is inevitable that western nations will be asked to support institutions in transition countries, and the ways in which justice systems have relied on barbaric techniques to serve politicized religious interests must be confronted. On what grounds might the international community engage in collaborative justice reform in MENA?

Development projects serve as an important intersection point between the past, present, and future. As a site of potential debate and deliberation, both formal and informal barriers to reform can be identified and explored by comparing and assessing international interactions through the narrative accounts of those who participated on these projects. Probation projects are of specific interest in this regard, because it allows countries to reduce prison populations while expanding community-based supervision. It usefully varies widely in its implementation and as such allows for a debate and deliberation among and between legal professionals and civil society groups in individual countries about the right mix of punishment and rehabilitation. As the global recession highlights the high cost of punitive corrections models, countries in North Africa, Asia, and elsewhere in the world may be ready for such a discussion. Yet before the applicability of the model can be considered, a clear description of the problem, the projects, and the development of probation in Latvia may be required.

Chapter 1 Bibliography

S. Asquith. *Report on alternatives measures for dealing with young offenders in Latvia.* Riga, Latvia, United Nations Development Project, 2002.

Association of Universities and Colleges of Canada. *Latvian legal reform program: Final report to CIDA.* Ottawa, ON, Association of Universities and Colleges of Canada, Ottawa, 2005.

S. Bell, R. Corrado, Y. Durand & C. Griffiths. Report of the LRCP advisory panel. Ottawa, ON: Association of Universities and Colleges Canada, 2002.

L. Berthiaume. *CIDA looks to private sector.* Ottawa: ON: Embassy Magazine. Retrieved from August 6, 2008 from <www.embassymag.ca/html/index.php?display=story&full_path=/2008/march/26/cida/>.

D. Black, & H. Smith. Notable exceptions? new and arrested directions in Canadian foreign policy. *Canadian Journal of Political Science,* Vol. 26, No. 4, 1993, pp. 745-774.

D. Black & R. Tiessen. The Canadian international development agency: New policies, old problems. *Canadian Journal of Development Studies,* Vol. 28, No. 2, 2007, pp. 191-212.

D.A. Blumental & T.L.H. McCormack (Eds.). *The Legacy of Nurenburg: Civilizing Influence or Insitutionalized Vengeance.* Leiden, GER: Martinus Nijhoff Publishers, 2008.

A.E. Bottoms. The Philosophy and politics of Punishment and Sentencing. In C. Clarkson and R. Morgan (Eds.), *The Politics of Sentencing Reform*, Oxford, UK: Clarendon Press, 1995, pp. 17-49.

S. Brown. CIDA under the gun. In J. Daudelin, & D. Schwanen (Eds.), *Canada among nations 2007: What room for manoeuvre?* Montreal: PQ: McGill-Queen's University Press 208, pp. 91-107.

S. Caldwell. *Evaluating the evaluation: Review of CIDA's work in the Baltics.* Toronto, ON: University of Toronto, 2005.

M. Campbell. Politics and Public Servants: Observations on the Current State of Criminal Law Reform. *Canadian Journal of Criminology*, Vol. 42, No. 3: 2000, pp. 341-354.

G. Cameron. *Between policy and practice*. Regina: Sk.: Saskatchewan Institute of Public Policy, 2006.

Canadian International Development Agenc. *Canada and the Baltics: Partners in Transition*. Gatineau, PQ: Canadian International Development Agency, 2004.

R. Canton. Taking Probation Abroad. *European Journal of Probation*, Vol. 1 No. 1: 2009, pp. 66-78.

T. Carothers. Promoting the rule of law abroad: The problem of knowledge (Working Paper No. 34.) Washington, DC: Carnegie Endowment for International Peace, 2003.

R. Carty & V. Smith. Underdevelopment assistance. In R. Carty, & V. Smith (Eds.), *Perpetuating poverty: The political economy of Canadian foreign aid*. Toronto, ON: Between the Lines, 1981.

S. Cohen. *Visions of Social Control: Crime, Punishment and Classification*. London, UK: Polity Press, 2005.

H. Chodosh. *Global justice reform: A comparative methodology*. New York: New York University Press, 2005.

Y. Dandurand. Effective technical assistance in crime prevention and criminal justice. *Maximizing the Effectiveness of the Technical Assistance Provided in the Fields of Crime Prevention and Criminal Justice*, Vienna, Austria. Paper No. 49, 2006.

Y. Dandurand, C.T. Griffiths & V. Chin. Training and effective support of comprehensive justice and security reforms: Outcomes to date and lessons learned. In K. Aromaa, & S. Redo (Eds.), *For the rule of law: Criminal justice teaching and training @cross the world*. Helsinki: FI: European Institute for Crime Prevention and Control, 2008.

M. Dean-Myrda & F. Cullen. The panacea pendulum: An account of community as a response to crime. In J. Petersilia (Ed). *Community Corrections: Probation, Parole, and Intermediate Sanctions*. Oxford: Oxford University Press 2008, pp. 3-18.

Y. Dezalay & B. Garth. Marketing and Selling Transnational 'Judges' and Global 'Experts': Building the Credibility of (Quasi) Judicial Regulation, *Socio-Economic Review*, Vol. 8 No. 1, 2010, pp. 113-130.

D. Dolowitz & D. Marsh. Who Learns What from Whom: a Review of the Policy Transfer Literature. *Political Studies* Vol. 44, 1996, pp. 343-357.

W. Easterly. *The White Man's Burden: Why the West's Efforts to Aid the Rest Have Done So Much Ill and So Little Good.* New York, NY: Penguin Press, 2006.

O.M. Fiss. The Autonomy of Law. Faculty Scholarship Series, Paper 1316, 2011. Available at: <http://digitalcommons.law.yale.edu/fss_papers/1316>.

H. Führer. The Story of Official Development Assistance: A History of the Development Assistance Committee and the Development Co-Operation Directorate In Dates, Names and Figures. Organization For Economic Co-Operation And Development Paris, FR, 1996.

F. Fukuyama. *The End of History and the Last Man.* NY: Free Press, 1992.

F. Fukuyama. *State-building: Governance and world order in the 21st century.* Ithaca, NY: Cornell University Press, 2004.

J.A. Gardner. *Legal Imperialism: American Lawyers and Foreign Aid in Latin America.* Madison: The University of Wisconsin Press, 1980.

D. Garland. Probation and the Reconfiguration of Crime Control. In R. Burnett (Ed.) The Probation Service: Responding to Change, Probation Studies Unit Report No.3/97, Oxford: Center for Criminological Research, 1997.

D. Garland. *The Culture of Control: Crime and Social Order in Contemporary Society.* Chicago, Il: University of Chicago Press, 2001.

Z. Gestautaite. *Penal and policy reform in Lithuania and the involvement of Canadian expertise.* Unpublished Masters Thesis, Carleton University, Ottawa, ON, 2001.

S. Golub. The legal empowerment alternative. In T. Carothers (Ed.), *Promoting the rule of law abroad: The problem of knowledge.* Washington, D.C.: Carnegie Endowment for International Peace, 2003, pp. 105-136.

F.J. Goodnow. Reform in China, *American Political Science Review* Vol. 9, 1915, pp. 209-219.

I. Hacking. *The Taming of Chance.* Cambridge: Cambridge University Press, 1990.

K.D. Haggerty. Displaced expertise: Three constraints on the policy-relevance of criminological thought. *Theoretical Criminology*, Vol. 8, No. 2, 2004, pp. 211-231.

L. Hammergren. *Envisioning Reform Improving Judicial Performance in Latin America.* Penn State Press: University Park, PA, 2007.

R. Harris. Probation Around the World: Origins and Development. In Hamai, K., Harris, R., Hough, M., Ville, R., Ugljesa Zvekic, U. (Eds.) *Probation Around the World: A Comparative Study.* London, UK: Routledge Press, 1995, pp. 25-70.

R. Harris & N. Timms. *Secure Accommodation in Child Care: Between Hospital and Prison or Thereabouts.* London: Routledge, 1993.

I. Head. *Farewell speech to IDRC.* Ottawa, ON: International Development Research Council, March 8, 1991.

C. Hedderman & M. Hough. Getting tough or being effective: what matters? In G. Mair (Ed.), *What Matters in Probation.* Cullompton, UK: Willan, 2004, pp. 146-169.

T. Heller. An Immodest Postscript. In E. Jensen & T. Heller. (Eds.) *Beyond Common Knowledge: Empirical Approaches to the Rule of Law.* Stanford University Press, 2005, pp. 382-412.

K. Hendley. Law and development in Russia: A misguided enterprise? *Proceedings of the American Society of International Law 90*, Washington, DC, 1996.

P. Igbinovia. Criminology in Africa. *International Journal of Offender Therapy and Comparative Criminology*, Vol. 33, No. 2, 1989, pp. 5-10.

International Development Association. Aid Architecture: An Overview of the Main Trends in Official Development Assistance Flows. World Bank, Washington DC, 2007.

W. Jacoby. Inspiration, coalition, and substitution: external influences on post communist transformations. *World Politics* Vol. 58, No.4, 2006, pp. 623-651.

T. Jones & T. Newburn. Learning from Uncle Sam? Exploring US influences on British crime control policy. *Governance*, Vol. 15, No. 1, 2002, pp. 97-119.

M. Joutsen. Managing international technical assistance projects in criminal justice: Experiences with assistance in the reform of crime prevention and criminal justice in central and eastern europe. United Nations European Institute for Crime Prevention and Control (HEUNI) Paper No. 8, 1996.

A.M. van Kalmthout & I. Durnescu. *Probation in Europe*. Nijmegen: Wolf Legal Publishers, 2008.

S. Karstedt. Comparing cultures, comparing crime: Challenges, prospects and problems for a global criminology. *Crime Law and Social Change,* Vol. 36, 2001, pp. 285-208.

S. Karstedt. The Nuremburg Tribunal and German Society: International Justice and Local Judgment in Post Conflict Reconstruction. In D.A Blumenthal & T.L.H. McCormack (Eds.), *The Legacy of Nuremberg: Civilizing Influence or Institutionalized Vengeance.* Leiden, GER: Martinus Nijhoff Publishers, 2008, pp. 13-32.

D. Kaufman, A. Kraary & M. Mastruzzi. Governance matters IV: Governance indicators for 1996-2004. World Bank, Washington, DC, 2005.

D. Kaufmann, A. Kraay & P. Zoido-Lobatõn. Governance Matters (World Bank Policy Research Working Paper No. 2196). Washington, DC, 1999.

D. Kaufmann, A. Kraay & P. Zoido-Lobatõn. (2008). Governance indicators: Where are we, where should we be going?: Policy researc working paper 4370. Washington, DC, 2008.

D. Kealey, D. Protheroe, D. MacDonald, & T. Vulpe. Re-examining the role of training in contributing to international project success: A literature review and an outline of a new model training program. *International Journal of Intercultural Relations,* Vol. 29, 2005, pp. 289-316.

D. Kennedy. Laws and Development. In A. Perry-Kessaris & J. Hatchard (Eds.), *Facing Complexity: Law and development in the 21st century*. London, UK: Cavendish, 2007, pp. 17-26.

R. Kleinfeld. Competing definitions of the rule of law. In T. Carothers (Ed.), *Promoting the rule of law abroad: The problem of knowledge*. Washington, D.C.: Carnegie Endowment for International Peace, 2003, pp. 31-74.

M. Lauristin. Contexts of transition. In M. Lauristin (Ed.), *Return to the western world: Cultural and political perspectives on the estonian post-communist transition*. Tartu: Estonia Tartu University Press, 1997, pp. 25-40.

C. Leys. *The Rise and Fall of Development Theory*. Bloomington: Indiana University Press, 1996.

J. Linn. *Legal and judicial reform in the transition economies of Europe and central Asia*. Washington, DC: Legal Department, World Bank, 1999.

M. Los. Crime in transition: The post-communist state, markets and crime. *Crime, Law & Social Change*, Vol. 40, 2003, pp. 145-169.

B. Luksenaite. Evaluation of CIDA programming in the Baltic states, 1990-2003. A Review. Toronto, ON: University of Toronto, 2005.

L. Macdonald. Unequal partnerships: The politics of Canada's relations with the third world. *Studies in Political Economy*, Vol. 47, 1995, pp. 111-141.

R. MacDonald *(Book review) the tools of government: A guide to the new governance by L. Salamon*. London, UK: Oxford University Press, 2002.

T.F. McInerney. Law and Development as Democratic Practice. *Vanderbilt Journal of Transnational Law*, Vol. 37, 2005: 935-970.

R. Morgan. G. Mair *What Matters in Probatio*, Cullompton, UK: Willan, 2004. In *The Howard Journal of Criminal Justice* 46 (1), 2007, pp. 85-86.

H. Morgenthau (1962). A political theory of foreign aid. *American Political Science Review*, Vol. 56, No. 2, 1962, pp. 301-309.

D.R. Morrison. *Aid and ebb tide: A history of CIDA and Canadian development assistance*. Waterloo, ON: Wilfred Laurier Press, 1998.

D.R. Morrison & N. Islam. Introduction. *Canadian Journal of Development Studies*, Special Issue on Governance, Democracy and Human Rights, 1996.

K. Nossal. Mixed motives revisited: Canada's interest in development assistance. *Canadian Journal of Political Science*, Vol. 21, 1988, pp. 35-56.

K. Nossal. *The patterns of world politics.* Scarborough, ON: Prentice Hall Allyn and Bacon, 1998.

S. Power. The Enforcer, *New Yorker.* January 19, 2009 (p. 52).

R. Pound. *Social control through law.* New Haven, Yale University Press, 1942.

B. Pratt. *Aid harmonisation: Challenges for civil society.* Ottawa: ON: International NGO Training and Research Centre, 2005. Available at <www.intrac.org/resources_database.php?id=275>.

C. Pratt. DFAIT's takeover bid of CIDA: The institutional future of the Canadian international development agency. *Canadian Foreign Policy*, Vol. 5, No. 2, 1998, pp. 1-14.

C. Pratt. Alleviating global poverty or enhancing security: Competing rationales for Canadian development assistance. In J. Freedman (Ed.), *In transforming development: Foreign aid in a changing world.* Toronto, ON: University of Toronto, 2000, pp. 37-59.

C. Pratt. Ethical values and Canadian foreign aid policies. *Canadian Journal of African Studies / Revue Canadienne Des &tudes Africaines*, Vol. 37, No. 1, 2003, pp. 84-101.

N. Pugach. Embarrassed Monarchist: Frank J. Goodnow and Constitutional Development in China, 1913-1915. *The Pacific Historical Review*, Vol. 42, No. 4, 1973, pp. 499-517.

G. Rist. *The History of Development: From Western Origins to Global Faith*, 3rd ed. Zed Books, London, 2008.

K. Rittich. Who's afraid of the critique of adjudication? Tracing the discourses of law. In development. *Cardoza Law Review*, Vol. 22, 2001, pp. 929-946.

K. Roach. The Effects of the Canadian Charter of Rights and Freedoms on the Canadian Criminal Justice System. *Israel Law Review*, Vol. 33, 1999 pp. 607-637.

E.M. Rogers. *Diffusion of innovations* (5th Ed.). New York, NY: Free Press, 2005.

R. Rose. *Learning from Comparative Public Policy: A practical guide.* London, New York: Routledge, 2005.

J. Sachs. *The End of Poverty: Economic Possibilities for Our Time.* New York, NY: Penguin Press, 2006.

M.J. Sandel, *Justice: What's the Right Thing to Do?* NY: Farrar, Straus and Giroux, 2009.

J. Schnitzer. *The Nuremberg Justice Trial 1947: Vengeance Of The Victors?* Unpublished LLM Thesis, University Of Victoria, 2010.

D. Shichor. Penal Policies at the Threshold of the Twenty-First Century. *Criminal Justice Review*, Vol. 25, No. 1, 2005, pp. 1-30.

A. Seidman & R. Seidman. Drafting legislation for development: Lessons from a Chinese project. *American Journal of Comparative Law*, Vol. 44, 1996, pp. 1-44.

L. Shelley. *Policing soviet society: The evolution of state control.* London, UK: Routledge, 1996.

J. Shklar. Political theory and the rule of law. In P. Hutchinson, & P. Monahan (Eds.), *The rule of law: Ideal or ideology*. Toronto, ON: Carswell Publishing, 1987, pp. 1-16.

M. Stephenson. *A trojan horse in China?* In T. Carothers (Ed.) *Promoting the Rule of Law Abroad* Washington, D.C.: Carnegie Endowment for International Peace, 2003, pp. 191-216.

S. Steinmo, K. Thelen & F. Longstreth. *Structuring Politics: Historical Institutionalism in Comparative Analysis.* Cambridge, UK: Cambridge University Press, 1992.

L.M. Sundstrom. Foreign assistance, international norms, and civil society development: Lessons from the Russian campaign. *International Organization,* Vol. 59, No. 2, 2005, pp. 419-450.

B. Tamanaha. *On the Rule of Law: History, Politics, Theory.* Cambridge, UK: Cambridge University Press, 2004.

K. Thelen. How institutions evolve: Insights from comparative-historical analysis. In J. Mahoney and D. Rueschemeyer (Eds.) *Comparative Historical Analysis in the Social Sciences,*. New York: Cambridge University Press, 2003, pp. 208-240.

J. Therien. (1999). *(Book review) Aid and ebb tide: A history of CIDA and Canadian development assistance* by D. Morrison. *Canadian Journal of Political*, Vol. 32, No. 3, 1999, pp. 586-587.

M.J. Trebilcock & R.J. Daniels. *Rule of Law Reform: Charting the Fragile Path of Progress* Cheltenham, UK: Edward Elgar, 2008.

D.M. Trubeck. The "Rule of Law" in Development Assistance: Past, Present, and Future. Working Paper, Center on World Affairs and the Global Economy, University of Wisconsin-Madison, 2003.

United Nations Office of Drug Control. *Criminal justice reform unit toolkit.* July, 2008, from <www.unodc.org/unodc/en/justice-and-prison-reform/Criminal-Justice-Toolkit.html>.

United Nations Development Program. *Making the Law Work for Everyone* (Volume 1). United Nations Development Program: New York, NY, 2008.

M. Valverde. *Law's dream of a common knowledge.* Princeton: Princeton University Press, 2003.

M. Vanstone & P. Priestley. Community Justice and a Model of Rehabilitation, *British Journal of Community Justice.* Vol. 6, No. 1, 2008 pp. 63-72.

J.R. Wedel. *Collision and Collusion: The Strange Case of Western Aid to Eastern Europe, 1989-1998.* New York: St. Martin's Press, 1998.

J.P. Wheeldon. Learning from Latvia: Adoption, Adaptation, and Evidence Based Justice Reform. *Journal of Baltic Studies*, Vol. 41, No. 4, 2010, pp. 507-530.

J.P. Wheeldon. The Paris Declaration: Challenges and Opportunities for Canada's Universities. Ottawa, ON, Association of Universities and Colleges of Canada Ottawa, ON, 2006.

J.P. Wheeldon & T. Sanford. Toward Integrated Community Justice in Latvia. *Law and Justice*, Vol. 9 No. 37, 2002, pp. 258-260.

P. Whitehead & R. Staham. *The History of Probation: Politics, Power and Cultural Change 1876-2005.* London, UK: Shaw and Sons, 2007.

A. Wolfe. *The Future of Liberalism*. New York: Knopf, 2009.

World Bank Legal Department. *Legal and judicial reform: Observations, experiences and approach of the legal vice presidency*. Washington, DC: Legal Department, World Bank, 2002.

2 From Incarceration to Community: Probation in the Baltics

As introduced in Chapter 1, a recent approach within legal technical assistance initiatives has been to concentrate on establishing, supporting, and reforming probation services. Operating at the centre of criminal justice systems around the world, they provide a means to ensure state supervision of offenders while promoting rehabilitation and crime prevention. Since the 1980s, however, probation as a concept has been re-imagined in Canada, the US and the UK. In place of a model of care and assistance, probation services today are often guided by the use of more punitive approaches to administer risk and manage crime. Despite these challenges, probation still offers an important means for developing and transition countries to reduce the numbers of individuals incarcerated in overcrowded and under-resourced prison systems, while promoting social inclusion and crime prevention.

Established in 2003, the Latvian State Probation Service (SPS) has grown significantly and withstood a number of administrative and operational challenges, including the recent economic downturn. While operationally similar to other European probation services, its development occurred through international collaboration and cooperation and represents an important example of a successful international justice reform project. By borrowing and adopting in some cases, and revising and adapting in others, the Latvians involved in the project established and continue to refine and improve the SPS. Their efforts have resulted in a significant reduction in the prison populations since 2004, promoted a new and important role for communities in crime prevention. It may suggest an important model of sustainable justice reform.

2.1 The Problem with Prisons and the Promise of Probation

Given the reliance on incarceration in North America and around the world, it may be surprising that the use of imprisonment as a punishment is relatively new. While prisons long existed for the temporary detention of debtors and those with unpopular political or religious beliefs, confining criminals was most often simply a means to keep them under control until corporal or capital punishment was administered (Peters, 1995). Before the 19th Century, whipping, flogging, beating, birching and a host of violent, painful, and harmful actions were not only sanctioned but also served as public spectacles designed to shame the offender and deter onlookers. By the end of the 18th Century, the penal system of Europe had changed drastically, with various forms of incarceration gradually replacing the "theatre of horror." Historian Michael Ignatieff (1978, p. xiii) explores how:

> ...it came to be considered just, reasonable, and humane to immure prisoners in solitary cells, clothe them in uniforms, regiment their day to the cadence of the clock, and 'improve' their minds with dosages of scripture and hard labor. Between 1770 and 1840 this form of carceral discipline 'directed at the mind' replaced a cluster of punishments 'directed at the body – whipping, branding, the stocks, and public hanging.

In one view, there were two distinct developments during this period that help explain this shift (Spierenburg, 1995). The first development concerns a shift in attitudes about the body of the offender. Historically, the use of torture and execution in Europe were connected to the authority of the King. In France, for example, the system was "planned to ruin citizens" (Radzinowicz, 1966, p. 1) from arrest through public displays of torture and execution. Police relied upon spies, covert letter opening, and holding people indefinitely, hidden from family and friends (Lilly, Cullen & Ball, 2011). Punishments were severe and ranged from burning people alive, to breaking them on the wheel and various other forms of mutilation, whipping, and branding. As public affirmations of the King's authority to rule, punish, and discipline (Foucault, 1975), this power was in some ways subject to public approval. In France, there are reports of crowds gathered around the event that rioted against the executioner, stopping the "discipline" if it was deemed too excessive (Spierenburg, 1984). In the early 18th century in Britain, there were 200 capital offences, and in London death by execution took place every six weeks, with between five and fifteen condemned people hanged on each occasion (Lofland, 1973, p. 35). By the end of the 18th century, protests against public execution and torture grew and new sorts of punishment were required.

One punishment in use since 1615 was what is euphemistically known as convict transportation – more accurately described as deportation. In both Britain and France, sending convicted criminals to a penal colony was seen as a useful solution to the problem of crime. Beginning in 1718, Britain relied on this punishment more frequently and sent tens of thousands to the American colonies. Following the American Revolution, those sentenced were sent on a more arduous journey to Australia, a practice that continued until 1868. During this same period, France sent criminals to penal colonies in Louisiana, and later to French Guiana, while Swedish courts sent convicts to regions of the Baltics that where under their dominion (Spierenburg, 1995). Throughout the 18th century, the brutality of the existing justice system was reduced. While France abolished the galleys in 1748 – a punishment that forced convicts to row a large boat – galley sentences remained popular, and came to mean a variety of manual labor in the shipyard. By 1780, torture as part of a trial or judicial sentence was abolished, and the use of other methods of public corporal punishments declined dramatically. Where their use continued, they were often combined with imprisonment.

These reforms, and others, were influenced by the publication of a small book by an Italian mathematician and economist (Lilly, Cullen & Ball, 2011). Cesare Bonesana Marchese de Beccaria's *On Crimes and Punishments*, published first in 1764 and translated to English three years later, argued that punishments should be limited and not go beyond what was necessary for crime prevention and deterrence. Beccaria argued that the unjust actions of the state in depriving liberty and inflicting pain would lead individuals to turn their back on the authority, or sovereignty, of the state. The results of Beccaria's thesis reverberated across Europe and found a home in America. In the UK, William Blackstone incorporated Beccaria's rational approach to punishment in his *Commentaries* and became part of a more general trend from the Magna Carta (1215) through the Bill of Rights (1689) to define individual rights against the arbitrary power of the state (Walker, 1997).

The second development was that imprisonment with forced labor and other forms of penal bondage grew increasingly popular. In addition to the influence of Beccaria, political philosopher and social reformer Jeremy Bentham offered another justification for rethinking prisons. Like Beccaria, as part of his groundbreaking work on utilitarianism, Bentham argued that the punishment of illegal offenses against society should be proportional to the amount of harm caused by them. In this regard, past models could not be justified if they were disadvantageous, needless, unjust, or arbitrary. Houses of Correction became more popular after 1800 and could compel convicts to work, attempt to correct bad habits, enforce morality, and reform behavior. Although Houses of Corrections had existed all over Northern Europe since the 16th Century, the first had been established at a former palace at Bridewell in the UK. Houses of Correction modeled on Bridewell were established in every British county and their use expanded throughout Europe, from Spain to Stockholm, to detain beggars, idlers, and vagrants. Germany and Holland most fully developed the model of the prison workhouse (Spierenburg, 1995).

In Britain, it was the conditions in county gaols that became of significant concern to John Howard – another reformer who would later be credited with spurring a series of changes designed to improve the prison system. Howard discovered that once prisoners from each local parish were transported from the lock up or "cage", their eventual destination was overcrowded county gaols. With poor conditions and subject to injurious ministrations, prison terms were based on practical necessity, and not guided by informed policy. As described by Howard:

> Ely Gaol was the property of the Bishop and because of the insecurity of the old prison, the gaoler chained the victims down on their backs on the floor,

> across which several iron bars, with an iron collar with spikes about their necks and a heavy iron bar over their legs.

Howard continued to visit gaols around Britain, and in 1777 published an extensive account entitled *The State of the Prisons in England and Wales.* His work took a decade to cross the Atlantic. By 1786 it had led to the formation of the first American prison reform societies and a variety of new approaches to incarceration. This included practices such as solitary confinement in the Walnut street jail, enforced silence in the Auburn systems, and eventually the education and vacational training programs that continue to this day (Walker, 1997).

In Britain, Howard's diligent efforts and reporting had led to local reforms, but it was only after 1810 that a national campaign, organized in part by the Quakers, aroused the consciences of the "enlightened" elite, who used their legislative influence to begin to compel counties to improve conditions and to nationalize penitentiaries (McGowen, 1995), the first of which was completed in 1816 at Millbank in London. In 1842, Pentonville prison was built, based loosely on the panopticon design allowing inmates to be watched, or appear to be watched, from a central hub within the prison. Created by Jeremy Bentham, this design attempted to use surveillance as a means to secure compliance. In place of barbaric corporal punishment, criminal rehabilitation sought to reform those imprisoned so that upon release, they would be contributing members of society. Foucault was the first to recognize that while based on altruistic goals, the expansion of prisons and the focus on discipline and social control would have profound consequences. This is a view that has since been updated and refined (Garland, 2001).

An early form of probation was personal supervision. It began in the 1820s, when Warwickshire magistrates began to release young and non-serious offenders conditionally to employers. Later, offenders could be released to other community members known as court missionaries or guardians, who would take responsibility and pay a surety or bail to ensure they had a financial incentive to produce the individual in court as required. American colonists continued this practice, although any supervision was strictly voluntary until John Augustus, a Boston boot maker, began visiting the police court in 1841. While he initially began undertaking pre-trial enquiries into cases of drunken offenders, he soon expanded his interest. He is today seen as the "father" of modern probation because he not only demonstrated how supervision could benefit those he sponsored, but he usefully coined the word "probation" itself. As Harris points out (1995, p. 8), the etymology is relevant:

> ...*probation*, a noun, is connected to 'proving oneself,' while *probator* is an 'approver'...[suggesting something more]...than unconditional support on a voluntary basis.

The Probation of First Offenders Act in the UK (1887) allowed courts to release those guilty of minor offenses "on probation." The Act provides for friendly supervision by some authority to which the offender would have to report – who in turn would report to the court. However, no formal mechanism existed for supervision and court missionaries, and other volunteers were to do their best without legal sanctions to enforce co-operation. The formal rise of non-custodial sanctions began in Belgium in 1888, with the suspended sentence used for first time offenders. Courts could determine the sentence and then "suspend" it, allowing the individual to enjoy freedom providing the conditions of the suspension were met. Beginning in the north and moving south and east, the suspended sentence moved slowly across Europe. After the First World War, the suspended sentence existed across the continent, and was incorporated into the Russian Socialist Federated Republic in 1919. Throughout the 20th century, this suspended sentencing spread to Asia, Latin America, Africa and the Middle East (O'Brian, 1995).

The importance of probation – or the supervision of a suspended sentence – as a non-custodial measure must be seen alongside the general recognition that an over-reliance on prison is a costly and ultimately ineffective solution to the problem of crime (Morris, 1995). While this observation is by no means new, recent contributions have gone further to suggest prisons are themselves "criminogenic" (Burnett & Maruna, 2004; Camp & Gaes, 2005). Western (2006) has convincingly shown how prisons model and instill anti-social behavior, undermine labor market skill sets, and devastate families – all central elements in successful post incarceration re-entry and re-integration. They also hide from society those whose experiences must be understood if the multi-faceted problem of criminal offending is to be properly addressed. As Western (2006, p. 87) notes:

> Imprisonment conceals criminal offenders by removing them from the poor communities that feed the penal system. These inmates occupy a shadowy status that affects a variety of official statistics that record the economic well being of a population. In many cases, prison and jail inmates are not counted in government measures of economic activity, joblessness, or poverty. The invisibility of the penal population in official statistics underlines the depth of inequality generated by incarceration.

Despite a lack of evidence to demonstrate a positive link between a higher rate of imprisonment and a reduction of the crime rate, "the less effective the prisons are in reducing crime, the higher the demand for more imprisonment" (Morris, 1995, p. 257). For disciples of Foucault, the prison system should not be viewed as a system that has failed to decrease crime by punishing criminals. Instead, the prison system is an effective means to allow for one group of individuals within a society to control others. Prison is just another form of discipline used to bring dissenters into line by incarcerating, isolating, and economically controlling those who refuse to accept the orthodoxy of the day (Foucault, 1975).

In the last decade, in addition to the general acknowledgement of its ineffectiveness for most offenders, this form of punishment is running up against the exorbitant costs associated with confining people humanely, and the challenges of maintaining a minimum level of safety for both inmates and the staff who work behind the walls. Ironically, while the costs of maintaining mass incarceration have resulted in cuts for community corrections, probation in the US, combined with other intermediate sanctions, is much more effective at keeping communities safer (Tonry, 1998). From a comparative and international perspective, the chief strength of probation is that it has and will continue to be developed differently, based on the historical context and immediate needs of a specific country. It offers a means, however, to shift from a sole focus on punishment to a more nuanced approach to sanctions as a socially responsible approach to crime. According to Joutsen & Zvekic (1994, p. 6), probation services are associated with a number of societal benefits:

> The arguments for non-custodial sanctions are essentially the mirror image of the arguments against imprisonment. First, they are considered more appropriate for certain types of offences and offenders. Second, because they avoid 'prisonisation', they promote integration back into the community as well as rehabilitation, and therefore are more humane. Third, they are generally less costly than sanctions involving imprisonment. Fourth, by decreasing the prison population, they ease prison overcrowding and thus facilitate administration of prisons and the proper correctional treatment of those who remain in prison.

In Europe, despite the broad differences between countries and traditions, many probation services share some core functions (Van Kalmthout & Durnescu, 2008). Figure 2.1 outlines some of these common functions.

Figure 2.1 Core Functions of European Probation Services

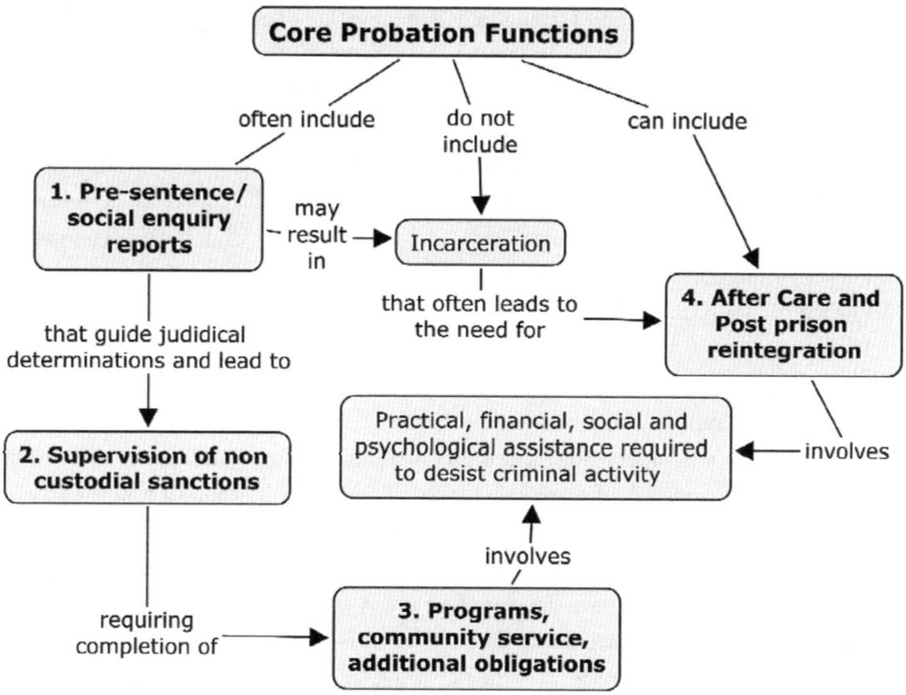

2.1.1 Probation in Europe and Baltic Variants

The scope, nature, and practice of probation in Europe are as diverse as the languages, cultures, and histories of the countries in which it has developed. In general, probation in many countries in Europe serves as a central site in the administration of the criminal justice system. In a useful overview, van Kalmthout & Durnescu (2008) suggest rudimentary probation activities have existed since the early 1800s throughout Europe, and specifically in France, the Netherlands, and the Nordic countries. As in the US, these activities were informally organized though religious groups or clubs, and individuals actively sought to assist offenders by diverting them away from alcohol, helping them find work, and supporting them to find a place to live. These informal arrangements were bolstered by efforts at the end of the 19th and the beginning of the 20th century to reform the system of criminal sanctions (O'Brian, 1995).

An important development during this period was the introduction of the conditional sanction that required the establishment of new supervising bodies. These bodies were initially supported by a number of volunteers who, on educational or religious grounds, sought to "cure" those in conflict with the law (Kalmthout & Durnescu, 2008). In countries where the rudimentary forms of probation already existed, the introduction of the new sanctions and supervisory bodies strengthened the position of organizations working with detainees and former detainees. Probation, as a fully realized concept with statutory implications, came into being in the UK with the 1907 Probation of Offenders Act. The recognition of the role of this work resulted in activities, once informally organized by volunteers, now officially mandated with a statutory legal basis. The sort of care required to supervise offenders conditionally sentenced or released by the courts led community-based charities to develop more specialized social casework. However, the professionalization of probation that would result may have proven to be something of a mixed blessing (Whitehead & Statham, 2007).

Probation services in Europe traditionally take place in the trial and enforcement phase. As in North America, most probation services are responsible for writing social enquiry and pre-sentence reports, for providing support and guidance to the offender during or after his detention, and supervising those under their jurisdiction. This might occur through a conditional, suspended or deferred sentence, a conditional release, or a non-custodial penalty. Sanctions might include an in-patient or out-patient order, a treatment or training program, or community service, known in Latvia as "Community Service Work." More recently, probation services have developed new ways to divert some offenders from the formal system at the pre-trial phase through various forms of "mediation", based on principles derived from the restorative justice movement (Kemshall *et al.* 2004).

Probation in the Baltics has developed in very different ways. In Estonia, the Ministry of Justice established probation in 1998 through a long-standing partnership agreement with the German Foundation for International Legal Cooperation (GFIC). While a Canadian-Estonian expert was involved in the initial phase of developing the probation system in Estonia it was through the GFIC that legal reform was achieved, and expert visits and exchanges were funded. A key partnership was with the German federal state Mecklenburg-West Pomerania (Randma-Liiv & Kruusenberg, 2010). Since study tours, training and probation projects in Estonia have been funded either by the European program PHARE or bilaterally, through the British Council. Probation was initially based in Estonian courts, but since 2008, has been united with the Prisons Department as part of the Ministry of Justice's Division of Social Rehabilitation. Probation in Estonia deals with both adults and juveniles, and is responsible for implementing all community sanctions and measures, including: pre-sentence reports, pre-trial diversion, and community service though supervision. Post prison, it may also supervise those released through parole orders and electronic monitoring.

In Lithuania, on the other hand, there does not exist a formally established system of probation. Correctional inspectors through the Prison Department of the Ministry of Justice carry some of what may be called probation tasks on an informal basis, especially related to aftercare, or reintegration. Between 1999 and 2002, the Canada Lithuania Corrections Project (CLCP), delivered programming by the Correctional Services of Canada (CSC) in partnership with the Lithuanian Ministry of Justice and in the Panevezys Women's Penitentiary. The project sought to support probationary activities by replacing the punitive and strict militaristic approach with a more rehabilitative model, and reduce overcrowding by supporting prisoner reintegration within their communities. CIDA (2004) has since suggested that Lithuanian programming reduced the number of inmates and supported new prison programming including education, job skills training, and increased community involvement with prisoners. A major result, it is argued, was the provision of psychological services and social services coordinated by new social workers.

Many Lithuanian participants involved in the Canada project who were interviewed through one independent study felt the project failed to comprehend the complex relationship between the state and community groups (Gestautaite, 2001). In one example, the failure to identify qualified social workers to support the reintegration of prisoners resulted in the hiring of former police officers. This decision alienated *Lygtinai Isleistu Asmenu Prieziuros Organizacija* (LIAPO), a project partner and central NGO established to assist with post-prison release and community reintegration. By choosing expediency over meaningful civil society engagement, Canadian results in Lithuania were not as pronounced as those in Latvia. Today, in Lithuania, correctional inspectors do not operate under a distinct legal basis or as a separate administrative body (Deveikyte, 2008). While some community volunteers assist, aftercare is mostly organized by a few established non-governmental organizations, like *Lithuanian Caritas*, and the Prisoners' Guardianship Association of Lithuania. Until recently, it appears engagement centers and support groups for at-risk juveniles were organized by the Red Cross.

While privileging the findings of one study over another is problematic, what CIDA viewed as a clear project success was not matched by independent research conducted on the ground. Policy transfer is difficult, and reforming justice systems is a process ill suited to the political impatience of our time. Latvian probation, discussed in more detail below, might be seen as a middle ground between the very formal state-based Estonian system and the more ad hoc community-based service approach in Lithuania. This might be usefully reconceived as a combination of care and control. Of immediate interest is the development of the State Probation Service (SPS) in Latvia.

2.2 Developing Probation/*Probācija* in Latvia

The creation of the Latvian Probation Service was a continuation of criminal justice reform activities that began in the mid 1990s, based initially on prison cooperation with Norway and Sweden. In 1997, this cooperation was formalized through the Nord Balt Prison Project

(NBPP), funded by the Council of Europe. The project sought to improve Latvian prisons, implement new programs, and increase opportunities among prisoners to access education, industrial training, and employment skills. Discussed in more detail in Chapter 5, these developments laid the groundwork for subsequent justice reforms. A central development through the NBPP was that the Latvian government and prison administration officials were first introduced to the concept of "probation." While based on a Northern European model, stressing aftercare and social rehabilitation, this introduction would lead a variety of Latvian actors to continue to support reforms, leading to the development of a probation service in Latvia. In January 1998, Concept Paper of Social Rehabilitation of Ex-Prisoners was approved. The term "probation" *(probācija)* first appeared in amendments passed in 1998 to the Sentence Execution Code (Jurevicius, 2008).

While the idea of providing state assistance to prisoners and suspending custodial sentences can be traced to the first period of independence (1918-1940), the practical development of the SPS took place only after Latvia regained its independence in 1991 (Zeibote, 2008). To understand the importance of probation in Latvia, some context may be useful. As discussed in more detail in Chapter 4, the criminal justice system the country inherited after independence was a product of Soviet occupation. There is a tendency to treat Soviet criminal justice uniformly as simply excessively punitive. Historically, however, the USSR was a leader in the development of non-custodial alternatives, such as community service orders, once called "corrective work". During Soviet rule in Latvia, there were some community sanctions and measures – like suspended sentences, correctional work, and early release from imprisonment. The limited supervision of offenders in the community that did exist, however, was organized and conducted by the police (van Kalmthout *et al.* 2003). The supervisory role by the police in Latvia limited the involvement of community members within the justice system. This had profound consequences in the early years of Latvian probation and recruiting volunteers was often very difficult (AUCC, 2005).

In occupied Latvia, as in other FSU countries, the criminal justice system often served ideological ends, and the justice system could be used to punish un-socialist thoughts and acts (Los, 2003). This legacy left a high rate of imprisonment, an over-reliance on pre-trial detention, and insufficient means for diversion programs and early release (Berzins, 2002). A central development was the new Criminal Law adopted in 1999, which included a new type of sentence – community service. Judges now had the discretion to impose a sentence of "Community Work" for less serious offenses, while retaining the ability to impose custodial sentences for more serious offenses. Central to the development of the SPS were project activities funded by CIDA between 1998 and 2004. Introduced in Chapter 1, these projects and their impact in Latvia are presented in some detail in Chapters 4, 5, and 6. In short, since 1999, the projects provided: financial and administrative support for pilot project competitions to model juvenile crime prevention and early probation services; the creation of a working group under the auspices of the Ministry of Justice that developed a Policy "concept paper" on the development of the probation service; amendments to the Criminal Procedure code, Criminal Law; and the drafting of the Probation Act ultimately establishing the State Probation Service as an institution under the Ministry of Justice in October 2003.

Beginning in 2003 and based on four years of project activities developing local alternatives, Canadians trained the first generation of Latvian probation officers (AUCC, 2005) to ensure the State Probation Service could practically function when the Law on the State Probation Service came into force on January 1, 2004. Its mission to promote community safety by reducing criminal offending and the strategy of the State Probation Service is closely linked to the Strategy of the Ministry of Justice. In 2010, the SPS worked with more than 27,000 clients and the Ministry of Justice has set additional priority areas for probation.

Figure 2.2 Probation Priority Areas (Dementjevs, 2011)

1) Strengthening of administrative capacity of sentence execution institutions including an increase of the salaries of probation officers, additional staff for work with specific categories of clients such as sex offenders and clients with mental disorders;
2) Development of the social correction programs and services for the resettlement of offenders including the introduction of prison programs to be carried out by probation officers;
3) Creation of unified Information system for State probation Service and prison Administration;
4) Expansion of mediation in criminal matters including the involvement and training of volunteers as mediators.

2.2.1 Legislation, Mission, and Organization

The main principles of the operation of the probation system are laid down in the Sentence Enforcement Code (1970), Law on the State Probation Service (2004), the Criminal Procedure Law (2005), and the Criminal Law (1998). The Sentence Enforcement Code prescribes the general procedure for the execution of all criminal sentences, including community work service. It also includes rules on supervision of persons with suspended sentences and persons on parole. The Law on Educational Measures for Juveniles contains rules on community work service – a possible diversion for juveniles that can be applied to juveniles as young as 11. The 2004 Law on the State Probation Service establishes the organization and operation of the SPS. The main principles of the SPS included in the law are:

1. *Principle of co-operation* – organization and facilitation of inter-institutional co-operation in order to use effectively the resources of the state, local governments and non-governmental institutions and to enchain resources for probation tasks;

2. *Principle of optimization* – the work of Probation Service is organized based on the economic principle of feasible functions, which allows for the delegation of some functions to local governments and NGOs, while retaining the prerogative nationally to control the implementation of these functions and set the criteria;
3. *Principle of social integration* – The basis for probation work is integration of clients in society, accomplishing the correction of behavior and supervision.

The 2005 Criminal Procedure Law outlines the process of the investigation of a criminal offence and the role of the probation service various stages in the criminal prosecution. It also defines the role of the probation service at the different stages of the criminal procedure. In Latvia, victims may choose to settle with an offender at any stage of a criminal prosecution, and the SPS can provide mediators to facilitate the process of mediation at no cost to the participants. Additional and secondary legislation in the form of twelve regulations of the Cabinet of Ministers defines and describes the operation of the probation service in greater detail. The Criminal Law defines Latvia's system of punishment and the process of suspending sentences. The law allows that anyone over the age of criminal responsibility (14 years) may become a client of the SPS.

The service was designed to allow for tasks to be phased-in. Until 2004 the service had competence over only the delivery of aftercare to ex-prisoners, preparation of pre-sentence reports to judges and prosecutors, and co-ordination of community work service. By 2005, the SPS consolidated its existing functions and completed its territorial development by creating its Headquarters in Riga and establishing 28 regional offices. By 2006, the SPS took on court-ordered supervision of persons and currently it plays an important role supervising non-custodial sanctions and court-ordered conditional sentences. The State Probation Service (SPS) states its mission as working toward the promotion of public safety. The main task of the service is to reduce offending by supporting crime prevention activities, mediation services, and a variety of projects in local municipalities in co-operation with secondary schools, the police, and local NGOs. Through consultative boards, crime prevention activities are coordinated with representatives from the court, police, prosecutor's office, and other social service organizations, who meet regularly to discuss problems and possible solutions in the area of crime prevention. As described on the SPS website:

> The creation of the State Probation Service is the proof that the sentencing system in our country does not have the retaliation characteristics that the offender is not lost for the society and that the state takes responsibility for the members of its society.

To administer these numerous activities, SPS is structurally divided into four units, with three deputy heads. The SPS structure is reproduced below.

Figure 2.3 Structure of the State Probation Service (Zeibote, 2008)

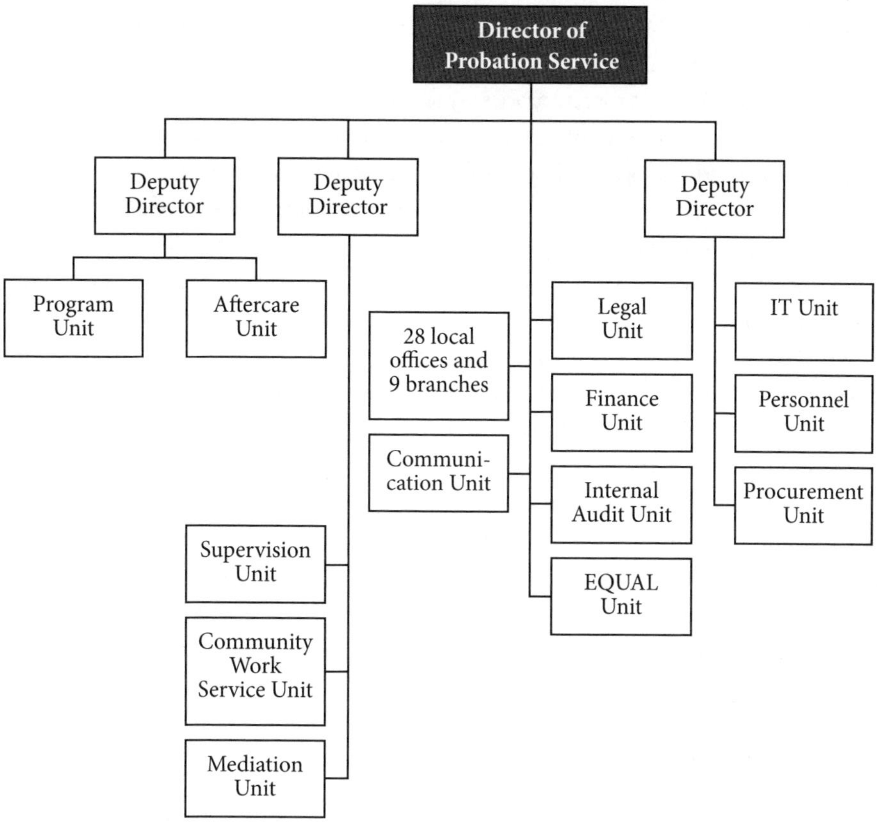

2.2.2 *Core Activities of the SPS*

The SPS in Latvia is involved in the work with offenders in all stages of the Criminal Justice process, including after-care outside the criminal justice system. Zeibote (2008) outlines three phases of the criminal procedure in which the SPS operates. These include: pre trial, trial and enforcement, and post release.

Pre-Trial Phase

At the pre-trial phase, a victim may choose to have the SPS organize a mediation process between them and the offender(s) to settle any issues arising from the offence. This settlement can be grounds for the termination of criminal proceedings in less-serious cases, under section 97(8) of the 2005 Criminal Procedure Law (CPL). In practice, most mediation cases are referred to probation by the police or prosecutors and rarely by the court.

In addition, a public prosecutor may divert an individual from formal criminal proceedings by conditionally releasing the accused from criminal liability. This may occur in two ways. The first is through a termination of proceedings where the criminal violation is less serious and the individual has not committed a criminal offense. The second is through an injunction by prosecutor where they believe that incarceration is not warranted. In either case, a prosecutor may end the criminal proceedings and sentence an individual to community service supervised by the SPS for a term of three to eighteen months. If the prosecutor decides either a termination or injunction is appropriate, they determine a time period of supervision from three to eighteen months, to be supervised by the SPS. Like a suspension of a sentence, if the person breaks any of the attached conditions or commits additional crimes during this period, the prosecutor may renew criminal proceedings.

To decide whether a termination or injunction is warranted, the prosecutor may require a report from the SPS. This report is called an "evaluation report" and is identical to a pre-sentence or pre-release report as discussed below. It is designed to present an individual's history and relevant characteristics. While voluntary, these reports represent the best way for an individual to avoid a custodial sentence. The SPS plays a central role in supervising the front-end diversions. An important additional development, identified by Zeibote (2008), is Section 243 of the CPL that provides for additional pre-trial measures. A bail-supervision program designed by Latvian-Canadian Andrejs Berzins (2002) to address the challenges posed by the overcrowded pre-trial detention facilities remains under consideration.

Table 2.4 Functions of Probation at Pre-Trial Phase

Activities	Relevant Law	Relevant Actors
Supervised victim-offender mediation	Sec. 66 of CPL (2005)	SPS coordinates after referral by police, prosecutors, or in rare cases by the court
Termination of criminal proceedings by Prosecutor – replace with community service	Sec. 415 of the CPL (2005)	SPS supervises based on decision of prosecutors
Injunction by Prosecutor – replace with community service	Sec. 429(1) of the CPL (2005)	SPS supervises based on decision of prosecutors
Write Evaluation Report	Sec. 415 (2) and/or Sec. 420 (2) of the CPL (2005)	SPS develops the report as required

2.2.2.1 Trial and Enforcement Phase

At the trial and enforcement phase, perhaps the most important activity of the SPS is the development of a pre-sentence report. This report, which is like the "evaluation report" in the pre-trial phase, is designed to assist judges to decide the most appropriate penalty, as set out in section 491 of the CPL. In practice, in the interests of efficiency, a request for pre-sentence report is most often sent by the prosecutor in advance of the court date. While there is no specific law or regulation governing the content of the report or the timeframe for its preparation, the SPS has developed internal guidelines that any request includes basic information about the person, the nature of the offense, and the deadline of submission. In theory, the request must be sent at least three weeks before the report is due. Like the evaluation above, the pre sentence report is based on meetings with family members, employers, and other institutions that may be relevant (schools, social clubs, etc.) and must include:

> ...a characterization of the probation client and an evaluation of his or her social circumstances, as well as the opinion of the State Probation Service regarding person.

In addition, the report identifies possible resources for the offender in the communities in which they live, and proposes conditions that would be advisable for the offender. During the process to develop the pre sentence report, the individual has the right to refuse to co-operate with SPS. In these cases a report is not prepared and the prosecutor or judge is informed.

In addition to the development of pre-sentence reports, the SPS may also supervise alternative sanctions such as 40 to 280 hours of Community Work Service. This work is to be completed outside of regular employment or studies in the area where the individual resides, and cannot include remuneration. Work providers may include local municipalities, NGOs, libraries, schools, among others. Sentenced persons draft a work execution plan and probation officers contact work providers or visit work sites to check if the person is working every day and according to the agreed plan. If those sentenced evade the work, a court may substitute custodial arrest for the un-served sentence, calculating two hours of work as one day of custodial arrest.

In addition, the SPS may supervise those on a suspended sentence to a maximum of three years. Currently, the court can suspend sentences, including: deprivation of liberty, custodial arrest, community work, or a fine. The sentence is suspended if a court, taking into account the nature of the offense, the harm caused, the personality of the offender, and other relevant circumstances, is convinced that the offender will not commit future violations. According to section 155 of the Sentence Enforcement Code, those serving suspended sentences must register at SPS within five days after the judgment has entered into force. They must comply with all legitimate requests, appear at the time and place set by a probation officer, and inform the probation officer about their place of residence, source(s) of income, and education. Those with suspended sentences must request permission to leave their place of residence for longer than fifteen days, and comply with any other obligations set by the court (Zeibote, 2008).

According to section 55(6) of Criminal Law, these additional obligations include agreements to offer reparations for the harm committed; not to change place of residence without the consent of the SPS; to keep away from specified places; to be present at place of residence at the time specified, and others as directed by the court. As discussed below, a new function of the SPS is to identify programmatic needs among clients, and supervise their participation in relevant programming such as anger management, substance abuse counseling, or cognitive skills development. Should a convicted individual who is granted a suspended sentence fail to fulfill the obligations imposed by the court, pursuant to a submission of SPS, the court may revoke the suspension of a custodial sentence or extend the term of probation for one year. Likewise, if a convicted person granted a suspended sentence commits a new criminal offence during the term of probation, his or her originally imposed sentence shall be implemented and further investigations launched.

Table 2.5 Functions of Probation at Trial and Enforcement Phase

Activities	Relevant Law	Relevant Actors
Write Pre Sentence Report	Sec. 15 of the Law on State Probation Service (2003)	SPS writes based on request from judge (often first requested by prosecutors)
Supervise Suspended Sentence	Sec. 55 of Criminal Law; Chap. 30 of Sentence Execution Law	SPS supervises sentence
Direct an individual to participate in probation programs	Sec. 55 (6) CPL (2007)	SPS identifies needs and supervises and implements programs

Presently, the service has a limited role during custodial sentences, although as discussed below, new programs are being developed to allow probation officers to begin to work with those in prisons to develop a sentence enforcement plan, and deliver programming within the prison.

Post Release Phase

Based on the observation that most offenders were not subject to any supervision or support following their release (Berzins, 2002), aftercare was one of the first functions of the SPS after it was created in 2003. As a separate activity, it is described in Law on the State Probation service and partly in the Sentence Enforcement Code. As a result of budget cuts, as of June 16, 2009 aftercare has been excluded from State Probation Service functions. Ironically, in a survey of public opinion in 2006, while only 28% of Latvians had heard about probation, the vast majority of those associate the SPS with post prison release and aftercare, rather than with community work service, supervision, or mediation (Zeibote, 2008). While this function is not presently included, if international experience is any guide, community re-integration will need to be revisited by the SPS. At present, there is no agency better placed in Latvia than the probation service to undertake it.

Originally, those who wish to co-operate with the State Probation Service after the full term of sentence may enter into an agreement for up to 18 months to receive aftercare, including consultations provided by a probation officer on issues of available resources such as housing, education, and employment. In addition, there may be an option for those releasing to participate in various probation programs, including cognitive behaviourial and resettlement programs, as well as half way house accommodation for up to nine months. During the aftercare phase, the SPS was originally to work in close co-operation with local municipalities, State Employment Agency and NGOs to assist clients in setting up their lives following imprisonment – this function, while formally suspended, continues on an ad hoc basis as discussed below.

A conditional release from a custodial sentence in Latvia is possible, provided the individual has not committed a violation and has attempted to compensate those harmed by his or her crime; served not less than half of the sentence of a serious crime, or two-thirds of the sentence imposed for a less serious crime. For those convicted of a serious crime and previously sentenced to a custodial term, the requirement for conditional release is not less than three-quarters of the sentence imposed. If life imprisonment has been imposed, conditional release is possible only after twenty-five years of a custodial sentence.

Under the original law, an administrative commission and the court must approve conditional releases based on the pre-release report developed by the SPS. In general, those conditionally released have the same obligations as those with suspended sentences, but are viewed by the SPS as requiring additional kinds of assistance. Should someone conditionally released prior to the completion of sentence commit a new criminal offence or violate any conditions required under the terms of their release, they are returned to court for additional sanctions (Zeibote, 2008). Although the SPS has ceased to provide after-care formally, they remain involved in informal assistance when requested, and in cooperation with a variety of NGOs. They will also cooperate with the Prison Administration in 2012 to deliver a Sex Offender program, currently in development, to incarcerated offenders. As a result of the discontinuation of aftercare, probation functions are today concentrated on four main duties.

Figure 2.6 Percentage of Main Duties of Probation Officers in 2010 (Jurevicius, 2011)

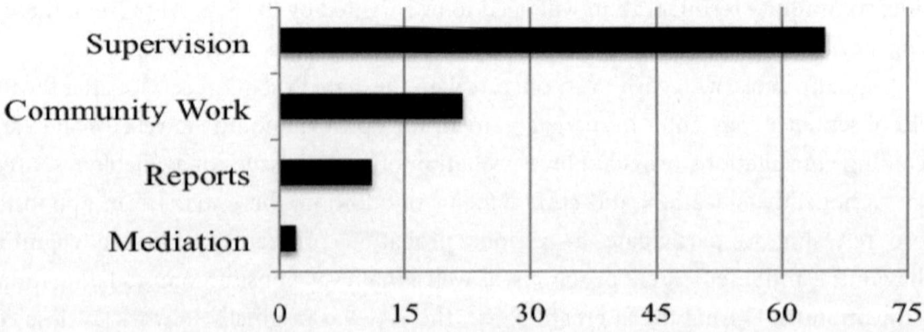

2.2.3 *Supervision Strategies*

As presented above, supervision is the most important function for probation officers and might usefully be seen based on the continuum of control and care model. Control is exercised through the courts that set the conditions, obligations, and requirements of probation clients, including participation in substance abuse programming, avoiding undesirable associates, and checking in with probation officers at the appointed time and place. Care and assistance is provided through the identification of basic needs like education, employment, housing, and criminogenic needs that inform treatment plans. Central to understanding how probation operates in practice in Latvia is the role of the risk/needs assessment approach. Developed through the Canadian project, and based on the assessment tool of the British Columbian government in Canada based on the Risk-Needs-Responsivity model (RNR) developed in the 1980s and first formalized in the 1990s (Bonta & Andrews, 1996), the RNR model is based on the three principles outlined in figure 2.7.

Figure 2.7 RNR Principles

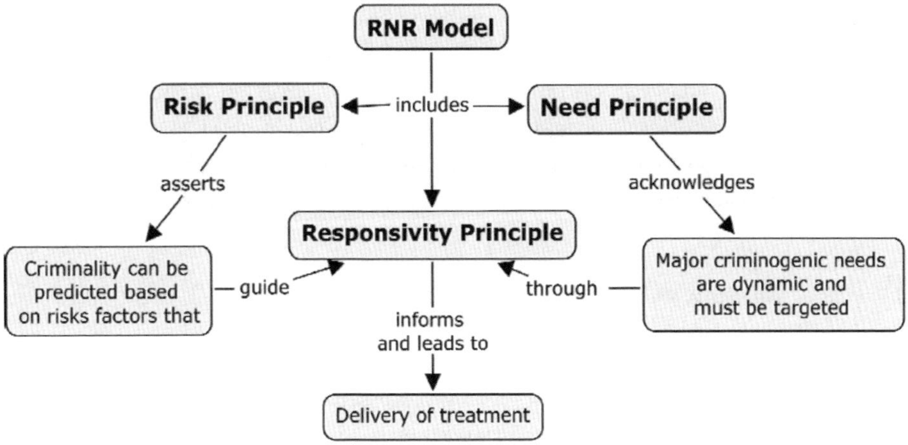

In Latvia, the supervision of a suspended sentence is outlined in internal SPS regulations based on how an individual scores on the Latvian risk assessment instrument. The score assigned corresponds to three levels of supervision - high, medium, and low - and the assessment is used to draft a plan with the involvement of the sentenced person. In practice, supervision is based on three principles. The risk principle is based on the idea that the SPS should offer more treatment to higher risk offenders - low risk offenders require minimal to no intervention. The need principle is based on the idea that programming should target criminogenic needs and dynamic risk factors. The responsivity principle is based on the idea that the SPS should offer treatment in a manner designed to help offenders become responsive to the programmatic intervention.

In Latvia, based on this matrix, a supervision plan may include one intervention per month for persons with a low risk of offending, with up to four interventions per month for those identified as having a high risk of offending. Each individual under supervision has a case manager that is responsible for supervising the plan, including identifying problems and potential solutions and directing them to participate in specially developed probation programs run by trained probation officers. Those with a high or medium risk of offending must participate in probation programs which are based on various cognitive-behaviorial approaches. The development and delivery of probation programs is discussed in more detail below.

2.3 Operational and Administrative Developments

The SPS has identified and overcome a number of hurdles since its establishment in 2003. While others remain, and are discussed in greater detail later, it may be useful to understand how the service has adapted, continued to build capacity, and extended beyond its limited beginnings to the position it occupies within the Latvian criminal justice system today. These might be usefully organized into staffing and training issues, probation programming, and the role of volunteers.

2.3.1 *Staffing, Demographics, and SPS Training*

Initially, staff recruitment was based on individuals who had been part of Latvia-Canadian programming, including the training sessions discussed in detail in Chapter 6. By law, all probation officers must be civil servants and thus need a Bachelor's degree. While there are no specific requirements for type of university degree, preference is given to staff with education in law, social work, social pedagogy, and psychology, as demonstrated by the educational background of probation staff in 2010, in figure 2.8.

Figure 2.8 Staff Educational Backgrounds (Jurevicius, 2011)

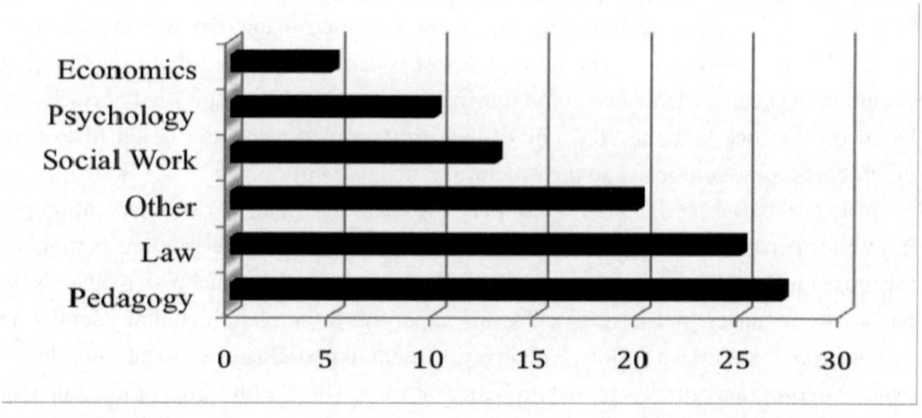

There is not yet a specific university-based program on probation, although the University of Latvia is working with the SPS to develop a two-year Probation program. To support staff to continue their education, the SPS co-funds Master's degree programs, provided the area of study is related to probation work. Presently, the majority of staff holds either a Bachelor's or Master's degree, as demonstrated below. Currently there are discussions on lowering academic requirements for workers organizing community work service and the supervision of low risk offenders.

Figure 2.9 Type of Educational Degree by Staff (Jurevicius, 2011)

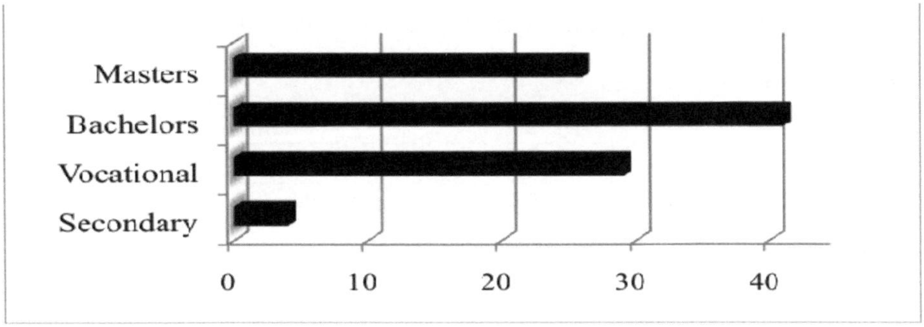

In 2010, 86% of probation staff was female and 14% male. Figure 2.10 shows the percentage of probation staff by age.

Figure 2.10 Percentages of Probation Staff by Age (Jurevicius, 2011)

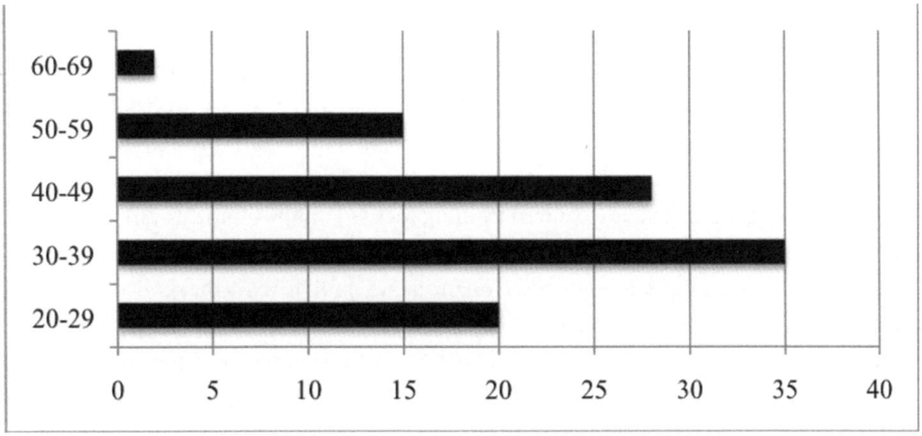

In the past, the turnover of staff has been quite high; 50 employees, for example, left the SPS from January to June 2007 (Zeibote, 2008). Since that time, the internal dynamics of the service have become more stable. In 2003, eight people were employees of the SPS, and by the end of 2006, quantity of staff members reached 430 and have since been reduced in recent years, as budget cuts and staff turnover has forced some consolidation of roles and responsibilities. At present, staff must comply with professional standards elaborated in 2008, which include specific duties, competencies, skills, and knowledge. Developed since the Canadian project ended, they were provided by past project participants from British Columbia who interviewed senior staff to identify the ten most important competencies of an ideal probation officer.

Table 2.11 Ten Core Competencies of a Probation Officer (Jurevicius, 2011)

Core Competencies
1. Ability to listen (and hear) the client
2. Ability to understand and to empathize with client
3. Ability to act adequately, in controlled manner (not impulsively)
4. Teamwork and cooperation within institution/organization
5. Decisive insight
6. Adaptability to changes in client's needs, and the organization of case management
7. Ability to extract and utilize necessary information for preparation of reports, plans, and to promote positive changes
8. Professional integrity/ honesty
9. Problem solving to identify and direct client-focused resources
10. Goal oriented to use appropriate tools to achieve results

In Latvia, these have been distilled into five skills. They include the ability to: motivate clients to cooperate; independently plan and organize work; identify and analyze client issues; locate and implement possible solutions; and make and justify supervision decisions. Following the initial training of Latvian probation officers in staff through the Canadian project, there was limited additional training in the early years of the SPS. While all civil servants had to complete state-required training focused on the political system of Latvia, ethical duties of civil servants, time and resource management, public procurements, and legal writing, the training was not focused on probation practices. As the service has grown, the training program has become more advanced.

Between 2006 and 2009, training was delivered by experts from headquarters and focused on the history and theory of probation. There were no tests or exams, and the approach was highly centralized with little practical discussion of what probation in Latvia involved or required. In response, a number of additional one-day in-service days for probation officers were developed as the service grew in experience and expertise (Jurevicius, 2011). These focused on the history and theory of punishment and probation, the functions of the State Probation Service of Latvia, the evidence-based "What Works" approach, cognitive behavioral theory and thinking errors, and basics for safety at work. Other one-day in-service training focused on supervision practices, the risk and needs assessment tools (RNA) for juveniles and adults, the preparation of assessment and "evaluation" reports for both pre-sentence and parole, and on community service and mediation and restorative justice.

2.3.3.1 Future Training

More recently, training has been moved to a hybrid model that combines independent study online with small group work and peer review. Training involves readings on recent developments in probation, case analysis of difficult supervision experiences, and individual consultations and feedback. Organized by headquarters, local probation managers submit training applications to the respective Department, including Supervision, Community Works, Mediation, or Probation Programs based on the training needs of staff. No special facilities exist for staff training, but a qualitatively new training model of Latvian Probation Service is to be implemented by 2013 (Jurevicius, 2011). Probation officers identified as specialists will undertake training of other colleagues for several weeks per year. These specialists will engage in site visits and case reviews, and the new focus of future training will be on conveying theory into practice and the development of core skills using a variety of hands-on and experiential models, including role-plays.

2.3.2 The Role of Volunteers and the Evolution of Probation Programming

In the early years of Latvian probation, volunteers worked exclusively to support youth-centered prevention programming, prison programming for juvenile offenders, and community reintegration efforts for juveniles and adults alike. An early focus was the development of a system to encourage community-based volunteers and mediators (Zeibote, 2008). Individuals who have expressed the wish to participate in the implementation of probation tasks, and who have participated in consultations with the officials of the State Probation Service, may be approved to work as volunteers. Approval is based on their education, experience, their age (over 18), and knowledge of the Latvian language. Today, in addition to nearly 400 staff, the service relies upon a network of more than 60 trained and certified volunteers who assist in the delivery of programs, and who work with offenders at the direction of and in cooperation with probation officers in their community and the SPS (Jurevicius, 2010).

Initially, programs offered through the SPS were limited. They included basic cognitive behavioral programming, anger management, and substance abuse programs (Zeibote, 2008). In 2008, a committee comprised of officials from the SPS, the Ministry of Social Welfare, the Ministry of Education and Science, and the Ministry of Health was established to streamline existing probation programs (Dementjevs, 2011). Today, probation programs include two social rehabilitation programs, such as the School of Life, targeted at offenders who have served long-term sentences in prison, and the Substance Use Management program, targeted at probation clients who have committed crime under the influence of alcohol or drugs.

In addition, the SPS coordinates seven social behaviorial correction programs. These include: the Forming Respectful Relationships program targeted at probation clients whose offenses are linked to violent behavior in the family; and the Violence Prevention Program for clients whose offenses are linked to impulsive aggressive behavior. Other social behaviorial programs include the EQUIP program for juveniles aged 14-25 who have engaged in delinquent behavior, and the Motivation for Change program for clients judged to need additional support and life skills. Two new sex-offender treatment programs are being developed with the assistance of the Norwegian government for offenders on some form of community supervision, and others who are incarcerated (Dementjevs, 2011).

2.3.3 Impacts, Outcomes, and the Role of Data

As discussed in Chapter 1, Canadian programming is largely seen as successful in Latvia based on the projects achieving their broad project-based goals. However, achieving Canadian-developed goals is a rather limited means to assess success. A more relevant indicator is the growth of the SPS and its impact on the criminal justice system itself. Since 2001, but especially evident since 2004, the SPS has grown and Latvia has experienced a decreasing prison population as Figure 2.13 illustrates. This drop in incarceration rate has occurred despite the fact that the crime rate in Latvia has remained relatively stable over the last five years, as suggested in Figure 2.14. One important development appears to be the development of the SPS in 2003, as incarceration rates between 2004 and 2007 were dramatically reduced just as probation clients increased.

Table 2.12 Latvian Probation Service in Numbers (SPS, 2011)

Year	2003	2004	2005	2006	2007	2008	2009	2010
Budget (Lats)	190 000	444 908	2, 516 816	3, 271 540	5, 368 111	5, 834 700	3, 851 375	2, 892 135
Staff	20	39	257	430	513	551	359	389
Probation Clients	n/a	204	2581	12 081	19 492	25 921	21 361	19 434
Case Load	n/a	5.23	10.04	28.09	37.99	47.04	59.50	49.96

Table 2.13 Latvian Prison Population Trends (ICPS, 2010)[1]

Year	1992	1995	1998	2001	2004	2007	2010
Prison Population	8340	9457	10,070	8831	8179	6548	6780
Per 100,000	314	374	410	373	353	287	319

Table 2.14 Latvian Overall Crime Rates (CSB, 2010)[2]

Year	1992	1995	1998	2001	2004	2007	2010
Recorded Crimes	16, 871	39,141	36,674	51,082	62,173	55,620	51, 108
Per 10, 000	237	158	152	217	269	244	228

Another important development is the careful compilation of data on probation and its online publication. Too often western probation services, and agencies of the justice system generally, have failed to invest in the sorts of research partnerships upon which to base a clear, articulate, and progressive vision of their public value (Wheeldon & Heidt, 2007). During the first years of the SPS, statistics were not always collected properly, and there are differences in numbers of clients for certain years between annual reports (Jurevicius, 2011). More recently, efforts have been made to improve the quality of data collection. In Latvia, the collection of reliable data is seen as central to establishing the benefits of these new approaches. The numeric indicators in the table below offer important insights into the development and operation of the SPS. Although as discussed in Chapter 3, numeric indicators alone are rarely sufficient to establish meaningful understanding about the utility of a criminal justice intervention, they should not be ignored. The collection and careful analysis of data must always inform broader policy discussions. Table 2.15 provides key data on the operation of the SPS.

Table 2.15 Number of clients under different activities of probation 2004-2010

Activities	2004	2005	2006	2007	2008	2009	2010
Mediation	-	51	251	744	1140	745	440
Pre-sentence reports	61	633	1156	1532	1725	930	176
Pre-release reports	-	-	1226	1406	1330	1468	1887
Suspended sentence	-	-	4925	9088	10634	11144	10563
Parole supervision	-	-	832	557	1956	1758	1778

1 See International Centre for Prison Studies (ICPS) Latvia Brief Retrieved from <www.kcl.ac.uk/depsta/law/research/icps/worldbrief/wpb_country.php?country=149> March 18, 2011.

2 See The Central Statistical Bureau of Latvia retrieved from <http://data.csb.gov.lv/Dialog/Saveshow.asp> on March 18, 2011.

Activities	2004	2005	2006	2007	2008	2009	2010
Conditionally released from criminal liability	-	-	445	319	871	678	409
Community work for juveniles – educational measure	-	77	138	188	190	212	163
Community work service	-	1059	2545	3159	3904	4290	4018
Aftercare	169	778	293	273	265	136	N/A
Clients placed in rehabilitation centers (half-way houses)	-	178	164	359	289	N/A	N/A
Clients involved in programs	-	-	679	1862	1669	1317	1291

2.4 Concluding Remarks

The development of the Latvian probation service since 2003 is unprecedented. Based on the general recognition of the problems with mass incarceration and a renewed focus on social inclusion, it is clear Latvia benefited from the experience of a number of countries in the region and beyond. While challenges no doubt remain, the service has reduced the prison population, and developed new programs and services for a growing number of clients. Although similar in some aspects to other European systems, the service is a uniquely Latvian creation. Today, the SPS works with 27, 000 clients facilitating mediation in criminal matters, preparing pre-sentence and parole reports, developing and implementing social behaviorial correction programs for offenders, organizing and supervising community work for juveniles and adults, and supervising those conditionally released or paroled from places of imprisonment.

Unlike probation in Estonia and Lithuania, the Latvian service better combines key elements of care and control through the local adaption of risk/needs frameworks and instruments used to categorize offenders, and the cooperation of the community who assist probation officers to organize and deliver programming. The SPS has also overcome key challenges related to building and sustaining administrative competence. This has included developing new training models, implementing staffing requirements, training volunteers, and the careful compilation of operational and administrative data. The commitment of probation staff to compile evidence and share both their successes and failures should be respected and encouraged.

Expanding the involvement of the community in crime prevention is neither a politically neutral nor easily achieved outcome. In Latvia, however, the community and civil society are seen as key elements in probation work, and increasing their role has been a priority. While numeric indicators provide an important lens through which to view the value of probation programming in Latvia, they may not be sufficient when trying to understand "how" and "why" programming was successful. Chapter 3 explores key questions to be asked when evaluating legal technical assistance projects based on the broader complexities of development, and the specific challenges related to probation programming, including country context, organizational constraints, and individual impediments. It argues that this three-tier model is relevant for any country emerging from authoritarian regimes and seeking to reform their justice system.

Chapter 2 Bibliography

Association of Universities and Colleges of Canada. *Latvian legal reform program: Final report to CIDA*. Ottawa, ON, 2005.

J. Batt. *The New Slovakia: National Identity, Political Integration and the Return to Europe.* London, UK: Royal Institute of International Affairs, 1996.

C. Beccaria. *On crimes and punishments.* Indianapolis: Hackett Publishing, 1764/1986.

G. Berman & A. Fox. *Trial and Error in Criminal Justice Reform: Learning from Failure.* Washington, DC: Urban Institute, 2010.

A. Berzins *Report to The Working Group on Probation in Latvia.* The Legal Reform Capacity Program in Latvia, Ottawa, ON: Association of Universities and Colleges of Canada, 2002.

J. Bonta & D.A. Andrews. A commentary on Ward and Stewart's model of human needs. *Psychology, Crime & Law*, Vol. 9, 2003, pp. 215-218.

R. Burnett & S. Maruna. So 'prison works', does it? The criminal careers of 130 men released from prison under home secretary, Michael Howard. *The Howard Journal*, Vol. 43 No. 4, 2004, pp. 390-404.

R. Canton. Penal Policy Transfer: A Case Study from Ukraine. *The Howard Journal*, Vol. 45, No. 5, 2006, pp. 502-520.

S.D. Camp & G.G. Gaes. Criminogenic effects of the prison environment on inmate behavior: Some experimental evidence. *Crime and Delinquency*, Vol. 51, pp. 425-442.

Central Bureau of Statistics. Court Decisions on Criminal Cases. Riga, LV, Central Bureau of Statistics, 2011.

A. Dementjevs. Innovations in State Probation Service of Latvia: The Impact of Alternative Sanctions and Electronic Monitoring. Presentation Delivered March 3, 2011 International Meetings of Ministries of Justice, Vilnius, Lithuania.

E. Deveikyte. Probation in Lithuania. In A.M. van Kalmthout & I. Durnescu (Eds.), *Probation in Europe*. Nijmegen: Wolf Legal Publishers, 2008.

P. Dutkiewicz, A. Keating, M. Nikoula & E. Shevchenko. *Juvenile Justice in Russia: Models, Design and the Road Ahead.* Gatineau PQ: Canadian International Development Agency, 2009.

M. Foucault. *Discipline & Punish: The Birth of the Prison*. NY: Vintage Books, 1975.

D. Garland. *The Culture of Control: Crime and Social Order in Contemporary Society*. Chicago, Il: University of Chicago Press, 2001.

Z. Gestautaite. *Penal and policy reform in Lithuania and the involvement of Canadian expertise.* Unpublished Masters Thesis, Carleton University, Ottawa, ON, 2001.

S. Golub. The legal empowerment alternative. In T. Carothers (Ed.), *Promoting the rule of law abroad: The problem of knowledge*. Washington, D.C.: Carnegie Endowment for International Peace, 2003, pp. 161-190.

R. Harris. Studying Probation: A Comparative Approach. In K. Hamai, R. Harris, M. Hough, R. Ville & U. Zvekic (Eds.) *Probation Around the World: A Comparative Study*. London, UK: Routledge Press, 1995, pp. 3-24.

J. Howard. *The State of Prisons in England and Wales*. London: Patterson Smith, 1777/1937.

M. Ignatieff. *A Just Measure of Pain*, London: Macmillan, 1978.

International Center for Prison Studies. World Prison Brief. International Center for Prison Studies, University of Essex, 2011, Available at: <www.prisonstudies.org/>.

W. Jacoby. *The enlargement of the EU and NATO: Ordering from the Menu in Central Europe*. New York: Cambridge University Press, 2006.

M. Joutsen & U. Zvekic. Noncustodial Sanctions: Comparative Overview. In U. Zvekic (Ed.), *Alternatives to Imprisonment in Comparative Perspective*, Chicago: Nelson-Hall Publishers, 1994, pp. 1-42.

I. Jurevičius. *Creation of the State Probation Service*. Unpublished Masters Thesis, University of Latvia: Riga, 2008.

I. Jurevičius. Implementing Probation programs in Latvia. Presented at STARR conference What Works in Reducing Re-offending? April 28-30, 2010. Downing College, University of Cambridge, UK.

I. Jurevičius. Recruitment and training of probation officers in Latvia. Presented May 26, 2011, Center for European Probation, Utrecht, Netherlands.

A.M. van Kalmthout, J. Roberts & S. Vinding (Eds.). *Probation and Probation Services in the EU Accession Countries*. Netherlands: Wolf Legal Publishers, 2003.

A.M. van Kalmthout & I. Durnescu. *Probation in Europe*. Nijmegen: Wolf Legal Publishers, 2008.

A. Kamenska. *Par piespiedu sabiedrisko darbu kā sodu Latvijā*. Cietumu un policijas reformu programmas apkārtraksts Alternatīva, Nr.1, 2000a.

A. Kamenska. *Probācijas dienests Lielbritānijā*. Cietumu un policijas reformu programmas apkārtraksts Alternatīva, Nr.1, 2000b.

A. Kamenska. Latvia. In A.M. van Kalmthout, J. Roberts & S. Vinding (Eds.), *Probation and Probation Services in the EU Accession Countries*. Netherlands: Wolf Legal Publishers, 2003.

H. Kemshall, P. Holt, R. Bailey & G. Boswell. Beyond programmes: organisational and cultural issues in the implementation of What Works. In G. Mair (Ed.), *What Matters in Probation*. Cullompton, UK: Willan, 2004, pp. 170-186.

L.H. Lofland. *A World of Strangers: Order and Action in Urban Public Space*. New York: Basic Books, 1973.

M. Los. Crime in transition: The post-communist state, markets and crime. *Crime, Law & Social Change*, Vol. 40, 2003, pp. 145-169.

J.R. Lilly, F.T. Cullen & R.A. Ball. *Criminological Theory: Context and Consequences.* Thousand Oaks: Sage, 2011.

R. MacDonald. *(Book review) The tools of government: A guide to the new governance by Salamon, Lester.* London, UK: Oxford University Press, 2002.

R. McGowan. The Well-Ordered Prison: England, 1780-1865. In N. Morris & D.J. Rothman (Eds.), *The Oxford History of the Prison: The Practice of Punishment in Western Society.* Oxford: Oxford University Press, 1995, pp. 227-262.

N. Morris. The Contemporary Prison 1965 – Present. In N. Morris & D.J. Rothman (Eds.), *The Oxford History of the Prison: The Practice of Punishment in Western Society.* Oxford: Oxford University Press, 1995, pp. 227-262.

R. O'Brien. The Prison on the Continent: Europe, 1865-1965. In N. Morris & D.J. Rothman (Eds.), *The Oxford History of the Prison: The Practice of Punishment in Western Society.* Oxford: Oxford University Press, 1995, pp. 199-226.

E.M. Peters. Prison Before the Prison: The Ancient and Medieval Worlds. In N. Morris & D.J. Rothman (Eds.) *The Oxford History of the Prison: The Practice of Punishment in Western Society.* Oxford: Oxford University Press, 1995, pp. 3-48.

L. Radzinowicz. *Ideology and crime.* New York: Columbia University Press, 1966.

T. Randma-Liiv & R. Kruusenberg. West-East policy transfer: motives, scope, role models and agents. Paper presented at IRSPM Conference held April 2-9, 2010, Berne, SW.

P. Spierenberg. The Body and The State: Early Modern Europe. In N. Morris & D.J. Rothman (Eds.), *The Oxford History of the Prison: The Practice of Punishment in Western Society.* Oxford: Oxford University Press, 1995, pp. 49-78.

M. Tonry. Evaluating Intermediate Sanctions Programs. In J. Petersilia (Ed.), *Community Corrections: Probation, Parole, and Intermediate Sanctions.* Oxford: Oxford University Press, 1998, pp. 79-96.

S. Walker. *Popular Justice: A History of American Criminal Justice,* (2nd Ed.) New York: Oxford Press, 1997.

B. Western. *Punishment and Inequality in America.* New York: Russell Sage, 2006.

J. Wheeldon & J. Heidt. Bridging the Gap: A Pragmatic Approach to Understanding Critical Criminologies and Policy Influence. *Critical Criminology*, Vol. 15, No. 4, 2007, pp. 313-325.

P. Whitehead & R. Staham. *The History of Probation: Politics, Power and Cultural Change 1876-2005*. London, UK: Shaw and Sons, 2007.

L. Zeibote. Probation in Latvia. In A.M. van Kalmthout & I. Durnescu (Eds.), *Probation in Europe*. Nijmegen: Wolf Legal Publishers, 2008.

3 Maps, Methods, and Meaning: Presenting a Three Tier Research Model

As described in Chapter 2, the establishment of the SPS in Latvia provides a possible counterpoint to what have been longstanding concerns about the role and value of legal technical assistance. In place of research, too often so-called expertise in this area is based on assumptive and conceptual arguments, accepted wisdom, and past practice. Too few studies consider how participants in a host country perceive components of specific capacity-building activities and training models. Renewed academic effort is needed to separate fact from opinion, and promote evidence-based approaches to better guide the delivery of legal technical assistance programming. Building on the pioneering work of Wedel (1998), who called for more study into the way interactions influence development outcomes, this chapter suggests more attention should be paid to the narratives of those who work on these projects.

To untangle some of the challenges connected with the study of international development projects and specifically, legal technical assistance projects, this chapter reviews existing international studies and research from Canada and the Former Soviet Union. It presents a discussion of research designs and data collection methods including the use of visual maps and diagrams that take seriously the challenges of cross-cultural research and can help participants locate their experience in their own terms. Finally, this chapter presents a three-tier model of project analysis that guides the remainder of the book. By studying the ways in which contextual, organizational, and individual factors augment or limit a project's success or failure, a more comprehensive approach to the assessment of development projects from Latvia might be undertaken, and lessons identified and applied elsewhere.

3.1 Development by Design or a Failure to Learn from the Past?

Despite the renewed focus on development assistance and the importance of broader integration with other government agencies, systemic problems affect organization and delivery of developmental assistance. Whatever the challenges, ample evidence exists that when properly designed, supported, and implemented, a competent network of individuals working together toward shared goals can facilitate important development successes. Rarely, however, is a development project examined in enough depth to allow the successes and failures to serve as a means to catalog these lessons. In one of the largest reviews of its kind – based on a sample of twenty-five evaluations completed over the past thirty years on projects ranging from rule of law to civil society, governance and general democracy in sub-Saharan Africa, Africa, Asia and the Middle East, Europe and Eurasia, and Latin America and the Caribbean – the authors conclude:

> We find a lack of methodological accuracy and inappropriate coverage of important information about the impact of assistance interventions. Most of the evaluations fail to provide key information about assistance activities, such as funding levels and personnel. We also find that the focus of evaluations tends to be on the immediate outcomes of very specific activities rather than on their link to agency goals and interests. Nearly all of the evaluations fail to discuss or rule out other possible explanations for a relation between a USAID activity and its alleged effects. The single-group, posttest-only design was the usual evaluation design, making it extremely difficult to attribute effects to USAID interventions. As a result of these problems, the USAID evaluations fail to show with a reasonable degree of certainty that the changes observed would not have occurred in the absence of USAID (Bollen, Paxton & Morishima, 2005, p. 199).

While rule of law and governance programming has increased exponentially since 1990, the knowledge and understanding about the effects of this assistance have not developed alongside these activities. Carothers (1999) in particular laments the serious consequences that result from the lack of systematic learning from within and outside the circle of practitioners. This is by no means an American phenomenon. In Canada, research on rule of law projects are often methodologically limited (Caldwell, 2005), and rarely disseminated. CIDA continues to operate through what has been called a "confusion of objectives," and a lack of consistency around aid practices which have been prone to "frequent twists and turns", and polices which have been adopted and rejected (Young, 1985, p. 13). Parpart and Veltmeyer (2004) argue that far from a hindrance, the "confusion" and "chaos" that is a hallmark of CIDA practice provides some needed nuance to development, a complex and sometimes contradictory endeavor.

In Canada, despite a research architecture including the International Development Research Agency (IDRC), universities, and think tanks, there is limited support for novel research into international development projects. In general, for many academics, research opportunities in development are negligible, and the policy community is unreceptive (Pestieau & Tait, 2004). Indeed, the lack of support within the development community itself may be based in part on the ascendance of more critical scholars skeptical about the colonial implications of international development and cynical about Canada's role in it. This has resulted in few empirical studies, and a lack of peer-reviewed and disseminated research. If justice reform projects are to continue as a central feature in democracy, human rights, and good governance programming, a central question is to what extent are lessons from these experiences being catalogued, considered, and integrated into current understanding.

While the failure to catalog lessons is consistently expressed among those who write about comparative development (Heller, 2005), there is a basic lack of understanding about how to study the context in which these projects have arisen. For Cameron (2006), this is not an organizational problem but a broad-based knowledge problem. As discussed in Chapter 1, the development assistance was initially constructed in response to geo-political needs and later based on what appeared to be compelling theories of economic transformation. There is simply no understanding among practitioners on the ground about how the rule of law is connected to democratic transformation (Perlin, 2003). Instead, just as assumptions about the rule of law have been unthinkingly exported from one country to another, so too have "results-based" approaches; as if indicators can be easily transposed from one development focus-area to another. This has resulted in a fetish for quantitative indices and management tools that attempt to replace complex human interactions with simplistic box-ticking exercises.

As presented below, when properly facilitated, those contemplating justice reform can better assess and understand the contextual, organizational, and individual challenges inherent in defining the role of law in society, both in theory and in practice. This requires, however, a focus on independent research and a willingness to acknowledge successes where they exist. Instead of complaining, more scholars should think carefully about how to study, measure and draw implications from the interactions within development projects. It may be useful to start with the failures.

3.1.1 *Learning From Failure: Legal Technical Assistance*

Thomas Carothers (1998, p. 95) warns against the rule of law's "...sudden elevation as a panacea for the ills of countries in transition from dictatorships or statist economies", a situation that "should make both patients and prescribers wary." He suggests that rule of law promotion programs can be categorized into three types. These include: the drafting and re-drafting of legislation; the fortification of legal institutions to make them more competent, efficient and accountable; and measures to curb governments into submission to the law. Carothers concludes that while some reform programs of the first two varieties have been successful, foreign and international assistance in 'strengthening' the rule of law has not fulfilled the expectation that it might encourage government compliance with the rule of law's 'fundamental principles.' Moreover, he has argued, development agencies do not appreciate what has failed and why (Carothers 2003).

The failure by developmental agencies to study, learn and apply the lessons of more than two decades of governance programming has not stopped their compilation. One problem, as discussed in Chapter 1, is that while the rule of law is considered a major aspect of modern governance (Sundstrom, 2006), legal technical assistance varies widely and is based on assumptions that are not well understood. Today, there is emerging academic interest in untangling these definitions and understanding democracy development based on an evaluation framework designed to investigate "what works for whom in what circumstances" (Wong, 2008, p. 38). Based on the acknowledgement in criminal justice and elsewhere that there is as much to learn from policy failures as there is from outright success (Berman & Fox, 2010), it may be useful to fully and fairly confront past critiques, in the service of broader democratic development. In the Middle East and North Africa, it offers a means to replace the burdens brought about by perpetual wars, and makes investing in collaborations that result in stability and peace look not only cost effective, but downright cheap by comparison.

Systematic treatments have placed the challenges of development assistance in political context (Morrison, 1998), and theoretical treatments have assisted in conceptualizing the challenges of justice reform and democracy development (Chodosh, 2005; Perlin, 2003). Useful recent contributions have provided qualitative insight into the challenge of democratic development through the civil society sector in Russia (Sundstrom, 2006). Some suggest, more generally, that the manner in which assistance is delivered is often as important as the type of assistance offered (Griffiths *et al.* 2005). Critiques of existing legal technical assistance initiatives are well documented and multi-faceted (Dandurand, 2006, pp. 21-22). Critics suggest a lack of sufficient funds, uncoordinated external attempts by multiple and under-informed donors (Protic, 2005), and the failure to promote coordinated and cooperative technical assistance among the numerous justice agencies within a country (Herman, 2001). Too often this has led to duplication and a poor utilization of development dollars. In part this is what drives the discussions around the *Paris Declaration* and the penetrating critiques of Bill Easterly. Others are included in Figure 3.1

Figure 3.1 Identifying Failures in Legal Technical Assistance

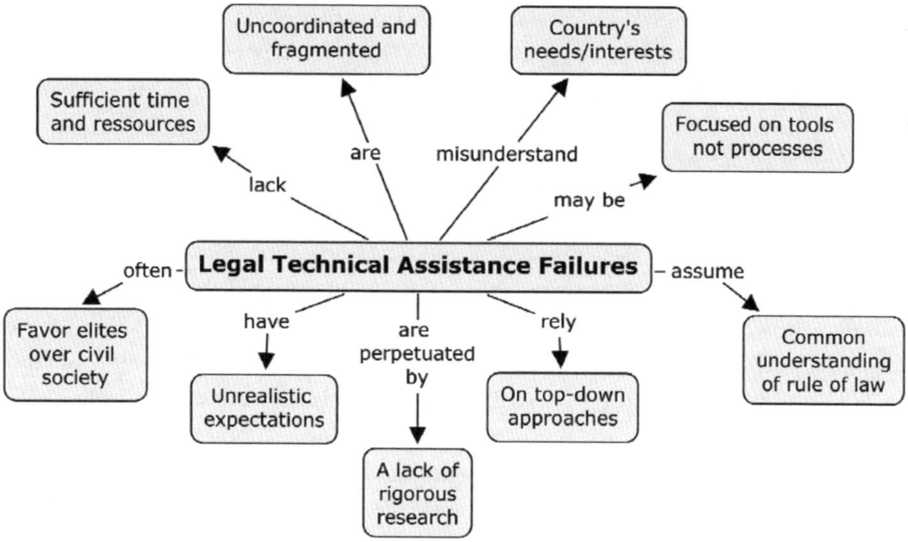

While the above critiques are significant, it does appear that most often it is the failure to meaningfully understand the context and needs of those on the ground that present the most difficult challenge for sustainable reform. In the place of longer-term engagement, it is too tempting to resist simply superimposing organizational structures and assume a "one size fits all" approach to social interactions will prevail. This has often resulted in short-term projects that are characterized by the pursuit of policies with unreasonable expectations and unrealistic timelines (Crawford, 2003; Griffiths *et al.* 2005). Since 2001, a growing focus within development has been on how an expanding security sector as part of the larger global war on terror has diverted funding away from democracy promotion and human-rights-based reforms (Shaw & Dandurand, 2006). The failure by the west to appreciate the complexities of terror as a technique has led to strained relationships and simplistic assumptions that play into broader critiques about the hegemonic nature of north-south relationships (Hardt & Negri, 2001).

A related problem is that past justice reform initiatives have rarely taken into account the communities in which these reforms are to be implemented (Chodosh, 2005). The over-reliance on formal structures and state institutions and top-down international interactions (Trubeck & Santos, 2006) is partly to blame. Common in the field of political science (Krasner, 1988), reform is seen as the result of either adding new institutions or restructuring old ones by altering the roles they perform (Thelen, 2003). Even if institutions are part of the answer, it has been demonstrated that without mechanisms to support the development of new kinds of programming and a means to demonstrate their local operability, then sustaining reforms and changing underlying practices may be impossible (Griffiths *et al.* 2005). Legal reform projects of any kind cannot succeed unless they penetrate the informal arrangements and socially shared rules that affect the behavior of those working within them (Helmke & Levitsky, 2004). This is relevant everywhere in the world and it is significant in the countries of the FSU and CEE.

3.1.2 Policy Transfer in the FSU and CEE

In the last decade, an increasing number of empirical studies on policy transfer in the new democracies of Central and Eastern Europe (CEE) demonstrated the complexity of the endeavor (Busch & Jörgens, 2005; Ivanova & Evans, 2004; Randma-Liiv, 2007). Lessons have nonetheless emerged. Based on the "families of nations approach," geographic, cultural and/or historical ties facilitate the transmission of policy ideas among states (Castles, 1993). Policy transfer often takes place between countries sharing a common language (Castles, 1993; Evans 2004), and psychological, ideological, and institutional proximity (Rose, 1993) are relevant. In addition, and too rarely acknowledged, is the role of informal connections. Relationships have been shown to play an essential role in understanding how policies are picked up, adapted, revised, or rejected (Wolman & Page, 2002).

While in general policy transfer in the FSU has a complex history, countries in Central and Eastern Europe are sometimes viewed as nations trying very hard to catch up, both politically and economically, to their more developed neighbors (Randma-Liiv & Kruusenberg, 2010). While imitation of western institutions has been a convenient and sometimes useful first step (Jacoby, 2001), there is evidence that in the early transition stages of the 1990s, several policies in post-communist states were copied from foreign role models without a thorough analysis of their suitability (Ivanova & Evans, 2004; Randma-Liiv, 2007). Even where suitability was assessed, the adoption of sustainable reforms is often challenged by time constraints, the lack of resources, and a failure to adapt international models to serve local needs (Rose, 1993).

Yet the tendency of transition countries to simply copy polices and programs from developing countries is sometimes overstated. Countries in transition with successful reform experiences grow in confidence, and are as likely to design their own policies as simply import models from abroad (Tavits, 2003). These projects can be used to obtain international legitimacy (Jones & Newburn, 2002), or to persuade political leaders of the desirability of certain policies or practices (Jacoby, 2000; Rose, 2005). In Russia and elsewhere in the FSU, one approach has been to explicitly focus on criminal justice reform projects that use existing legislation to promote alternative programs, support local ownership, and improve the use and acceptability of community-based programs (Hendley, 1996). While some credit ROL initiatives with playing an important catalyzing role in the complex process of reforming dysfunctional legal systems (Spence, 2003), others are far less complimentary (Wedel, 2001).

In addition to the unintended consequences of attempts to develop civil society (Sundstrom, 2006), Channell (2005) argues that insufficient resources have characterized the attempts, with scant attention paid to the broader, more systemic problems within the country (Karstedt, 2002). For example, USAID's success in assisting the development of a new Russian criminal procedure code in 2001 was the culmination of a decade of projects, effort, resources, and tens of millions of dollars. It was of little use, however, to Mikhail Khodorkovsky. Despite a case riddled with procedural errors, outright falsehoods, and overt political interference, he was found guilty in 2011 and sentenced to prison for five additional years in Siberia. The experience in other FSU countries may suggest a possible explanation. In Poland, the premature adoption of international standards can result in political manipulation and superficial reform. Ironically, the naïve impulses of the development community can be used to entrench the very legal apparatus reforms were designed to replace (Los & Zybertowicz, 2000).

One way to assess the value of the lessons from Latvia is to consider similar projects in other countries of the FSU. It should be noted that there is no evidence that the legal framework per se exists as an impediment to probation in the FSU. The formal legal barriers are less pronounced than in other places. Courts are often able to suspend sentences with conditions attached, a legal disposition that is analogous to a probation order (Cartledge *et al.* 1981). More complex, however, is how to build the capacity on the ground to allow the role of the judgment of officers and judges who used their own discretion to find the right mix of sanction and treatment (Hamai *et al.* 1995). Yet probation is but one aspect of justice reform. In Latvia it emerged only after years of developing local alternatives and engaging Ministry officials.

One telling example related to complications of applying models from one country to another is the Canadian-Russian Youth at Risk project. Designed to assist Russian authorities and social service workers to revamp youth justice in the country, the overall goal of the $3.5 million dollar, 4-year project (2004-2009) was to support democracy and good governance in the Russian Federation. In a key report, published though the project, outcomes are divided into 5 main focus areas (Dutkiewicz *et al.* 2009) and are based on the improvements achieved through pilot projects in regions such as Moscow, Rostov, and Stavropol, and Cheboksary. Each region focused on different aspects of juvenile justice reform. These areas included: Prevention, Case Management, Courts, Corrections, Post Custody and together sought to showcase a variety of alternatives that could together lay the groundwork for a coherent and integrated system of services for youth at risk throughout Russia.

Prevention programming, through the YAR Project, focused on child rights, youth participation, peer education, workshop design, community consultations, results-based management, employment services and school-based peer mediation programming. In Rostov Oblast, the Project supported the establishment of the first Russian language website devoted to educating children and youth about their rights and responsibilities in an interactive and child-friendly format and language. In Moscow Oblast, the pilot project team developed a highly successful youth at risk project that policymakers are studying for replication in other regions of the country. School-based peer-mediation programming was another focus within prevention. A tool developed through the project was introduced into four pilot schools in the Rostov and Stavropol regions to focus on early prevention and conflict resolution for youth. It is expected to be rolled-out in school districts throughout the project pilot regions throughout Russia.

Other focus areas were the development of a case management system and better coordination between community resources and judges. The case management approach applied to those working with youth at risk focuses on assisting youth justice agencies and community partners to coordinate the provision of ongoing supervision and targeted rehabilitative services for each young offender. Through the project, regional models were developed through pilots that developed early models of 'probation ' and 'parole,' adapted previously provided Canadian examples of Risk and Needs Assessment (RNA) as an instrument, and promoted the use of a 'case management tool' throughout the Russian Federation. In addition, these approaches have allowed for a new approach to foster greater coordination between the courts and other relevant youth justice stakeholders.

As part of the focus on corrections and post custody, the YAR Project focused on exposing Russian stakeholders to Canadian principles and best practices in the field of youth corrections. Project-supported capacity-building activities have assisted pilot project teams and stakeholders in the corrections services to improve their ability to design and introduce targeted rehabilitation and pre-release re-integration programs as part of their interventions with young offenders in custody. The pilot teams have established partnerships with seven youth colonies (prisons) and have been instrumental in developing and delivering new and improved sustainable rights-based services to youth in detention that involve both traditional and non-traditional partners. In terms of post-custody, the project focused on establishing models of rights-based reintegration and rehabilitation services for youth to help them make the transition from correctional facilities back into the community.

Project documents refer to the Latvian experience in a number of ways. Like in the Ukraine project, the diaspora community has been involved. Russian-Canadian project staff such as Piotr Dutkiewicz, played a key role in the delivery of project activities. A Professor of Political Science and Director of the Institute of European and Russian Studies at Carleton University, Dutkiewicz was one for key advisory committee made up of Canadian and Russian members who together reviewed project plans, the implementation of the activities, and their outcomes. While not specified as an attempt to address the challenges of country context, the inclusion of key project staff like Tawnia Sanford, Walid

Madhoun, Gail Bowkett, Maryana Nikoula, and Evgeni Shevchenko suggest an awareness of the need to ensure the project was implemented by those with in-country experience and regional expertise. In addition, the list of Canadian experts – including a former Nova Scotia Crown Prosecutor Bob Lutes, Restorative Justice specialist Jane Lutes, an Ontario probation officer Gail Steeds, a Northern Ontario wilderness specialist from DARE Keith Zehr, and an Ottawa Youth Courts Judge Peter Wright all worked in Latvia. While there is no detailed review of their approach to delivering project activities, this at least suggests that their approach to training may mirror training activities in Latvia.

One critical aspect of the report that deserves more attention is related to the organizational and institutional impediments associated with overcoming the challenges inherent in scaling up reforms. For example, the project sought to support the development of a separate system of justice for minors, including the establishment of specialized courts for youth. While specialized pilot youth courts in Rostov, Bryansk, and Chuvashia were established, no legislative support for the development of separate juvenile courts exists throughout the country. In addition, Russia has not yet established specific federal procedures and courts for juvenile offenders to be dealt with separately under the justice system and the draft law on the establishment of juvenile courts in the Russian Federation has been stalled. Another challenge has been how to translate the establishment of the National Association of Colonies from a nationwide forum to facilitate the formulation and dissemination of innovative, rehabilitative, and youth-oriented policies to one capable to articulating and advocating for specific youth justice reforms.

While no independent scholarly reviews of the project exist to date, it is shame more attention was not paid to how the contextual and organizational challenges the project faced undermined the kind of reforms instituted in Latvia. Although the idea that we can only learn from successes has a long pedigree, learning from failure is of increasing interest (Berman & Fox, 2010). In the Russia project documents, for example, there is no discussion of the lack of effective regional pressures or an acknowledgment that the since Putin's consolidation of power in the early 2000s regions have little authority to institute reforms. According to a senior project manager:

> In Latvia the success of justice reform was a result of the grass-roots approach and the way local communities formed strong partnerships and worked within a more decentralized governance structure. In Russia and Ukraine the top-down approach to anything justice-related is a must and without independent municipalities and creative regional authorities, reform may be hard to sustain.

Another limitation is the failure to recognize the systematic dysfunction of the justice system and corruption by authorities, despite clear inarguable evidence of the systemic challenges to the justice system in Russia. These challenges were brought to light in a 2011 meeting of the European Parliament's Delegation to the EU-Russia Parliamentary Cooperation Committee on Human Rights. Mr. William Browder testified about the murder and cover up of Russian lawyer Sergei Magnitsky and argued the case was just the latest example to highlight the:

> ... depth and reach of corruption in Russia. The justice system is broken and criminalized. Officials steal from their own country's coffers with impunity, unabashedly murder the innocent people who stand in their way, and use the very system that is meant to protect ordinary citizens to protect themselves in their crimes.[1]

It may be that just as the 1990s were a period in which economic aid from the West was used to create tycoon capitalism in Russia (Wedel, 1998), this last decade will demonstrate how legal reform programming in some cases entrenched the powerful to the detriment of the powerless. Despite tens of millions of dollars in legal technical assistance, it is not clear what has been achieved in Russia, nor is it clear that more people have a meaningful voice in the creation and revision of laws, policies, and the administration of justice (Sundstrom, 2006).

The most recent project of interest is a CIDA-funded Juvenile Justice Reform Project in Ukraine. Designed to support the development of a national legislative and policy framework and train judges and other stakeholders involved in the delivery of the juvenile justice system, the project builds on previous cooperation with governments, NGOs, and academics from the Ukrainian-Canadian community. The role of the diaspora network in the project has been adopted, and the project's implementation continues to rely upon the role of local pilots and some form of the interactive training methods developed in Latvia. While it is far too early to assess the overall success of the project, it does appear the approaches modeled in Latvia are being continued in Ukraine.

Two questions are of immediate relevance. The first is related to the external pressures that may be relevant to understanding country context. One assumption of this book is that Latvian-Canadian cooperation was a collaborative endeavor that while influenced by international, regional, and even local pressure, remained voluntary, cooperative, and participatory. Nevertheless, it cannot be doubted that Latvia's economic and security interests were and remain tied up with the EU. While Latvia chose which model of probation to adopt, adapt, and institute, the impetus for reform cannot be divorced from the international pressure through reports, evaluations, and critiques. It is not clear to what extent these conditions exist in Ukraine. With a similar history of occupation, and a justice system

1 <http://lawandorderinrussia.org/2011/in-european-parliament-testimony-william-browder-exposes-10-facts-proving-the-russian-government-cover-up-of-sergei-magnitsky%E2%80%99s-murder/>.

not unlike the dysfunctional systems that existed in the Baltics, project managers in Ukraine report little on the ground energy among community members, NGOs, and government officials. The second is to what extent observations by Canton (2006) based on three years working in Ukraine about the lack of organizational research capacity to investigate key questions for any probation initiative can be addressed. He asks:

> What counts as a successful transfer? For example, suppose the attempt was being made to introduce community service into a jurisdiction as part of a strategy to provide alternative measures to custody. The attempt would count as unsuccessful, presumably, if no community service orders were made. But what if some orders were indeed made, but, instead of displacing prisoners from a burdened prison estate, simply added to the overall penal weight imposed upon quite minor offenders: would this count as a successful transfer? Or again what if orders were made in respect only of defendants who were powerful or privileged, with custody remaining for the poor? Or if orders involved undertaking tasks which brought personal profit to individuals rather than a wider community benefit? (Canton, 2006, p. 16)

Without a deliberate focus on data gathering, there maybe no way to assess the impact of the project should the proposed reforms through international engagement be subsequently taken up. This is not always the case of course and this is the element that makes Latvia especially unique.

3.2 Probation and an Integrated Evidence-Based Model

Chapters 1 and 2 provided a general argument for the value of looking to development projects generally as a means to understand the formal and informal impediments to reform. In addition, these chapters suggested how establishing, re-building, or reforming probation services can serve broader justice reform goals – given the centrality of probation within many justice systems. It may be useful to say a bit more about the important role of probation services within European debates about criminology and criminal justice (Walters, 2003). The interest in Eastern Europe surrounding probation can be seen as a desire to reduce prison populations, among the highest in Europe, and to reject prison as a reflexive response to any and all social problems. On this view, probation offers a means to displace offenders from custody while affirming the principles of social inclusion through rehabilitation (Canton, 2009). It may have other consequences as well. Chapters 4, 5, and 6 explore how Latvia's efforts to develop a probation service also resulted in a broadening of the discussion about law and society, the proper role of punishment, and the place of community within crime prevention. Of immediate interest is how to design meaningful development research methodologies.

3.2.1 *Studying Latvian Probation*

Following the fall of the Soviet Union, a number of European countries have become involved in knowledge exchange – in part, because probation cannot be easily separated from broader dialogue and debates about the policies and practices of criminal justice within Europe (Gründler, 1997). According to Canton (2009), these include questions about how these activities are to be understood, the prospects of successful policy transfer between countries with different backgrounds, and how projects are to be evaluated. To this, one might add: how should these projects be understood in the larger developmental context, based on assumptions about the importance of human rights, democratic development, and good governance?

Past efforts to understand Latvian probation have reported on basic functions (Zeibote, 2008) or pursued more exploratory designs, including traditional qualitative (Jurevičius, 2008; Randma-Liiv & Kruusenberg, 2010) and emergent mixed methods approaches (Wheeldon, 2009; Wheeldon, 2011). The approach taken here borrows heavily from past scholarship but combines the arguments and types of evidence gathered in novel ways. The goal is to advance a developmental model that can be applied to legal technical assistance focused on probation. Central to the assessment of this model is the need to think clearly about research designs, relevant data, and appropriate data collection methods. The failure to learn from the past demands a more integrated approach to research and a renewed focus on the value of evidence-based aid in the context of international development projects.

In general, the challenges of policy transfer in post-communist societies are shaped by a variety of considerations. Although problems common in policy transfer matters in Western countries are also present in developing and transition countries, specific issues related to transitional administrations compound these more general concerns. Governance programming is based on the assumption that social and legal institutions are simply too important to leave to chance. Thus, to understand both the variety of challenges facing transitional societies and the role of policy transfer, international development research models need to go beyond simplistic macro-level numeric measures, or context-specific micro-level narratives. This may be difficult for some.

There is emerging interest in how to apply experimental research methodologies used in education (Banerjee *et al.* 2007; Miguel & Kremer, 2004) and health (Duflo *et al.* 2006; Dupas 2007), to development. By replacing the inconsistent and theoretical-limited approach to existing practice with a model designed to uncover 'what works' (Fissman &

Miguel, 2008). To begin, existing projects must be reviewed in far more depth than commonly occurs. Researchers must be modest about what lessons can be generalized, and which indicators need further exploration. A major challenge is that development projects are often assessed as part of ongoing project-based evaluations or macro-level reviews (Luksenaite, 2005; Caldwell, 2005). Unfortunately they also often employ questionable or purposively limited methodologies (Brown, 2008) and tend to serve organizational needs without contributing more broadly to the field (Gilley, 2004). Embracing approaches based on new and more rigorous assumptions about what constitutes empirical evidence can have the effect of challenging the conventional wisdom of the past. Whatever the potential for 'evidence-based aid' to lead to greater support, dissemination, and integration of lessons learned though past project implementation is clear, a number of critiques have been leveled (Banerjee & Duflo, 2008). Some include the challenge of data collection techniques that rely upon western assumptions about language, and incomplete understandings of the way questions influence outcomes (Wheeldon & Faubert, 2009).

There may be no more important issue to understanding the means and mechanisms of individual knowledge transfer than that of translation and interpretation. When researchers who do not speak the native language organize data collection, they must rely upon interpreters who are not always able to provide a firmly defined one-to-one correlation between the words and phrases of different languages. This is a specific challenge in criminal justice, where core concepts may vary greatly based on western notions of individual rights and eastern notions of social order, but it exists as a significant research challenge (Castles, 1993). In addition, all research must be based on data and credible empirical evidence must assume participants can meaningfully share their thoughts, reflections, and opinions.

Other challenges are inferential in nature. They include questions surrounding the generalizability of findings between and within different countries, regions and even communities, and the problem of selection bias among those who agree to participate in development experiments. In general, there is a difficulty in assessing to what extent one can extrapolate successes from small and localized trials (Heckman, 1992). In addition to the ethical issues of selecting to whom to provide an intervention suspected of assisting the administration of justice, in practical terms only a fraction of projects that currently receive aid could be subject to randomized controlled trials (Deaton, 2006). This may be because development initiatives are fraught with political, technical, and interactional difficulties that defy easily controlled experimentation. As a human endeavor full of complex interactions, the attempt to apply methodologies perfected in sealed laboratories may have little relevance in the convoluted and multi-faceted world of development.

3.2.2 Designs and Development: Case Studies and a Three-Tier Model

One reply to the above challenges is to acknowledge that the role of localized international 'experiments' must be seen in the context of multiple interconnected constraints and challenges (Kealey & Protheroe, 1995). These challenges include, but are certainly not limited to, epistemological assumptions about which research designs can best generate meaningful evidence, what counts as data, and how data can best be collected. Researching international projects without acknowledging the unique social, cultural, and political context in which cross national collaboration occurs is a significant challenge for the compilation of meaningful empirical evidence. Credible attempts require a willingness to review projects in ways that are modest and open to review, revision, and interrogation by those working within, under, and through its expanse. One must always make clear core assumptions. One that informs this book is the idea that governance will remain an international goal, and that the criminal justice system will remain an important site of engagement through legal technical assistance projects and programs.

In a variety of countries emerging from authoritarian rule and dysfunctional regimes, probation may be an especially useful service upon which to base cross-national collaborations. Indeed, it might be said that it is through the mechanisms of justice that people define their relationship with the state and other communities, all of which incur local contextual, organizational, and individual constraints. Only by considering how these elements, separately and together, impact a project can the development community get a better sense of what works. Case studies have been widely used in development studies because they can improve understanding about the relationships between individual, organizational, and socio-political phenomena (Yin, 2003).

While one must be careful about attempting to generalize from specific cases to more general theories, empirical evidence examined through analytical extrapolation can allow for the comparison of processes that are relevant in similar regions (Chima, 2005). Given the observation that international development projects are important sites of international interaction, in-depth case studies may involve contextual, organizational, and individual challenges. Contextual challenges might be environmental and related to the host country, institutional and connected to the cooperation between host and donor organizations and agencies, or interpersonal related to the interactions between individuals involved in the development initiative (Kealey *et al.* 2005). Together, these factors may be of special relevance to legal technical assistance projects.

Environmental factors are broad and can be related to country readiness, institutional transparency and accountability, and the involvement of civil society (Dandurand *et al.* 2004). Kealey and his colleagues (2005) suggest the most significant environmental factors include the friendliness of the host country's national culture to the project's aims; the overall well-being of the host country and international economy and other economic factors; the host country's legal framework; the amicability, efficiency, and well-being of the project's interest groups; and the host country's political and social stability. In addition to the factors identified by Kealey *et al.* (2005), Shaw and Dandurand (2006) consider other broad-based external conditions specifically relevant to legal technical assistance. These can include political context, geopolitical factors, psychological attributes, economic circumstances, institutional context, and civil society involvement (2006:46).

Organizational and institutional understanding is another barrier to project success often identified within the literature (Kealey *et al.* 2005). Overcoming this barrier requires a foundation of mutual commitment, and a shared understanding among development partners. It is also integral that those working abroad have an understanding about the culture they are to live and work in, including its historical, political and socio-economic features, and social models. This knowledge can assist in the understanding of the organizational and institutional realities on the ground and the appropriate technical and training resources that may be useful in building strong partnerships, local ownership, and positive, sustainable outcomes (Kealey & Protheroe, 2002). Others suggest that this can also be related to the ability of project managers to implement the proposed reforms with stakeholders' approval, based on the compatibility of norms (Sundstrom, 2006, p. 169).

The organizational factors most frequently identified include partner selection, clarity of objectives, management structures and responsibilities, and the fit between organizational cultures among collaborating organizations (Kealey *et al.* 2005). Introduced in Chapter 1, organizational training tools developed for legal technical assistance projects can include manuals, handbooks, and toolkits (Dandurand *et al.* 2008: 63), and are widely used in training and technical assistance to enhance overall organizational ability (Griffths *et al.* 2005). As Dandurand (2006) suggests, this requires effective needs assessments that consider not only legislative or human resource gaps or weaknesses, but also acknowledge the organizational context. One useful development has been the UNODC Criminal Justice Reform Unit Tool Kit,[2] a practical set of assessment tools that provides a means to understand the context in which various justice reforms are proposed (Dandurand, 2006, p. 43).

Finally, individual and interpersonal elements to project success have been studied for more than two decades in Canada. Identified by Kealey *et al.* (2005) as the most important element for international projects, and based on the shift toward the 'knowledge economy' (Toffler, 1990), intercultural competence (Kealey & Protheroe, 1995) allows outside trainers to be able to develop an adaptive capacity, altering their perspective to understand and accommodate the demands of the host culture effectively (Taylor, 1994). Kealey's early work considered the role of communicative competency in cross-cultural adaptation and the importance of the selection of technical assistance personnel to development effective-

2 See UNDOC Tool Kit retrieved from <www.unodc.org/unodc/en/justice-and-prison-reform/Criminal-Justice-Toolkit.html> on July 15, 2008.

ness (Hawes & Kealey, 1981). A significant contribution is the notion that effectiveness in technical assistance requires more than knowledge and expertise. Kealey and Protheroe (1995) argued that, to be effective at creating positive learning environments, Canadian trainers had to understand the importance of professional modesty, to rely on local experts through mutual learning, and consider cultural dimensions.

Based on a model of the levels of cooperation and constraints developed in Canada (Kealey & Protheroe, 1995), I have revised these constraints to focus on country context, organizational constraints and individual challenges, present in Figure 3.2. These three concentric levels individually and collectively impact project success, and might usefully be used in the analysis of legal technical assistance projects.

Figure 3.2 A Three-Tier Model of Project Analysis

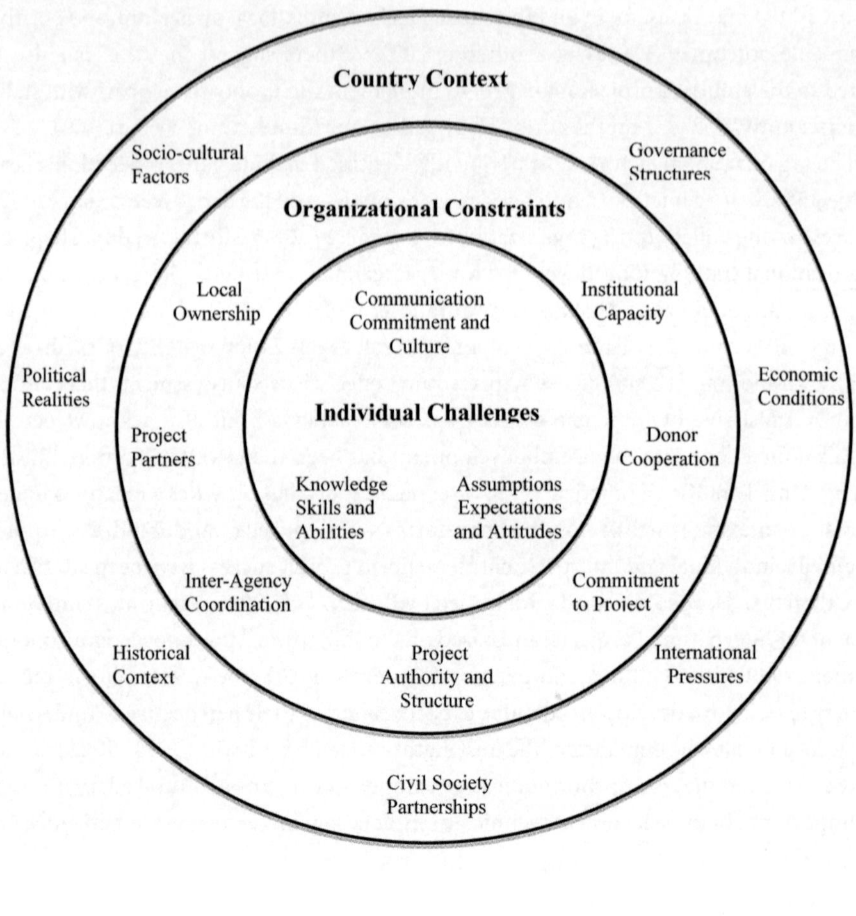

Using this model, there are specific considerations that may be relevant for probation projects. Based on Canton's (2009) useful overview, Figure 3.3 presents some considerations about how to design research and where to look for tensions, opportunities, and experiences as part of an in-depth case study methodology.

Figure 3.3 A Three-Tier Model of Probation Programming

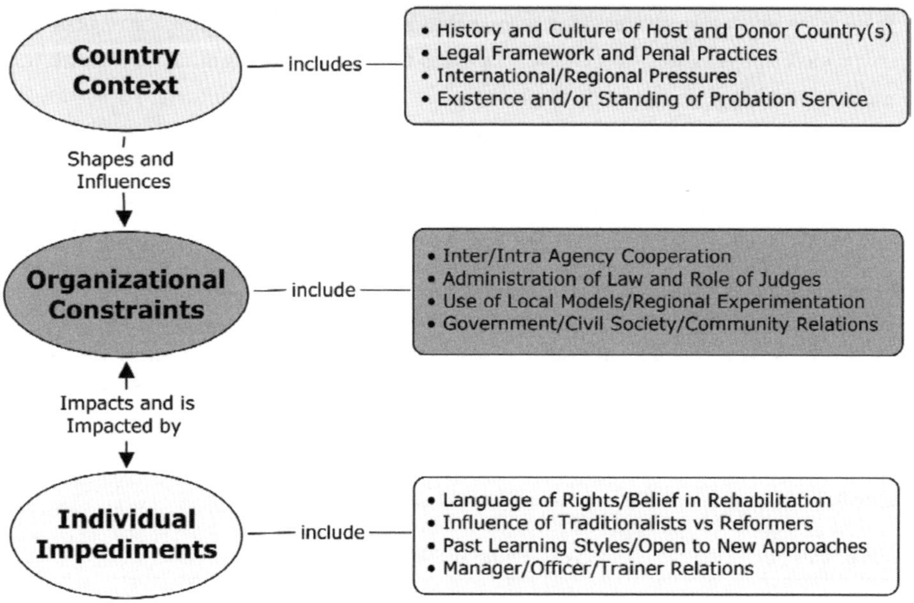

3.2.3 *What Counts as Data in International Development?*

The three-tier model provides a useful general means to understanding the variety of challenges and constraints in all international projects, and Canton (2009) outlines some additional considerations. However, all models require data. A variety of data exists on governance, but these measures are of varying quality. A central question is what to measure and whose views to rely upon. This question underlies a disagreement about whether one should focus on measuring the formal laws 'on the books,' or the practical application of these rules as they are perceived to apply 'on the ground.'

Rules-based indicators of governance focus on the formal laws related to the elements of the constitutional, legal, or macro-level structures within a country. These include: a focus on economic freedom, human rights, and governmental transparency; analyses of reports of government agencies; or a range of domestic and regional, non-governmental, civil society groups. For example, many studies have been conducted to develop indicators or indices that illustrate the level of attainment of the ROL in different countries, with a focus on criminal justice as these institutions determine whether people will be denied life or liberty, and attempt to mediate between the competing interests of individual rights and collective public safety.

In Latvia, as discussed in Chapter 2, a variety of numeric indicators suggest the value of probation to the broader criminal justice system. At issue is the application by international development agencies of result-based management approaches and logical frameworks. Instead of robust measures of association and interaction, they have produced narrow, descriptive, and project-based analyses that rely upon quantitative assumptions about operational performance indicators that are insufficiently grounded in the complexities of the political context in which such assistance takes place (Crawford, 2003). Beyond project-based evaluations, a variety of international and regional measures and indices exist that often employ similar quantitative techniques to attempt to assess various aspects of the ROL. As outlined in Table 3.4, some focus on economic freedom, while others consider human rights. Some have a regional focus, whereas others have covered a global span. Still others have been conducted by non-private domestic, regional, or international organizations. This renewed interest has resulted in a wide variety of definitional considerations and empirical measures but as Kaufmann and Kraay (2008) remind us, by quoting Albert Einstein: "not everything that can be counted counts."

Table 3.4 Examples of ROL Measures and Indexes

Rule of Law Measure	Surveys, Polls, and Indexes
Economic	World Business Environment Survey World Competitiveness Yearbook Global Competitiveness Report
Human Rights	CIRI Human Rights Dataset Political Terror Scale Amnesty International Reports US State Department Country Reports on Human Rights Practices.
Regional Matrices	Bertelsmann Transformation Index
Global Measures	Freedom in the World
Additional Development Assessments	Progress towards Good Governance in Africa (United Nations) Country Policy and Institutional Assessment (African Development Bank) Country Policy and Institutional Assessment (Asian Development Bank)

Other indicators consider individuals' perceptions of how laws or provisions are applied (Kaufman *et al.* 2005). For example, emergent approaches look to the perceptions of a country's populace about the governance structures of their state, and target both legal professionals and ordinary citizens. Whether one privileges the opinion of experts with an intimate knowledge of the existence of formal rules, or the perceptions of individuals and their experience with and concerns about the structures of the state, both have built-in limitations. As funders have moved toward more targeted and specific development approaches, scholars, policy makers and the broader legal and development community have sought to develop more refined, nuanced, and policy-relevant indicators of governance (Kaufman & Kraay, 2008). A mixed methods approach to data collection in justice reform projects can overcome attempts to rely upon numeric governance measures and indicators. It can focus on data collection that can uncover how formal and informal structures impact broader reform initiatives and explore if, how, and why formal rules are implemented on the ground.

An innovative methodology has recently been advanced by the American Bar Association (ABA) through its World Justice Project. By rejecting the either/or approach, this methodology focuses on combining attitudinal qualitative data from legal professionals and ordinary citizens, while validating this data using existing quantitative cross country ROL indexes. By providing aggregated and disaggregated data, this methodology has the potential to promote a more integrated approach to measuring governance through ROL structures (Wheeldon, 2008). Within probation, this could include quantitative and numeric analysis of a particular probation function – such as mediation. Regional variance might then be explored through more in-depth qualitative techniques to collect data upon which to contextualize the numeric counts. This approach can also work in reverse by investigating how individual officers view the development of pre-sentence reports through qualitative interviews, which could be combined with numeric analysis of the acceptance by a judge of recommended treatment and the client outcome following a probation term.

These types of integrated approaches acknowledge that contrasting understandings of the same concept exist, and that laws, policies, and practices presumed as central to the rule of law may in fact be 'contested' (Waldron, 2002). While justice and the good of the community should be considered in any evaluation of the ROL, more important may be the "...pervasive societal attitudes about fidelity to the rule of law...[and] the mysterious quality that makes the rule of law work" (Tamanaha, 2004, p. 141). Whatever design is selected, and whatever data is deemed both valid and reliable, questions persist about how best to collect this data, and which instruments can best serve various research areas. International development ought to be of particular concern.

3.2.4 Data Collection and the Role of Maps

Traditionally, uncovering the broader trends in international development required gathering data through in depth interviews (Mikkelson, 2005). Based on qualitative research traditions, interviews can draw out individualistic accounts of knowledge, experience, and perception. Meaning can be discovered through social interactions and the ways in which an individual constructs, frames, and describes one's past. One example, discussed in Chapter 1, is the work of Janine Wedel. Based on what she calls an "extended case method" and "ethnography across levels and processes" (1998, pp. 205-208), Wedel engaged in participant observation and conducted more than 1,750 interviews to conclude that western aid to Eastern Europe in the 1990s often relied upon numerous processes of interactions between elites – both donors and recipients. While her account is ultimately pessimistic, she does acknowledge that questions remain about how to understand the nature of these relationships.

An important development within qualitative research is the acknowledgement that there are many possible interpretations of the same data, and qualitative researchers cannot assign value to one interpretation of meaning without acknowledging the role they themselves play within this construction (Guba & Lincoln, 1989). This requires that researchers study the experiences, influences, and activities of researchers themselves, and by focusing on precision (Winter, 2000) and credibility (Hoepf, 1997), qualitative researchers have begun to acknowledge that the approach chosen by the researcher shapes subsequent research interactions (Feyerbend, 1978). While the trend toward reflexivity (Macbeth, 2001) has helped to explicitly outline the role of the researcher in qualitative research, it historically has not been applied to development research. This is a significant oversight (Wheeldon & Faubert, 2009; Wheeldon, 2010; Wheeldon, 2011).

Reflexivity requires not only awareness that one's subjective past experiences contribute to how one constructs social meaning, but also of the ways in which economic, social or other interests may influence our decision-making process (Willig, 2001). Today, there is a renewed focus within research and reputable publications on credibility through this sort of transparency, and researchers are generally required to discuss not only counter evidence but also other possible interpretations of their findings. In addition, credible researchers explicitly acknowledge who funds their research and how their own personal biases impact the conclusions they draw. These admissions are part of most peer-reviewed processes and often the researcher's reflections are published within the paper as a means to promote the integrity of the research process.

Another approach is the development of new means of data collection – the visual map. Seen alongside other more participant-centered data collection like vignette responses, subject-operated cameras/videos/sound recordings, focus groups, and journaling (Wheeldon & Faubert, 2009), maps may serve a variety of purposes for cross-national research. One is the way the construction of the maps could address or mitigate bias for those attempting to study a phenomenon to which they themselves have been a party. By giving a voice to the participants through more user generated and unsolicited means, maps can allow themes to emerge from participants themselves that could be used to guide subsequent interviews. Instead of asking questions based on the researcher's own assumptions, these questions could be based on views compiled through the maps.

Other benefits are more practical. Maps can provide an opportunity for an individual to demonstrate the importance of various concepts and their relationships in unique ways. When data are being gathered through cross-cultural research, maps may offer a means to capture experience in a way that minimizes the challenges of translation discussed earlier. By providing a window on how the mind's eye uses visual images, maps have been shown to limit the canned responses that are often a feature of interview-based research. This can allow the researcher to collect data by distance – as maps can be created by hand, faxed or scanned and emailed, or created using a computer program or word processor. Mind maps may be especially valuable in participatory models within international development (Wheeldon & Ahlberg, 2012).

Mind maps are often less formal than other sorts of visual maps, do not require linking phrases, and generally focus on one topic at a time. They have the potential to be far more creative and can use color, graphics, bold lines, or other less conventional techniques to construct a very personal reflection of individual views. They often begin in the center of the page with central ideas or themes and 'radiate' out, connecting associations and examples with the central topic on the page. It is the free-form possibilities of the mind map that may be of the most interest to international development researchers seeking new kinds of data collection tools.

Figure 3.5 Constructing a Mind Map (Wheeldon, 2010, p. 91)

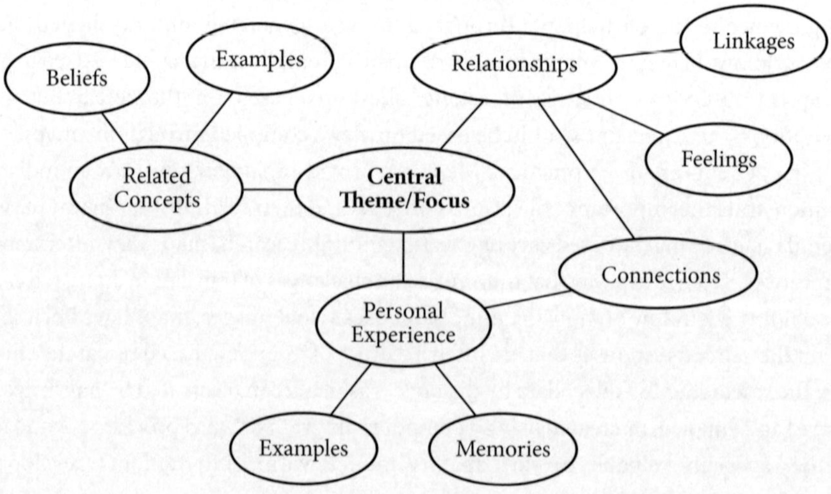

To understand the potential of maps as social science data, it is useful to see that creating visual maps requires people to make decisions about how topics relate to each other. These decisions provide a way to understand how participants view the topic, and the nature of the connections between relevant issues, ideas, and concepts. It also allows researchers to "see" these connections and consider what the organization of these concepts means, and assess the hierarchical and multi-dimensional levels of different sorts of relationships. Ebener *et al.* (2006, pp. 638-640) suggest that:

> ...mapping offers an opportunity to elucidate and assist with analysis of complex processes and hence play a role in knowledge translation... [it] has the advantage of being concrete and tactical... [and] makes tacit and explicit knowledge graphic and visual.

For data collection in social science research, this may mean that maps in their various forms offer a means to break out of conventional representations of experience through language. This view is based on the acknowledgement that people learn in different ways and think using a combination of words, graphics, and images. It avoids the sole reliance upon data collection based on psycho-linguistic assumptions about the meaning of syntax, semantics, and context (Cassirer, 1946). This may be especially relevant for researchers working in international development where individual understanding is mediated by the social, cultural, and linguistic realities of different groups (Habermas, 1976). If consciousness is a combination of individualized experiences and those based on interactions with others

(Husserl, 1970), maps may provide one strategy to break out of conventional and linguistically limited representations of experience, rehearsed narratives, and canned responses (Hathaway & Atkinson, 2003).

Mapping Participatory Action Research

While all maps provide a means to make invisible internal maps of understanding apparent, a useful way to see maps in international development is to understand their use as part of participatory research models. Participatory action research (PAR) refers to research that focuses on addressing problems, issues, or concerns as expressed by the community members themselves. This approach is seen as a continuous process and a revisable endeavor (O'Brien, 2001). By using more collaborative methods to test new ideas and implement action through the active participation of community members, it is assumed more meaningful outcomes will result. McIntyre (2008) provides a useful overview of a number of projects that can be defined as participatory. These include community projects focused on violence against women (Maguire, 1987), HIV treatment (Maglajlic, 2004), prison education (Fine & Torre, 2006), and practical matters like water sanitation (Jackson & McKay, 1982) and improving communication and efficiency in a hospital emergency room (Eisenberg, Baglia & Pyrnes, 2006).

As PAR has grown, so have the methods used to capture, analyze, and present the data collected through these approaches. Indeed, one of the characteristics of participatory approaches lies in innovative adaptations of methods drawn from conventional research, and their use in new contexts, in new ways – often by, as well as with, local people. Participatory approaches to international development have involved the construction of maps of watersheds, fields, and other relevant agricultural features (McCracken, 1988), and as part of rural development appraisals (Chambers, 1994). These early experiences were augmented by the use of maps to consider issues of social significance. Maps have been used to study the uptake of health services and evaluations of disease prevention programs. Based on exploratory maps made by patients of their own body, warts and all, (Cornwall & Jewkes, 1995), new participatory public health research methods have been explored (Burke *et al.* 2005). In general, the utility of participatory mapping is that it can provide both useful data while explicitly valuing the local sources of that data. They might be usefully applied to new directions in development research, as outlined in Figure 3.6.

Figure 3.6 Key Challenges for Development Research

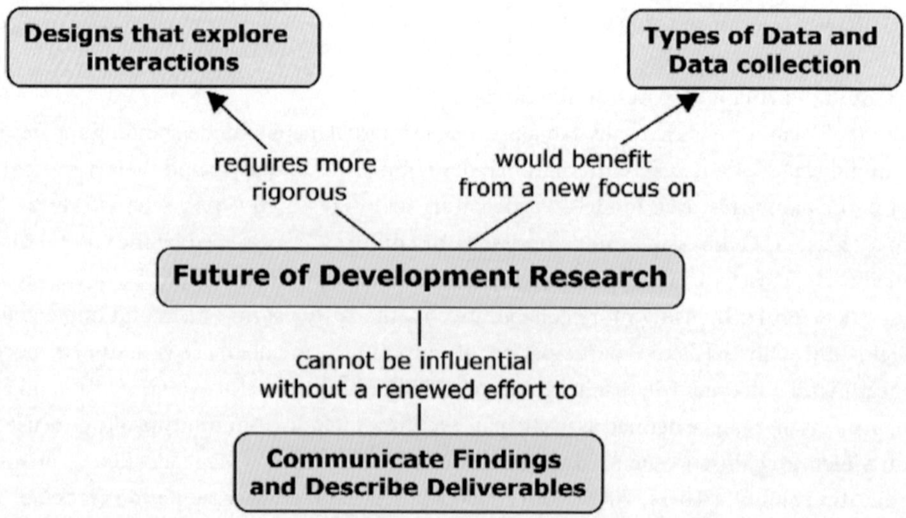

3.3 INCARCERATION, COMMUNITY, AND CONTROL: METHODOLOGY AND APPROACH

This book is based on interviews of both Latvian and Canadian participants involved in the LLRP conducted over a four-year period. The data presented in this book is based on three separate studies. All relied upon maps as a means to provoke deeper recall, prime the pump of past events, guide follow up questions, and compile mixed methods measures (Wheeldon & Faubert, 2009; Wheeldon, 2010; Wheeldon, 2011). As presented in Intermission 1, participants completed visual maps based on an exemplar map and were asked to record positive and negative experiences of the LLRP. Based on the graphic representation of their experiences, themes were identified and interview questions were developed to explore how they framed their understanding of the project, and how each viewed the role and value of Latvian-Canadian cooperation.

In order to be part of the studies, all participants signed an informed consent document that outlined the nature of the research and the means of data collection. In addition to assuring all participants of anonymity and confidentiality, an exemplar map was provided that demonstrated a variety of ways the concept of St. Nicholas was understood. It is reproduced in Figure 3.7. This map was selected because it was international, included different names, physical features, activities, linking words, and additional characteristics.

Figure 3.7 Concept Maps of St. Nicholas (Lanzing, 1996)

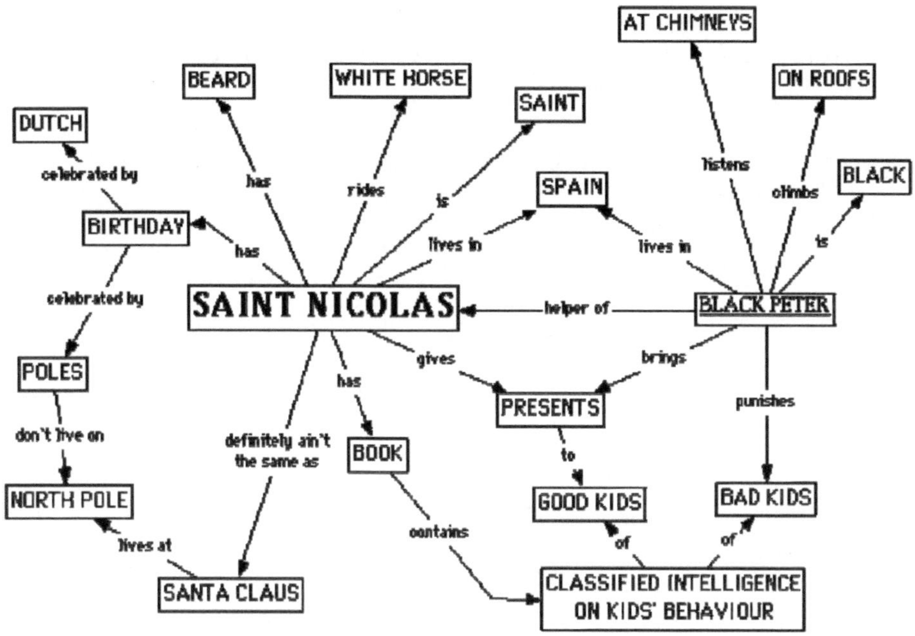

In addition to the above example, the following instructions were provided to participants:

- Visual maps can demonstrate how people visualize relationships between various concepts.
- Maps do not require complete comprehensiveness; however, the map should reflect key experiences and perceptions related to your experience.
- You are encouraged to include both challenges and successes (where applicable) in the creation of your concept maps
- Please limit your concept map to one page (8.5/11).

Based on approaches that seek new partnerships between quantitative and qualitative research, a mixed-methods approach was employed. By presenting both general numeric findings and more specific thematic reflections, the approach used harnessed both the power of quantitative counts and the perspective of qualitative interviews.[3] In short, participants were first requested to complete a visual map and later participated in follow-up interviews on their experience of the Canadian training and/or their role as trainer through the Latvian Legal Reform Program. While a selection of maps is reproduced in the first

3 Readers who are interested in the methodological process and analysis strategy might enjoy more detailed treatments published in the *Journal of Mixed Methods Research*, and *Journal of Baltic Studies*.

intermission, figure 3.8 is a useful exemplar of a map gathered through that research. Of specific interest was how the responses of both Canadian and Latvian participants could assist the understanding of organizational and pedagogical challenges within international justice reform, and what this might mean for the design and delivery of future probation programming round the world.

Figure 3.8 Exemplar Visual Map on Latvian-Canadian Cooperation

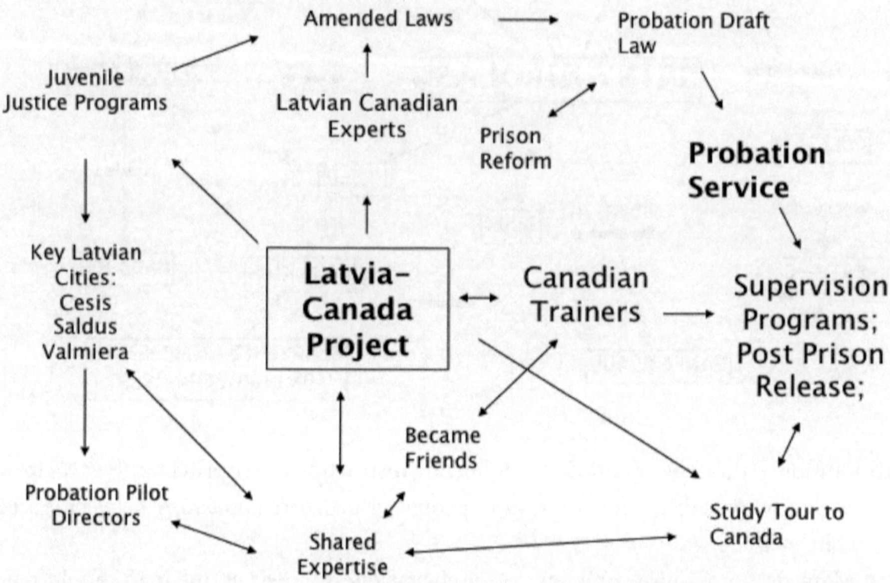

To guide subsequent interviews, maps were analyzed both in terms of their construction and the substantive elements participants included represented in Figure 3.9.

Figure 3.9 Analyzing Maps and Interviews (Wheeldon, 2007)

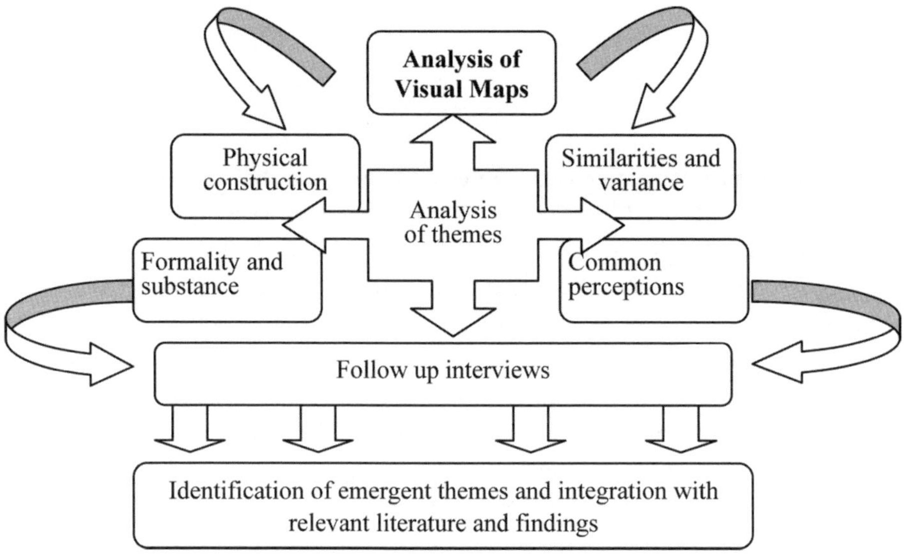

This book is based on dozens of follow up interviews to validate findings, double check quotes, and triple check the conclusions drawn, as well as suggestions provided in these pages. In total, more than fifty Canadian consultants, trainers and project staff, along with Latvian participants from the government, local municipalities, and legal system, were interviewed. Additionally, a number of project documents, reports, books, articles, and international project evaluations were consulted. Together, they provided a wealth of data about the role of expertise, the utility of various training approaches, and the need for international development to focus on the role of local trials, inter-personal networks, and interactive trainings as a means to promote sustainable, locally led reform. Chapters 4, 5, and 6 include these observations based on the trends, commonalities, and differences that emerged through the maps and follow up interviews.

In addition, this book has benefited from the contributions of Latvian, Lithuanian and Estonia academics, researchers, and practitioners (Gestautaite, 2001; Jurevičius, 2008; Randma-Liiv & Kruusenberg, 2010; Zdanevicius, 2006; Zeibote, 2008), whose insights have brought significant perspective to the analysis. Another incredible resource is the first comparative study of probation services around the world – published in 1995. Co-authored by Koichi Hamai, Robert Harris, Mike Hough, Renaud Ville, and Ugljesa Zvekic, this effort provides a comprehensive overview of probation, and is an indispensable resource. It has inspired this book in a variety of ways. Another resource is the first compendium of probation services in Europe, edited and compiled by Anton Van Kalmthout and Ioan Durnescu, and published in 2008. By involving officials within each country's probation service, they have begun a process of information sharing that will hopefully continue.

3.3.1 *Reflexivity and Acknowledging "Self"*

Researchers frequently fail to realize, recognize, or acknowledge how they are caught up in a historical moment and cultural context that shapes their views and thinking. As part of any social endeavor, it may be impossible to escape the ways in which experiences, ideology, or assumptions shape expectations. The recognition that past experiences are connected to future actions, the question of personal credibility becomes related to the extent to which researchers acknowledge how their interests, interactions, and beliefs influence their actions. In addition to the unique use of maps, wherever possible the book relies upon the participant's own words. To address the multiple roles played by the author, this book intersperses more scholarly analysis, with personal reflections – through the preface, two intermissions, and the epilogue. Finally, the remaining chapters include more critical voices and views to ensure the goal of this book do not outpace the data upon which it is based. This may not fully address the limitations involved in researching a project in which one is involved. However, the clear acknowledgement of the author's own journey as part of this project hopefully provides some useful perspective for the reader.

3.4 Concluding Remarks

While development agencies have been slow to catalog, lean, and apply the lessons of the past, it does appear there are both considered observations and empirical findings that can guide subsequent activities. To understand the quality of existing evidence it may be useful to understand how questions surrounding designs, data, and data collection dictate the reliability of what is reported. Moreover, development projects are a series of complex interactions in which contextual, organizational, or individual challenges may overcome any successes, or may confound attempts to draw meaningful conclusions. One research model of enormous utility may be the three-tier model of project analysis.

This approach would be assisted by the combination of different sorts of data gathered through valid methods. By considering these elements separately and together, the development community can build evidence-based policies rooted in careful empirical study. This chapter has presented mind maps as a novel means to collect data in legal technical assistance projects and probation programming, and demonstrated how maps may be useful for organizing lessons and themes, and rendering complex concepts more accessible. Collecting maps may provide a more nuanced picture of a project, a training session, or an event. As discussed in this chapter, it also requires that researchers think about how to balance allowing participants to reflect and create maps, while ensuring the researcher can make sense of these visual records of experience.

Studying probation and legal technical assistance has a valuable role to play in understanding how governance reform can occur. Beyond the short and medium term outcomes, this type of programming may also usefully stimulate dialogue and deliberation about how the law interacts within different aspects of societies and groups. By considering contextual, organizational, and individual factors at play in a project's success or failure, a more rigorous academic approach to the assessment of development projects might be undertaken.

Chapter 3 Bibliography

A. Banerjee & E. Duflo. The Experimental Approach to Development Economics. Abdul Latif Jameel Poverty Action Lab, Department of Economics, Cambridge MA: Massachusetts Institute of Technology, 2008.

A. Banerjee. (2007). *Making Aid Work.* MIT Press: Cambridge, MA

G. Berman & A. Fox. *Trial and Error in Criminal Justice Reform: Learning from Failure.* Washington, Dc: Urban Institute, 2010.

K. Bollen, P. Baxton & R. Morishima. Assessing International Evaluations: An Example from USAID's Democracy and Governance Program. *American Journal of Evaluation*, Vol. 26, No. 2, 2005, pp. 189-203.

S. Brown. CIDA under the gun. In J. Daudelin, & D. Schwanen (Eds.), *Canada among nations 2007: What room for manoeuvre?.* Montreal: PQ: McGill-Queen's University Press, 2008.

J.G. Burke, P. O'Campo, G.L. Peak, A.C. Gielen, K.A. McDonnell & W.M.K. Trochim. *Qualitative Health Research*, Vol. 15, 2005, pp, 1392-1410.

P. Busch & H. Jörgens. The international sources of policy convergence: explaining the spread of environmental policy innovations. *Journal of European Public Policy*, Vol. 12 No. 5, 2005, pp. 860-884.

S. Caldwell. *Evaluating the evaluation: Review of CIDA's work in the Baltics.* Toronto, ON: University of Toronto, 2005.

G. Cameron. *Between policy and practice.* Regina: Sk.: Saskatchewan Institute of Public Policy, 2006.

Canadian International Development Agency. *Canada and the Baltics: Partners in Transition.* Gatineau, PQ: Canadian International Development Agency, 2004.

R. Canton. Taking Probation Abroad. *European Journal of Probation* Vol. 1, No. 1, 2009, pp. 66-78.

R. Canton. Penal Policy Transfer: A Case Study from Ukraine. *The Howard Journal,* Vol. 45, No. 5, 2006, pp. 502-520.

T. Carothers. The rule of law revival. *Foreign Affairs,* Vol. 77, No. 2,1998, pp. 95-107.

T. Carothers. *Aiding Democracy Abroad: The Learning Curve.* Washington, D.C.: Carnegie Endowment for International Peace, 1999.

T. Carothers. Promoting the rule of law abroad: The problem of knowledge (Working Paper No. 34). Washington, DC: Carnegie Endowment for International Peace, 2003.

T. Carothers. *Critical Mission: Essays on Democracy Promotion.* Washington, DC: Carnegie Endowment for International Peace, 2004.

T. Carothers. *Promoting the rule of law abroad: In search of knowledge.* Washington, D.C.: Carnegie Endowment for International Peace, 2006.

C. Cartledge, P. Tak, & M. Tomic-Malic. *Probation in/en Europe.* Hertogenbosch, NE: European Assembly for Probation and After Care, 1981.

F.G. Castles. Introduction. In F.G. Castles (Ed.), *Families of Nations. Patterns of Public Policy in Western Democracies.* Dartmouth: Aldershot, 1993, pp. 1-4.

E. Cassirer. *Language and Myth.* New York, NY: Harper & Brothers, 1946.

R. Chambers. Participatory rural appraisal (PRA): Analysis of experience. *World Development,* Vol. 22, No. 9, 1994, pp. 1253-1268.

W. Channell. Lessons not learned: Problems with western aid for law reform in post-communist countries (Working Paper No. 57), 2007.

H. Chodosh. *Global justice reform: A comparative methodology.* New York: New York University Press, 2005.

J. Chima. What's the Utility of the Case-Study Method for Social Science Research? A Response to Critiques from the Qualitative/Statistical Perspective. Paper presented at the annual meeting of the American Political Science Association, Marriott Wardman Park, Omni Shoreham, Washington Hilton, Washington, DC, September 1, 2005.

A. Cornwall & R. Jewkes. What is participatory research? *Social Science Medicine*, Vol. 41, No. 12, 1995, pp. 1667-1676.

G. Crawford. Promoting Democracy From Without – Learning From Within (Part I), *Democratization*, Vol. 10, No. 1, 2003, pp. 77-98.

Y. Dandurand. Enhancing criminal justice reforms, including restorative justice. 11th UN Congress on Crime Prevention and Criminal Justice, April 18-25, 2005, Bangkok, Thailand.

Y. Dandurand. Effective technical assistance in crime prevention and criminal justice. *Maximizing the Effectiveness of the Technical Assistance Provided in the Fields of Crime Prevention and Criminal Justice*, Vienna, Austria. Paper No. 49, 2006.

Y. Dandurand, C. Griffiths, & V. Chin. *Justice and security reform and development: Discussion note.* Gatineau, PQ: CIDA Americas Branch, 2004.

Y. Dandurand, C. Griffiths, & V. Chin. Training and effective support of comprehensive justice and security reforms: Outcomes to date and lessons learned. In K. Aromaa & S. Redo (Eds.), *For the rule of law: Criminal justice teaching and training @cross the world.* Helsinki: Fi: European Institute for Crime Prevention and Control, 2008.

Y. Dandurand, C. Griffiths, V. Chin, M. Lalonde, M. Montgomery, & B. Tkachuk. *Programming opportunities in the justice and security sectors in the Caribbean. A report to the CIDA.* Vancouver, BC: International Centre for Criminal Law Reform, 2004.

A. Deaton. Evidence-based aid must not become the latest in a long string of development fads. Boston Review July/August 2006 Available at: <http://bostonreview.net/BR31.4/deaton.html>.

E. Duflo, D. Pascaline, K. Michael & S. Samuel. Education and HIV/AIDS Prevention: Evidence from a randomized evaluation in Western Kenya. World Bank Policy Research Working Paper No. 402, 2006.

P. Dupas. *Relative Risks and the Market for Sex: Teenage Pregnancy, HIV, and Partner Selection in Kenya*. MIMEO, UCLA, 2007.

P. Dutkiewicz, A. Keating, M. Nikoula & E. Shevchenko. *Juvenile Justice in Russia: Models, Design and the Road Ahead*. Gatineau PQ: Canadian International Development Agency, 2009.

S. Ebener, S. Khan, R. Shademani, L. Compernolle, M. Beltran, & M. Lansang. *Knowledge mapping as a technique to support knowledge translation*. Geneva, Switzerland: World Health Organization, 2006.

E. Eisenberg, J. Baglia, & J. Pynes. Transforming emergency medicine through narrative: Qualitative action research at a community hospital. *Health Communication*, Vol. 19, 2006, pp. 197-208.

M. Evans. Understanding Policy Transfer. In M. Evans (Ed.), *Policy Transfer in Global Perspective*. Ashgate: Aldershot, 2004, pp. 10-42.

P. Feyerbend. *Science in a free society*. London, UK: New Left Press, 1978.

M. Fine & M. Torre. Intimate details Participatory action research in prison. *Action Research*, Vol. 4, No. 3, 2006, pp. 253-269.

R. Fisman & E. Miguel. *Economic Gangsters: Corruption, Violence and the Poverty of Nations*. Princeton University Press, Newark: NJ, 2008.

Z. Gestautaite. *Penal and policy reform in Lithuania and the involvement of Canadian expertise*. Unpublished Masters Thesis, Carleton University, Ottawa, ON, 2001.

B. Gilley. *China's democratic future: How it will happen and where it will lead*. New York: Columbia University Press, 2004.

C. Griffiths, Y. Dandurand & V. Chin. Development assistance and police reform: Programming opportunities and lessons learned. *The Canadian Review of Policing Research*, Vol. 2, 2005, pp. 101-113.

P. Gründler. The Permanent European Conference on Probation and After Care. In R. Villé, U. Zvekic and J. Klaus (Eds.), *Promoting Probation Internationally.* Rome and London: United Nations Interregional Crime and Justice Research Institute, 1997, pp. 150-156.

E. Guba & Y. Lincoln. Paradigmatic controversies, contradictions, and emerging confluences. In N. Denzin & Y. Lincoln (Eds.), *Handbook of qualitative research* (3rd Ed) Thousand Oaks, CA: Sage, 2005, p. 191-215.

J. Habermas. *Communication and the evolution of society.* London, UK: Polity Press, 1976.

K. Hamai, R. Harris, M. Hough, R. Ville, Z. Ugljesa (Eds.). *Probation Around the World: A Comparative Study.* London, UK: Routledge Press, 1995.

M. Hardt. & A. Negri. *Empire.* Cambridge, Harvard University Press, 2001.

A. Hathaway & M. Atkinson. Active interview tactics in research on public deviants: Exploring the two-cop personas. *Field Methods,* Vol. 15, 2003, pp. 161-185.

F. Hawes & D. Kealey. (1981). An empirical study of Canadian technical assistance: Adaptation and effectiveness on overseas assignments. *International Journal of Intercultural Relations,* Vol. 1, No. 5, 1981, pp. 239-258.

J. Heckman. Randomization and social policy evaluation. In Charles Manski and I. Garfinkel (Eds.), *Evaluating Welfare and Training Programs.* Cambridge, MA: Harvard University Press, 1992, pp. 201-230.

T. Heller. An Immodest Postscript. In E. Jensen & T. Heller (Eds.), *Beyond Common Knowledge: Empirical Approaches to the Rule of Law.* Stanford University Press, 2005, pp. 382-412.

G. Helmke & S. Levitsky. Informal Institutions and Comparative Politics: A Research Agenda, *Perspectives on Politics,* Vol. 2, No. 4, 2004, pp. 725-740.

K. Hendley. Law and development in Russia: A misguided enterprise? *Proceedings of the American Society of InternationalLaw* Issue 90, Washington, DC, 1996.

T. Herman. Aspects in international technical assistance – lessons learned. *HEUNI Conference Crime Prevention and Criminal Justice,* Helsinki: FI, 2001.

M. Hoepf. Choosing qualitative research: A primer for technology education researchers. *Journal of Technology Education*, Vol. 9, No. 1, 1997, pp. 47-63.

E. Husserl. *The crisis of European sciences and transcendental phenomenology* (D. Carr, Trans.) Evanston, IL: Northwestern University Press, 1970.

V. Ivanova & M. Evans. Policy Transfer in a Transition State: The Case of Local Government Reform in the Ukraine. In M. Evans (Ed.), *Policy Transfer in Global Perspective*. Ashgate: Aldershot, 2004, pp. 101-118.

T. Jackson & G. McKay. Sanitation and water supply in Big Trout Lake: Participatory research for democratic technical solutions. *Canadian Journal of Native Studies*, Vol. 2, No. l, 1982, pp. 129-145.

W. Jacoby. *Imitation and Politics: Residing Modern Germany*. Cornell: Ithaca, 2000.

W. Jacoby. Tutors and Pupils: International Organizations, Central European Elites, and Western Models. *Governance* Vol. 14, No. 2, 2001, pp. 169-200.

T. Jones & T. Newburn. Learning from Uncle Sam? Exploring US influences on British crime control policy. *Governance*, Vol. 15, No. 1, 2002, pp. 97-119.

I. Jurevičius. *Creation of the State Probation Service*. Unpublished Masters Thesis, University of Latvia: Riga, 2008.

A.M. van Kalmthout & I. Durnescu. *Probation in Europe*. Nijmegen: Wolf Legal Publishers, 2008.

S. Karstedt. Durkheim, tarde and beyond: The global travel of crime policies. *Criminal Justice*, Vol. 2, No. 2, 2002, pp. 111-123.

D. Kaufman, A. Kraary, & M. Mastruzzi. *Governance matters IV: Governance indicators for 1996-2004*. World Bank, Washington, DC, 2005.

D. Kaufmann, A. Kraay & P. Zoido-Lobatõn. Governance Matters (World Bank Policy Research Working Paper No. 2196). Washington, DC, 1999.

D. Kaufmann, A. Kraay & P. Zoido-Lobatõn. Governance indicators: Where are we, where should we be going?: Policy research working paper 4370. Washington, DC, 2008.

D. Kealey. A study of cross-cultural effectiveness: Theoretical issues, practical applications. *International Journal of Intercultural Relations,* Vol. 13, 1989, pp. 387-428.

D. Kealey. *Cross-cultural effectiveness, A study of Canadian technical advisors overseas.* Gatineau, PQ: CIDA Briefing Centre, 1990.

D. Kealey. The challenge of international personnel selection. In D. Landis & R.S. Bhakat (Eds.), *Handbook of intercultural training* (2nd Ed.). Thousand Oaks, CA: Sage Publications, 1996, pp. 81-105.

D. Kealey. *Cross-cultural effectiveness – A study of Canadian technical advisors overseas.* Gatineau, PQ: Centre for Intercultural Learning, Canadian Foreign Service Institute, 2001.

D. Kealey & D. Protheroe. *Cross-cultural collaborations: Making north-south cooperation more effective.* Hull, Québec: Centre for Intercultural Learning, Canadian Foreign Service Institute, 1995.

D. Kealey & D. Protheroe. *Getting International Projects Right: A Challenge for the 21st Century.* Hull, Québec: Centre for Intercultural Learning, Canadian Foreign Service Institute, 2002.

S. Krasner. Sovereignty: an institutional perspective. *Comparative Political Studies,* Vol. 21, 1988, pp. 66-94.

J. Lanzing. Everything you always wanted to know about...concept mapping, 1996. Retrieved October 24, 2008, from <http://utto1031.to.utwente.nl/artikel1/>.

M. Loś & A. Zybertowicz. *Privatizing the police state.* New York: NY: MacMillan, 2000.

B. Luksenaite. Evaluation of CIDA programming in the Baltic states, 1990-2003. A review. University of Toronto, Toronto, ON, 2005.

D. MacBeth. On reflexivity in qualitative research: Two readings, and a third. *Qualitative Inquiry,* Vol. 7, No. 1, 2001, pp. 35-68.

R.A. Maglajlić. Right to Know, UNICEF BiH Developing a Communication Strategy for the Prevention of HIV/AIDS among young people through PAR. *Child Care in Practice.* Vol. 10, No. 2, 2004, pp. 127-139.

P. Maguire. *Doing participatory research: a feminist approach*. Amherst, MA: Center for International Education, 1987.

J. McCracken. Participatory Research in Gujerat: a Trial Mmh'l /or the Aga Khan Rural Support Program (Italia). International Institute for Environment and Development, London, UK, 1988.

A. McIntyre. *Participatory action research*. Thousand Oaks, CA.: Sage Publications, 2008.

E. Miguel & M. Kremer. Worms: Identifying Impacts on Education and Health in the Presence of Treatment Externalities, *Econometrica*, Vol. 72, No. 1, 2004, pp. 159-217.

B. Mikkelson. *Methods for Development Work and Research: A New Guide for Practitioners*. New Delhi: Sage Publications, 2005.

D. Morrison. *Aid and ebb tide: A history of CIDA and Canadian development assistance*. Waterloo, ON: Wilfred Laurier Press, 1988.

R. O'Brien. An overview of the methodological approach of action research. In Roberto Richardson (Ed.), *Theory and Practice of Action Research*. João Pessoa, Brazil: Universidade Federal da Paraíba, 2001, pp. 3-11.

J. Parpart. & H. Veltmeyer. The Development Project in Theory and Practice: A Review of its Shifting Dynamics. *Canadian Journal of Development Studies*, Vol. 25, No. 1, 2004, pp. 38-59.

G. Perlin. *International assistance to democratic development: A review*. Montreal: PQ: Institute for Research on Policy Practices, 2003.

C. Pestieau & S. Tait. Academic Research and Development Policy in Canada. *Canadian Journal of Development Studies*, Vol. 25, No. 1, 2004, pp. 119-145.

D. Protic. Judicial reform in Serbia: Enhancing judicial performance through training. In EBRC (Ed.), *EBRC in transition 2005 courts and judges*. London: UK: European Bank of Reconstruction and Development, 2005.

T. Randma-Liiv. From Policy Transfer to Policy Learning in Central and Eastern Europe. In D. Coombes and L. Vass (Eds.) *Post-Communist Public Administration: Restoring Professionalism and Accountability*. Bratislava: NISPAcee, 2007, pp. 27-36.

T. Randma-Liiv & R. Kruusenberg. West-East Policy Transfer: Motives, Scope, Role Models and Agents. Paper presented at IRSPM Conference held April 2-9, 2010, Berne, SW.

R. Rose. *Lesson-drawing in Public Policy: A Guide to Learning across Time and Space.* New Jersey: Chatham House Publishers, 1993.

R. Rose. *Learning from Comparative Public Policy: A practical guide.* London, New York: Routledge, 2005.

M. Shaw & Y. Dandurand (Eds.), Effective Technical Assistance in Crime Prevention and Criminal Justice: Maximizing the Effectiveness of the Technical Assistance Provided in the Fields of Crime Prevention and Criminal Justice, Working Paper 49 (Helsinki, HEUNI), 2006.

M. Spence. The complexity of success in Russia. In T. Carothers (Ed.), *Promoting the rule of law abroad: The problem of knowledge.* Washington, D.C.: Carnegie Endowment for International Peace, 2003, pp. 217-250.

L. Sundstrom. *Funding civil society: Foreign assistance and NGO development in Russia.* Paulo Alto, Ca: Stanford University Press, 2006.

B. Tamanaha. *On the Rule of Law: History, Politics, History.* Cambridge, UK: Cambridge University Press, 2004.

M. Tavits. Policy Learning and Uncertainty: The Case of Pension Reform in Estonia and Latvia. *Policy Studies Journal,* Vol. 31, No. 4, 2003, pp. 643-660.

E. Taylor. A learning model for becoming interculturally competent. *International Journal of Intercultural Relations,* Vol. 18, No. 3, 1994, pp. 389-408.

K. Thelen. How institutions evolve: Insights from comparative-historical analysis. In J. Mahoney and D. Rueschemeyer (Eds.), *Comparative Historical Analysis in the Social Sciences,* New York: Cambridge University Press, 2003, pp. 208-240.

A. Toffler. *Powershift: Knowledge wealth and violence at the edge of the 21st century.* New York: Bantam Books, 1990.

D. Trubek & A. Santos. Introduction: The Third Moment in Law and Development Theory and the Emergence of a New Critical Practice. In D. M. Trubek & A. Santos (Eds.), *The New Law and Economic Development: a Critical Appraisal.* London, UK: Cambridge University Press, 2006, pp. 1-18.

J. Waldron. Is the rule of law an essentially contested concept? (in Florida). *Law & Philosophy*, Vol. 21, No. 2, 2002, pp. 137-164.

R. Walters. *Deviant Knowledge: Criminology, Politics and Policy.* Cullompton: Willan Publishing, 2003.

J. Wedel. *Collision and collusion: The strange case of Western aid to Eastern Europe 1989-1998.* New York, NY: St. Martin's Press, 1998.

J. Wheeldon. *Bringing British Columbia to Latvia: Canadians reflect on expert designation in an international criminal justice project.* Unpublished Manuscript. Burnaby, BC: School of Criminology, Simon Fraser University, 2007.

J. Wheeldon. *Rule of law indexes: Methodological challenges and approaches for the world justice project.* Washington, D.C.: American Bar Association, 2008.

J. Wheeldon. *Mapping Knowledge Transfer: Latvian-Canadian Cooperation and Justice Reform.* Unpublished PhD Dissertation. Burnaby, BC: School of Criminology, Simon Fraser University, 2009.

J. Wheeldon & J. Faubert. Framing Experience: Concept Maps, Mind Maps, and Data Collection in Qualitative Research. *International Journal of Qualitative Methods*, Vol. 8, No. 3, 2009, pp. 68-83.

J. Wheeldon. Learning from Latvia: Adoption, Adaptation, and Evidence Based Justice Reform. *Journal of Baltic Studies*, Vol. 41, No. 4, 2010, pp. 507-530.

J. Wheeldon. Mapping Mixed Methods Research: Methods, Measures, and Meaning. *Journal of Mixed Methods Research*, Vol. 4, No. 2, 2010, pp. 87-102.

J. Wheeldon & M. Ahlberg. *Visualizing Social Science Research: Maps, Methods, and Meaning.* Thousand Oaks, CA: Sage Publications, 2012.

J. Wheeldon. Is a picture worth a thousand words? Using mind maps to facilitate participant recall in qualitative research. *The Qualitative Report*, Vol. 16, No. 2, 2011, pp. 509-522.

C. Willig. *Introducing qualitative research in psychology: Adventures in theory and method.* Buckingham, UK: Open University Press, 2001.

G. Winter. A comparative discussion of the notion of validity in qualitative and quantitative research. *The Qualitative Report*, 4(3&4), 2000. Retrieved March 6, 2010 from <www.nova.edu/ssss/QR/QR4-3/winter.html>.

H. Wolman & E. Page. Policy Transfer among Local Governments: An Information-Theory Approach. *Governance: An International Journal of Policy and Administration*, Vol. 15, No. 4, 2002, pp. 477-501.

G. Wong. Creating Democratic Value: Evaluating Efforts to Promote Democracy Abroad: Approaches to the Evaluation of International Democracy Assistance. Center for Democracy, Queen's University Prepared for Foreign Affairs and International Trade Canada (DFAIT), 2008.

R. Yin. *Case Study Research: Design and Methods.* (3rd ed.) Thousand Oaks, Ca: Sage Publications, 2003.

R. Young. Canada foreign aid: facing a crisis of its own? *Journal of Canadian Studies*, Vol. 19, No, 4, 1985, pp. 31-49.

A. Zdanevicius. *Experts as agents in criminal policy making.* Kaunas, Lithuania: Vytautas Magnus University, 2001.

L. Zeibote. Probation in Latvia. In A.M. van Kalmthout & I. Durnescu (Eds.), *Probation in Europe*. Nijmegen: Wolf Legal Publishers, 2008.

Intermission 1: The Power of Personalities and Mapping Cooperation

Scholarly approaches to writing about international development projects are still evolving. One challenge is that those able to access the kind of data required for useful empirical explorations often are, or perhaps were, themselves involved in those same projects. This is certainly the case in my experience. Based on my admittedly limited time working in international development, it seems to me that the inherent challenges of this field require a certain sort of dedication and worldview. Indeed, while it is rare to find someone who is unattached to the work he or she does, one's prior involvement in development projects can complicate objective analysis in myriad ways. While the events that brought me to the Baltics seem in many ways happenstance, the relationships that I made through my time were anything but. There is no doubt that the people and personalities I met in Latvia greatly influenced my experiences and my views.

A particularly important time for me, it turned out, was January and February of 2002. Through the LRCP, Tawnia Sanford had brought an Advisory Team to Latvia to write a report on the successes and challenges of the project to date. The team was comprised of University professors in criminal justice with varying levels of international experience. Over a two-week period I accompanied Curt Griffiths, Ray Corrado, Sandra Bell, and Yvon Dandurand as they visited Latvia, and listened intently as they talked about different countries, projects, and development approaches. It quickly became apparent that what was happening in Latvia was unique. It also became clear that applying traditional social science research methods, which tend to assume a common language and reference point, to international development projects was challenging. It was fascinating to watch these experts interview judges, legislators, and government officials and I began to understand how language and culture could influence data collection.

To address these challenges, the projects relied upon a network of interpreters and translators – some of whom were fantastic and others perhaps out of their depth. Unless those assisting had a basic understanding of the language of criminal justice and could ask clarifying questions when necessary, the meetings often broke down and the information gleaned seemed superficial. Yet, by watching how they worked and listening in to the debates in the van on the way to or from one meeting or another, I began to put what I was seeing into context. Working with this experienced group of international researchers, authors, and justice experts allowed me to frame my role in this endeavor in a way that gave me a new sense of purpose.

Working in development requires about the complexities of another culture, and accepting new rules and social norms. Through this experience frustrations are inevitable, borne of one's expectations and assumptions about how the world is *supposed* to work. Invariably, as a social creatures, we develop relationships, build safety nets, and accrue memories. What once was strange becomes the norm, and those working abroad find it increasingly difficult to relate to their own culture, and the expectations of visitors from home. *It's just not done that way here,* you say. While this process can make one more interculturally competent, flexible, and open, it also makes it difficult and maybe impossible to remain an unbiased observer. The relationships I formed and my personal experiences might be usefully framed using the three-tier model presented in Chapter 3. In the place of country context, organizational constraints, and individual impediments, I use personal relationships, administrative realities, and socio-cultural differences.

One of my first personal connections in Latvia was with someone who identified as Russian. Erik Bergman attended the University of Latvia and worked at the VBTAC in a variety of roles. Erik gave me insights into the people we were meeting, office politics, and the complicated role of Latvian-Russian relations. I remember arguing with him about Chechnya the first week I met him. As he sided with Putin and the need to crush dissent, I could not resist asking about USSR activities in Latvia. With this he became uncharacteristically obtuse. The reports of the past atrocities were false, he said, or at least trumped up. While we disagreed on very little else, this was my first introduction to Latvia's complicated history from a Russian perspective. It was through Erik that I began to appreciate the role of language in Latvian society.

While Tawnia spoke some Russian and never learned Latvian, Erik spoke excellent English, Russian, and Latvian. I noticed early on that he often reverted to Russian when interacting with older Latvians. I remember thinking that this seemed to me both practical and at times somehow menacing. I threw myself into learning Latvian. It is a beautiful language that is easier to learn than Russian, and I thought more sensitive, given the political history of the region. While my language facility improved over the years, I never became fully fluent. Today throughout the Balitics, young Russians, Estonians, Latvians, and Lithuanians communicate together easily. They all speak English, which in this part of the world has replaced Russian and German as the *lingua franca*.

Another integral relationship I had was with Liene Zeibote. Although a Ministerial Assistant at the Ministry of Justice when I first met her, she became affiliated with the Latvia project through the LRCP and was named Local Coordinator when the project was extended. During this time she was indispensable, acting as a bridge between project activities as initially outlined and the ever-changing needs of the nascent probation service. As her experience negotiating the Latvian bureaucracy increased, she was able to grasp the sea change approach to justice presented by the Canadian trainers involved in the project. In 2004, she was hired as Deputy Director at the SPS and continues today to play an integral role in building the service and mediating the challenge of the rehabilitative ideal in the face of the hard-nosed reality of Latvian political culture. She has also remained a friend.

Other significant relationships were forged with the Canadian trainers. As both chief cook and bottle washer, my role as project manager involved everything from writing proposals, negotiating contracts, and taking meetings to less impressive feats such as facilitating airport transport in the early hours of the morning, and acting as de facto tour guide and local travel agent. While in Latvia the trainers faced a host of challenges, not the least of which was my inexperience. They often needed to adjust their training style and schedules to suit local needs and the Ministry often changed interpreters in the middle of training sessions, complicating the already intricate process of communication. Cell phones rang and were answered in the middle of a presentation and one half of a loud Latvian discussion would drown out the information these experts had travelled thousands of kilometers to share.

In a practical sense, the most challenging obstacles I encountered were the administrative complications. Some were a function of legal frameworks and other were the result of Latvian practices. I recall sitting with a high level official at the Ministry of Justice. As was sometimes the case, once I got to know the officials I would speak in my basic Latvian, while they would speak to me in slightly better English. At one meeting fortified by a brandy, this official pointed to a bookshelf on which more than 30 thick volumes were arranged. He explained to me that after the collapse of Banka Baltija in 1995, many Latvians had filed civil actions against the bank. At the time, however, there existed no means for a class action lawsuit, and the books contained every individual claim that the courts were required to review. "Imagine the time it will take," he said. "It will be years." I was not sure if the story was meant to highlight the complications of legal reform in Latvia, provide a basis for future excuses about why it would be impossible, or perhaps both.

For the nascent probation service, the biggest administrative challenge was whether judges could be convinced to rely upon the service. This had been an issue with other reform attempts, and to address it the project funded a 2002 seminar with judges through the Latvian Judicial Training Center, run by Latvian-American Robert Rusis. Sitting in a well-appointed room with thirty judges from small towns and cities throughout Latvia, I was perhaps never more doubtful that probation could ever be effectively instituted. The judges were openly dismissive, disinterested, and perhaps even hostile to the team of international experts. At first I thought this was perhaps a result of the vaulted position of judges within Latvia. I have since come to view that experience as part of a larger aspect of Latvian social practices – and at least at that time a certain type of xenophobia that often frustrated my youthful optimism.

A frequent traveler, I have often had occasion to ask for directions in unfamiliar cities, and in new and perhaps inexact dialects of the local language. In Latvia taxi drivers, shopkeepers and wait staff would ignore me, laugh in my face, or meet my queries with a dismissive air bordering on contempt. At times it was amusing. There was an older woman who swept the street near my room with what looked to me to be branches tied together on a stick. I would practice my good morning to her "Labrit," and greet her morning after morning and month after month. She would snort and look away – as if to say, "what's so good about it?" I did win her over in the end – "Labrit, labrit" she would say hurriedly, roll her eyes, and turn away. Limited successes like these were rare and I could never quite shed my role as privileged outsider.

On an international project, consultants and managers are paid a per diem. While these are rarely enough to cover the "total" expenses involved with living abroad, they can be used purposively and generously. To me this meant picking up the check, when I could, and hosting events when required. Project Managers do a bit better than interns, and it was nice to move out of my one-room accommodation. I consciously tried not to be "too generous" but I never lost the sense that while people were happy not to have to pay for things, they sometimes resented the fact that I could. One interesting aspect that I got to witness was the development of Latvian consumer culture in the early 2000s. Beautiful new stores full of consumer electronics by and large sat empty. After a couple weeks in Latvia, I decided to visit a few to figure out options on a CD player for my small room. After waiting for ten minutes in an empty store, I had to approach someone who hesitantly began to help me. Growing up as a creature of consumer capitalism in North America I expected the customer to be number one – I mean why take a sales job if selling things to customers was not something you cared about? I guess I assumed there were lots of jobs going and everyone could just choose where they wanted to work. A foolish assumption in hindsight but born out of my experience at the Malls of North America. In fairness though, service in bars and restaurants was the same – horrible.

Sometimes it was on purpose. One of my favorite spots was a Soviet style restaurant *Austrumu Robezaand*, which offered an ironic look at communism and totalitarian regimes. Although there was decent food available, the inclusion of ironic Soviet menu items could lead to unfortunate culinary outcomes. Mostly I liked the busts of Hitler, Stalin, Lenin, and Putin. The service was deliberalty rude, and occasionally poets and would take to the stage in mock earnestness. The bathroom key was a bullet from WW1. Not all my consultants got the joke. Living in it everyday, I could appreciate what humor existed. Sometimes I would try to tease out the social situation to try to better understand expectations; mostly I was just confused.

Over the next few years, I got to revisit this feeling every time a new consultant arrived. Sales people did not smile and no one wanted to make conversation. I recall returning to Canada for a couple of weeks and being irritated at the meaningless "have a nice days" that would punctuate nearly every commercial interaction. Maybe they had it right, I thought. Superficial smiles still annoy me but there is something to be said for helping strangers. I have since come to understand that this is what people mean by Latvians' reputation for a 'passive' approach to life. I still do not get it though. During a 2008 trip to to gather data for this book, I stood near the bus station asking more than fifty people in clear, understandable Latvian which bus went to Mezaparks. For over approximately 20 minutes I had to endure people rushing past me, avoiding eye contact, and in one case crossing the street, to avoid the strange Westerner speaking their language. On that occasion I gave up, hailed a taxi, and stated the address in Latvian. I was there within minutes, although I then had to negotiate the 'foreigner fare' that I had been assigned. Too often my accent (or lack thereof) betrayed me. I can recall being told in no uncertain terms that I should stay quiet as my Latvian friends negotiated prices on my behalf.

During my early years in Latvia these sorts of experiences frustrated me to no end. As I got to know some of the Latvians working on the project, it became clear that initial coldness could become amazing warmth in a very short time. Latvian colleagues have offered me a place to sleep, food and drink, and help with translation and interpretation. They have rearranged schedules, dropped everything, and helped me in ways I probably do not even know about. Perhaps the most significant challenge was that while Latvia had formally embarked on a process of reform though the development of a probation service, not all of those in the training session saw eye to eye about the need or means of this reform. More than once, the solution to complex scenarios provided through the training was the most punitive and least creative possible. I often exchanged meaningful looks with the trainers, when senior officials – who had been disregarding the views of those in some Latvian communities for years – began to monopolize discussion.

Looking back, I can see how privileged I was to work with a number of experts from a variety of justice agencies in Canada from coast to coast. They came for very little money, by international development standards. Their flexibility in selecting which aspects of their expertise to present was impressive and they perhaps unknowingly educated me about the Canadian justice system. I can recall often feeling as though I was putting together a complex puzzle that I should know better than I did. Each of these individuals contributed a piece. Too numerous to list by name, each brought his or her knowledge and energy to the project, and many have remained involved with the SPS even today.

As the project was nearing completion, it became clear to me that no one was chronicling what was happening in Latvia. The embassy was in full wrap up mode, downgrading from a large formal presence to a tiny office with reduced staff. CIDA was not considering how the Latvian experience could be leveraged in other countries of the FSU, let alone other countries emerging from authoritarian regimes. After observing a number of interactions between Latvians and North American or European researchers, I began to put what I was seeing into context. I began to imagine how this project might form the basis of a dissertation proposal. To study the Latvian experience developing probation, I faced at least two substantive problems. The first problem was my involvement in the project and the potential for bias that may emerge or could be reasonably assumed by others. As Project Manager for the LLRP, I wrote the proposal, negotiated the contract and managed all aspects of project delivery – including the selection of Canadian trainers. How could I investigate something in which I had been so intimately involved?

The second issue was based on my experience watching Latvians interact with researchers from other countries. Too often, the interviewers assumed a certain level of linguistic facility, and too often I watched participants agree with the implicit assumptions embedded in their questions. As I learned more about grounded approaches to research, and understood in greater detail the role of the researcher in the research process, I sought to uncover and understand new approaches to data collection. How could new methods be more explicitly user-generated and unsolicited? One answer was a creative use of visual maps.

I first became interested in maps through my teaching. When pressed to explain a relationship or interconnection, I would invariably revert to quickly constructing diagrams, maps, and graphs easily created on a black or white board. There is something about visually representing a concept or relationship that can quickly cut through jargon or complex explanations. The famous quote that a picture is worth a thousand words is true for many. Soon I began experimenting in class. I asked students to complete maps during the first week and then again in the last week and had them compare their maps. How were they different? How were they similar? It was clear that the way the students presented their ideas before and after course delivery had changed. It was not always clear why. While I knew that maps could be used to organize and explain ideas, it also seemed that how individuals visually presented their ideas was unique and inherently valuable. I became fascinated with how maps could be used to gather social science data from international participants.

As discussed in some detail in Chapter 3 visual maps offer a creative means of engagement and can be used to probe the backstage of participant experience. This graphic means to capture perceptions represents a new data collection strategy that seeks to go beyond soliciting rehearsed forms of narrative communication. Using visual maps as data might be seen alongside other participant driven mediums such as vignette responses, subject-operated cameras/videos/sound recordings, journaling, and blogs. As part of my work in Latvia they offered me yet another benefit. To ensure that my interviews were not based on my subjective, personal experiences, I used visual maps to first gather unsolicited views of the way participants framed their experience of the project. The data collected from maps created by Canadians and Latvians has proven invaluable. I have spent more than three years exploring different strategies for understanding what these maps mean and how they might be analyzed. The result was my first book, entitled *Visualizing Social Science Research.* Here in Intermission 1, I have chosen to describe the process I used to collect data, and include some of these maps as a means to both locate my findings and showcase this unique method for data collection in international development. Through my research since 2006, I have gathered a variety of maps from Canadian trainers and Latvian participants. A select sample is included below.

Figure 1 Map from a Canadian Trainer

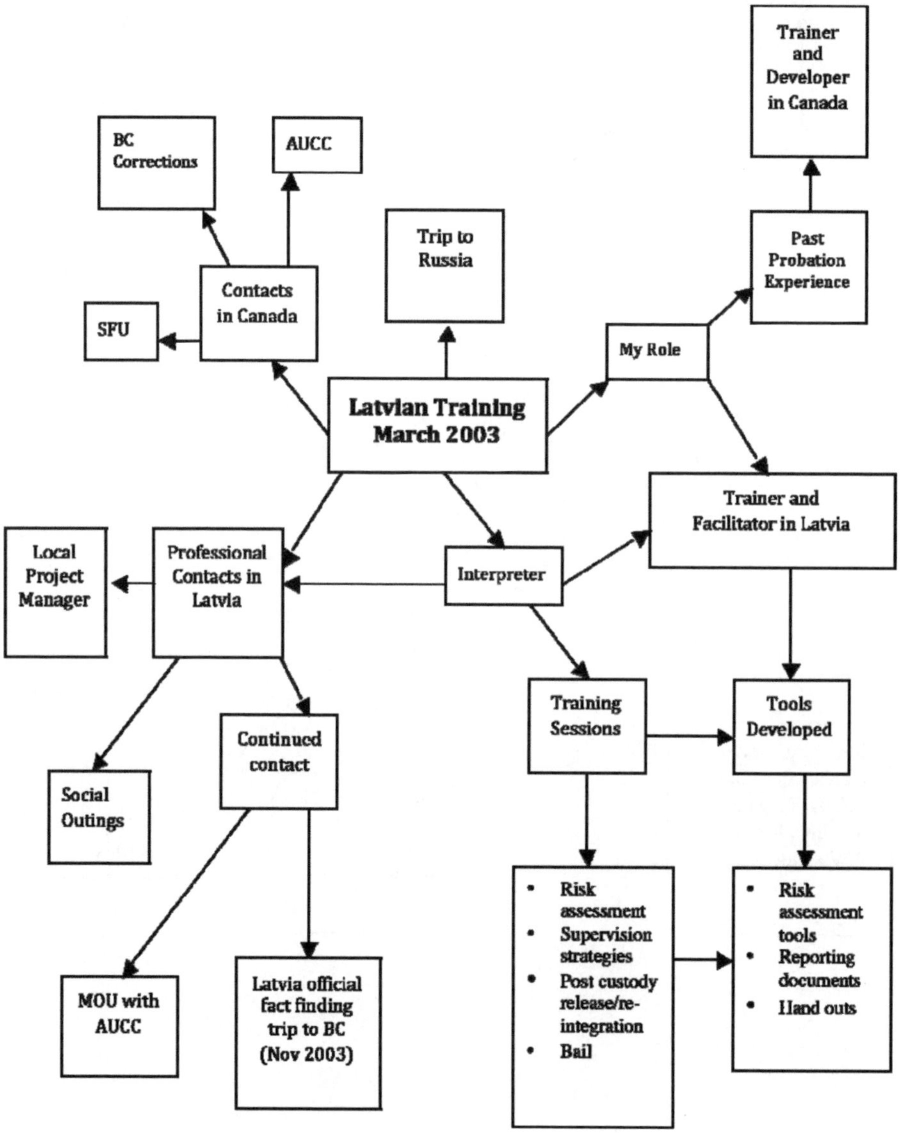

Figure 2 Map from a Latvian Participant

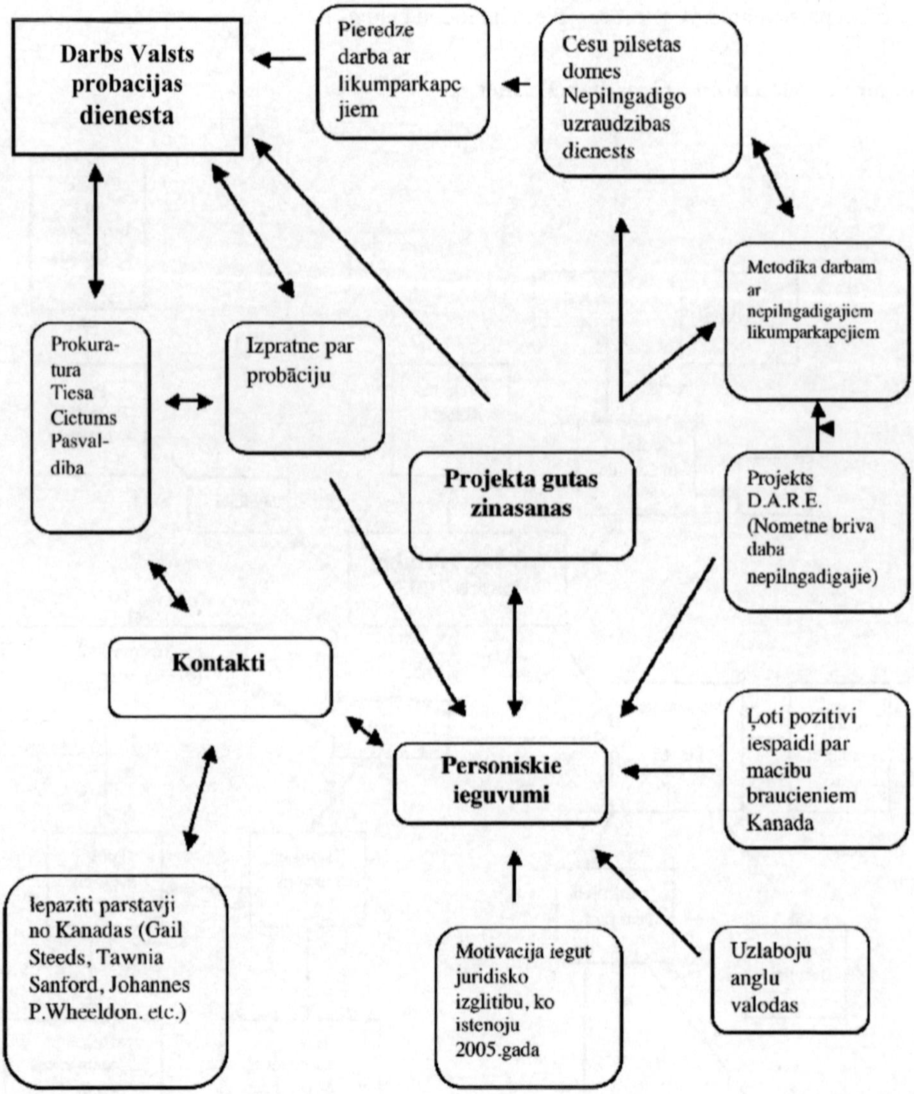

Figure 3 Map from a Canadian Trainer

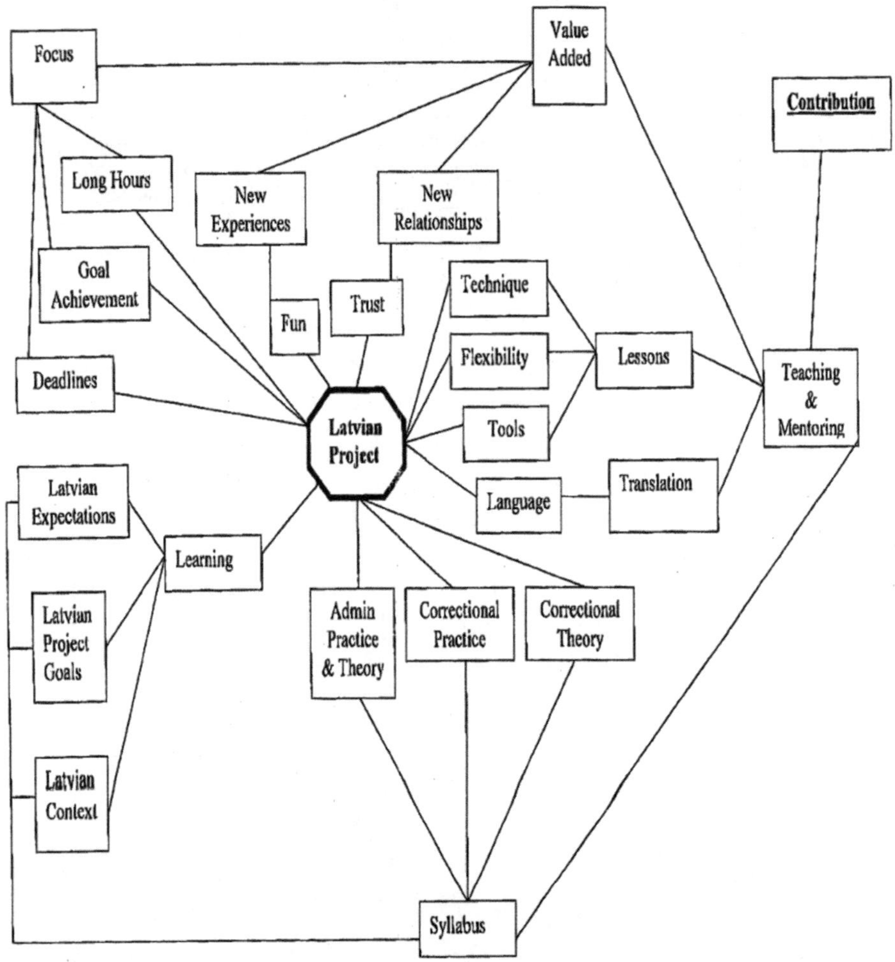

Figure 4 Map from a Latvian Participant

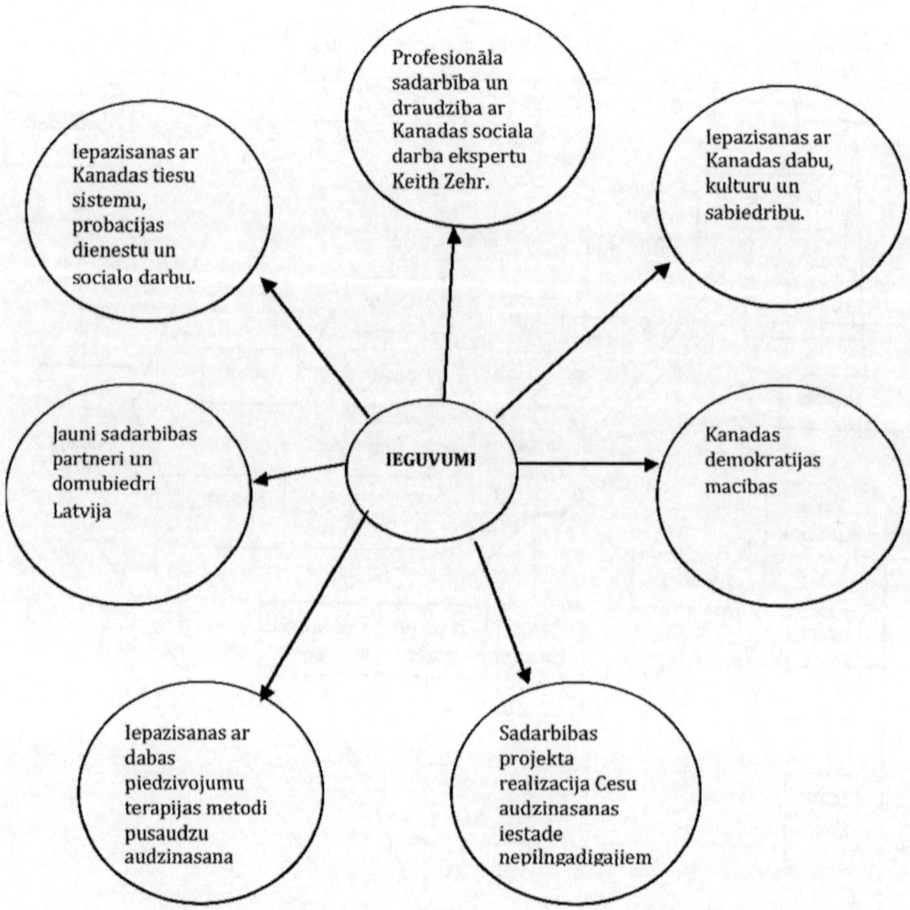

Figure 5 Map from a Canadian Trainer

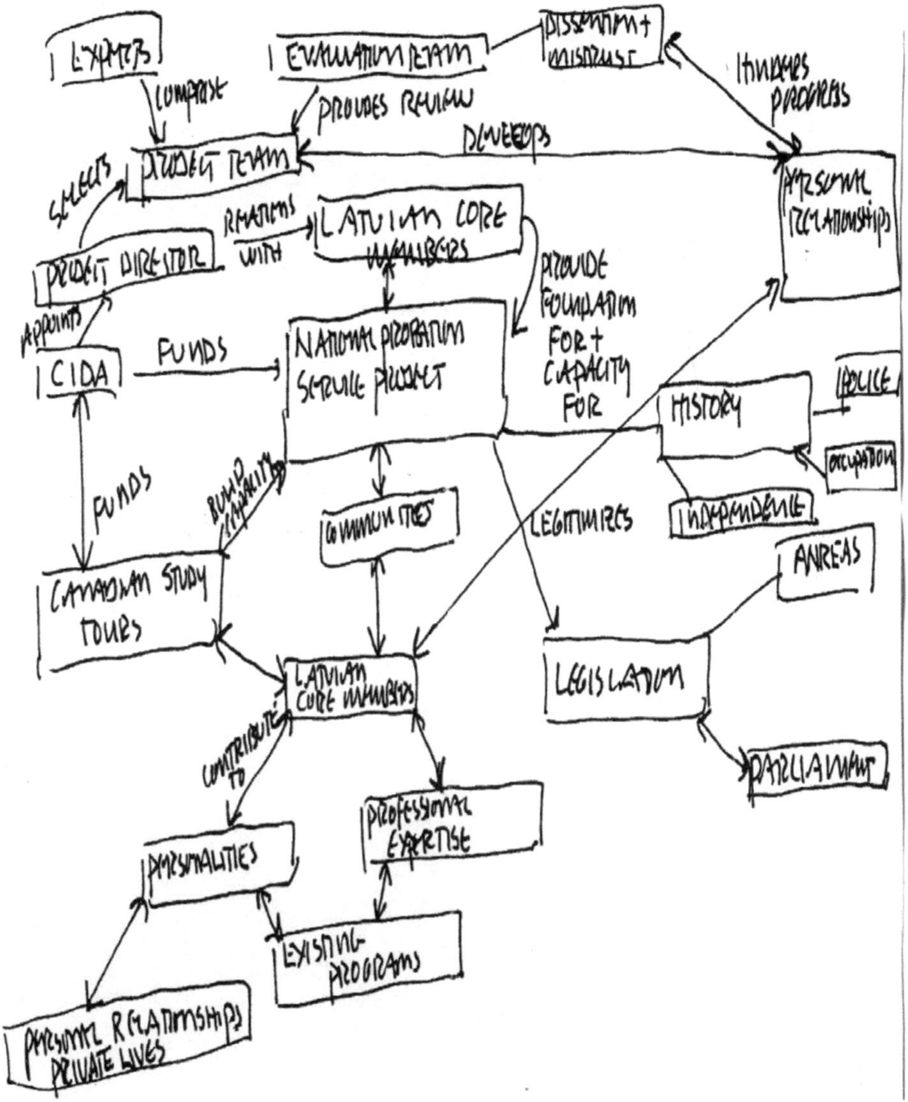

Figure 6 Map from a Latvian Participant

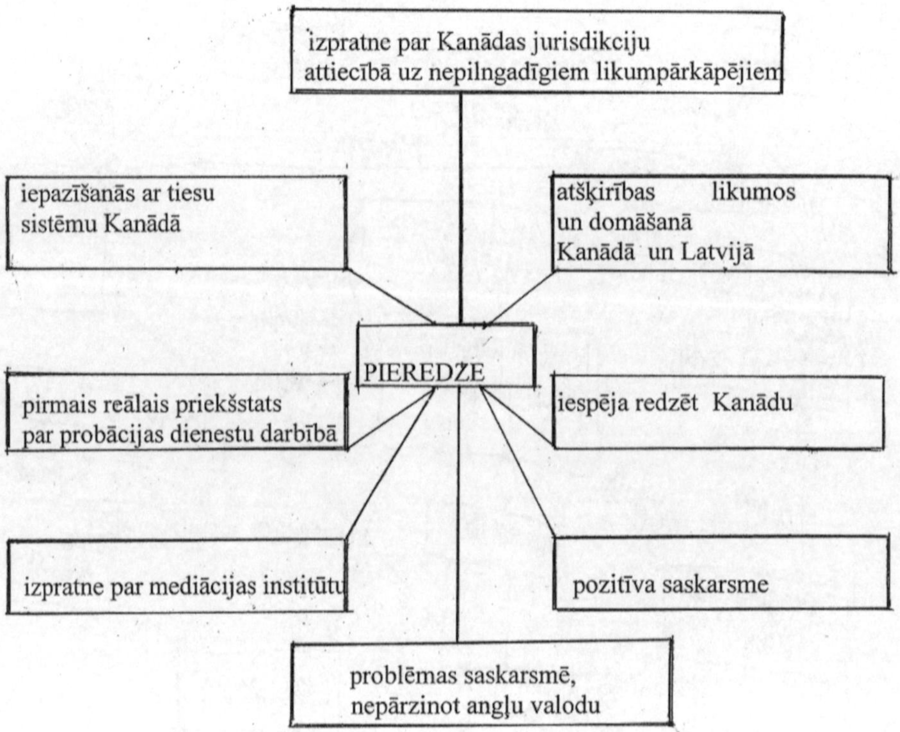

Figure 7 Map from a Canadian Trainer

Figure 8 Map from Latvian Participant

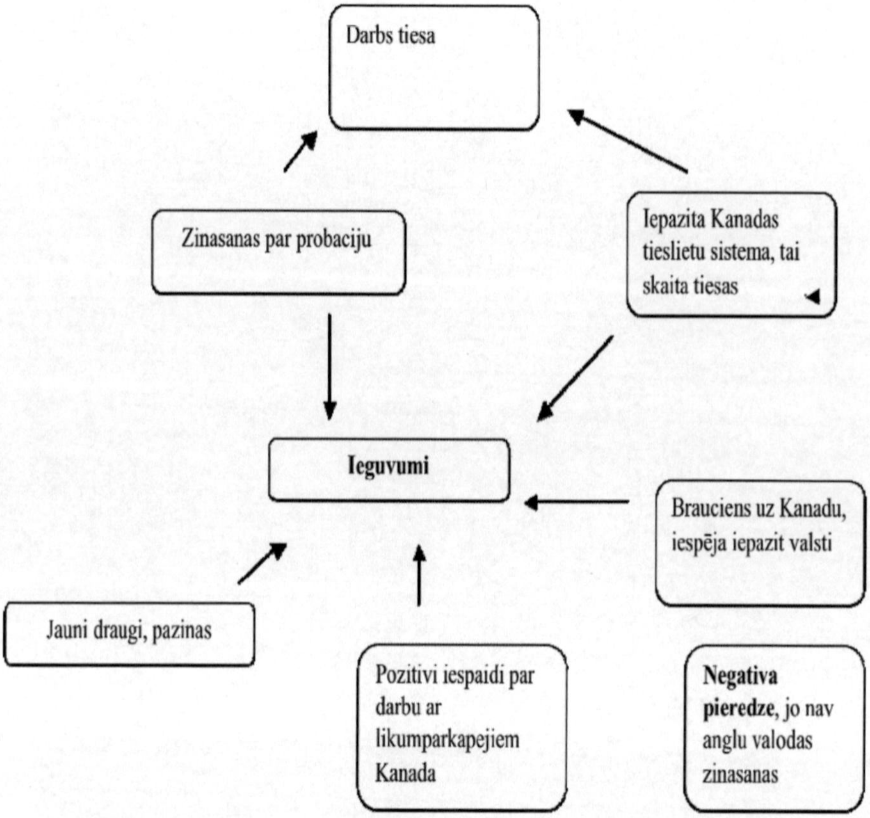

Taken together these maps provide a tangible sense of how participants experienced Latvian-Canada cooperation. When used to design follow up interviews, the combined data provided perhaps the most complete review of their experiences – both positive and negative. The maps and the interviews have served to provide me a means to put different aspects of the project into context and allowed to quote project participants in their own words, based on questions drawn from the themes within their maps. As is clear, some maps were completed in Latvian and others in English and to ensure the maps were translated properly, I had the maps translated by two translators well known to the project. In the few cases in which there were differences in interpretation, I contacted the mapmaker to seek clarification. While my previous work has focused on how to compile, consider, and quantify some of these maps, in this book, I have chosen to leave them as unique artifacts. For readers who speak Latvian, I hope you enjoy them. For others, I hope they are a reminder of the challenges of data collection in international contexts, and the ways in which maps can demonstrate meaning, even when they are in another language.

In Chapter 1, I set out the challenges of governance reform, and argued for the importance of the justice system as a site of reform. Based on my experience in Latvia, I also suggested that Probation might provide the best means to ensure some form of state control, while reducing incarceration and expanding community-based programming and rehabilitative models. Chapter 2 provided a more in-depth discussion of the challenges for probation as a concept and outlined the operations and function of the Latvian State Probation Service (SPS). In Chapter 3, my focus was to present some of the methodological challenges that exist when trying to evaluate justice programming and suggested that visual maps may offer a means to gather more unsolicited and thus credible data that can be used to develop mixed methods measures. In addition, I argued for an international model of justice reform that takes seriously the country context, organization impediments, and individual challenges. As evidence should always precede inference, before suggesting why this model can usefully be applied in the MENA region, it is instructive to look the Latvian-Canadian experience.

In Chapters 4, 5 and 6, I present one way in which this model can be used to explore Latvian-Canadian programming between 1999-2004. There is something of a tendency to see the Latvia project in simplistic terms, I argue in the next three chapters that it was the confluence of three projects that built one on top of the other to produce alternatives. The experience of developing and delivering these models was then used to develop a legal basis for alternatives to incarceration, and formed the basis of State-led justice reform initiatives. These furthered, deepened, and institutionalized what were local pilot projects designed and delivered by community-based reformers, who were now experts. Chapter 7 represents an attempt to apply the lessons learned in Latvia to the emergent interest in justice reform and probation programming in the Middle East and North Africa. It is by necessity tentative. My hope is to better define the framework by which developments on the ground can be understood. This involves an exploration of if and how the three-tier model, introduced in Chapter 3 can be used to understand the regional, organizational, and individual impediments to reform. One argument that needs more study is the extent to which justice reform can be seen as an important example of modeling democratic values of inclusion and exploring the inherent balancing act required within justice systems between individual rights and collective security. This book provides some initial insights into that process, and the subsequent chapters offer a means to understand – if not completely overcome – the conceptual challenges inherent in international collaborative justice reform.

4 Country Context: Occupation, Transition, and the Latvian Diaspora

Chapter 3 explored some challenges associated with compiling knowledge on legal technical assistance and studying meaningful outcomes and impacts of international development initiatives. One approach that departs from singular project-based evaluations or development agency funded reviews involves in-depth mixed methods case studies based on a three-tier model of project analysis. At the macro level this involves understanding the historical context of the country. Latvia's central location along trade routes in the Baltic region has made it long sought after by its larger neighbours. In the 20th century, it has been governed by Sweden, Poland, Germany and Russia and occupied for far longer than it has been independent.

Of specific interest in this chapter is how Latvia's history, penal policy, and legal framework presented challenges for Latvian-Canadian cooperation, and how the project overcame these in some cases, and mitigated against them in others. Central to these constraints was a dysfunctional criminal justice system – a legacy of Soviet occupation. This system resulted in high numbers of imprisoned youth and adults in facilities described as inhuman and degrading. As international and regional pressures from Europe, the United Nations, and a variety of civil society groups mounted, Canada emerged as a central partner in justice reform. Initially the Baltic Diaspora assisted to bridge cultural differences between Canada and Latvia, and overcome differing understandings of law, justice, and society.

4.1 An Ancient History of Occupation

The territory known today as Latvia was first inhabited in 9000 BCE by the ancient Finnic peoples. In the first half of 2000 BCE, the first Balts arrived. Generally acknowledged as the forefathers of the Latvian people, the Finnic tribes are also considered the early ancestors of contemporary Estonians, Finns, and Livs (Gimbutas, 1963). Latvia became famous as a trading crossroads, and Latvia's largest river – the Daugava – served as an integral route connecting Scandinavia, Russia and the Byzantine Empire (Abols, 2002). The Balts of this time actively participated in this trading network. Amber from the eastern shore of the Baltic Sea was known as far away as ancient Greece and the Roman Empire and considered more valuable than gold (Bilmanis, 1951). It remains special to Latvians even today.

Latvia's location made it a tempting prize for Swedish Vikings, German conquerors and invaders from Poland and Russia, who all ruled different parts of the Latvian territory (Bilmanis, 1951). By the 1520s, Rīga became an important centre of Reformation in Northern Europe and between mid-16th and the early 18th century Latvia was relatively stable, ruled again by a German landowning class (Rutkis, 1967). By the end of the 18th century, expansionist Russia had annexed the whole of Latvia. Although German landowners retained influence, the emancipation of the serfs throughout the Russian Empire in 1861 brought a new measure of stability to Latvia (Plakans, 1995). Nationalistic sentiment was revived as the economy grew and educational and other institutions were established. The idea of an independent Latvian state was introduced during the Russian Revolution of 1905, but did not gain popularity until 1917 (Abols, 2002).

4.1.1 *The Russian Revolution and Latvian Independence*

Following the Russian Revolution of 1917, Latvia declared its independence on November 18, 1918, after a confused two-year period of fighting in which both Latvian and Soviet forces controlled different parts of the country (Plakans, 1995). During this time, Germany and the United Kingdom fought separately and together to repel the Russian Army, and when they withdrew, Latvia was recognized as a nation both by Soviet Russia and Germany in 1920 (Rauchs, 1974). The Latvian constitution of Feb. 15, 1922 provided for a republic with a president and a unicameral parliament, the Saeima, where 100 members were elected for three years. During the next decade, governing an independent Latvia proved to be a challenge. The multiplicity of parties in the Saeima made governing difficult and, in 1934, Prime Minister Ulmanis proposed constitutional reforms that were widely opposed.[1] One vocal group, the *Baltischer Bruderbund,* was composed of Latvian fascist groups who waged a fierce propaganda war. On May 15, 1934, Ulmanis issued a decree declaring a state of siege and the Saeima and all the political parties were dissolved. Between 1934 and 1939 Ulmanis ruled quasi-dictatorially. He outlawed the *Baltischer Bruderbund* and attempted to consolidate power through economic reforms. Although Ulmanis strengthened the economy, this centralization of power set the stage for a later and much more pernicious siege (Spekke, 1957).

---

1 In 1922 the Latvian Saiema had 22 parties and 24 in 1931 and by that time Ulmanis had at that time been Prime Minister four times since 1918. In a variation on an old joke, in Latvia it is said when three Latvians get together four political parties are created. See The Latvian Institute's useful and detailed website: <www.li.lv/index.php?option=com_content&task=view&id=95&Itemid=173> retrieved on June 29, 2008.

4.1.2 *Molotov-Ribbentrop and Occupation*

While Latvia declared neutrality during the early phases of World War II, it soon fell prey to the *realpolitik* of geo-political interests. On Aug. 23, 1939 Nazi Germany and Communist Soviet Union concluded a Non-Aggression Treaty known as the Molotov-Ribbentrop Pact. Through the pact, Russia allowed Germany to invade Poland on September 1, 1939 in exchange for the establishment of a Soviet Sphere of Influence in Eastern Europe, which included Estonia, Latvia, and Lithuania. On June 15, 1940, the USSR invaded Latvia. USSR proxy candidates won the elections of July 15, 1940 by outlawing non-Soviet approved parties and arresting all opposition parties including Prime Minister Ulmanis, who was sent to Russia and imprisoned until his death (Misiunas & Taagepara, 1983).

As in other occupied countries, the USSR legitimated its rule by forcing an unconstitutional petition to join the USSR through the Latvian Saeima. A number of countries refused to recognize the illegal annexation, but the USSR consolidated power anyway. During this period officials identified, arrested, and imprisoned hundreds of former government officials, and introduced new laws with retroactive power designed to track anti-Soviet activity. While imprisonment and deportation was common for former Latvian elites, on the night of June 13, 1941, the Soviet government ordered a mass deportation that removed more than 15,000 people from Latvia to Russian camps. During the night, the Latvian Museum of the Occupation and the Latvian Institute reports that throughout the Baltic States more than 57,000 people were forcibly removed in cattle cars, including more than 5,000 children.

Despite the mass deportations, Soviet domination proved to be short lived in Latvia and, on June 22, 1941, the German army began advancing into Latvian territory as part of the broader Nazi invasion of Europe. Initially greeted as liberators, by July the Nazis had fully occupied Latvia and the retreating Soviet Army "evacuated" thousands more Latvians to the USSR. Between 1941 and 1944, Nazi Germany held Latvia, governed now under *Reichskommissariat Ostland,* a bureaucratic creation tasked with administering the Nazi occupied territories (Dallin, 1957). Latvian paramilitary and Auxiliary Police units established by occupation authority actively participated in the Holocaust. More than 200,000 Latvian citizens died during World War II, including approximately 70,000 Latvian Jews murdered during the Nazi occupation and a further 20,000 German Jews who were transported to Latvian death camps (Ezergailis, 1996). Latvian soldiers fought on both sides of the conflict, including in the Latvian Legion of the Waffen-SS (Vardys & Misiunas, 1978). While the occupying Nazi authorities conscripted many by threatening them with imprisonment, the killing of their relatives, or even death, the Museum of the Occupation suggests other Latvians willingly joined in the destruction of Jewish property and the eventual attempt at mass extermination, which began in 1941.

The role of Latvians in the Holocaust is complex and pains are often taken to differentiate between Latvia and other countries. Although some Latvians collaborated with the

Nazis, the spontaneous pogrom against the Jewish population that often occurred in other countries did not in Latvia (Ezergailis, 1996). Yet the Latvian Institute acknowledges that the proliferation of Nazi propaganda that blamed Latvian Jews for Soviet policies through the slogan "Jew-Bolshevik" was effective in Latvia. Although some suggest the scale of the murderous plan was not commonly known, others note that some brave Latvians did help some Jews escape (Gordon, 1990, pp. 37-40). There were underlying tensions, however, that may have led many Latvians to be reluctant to get involved (Levin, 1975). For the Jewish population, given the choice between the USSR and Nazi Germany, occupation by the former would not immediately result in detention, deportation, and/or death as was likely under the Nazis. While the Latvian Holocaust devastated the Jewish population leaving only 1,000 Latvian Jews in Latvia, other Latvians fared better. Nazi occupiers reversed the collectivist polices of the Soviets, returned land and businesses, and relaxed free speech provisions allowing Latvian authors to publish prose and poetry (Dreifelds, 1996).

To administer the Eastern Occupied Territories, Nazi Germany sent more than 15,000 civil servants to Latvia in the latter half of 1941. These bureaucrats took advantage of human and material resources in Latvia allowing Germany to buy products at far lower prices than possible elsewhere (Abols, 2002). As a result of the deterioration of the Eastern Front, in 1943 Hitler declared total war and Latvia again served as a key battleground between USSR and Nazi forces. In 1944 as the Soviet Army approached Latvia, more than 10% of the Latvian population – approximately 200,000 – people fled to North America and Western Europe (Plakans, 1995). On May 8, 1945 Germany surrendered. As a result of the Yalta conference in February, 1945, the USSR was able to retain its "influence" over territory in Eastern Europe, a move famously decried by Winston Churchill (1946) who stated: "this is not the liberated Europe we fought for."[2]

The reoccupation by the USSR resulted in harsh measures applied to punish alleged Nazi collaborators. Latvia lost more than a third of its population between 1945 and 1950. In 1947, the International Refugee Organization (IRO) began to process this mass emigration of refugees, many of whom ultimately settled in the USA, Canada, and Australia. For those who stayed in Latvia, the first post-war decade proved particularly difficult. As in other occupied countries, the USSR tried to transform the country into a typical Soviet satellite state. Directives from Moscow were rubber stamped through proxy governments in Riga, a city now controlled by non-Latvians. Severe political repression accompanied radical socioeconomic change, compounding the devastation of the war. In the first year of Soviet occupation 35,000 Latvians, mainly from the intelligentsia or intellectual elite, were deported to Russia. These policies existed throughout the 1940s, during which time

2 Churchill, Winston (1946), "The Sinews of Peace Address" delivered March 5, 1946, Westminster College, Fulton, Missouri. Retrieved June 27, 2008 from <www.hpol.org/churchill/>.

more than 100,000 people were deported through campaigns to collectivize agriculture and end the remaining armed resistance against the occupation regime (Plakans, 1995). In just over 40 years, the proportion of Latvians in the population dropped from roughly three-fourths to little more than one-half. Those who were not deported faced a program of extreme '*Sovietization*' that overtook national cultural life. Large-scale immigration from Russia and other parts of the Soviet Union began and continued throughout the post-war period (Lieven, 1994).

4.1.3 Soviet Collapse and Independence

The importance of the Baltic States to the collapse of the Soviet Union cannot be understated. Despite constituting a tiny minority of the Soviet population, the Baltic States played a major role in upending the horrors of occupation. In fact, as Gerner and Hedlund (1993, p. 7) suggest this was where it all began. Resistance in Latvia to the various occupations had existed from the earliest days of the unconstitutional annexation. Aid movements offered non-sanctioned care in hospitals, sanatoriums, and schools and supported various guerrilla movements by students, former politicians, and police who published leaflets and provided shelter to those threatened by deportation. In the late 1970s and 1980s, a national cultural renaissance developed, led by poets and folk culture groups (Dreifelds, 1996). This national "re-birth" was supported by the increased participation of Latvians in international academic conferences and the growing condemnation by Latvians living outside of the situation in Latvia that had resulted from occupation.

In 1985, a Baltic Tribunal held in Copenhagen featured several prominent Latvian-Americans who openly addressed a variety of human rights abuses reported from Latvians within Latvia. In 1986, external pressure was also applied when Helsinki-86, a human rights group comprised of persecuted Latvians forced to flee their homeland, demanded the restoration of Latvian independence. This international pressure coincided with campaigns by Mikhail Gorbachev for *glasnost* – political openness – and *perestroika* – economic restructuring, which together demolished the Soviet central planning apparatus without replacing it with anything new (Gerner & Hedlund, 1993, p. 33). As falling energy prices threatened economic stability the democratic reforms of Gorbachev may have allowed the forces of Latvian nationalism and independence to organize, resulting in organized efforts to compete in free elections. Three major factions emerged in the late 1980s: The radical nationalists of the Latvian National Independence Movement, the more moderate and inclusive Latvian Popular Front (LPF), and the anti-reform Interfront movement, an amalgamation of pro-Soviet forces primarily composed of ethnic Russian Latvian Communist Party members, as well as Soviet officers who had settled in Latvia after their retirement. The contemporary Latvian party system still largely reflects this order.

Among the Baltic States, Latvia was the first in which mass demonstrations occurred. Organized to protest environmental issues (Klavin *et al.* 2000), the Environmental Protection Club (VAK) hosted and staged a number of non-sanctioned political meetings and demonstrations in 1987, popularizing the idea of Latvian public empowerment. The "calendar" demonstrations were organized to commemorate long-suppressed critical turning points in Latvian history. Although the Soviets sent 6,000 troops to prevent these demonstrations, the momentum could not be stopped and in 1988, the Latvian Popular Front emerged in opposition to the ruling establishment. The decision of the Latvian Supreme Soviet in December 1989 to declare sovereignty effectively ended the Communist party's monopoly on political power in Latvia. As opposition grew, smaller groups merged through the Latvian writers' union, and led to the creation of the Latvian National Independence Movement. Bolstered by wins in elections in all three of the Baltic States on Aug. 23, 1989, millions of Balts joined hands from Vilnius, Lithuania through Latvia and ending in Tallinn, Estonia to mark the fifty-year anniversary of the Molotov Ribbentrop pact. The "Baltic Way" event connected people for 650 kilometers and marked a participatory political turning point and an important symbolic end to Soviet occupation.[3]

On May 4, 1990, Latvian independence was formally restored. The Latvian Supreme Council declared the Soviet annexation of Latvia illegal and restored certain articles of the constitution of February 15, 1922. Soviet efforts to restore their rule culminated in violent incidents in Riga in January 1991 (Marx, 1994). In the aftermath of the failed coup in Moscow in August of the same year, the Latvian legislature declared full independence (Lieven, 1993). Soon after reinstating independence, Latvia was welcomed to the international community, first by Iceland and soon after by the United States. A member of the League of Nations prior to WWII, Latvia almost immediately became a member of the United Nations (UN). In 1992, Latvia became eligible for the International Monetary Fund (IMF) and, in 1994, took part in the North American Treaty Organization (NATO) Partnership for Peace program and signed a free trade agreement with the European Union (EU). Soon after, Latvia became a member of the European Council as well as a candidate for membership in the EU and NATO. Latvia was the first of the three Baltic nations to be accepted into the World Trade Organization (WTO).

Since the restoration of independence, Latvia has embarked on a concentrated campaign to engage with the world. By 1997, Latvia had acceded to most of the major international human rights instruments including the International Covenant on Civil and Political Rights, the International Covenant on Economic, Social and Cultural Rights, the Convention on the Rights of the Child, and others. In June 1997, the Latvian Parliament ratified the

---

3 Hands Across the Baltic is a collection of pictures which chronicles this incredible event. Retrieved from <www.warresisters.org/images/latvia_statue.jpg> on March 31, 2008. A number of other images were made available to this study by the Latvian Museum of Photography in Riga, Latvia.

European Convention for the Protection of Human Rights and Fundamental Freedoms and thus recognized the compulsory jurisdiction of the European Court of Human Rights (ECHR). In September 1997, Latvia signed the Council of Europe's Convention Against Torture and Inhuman or Degrading Treatment and Punishment. Following Soviet occupation while Lithuania and Estonia developed new constitutions on the basis of pre-war documents, Latvia chose to maintain its original constitution, introduced in 1922. This was done to reinforce the perception of continuity from the first independence period (1918-1940) and to accentuate the illegitimacy of the long Soviet occupation (Dreifelds, 1996). A major addition was made in October 1998, when the Saeima added an extensive body of rules protecting human rights.

Since the 1990s efforts to strengthen key institutions, and engage in knowledge exchange and transfer through international assistance were funded. These early efforts became more formalized and Latvia has been the recipient of a large amount of international assistance. The European Community (EC) made significant financial investments in the countries of Central and Eastern Europe, through the Program of Community Aid program, funded through the Poland and Hungary: Assistance for Restructuring their Economies (PHARE). Between 2001-2002, funding included EUR 31.4 million for the national program, including economic and social cohesion measures in rural Latvian municipalities, and anti fraud and corruption measures, and EUR 6 million for the Baltic cross-border cooperation program. An additional EUR 32 million was made available to strengthen the key Latvian institutions. This assisted the implementation of EC policies, and built capacity among national, regional administrations and regulatory bodies, to bring Latvian industries and basic infrastructure up to EC standards. Key areas included: environment, transport, industry, product quality, working conditions, and the environment.[4] In addition to EU pre accession funding, individual countries such as Germany, France, and Japan made significant contributions in education, agricultural, and social services, as well as in the financial sector and trade policy. Contributions from the US focused on border protection and export control, non-proliferation, and international security projects, often through military linkages.[5]

Some argue the collapse of socialism in the countries of Eastern Europe and the former Soviet Union has created a void that various global and regional actors have begun to fill. Militarily, as a result of its oft-noted strategic location Latvia has become central for regional forces along the eastern shore of the Baltic Sea and is the site of the headquarters of the

4 For more details on the Phare program in Latvia see <http://europa.eu/scadplus/leg/en/lvb/e40104.htm> retrieved March 16, 2009.

5 For a useful overview of many the international development projects funded in Latvia see <http://aida.developmentgateway.org/aida/SearchDo.do?iso3=LVA&archive=0&page=1&order=name&orderDirection=asc&sourcePage=country&sector=All&donor=All&exportType=0> retrieved March 16, 2009. Of some interest is that Canadian, United Nations, and Soros funding is not listed in an otherwise a comprehensive collection of projects.

United Land Forces of the Baltic States. In 2004 Latvia fulfilled a major foreign policy goal becoming a member of NATO and ensuring a greater measure of protection should Russia reinvade, a possibility perhaps considered academic before the Russian-Georgia skirmishes of 2008. NATO membership also coincided with the Latvian government's decision to contribute 125 troops to the Iraqi operation, a mission that was extended through 2007. Politically, Latvia's efforts to reintegrate with Europe were recognized in 1999 when the heads of the European nations invited Latvia to begin negotiations regarding accession to the EU. In 2003, a referendum resulted in Latvia, along with the other two Baltic States, becoming a member of the European Union (EU) in 2004.[6] While these developments have drastically altered social, economic, and political structures in these regions (Berberoglu, 2005), there is no doubt that significant challenges remain for Latvia and other countries emerging from occupation. An abbreviated timeline is presented in Figure 4.1.

6 In the days leading up to the vote, concerns were expressed the Latvians might eschew another "occupation." In the end the referendum passed and 67% voted in favor of EU membership with turnout at 72.5%. See <http://news.bbc.co.uk/2/hi/europe/3126100.stm> retrieved July 22, 2008.

Figure 4.1 Latvian Timeline 1918-2004

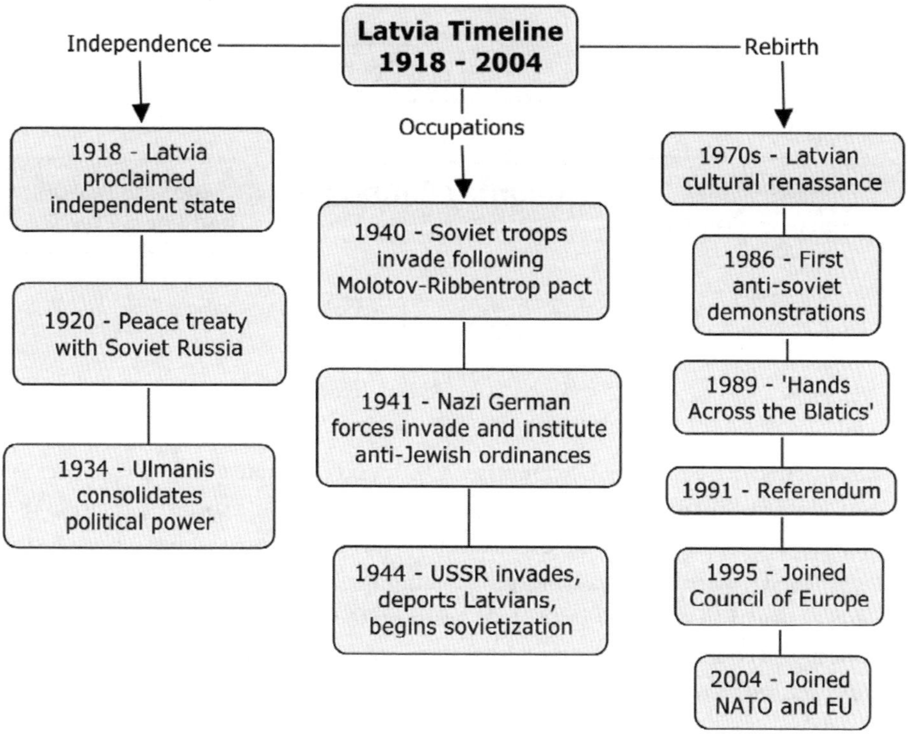

4.2 Country Context in Latvia: The Challenges of Transition

As presented in Chapter 3, contextual challenges to reform are broad and can be related to country readiness, institutional transparency and accountability, and the involvement of civil society (Dandurand *et al.* 2004). Kealey *et al.* (2005) suggest the most significant environmental factors include the friendliness of the host country's national culture to the project's aims and the overall political and economic stability of the host country. In addition, other broad-based external conditions are specifically relevant to legal technical assistance. These include: Political Context; Geopolitical Factors; Psychological Attributes; Economic Circumstances; Normative Accountability; Government Effectiveness; Corruption; Institutional Context; and Civil Society Involvement (Shaw & Dandurand, 2006:46). As discussed in Chapter 3, other important factors include the existence of international pressures, existing governance structures, and historical context; these are especially relevant in Latvia and other countries of the FSU. Figure 4.2 presents these.

Figure 4.2 Key Aspects of Country Context in Probation Programming

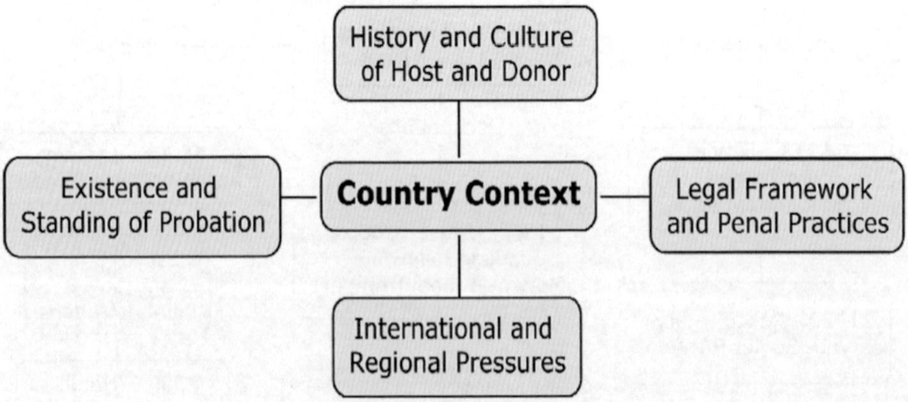

The Former Soviet Union (FSU) comprises a wide and disparate group of countries and people. However, many share a common political, economic, and social legacy from their experience of occupation and state socialism. As a small country with a unique history within the FSU, there may be a danger in attempting to draw too many inferences about the experience of all countries in the FSU based on the Latvian transition. Nevertheless, as an occupied country, Latvia was under the control of the USSR who promoted an ideologically framed view of a socialist state of the people and enforced a blueprint for political organization. Since the function of the state was to facilitate the transition to an ideal Communist society, it justified the exercise of control and coercion to that end (Fatic, 1997). As a result, all laws were intended to facilitate this transition and the justice system existed to enforce conformity with political ideology (Shelley, 1996).

In Latvia, independence brought about a number of contextual challenges, including the pressure of internal relations as well as language and citizenship issues between Latvians and the many others who identify as Russian (Vīķe-Freiberga, 2000). These citizenship issues are significant and too few treatments exist that consider the ethnic factor in patterns of crime and criminal justice in Latvia. Indeed, the working class in Riga and other urban centers in Latvia are disproportionately Russian. While this group has faced more unemployment than ethnic Latvians, who dominate among rural and educated groups, little data exists about whether ethnicity, unemployment, or other factors are connected to imprisonment in Latvia. There is, however, some suggestion that ethnic differences in Latvia relate to how people view the role of society, crime, and punishment (Kim & Pridemore, 2005).

A key challenge for the SPS was the dysfunctional criminal justice system that remained as a legacy of the Soviet occupation. There is something of a tendency to treat Soviet criminal justice uniformly as excessively punitive. This is simplistic, however, as discussed in more detail in chapter 5. Beginning in the 1990s, Latvia and other countries of the FSU attempted to diversify criminal sanctions by reforming existing sentencing laws and relying on non-custodial sanctions like fines and community service (Joutsen, 1996). Both the international pressures to reform that system, and cultural differences that often complicate East-West exchanges made the process of building criminal justice systems that were more democratic and transparent difficult. As discussed in Chapter 3, a key macro level challenge for justice reform and the development of probation relates to the existing legal framework in countries seeking reform. For Canadian-Latvian cooperation, one issue was differences between legal traditions in common law and civil law countries.

4.2.1 Legal Framework, Social Instability, and the Justice System

The role of probation in the development and supervision of alternatives is complicated by the differences between two distinct legal traditions: common law and civil (or statute) law. As discussed in Chapter 2 probation's origins lie in the practices of either releasing offenders on recognizance with no supervision required, or more commonly the surety system in which a willing third party agrees to supervise, monitor, and take responsibility for the offender. In practice this has come to mean a degree of professionalization among those who advise and monitor the offender and 'manage' the state-imposed requirements and/or obligations. These requirements often assume an approach to discretion that is traditionally associated with common law systems, which give broad deference to judges and their interpretations of law (Hamai *et al.* 2005).

By contrast, in the civil law tradition, priority is given to legislation based on a strict theory of separation of powers. In practice, this means that legislators legislate, while courts apply the law as written. In this tradition probation has developed from the suspension of the execution of sentence – an idea that spread rapidly after World War I. While originally not requiring supervision of any kind as per the Penal Code, this evolved in the years following World War One, as the notion of professional expertise gained acceptability. Across much of Western Europe supervision was added to the suspension of a sentence. One practical challenge commonly noted relates to an important function for probation services: the pre-sentence report. According to Perry and Barrows (2009, p. 74) there are:

> ...differences between Anglo-Saxon and Roman Law concepts and procedures. In the majority of Roman law jurisdictions the finding of guilt and sentencing processes are not separate, so introducing Pre-sentence reports that are designed to be used after a finding of guilt and before the sentence is passed can present a major process problem.

Another complication relates to the Soviet occupation of Latvia. While, in general, private property is protected in civil law countries, during the occupation some scholars argue a variant of civil law known as "Socialist law" operated in countries of the USSR. While the impact of this law ought not be ignored, legal systems in all socialist states preserved the formal criteria of the Romano-Germanic civil law. As a result many today consider the Socialist law as merely a particular case of this approach to civil law and not an independent legal tradition (Markovits, 2007). In the post-World War II period, once strict distinctions between common law and civil law have become more difficult to untangle. They may retain little explanatory power given the developments in many common law and civil law countries because:

> ...in common law countries probation moved from informal and marginal beginnings to become a dimension of law and policy, in civil law countries the reverse process occurred, with supervision being grafted on to a sursis whose main function was to suspend the execution of sentence (Harris, 1995, p. 25).

Nevertheless, the distinction between them remains relevant to the underlying assumptions about the role of judges, discretion, and the decentralization of justice related decision-making for probation to work as a meaningful sanction. In the UK, Canada, and the US, probation focuses on the judgment of officers and flexibility of judges who often use their own discretion to find the appropriate mix of sanction and treatment. This flexibility and focus on assistance is not a natural fit in the more formal legislation-driven and sometimes punitive countries of Eastern Europe. Yet, this distinction is too simplistic. In recent years, common law countries have introduced more explicitly statutory bases to guide probation, and civil law countries have begun to soften theirs (Hamai *et al.* 1995). As discussed in Chapter 5, Latvia provides an example of how these sorts of legal conversations may occur.

In general, the need for a more flexible approach to the formality of the civil law system was part of a trend brought about by the instability in the Baltics during the post independence era. During occupation, the structure and functioning of the Soviet socialist states influenced criminal justice policy and practice. Historically the USSR was a leader in the development of non-custodial alternatives, such as community service orders, once called "corrective work." In occupied Latvia, as in other states of the FSU, incarceration was used as a tool of social control to punish dissent and to facilitate the use of psychiatric evaluations for un-socialist thoughts and acts (Los, 2003). Compared with Western European states, official crime rates in the USSR were very low. State socialist ideology held that crime was by definition a capitalist phenomenon that would disappear with the achievement of communism and thus a lower crime rate would confirm the superiority of the communist system over the capitalist system (Butler, 1992).

When the USSR fragmented and the command economy collapsed in the late 1980s, the criminal justice system inherited policing without popular legitimacy, political management of the courts, remarkably low acquittal rates and poor representation of defendants (Bowring, 2009). The deep-rooted culture of imprisonment and a vast estate of remand centers and prisons resulted in overcrowding, TB, and commonplace inhuman treatment (Piacentini, 2007). New pressures, born of the social, political, and economic realities in many countries of the FSU, challenged court administration and the existing justice system apparatus (Botchkovar *et al.* 2009). During this period of social malaise, Baltic incomes decreased sharply as crime rates rose (Clemens, 2001). As a result of unsatisfactory health care, uncertainty about the future, and high levels of corruption, studies suggest many lost faith in the institutions of the state (Foglesong & Solomon, 2001; Kim & Pridemore, 2005).

Significant challenges for the criminal justice system specifically was the role of corruption, organized crime, and the shadow economy (Los, 1988). While, through the International Police Organization (INTERPOL), Latvian authorities gradually began to replace Soviet-trained police, allegations of police corruption persisted throughout the 1990s. While many Latvians feared organized and violent crime, other more widespread crimes were committed daily. Stealing from one's place of employment was considered criminal, but commonly occurred. Fostered by State Socialism and entrenched by poverty, in Latvia, pilfering was a way of life (Lieven, 1999, p. 371). Vested interests in old criminal justice practices existed alongside emotional, habitual, and ideological allegiances to Socialist criminal justice policies that could be harsh. This more punitive approach did not change with independence. As presented in Chapter 2, in 1992 Latvia imprisoned 314 persons per 100,000 of the national population. This climbed to 410 per 100, 000 in 1998[7] as both reported crimes and convictions increased.[8] In many prisons, such as the notorious wing of the Riga Central Remand Prison, conditions remained inhumane and degrading. As recently as 2004, tuberculosis was widespread in prison facilities and 70-80 prisoners were held in one overcrowded and unsanitary cell in Latvia's capital Riga.[9]

It was these conditions that first brought international and regional attention to the challenges within the criminal justice system and the need for alternatives. In general as Kalmthout & Durnescu (2008, p. 18) note:

7 Retrieved from <www.kcl.ac.uk/depsta/law/research/icps/worldbrief/wpb_country.php?country=149> March 18, 2009.

8 The total number of reported crimes increased from 34,686 in 1990 to 61,871 in 1992 while the number of convictions rose from 7,159 in 1990 to 11,280 in 1993. See Stewart Asquith (2002) *Report on Alternatives Measures for Dealing with Young Offenders In Latvia* (UNDP: Riga, Latvia) Retrieved from: <www.un.lv/down/Press/youth/rep_en.pdf> on August 10, 2008.

9 See Council of Europe (2005), *Tackling Tuberculosis in Latvia. Report to Committee for the Prevention of Torture and Inhuman or Degrading Treatment or Punishment (CPT) Based on ad hoc visit to Latvia*, May 5-12, 2004.

This need for alternatives is stimulated by two factors: 1) the rapid increase of criminality in many countries, mainly due to less serious (property) crimes, which has resulted in an overburdening of the criminal justice and penitentiary systems; and 2) the relatively large number of pre-trial detainees – in some countries amounting to about 50% of the total number of detainees.

4.2.2 *International and Regional Pressures*

From the mid late 1990s, Latvia faced mounting international criticism for inhuman conditions in prisons, rates of imprisonment, and the high number of prisoners awaiting trial.[10] Critics included the European Commission (EC), the United Nations (UN), the European Court of Human Rights (ECHR), and other NGOs and Human Rights organizations, including UNICEF. Site visits to Latvia resulted in a 2001 European Committee for Prevention of Torture (ECT) report,[11] urging immediate implementation of Council of Europe recommendations concerning pre-trial detention and consistency in sentencing.[12] But a year later the problems remained and 43% of those in Latvian prisons were awaiting trial. For juveniles alone the rate was 63% (Berzins, 2002).

In addition to incarceration rates and prison conditions, a principle issue was the lack of effective alternatives to imprisonment that resulted in long periods of pre-trial detention (Asquith, 2002). As pointed out by Randma-Liiv & Kruusenberg, (2010), the European Commission's (EC) pre-accession progress reports from 1998 to 2002 consistently drew attention to the lack of a probation system:

> ... Probation under strict conditions would probably help to ease the current pressures" (1998b:17); ... Probation service has not yet been established (2000:17); ... Probation service has still not been established (2001:18); ... The establishment of probation has been postponed (2002, p. 23).

In addition to this pre-accession external pressure, another politically relevant event occurred in 2002 when the European Court of Human Rights (ECHR) issued a ruling in

10 See Towards Accession. 9 October 2002, No. SEC(2002) 1405. pp. 22-24, 27-28. Pieejams Internetā: European Comission Regular Report from the Commission on Latvia's Progress Towards Accession.

11 Council of Europe Report to the Latvian Government on the Visit to Latvia Carried out by the European Committee for the Prevention of Torture and Inhuman or Degrading Treatment or Punishment (CPT) from 24 January to 3 February 1999. Strasbourg, 22 November 2001, No. CPT/Inf (2001) 27.

12 See Council of Europe Recommendation No. R (80) 11 of the Committee of Ministers to Member States Concerning Custody Pending Trial. Adopted on 27 June 1980 at the 321st meeting of the Ministers' Deputies, and Council of Europe Recommendation No. R (92) 17 of the Committee of Ministers to Member States Concerning Consistency in Sentencing. Adopted on 19 October 1992 at the 482nd meeting of the Ministers' Deputies.

the long-running case of *Lavent v. Latvia.*[13] The Court ruled that the trial court had not been independent and impartial, and that Lavent had been denied the right to a fair hearing within a reasonable period of time. Lavent was awarded costs and the international attention that resulted had a significant effect on the Ministry of Justice. These combined pressures were augmented by an especially strongly worded criticism in the Progress Reports of 2002, suggesting that accession would be delayed unless the Latvian government sought the means to better harmonize its criminal justice policy with international regulations and EU legislation.[14] As usual within international development, this is easier said than done.

Another contextual challenge to the success of Latvian-Canadian programming was cultural. A concept with multiple meanings, culture may generally be described as "...a configuration of learned behaviour... whose component elements are shared and transmitted by the members of a particular society" (Linton, 1945, p. 32). It is a complex frame of reference that consists of patterns of traditions, beliefs, values, norms and symbols, all shared to varying degrees by members of a community (Ting-Toomey, 1999, p. 10). In this way, cultural systems may on the one hand be considered as "...products of action, on the other as conditioning elements of further action" (Kroeber & Kluckhohn 1952, p. 181). Since 1991, Latvia and the other countries of the FSU have had to face the challenges posed by societal restructuring following a history of occupation and the sudden advent of independence (Joutsen, 1996). By seeking to reform their criminal justice system so as to place it in line with international standards, and to meet public demands for safety and security, the Baltic transition to independence has altered what Lauristin calls the 'symbolic environment' (1997, p. 38).

While this shift forced a rethinking among the peoples of the FSU about the interactions between individuals, communities, and the state, it has not replaced the different cultural and historic expectations of those from the East versus the West (Hebenton, 2001). In an adapted table (4.3) based on Lauristin (1997), the conceptual differences in expectations and assumptions are usefully outlined.

---

13 See *Lavent v. Latvia* (2002) ECHR no. 58442/00 retrieved from <www.echr.coe.int/ECHR/EN/Header/Case-Law/Caselaw+information/Lists+of+judgments/> on June 28, 2008.

14 See European Commission Regular Reports from the Commission on Latvia's Progress Towards Accession (1998-2002). Retrieved from <http://ec.europa.eu/enlargement/archives/pdf/key_documents/2002/lv_en.pdf> on May 14, 2008.

Table 4.3 Assumptions, Expectations and Interactions

Individualism (West)	Collectivism (East)
Individual identity – use of 'I', 'Me'. Loose in Group relationships.	Group identity. Use of 'We', 'Us'. Tight in Group relationships.
Self and Immediate Family only. Looking after self.	Extended Family and in-group networks. Protection for loyalty.
Belief in competition. Challenge. Express self and assert uniqueness.	Belief in cooperation. Harmony, deference. Avoid confrontation.
Personal responsibility. Independence, maximize outcomes.	Shared responsibility. Interdependence and shared resources
Doing one's own thing. Personal time. Honesty to speak one's mind.	Little time for self. Opinion pre-determined by Group.
Individual Freedom. Right to privacy	Equality and Group Consensus. Private life concealed.
Confrontation with authority. Resentment of conformity.	Acceptance of authority. Conformity.
Value originality, youth and initiative.	Value tradition, structure, and hierarchy.
Control by guilt, conscience	Control by shame and loss of face.

While these outlined differences are useful in understanding some of the broad differences between East and West, Latvia's history of occupation is also relevant. Both the organization of society through the Soviet state apparatus (Los, 2003), and the use of the justice system to enforce conformity with Socialist ideology (Shelley, 1996) impacted public confidence in the institutions of the state (Gestautaite, 2001). It has been suggested that Latvians have a history of indifference to others and a passive approach to life (Ezergailis, 1996), but the ways in which society was controlled by means of shame and political repression influenced the social and psychological fabric of those in the FSU (Lauristin, 1997). They shaped how Latvian society in general views the role of justice, punishment, and rehabilitation at the macro level. They may also be important in understanding how societies respond to new – and less punitive – approaches to crime control.

4.3 Project Programming: The Role of Latvian-Canadians

The contextual constraints to reform faced by Latvia were many and varied. By 1998, the dysfunctional realities of the justice system had led to a variety of international and regional pressures on Latvia to engage in a process of justice reform. Additional contextual constraints were related to Latvian culture and post occupation psychology that influenced the readiness of its people to consider new approaches to existent problems. One strategy, employed in Canada, was to look to the Latvian community living in Canada, displaced during the Second World War. Indeed this community, according to Judt (2005), made the Baltic States distinctive when compared with other occupied countries of the USSR. While Estonia, Latvia and Lithuania were all relatively prosperous, it was Latvia's history of independence and connection to the West that is of immediate interest. Latvia's twenty years of independence had allowed Latvia to establish borders, strengthen national cohesion, and demonstrate a viable economy (Dreifelds, 1996, p. 5). This period also served as a commonly invoked nationalistic reference throughout the 1980s. In addition, many Latvians had some exposure to the West and remained in touch with those outside the USSR. Independence allowed those who had remained in Latvia to rely upon the experience and expertise developed by Latvians abroad (Hinkle, 2006).

The term diaspora refers to the voluntary or forced movement of a people from a homeland to a new region. One of the central characteristics of such a movement is the generational continuity of identification with the former "homeland." Wyman (1998, p. 206) describes one aspect of this group solidarity among the Baltic émigrés:

> ...Baltic girls were crossing the ocean to Canada, presumably to become Canadian, they did not attempt to mix with other immigrant groups but filled their shipboard life with close identification with members of their own ethnic group.

Among the Latvian diaspora there was a view that Latvia itself had to "be kept alive" during occupation and young people were taught to keep Latvia close, by creating and sustaining an active community and culture, speaking Latvian, singing Latvian folk songs, and raising Latvian-speaking children and grandchildren. A common sentiment among some in Canada's diaspora community was:

> I was terribly upset about Russification in Latvia.... I thought that when [independence] comes, no Latvian-speakers will be left and the Russians will have won. We had to decide whether Latvian culture should continue to exist or not.

An often under discussed aspect of the Latvian diaspora community in North American is the variance in approach to their occupied homeland. This split was most pronounced between Daugavas Vanag and Latvian organizations in Canada and elsewhere. Many central Latvian organizations in Canada declared that all contact with Soviet Latvia – including travel, literature published in Soviet occupied territories, or welcoming Soviet Latvian cultural or religious figures in one's home – was treason (Hinkle, 2006). Other Latvian groups in America were less restrictive and used contacts with artists in Soviet Latvia or travel to Soviet Latvia to share their experiences and recount the various repressions they encountered (Liepiņš, 2004). When independence came, for many it was a surprise. The former President of the World Federation of Free Latvians, Kārlis Ķuzulis (2006), explained:

> [Although] we had always said that we are ready to return to Latvia even with bare feet, if only it were independent,… when this moment had arrived, and we were asked to fill three posts in the newly formed Supreme Council of Ministers in Latvia, we could find only one man, and that was Valdis Pavlovskis, who was willing to give up his job in the United States, move to Latvia and get to work. […] The period of exile had simply been too long to keep the love and enthusiasm alive…. Still there are many who have returned and work there.

A number of American-Latvians moved to Latvia in the early 1990s. Many took up leadership positions in various governmental and non-governmental structures. In June of 1993, during the first free democratic elections after the end of Soviet rule, a number of Latvian Americans were elected to Parliament – including twin brothers Olgerts Pavlovskis and Valdis Pavlovskis. Others like Vita Matisa and Vita Terauda served as directors of Soros Foundation – Latvia. Still others such as Kaija Gertnere, Ilga Berzkalns, Peteris Elferts, and Mara Simane are well known in civil society circles for their commitment and legacy in shaping the Latvian civil society. Although much smaller than the American-Latvian community, 80,000 Baltic-Canadians of Lithuanian, Latvian, and Estonian descent actively kept track of the independence movement and played an integral role in the early days of Canadian development programming in the region.

In Canada, as early as 1989, Lithuanian-Canadians Gabyija Petrauskas and Algis Pacevicius played an especially important initial role in turning Canadian attention to Lithuania, and Peeter Mehisto and Janis Eichmanis in Estonia and Latvia respectively (CIDA, 2004). In 1999, Canadian-educated Vaira Vīķe-Freiberga was elected President of Latvia. The result of this election was a further strengthening of ties between Canada and the Baltic region. In Latvia and Lithuania, the Baltic Diaspora in Canada provided both linguistic capacity and legal expertise, and played integral role in helping project staff to understand some of the more informal challenges to justice reform (AUCC, 2005). Key individuals included Vanda Simanis and Juris Dreifelds who shared their expertise during the early years of independence and returned to assist project activities in both Lithuania and Latvia (Lukensaite, 2005). Later in Latvia, other Latvian-Canadians played important roles advising the Ministry of Justice on legal reform and legitimizing community-based reforms through reports to National working groups, laying the groundwork for the transition from local experimentation to national implementation (Wheeldon, 2009).

One participant in Latvia whose contribution is widely acknowledged is Latvian-Canadian Andrejs Berzins. As Chief Crown Attorney for 16 years in Ottawa-Carleton, he helped implement the first victim offender mediation program in Ontario. Although Mr. Berzins had been involved since 1995, in 2002 he returned to Latvia and served as the Legislative Consultant for the LLRP, where he worked with Senior Ministry officials (AUCC, 2005). Discussed below, his legislative contribution should not be overlooked. Informal connections also appear to have been relevant between Berzins and then Latvian President Vaira Vīķe-Freiberga. Born in 1937 in Riga she fled with her parents to Germany and later to Canada. In 1965, she earned her PhD from McGill University, while remaining active in the Latvian community, and used Latvian folklore, such as the dainas, as part of her academic research. In scholarly articles on Latvian identity, she was critical of the Soviet Union and outlined her views of the political future of Latvia (Viīķe-Freiberga, 1980; 1989; 2000). In June 1998, she was made a Professor Emerita and took this opportunity to return to Latvia, where she was offered the Directorship of the Latvian Institute. While the exact role of Latvia's Canadian educated President during the project years is difficult to ascertain, it may be that the reforms that resulted through Latvian-Canadian collaboration were more acceptable given that Vīķe-Freiberga had lived and studied in Canada before returning to Latvia following independence.

4.3.1 *Psychological Proximity and Study Tours to Canada*

Psychological proximity (Rose, 2002) is based on geographical, linguistic, cultural and/or historical ties that facilitate the transmission of policy ideas among states (Castle, 1993). Randma-Liiv & Kruusenberg (2010) suggest this was a contributing factor to the project's success. Close relations between Latvians and Canadians of Latvian descent appear to explain why Canada turned out to be an exporter jurisdiction for Latvia. By taking advantage of Canada's large Latvian diaspora and their desire to return to Latvia, Canadian programming was able to provide integral context, political leadership, and criminal justice expertise by assisting to bridge existent cultural differences. One aspect of project activities was the use of study tours to Canada in 2000 and 2003. Latvian-Canadians played a central role during the study tours and organized meetings, participated in a variety of professional functions, shared materials, and hosted social events in Ottawa, Ontario.

Widely used in development, study tours offer a means to showcase the successes and failures of one country to a group of individuals from another. They provide real life examples of other ways of doing things and have been used as part of education initiatives and coursework on human rights and justice in Iraq and Afghanistan (Shaw & Dandurand, 2006). Within criminal justice, study tours provide increased understanding about the philosophy, approach, and operation through "...firsthand observation and meaningful discussion with frontline personnel in the host jurisdiction" (Dandurand *et al.* 2008, pp. 60-61). The first study tour occurred in 2000 through the LCJRP and many Latvians involved in subsequent project activities recall that first trip and an experience at Project DARE in Northern Ontario.

Project DARE, a youth justice therapeutic adventure program, is Canada's only organization accredited by the Association for Experiential Education. Latvian participants were exposed for the first time to DARE's unique blend of adventure/wilderness programming, unconventional classroom experience, and highly structured program design in 2000. It had a lasting impact. Project DARE would inspire a Latvian Wilderness Therapy program for juveniles incarcerated in the Cesis Juvenile Detention facility, and the model was used to train youth workers through funding from the World Bank, as well as Soros-Latvia, the UK, and CIDA. The experiences of the group at DARE came up again and again among those who participated in that first tour. One probation officer recalled an exercise in which the group was split up and had to tunnel through a snow bank in pairs.

> ...the exercises there [DARE] were at times very scary for me. I remember we had to tunnel through the snow and I was trapped...I couldn't get out. I wanted to cry and I had to overcame my fears...I had to trust the other [person].

Another study tour focused more explicitly on probation occurred in January of 2003. Twenty-two (22) participants travelled to Ontario and Quebec. Presentations and site visits during the first study tour included representatives from Correction Services Canada, Ontario Ministry of Public Safety, Ministère de la Santé et des Services sociaux du Québec, the John Howard Society, and a number of smaller community based organizations which work with probation. For some the tour was not as powerful as the first and there were complaints about the "...lack of free time and too much reading." Some wished the tour had returned to Camp DARE. More frequently participants saw the value of the tour and especially the variety of programming participants were exposed to during the two weeks. Many participants suggested that the study tour was an integral time in building networks among the Latvians who travelled to Canada. Through smaller group visits to Federal and Provincial justice agencies including Provincial probation offices, Federal Parole offices and the Ottawa Police station, the wide array of justice agencies in Canada was presented. For one probation officer, new to Canada and probation, the 2003 study tour:

> Changed how people saw justice and criminal justice system, how it could be and how Latvia could change, changed the people involved...Canada not perfect but [the tour] opened our eyes...mediation, restorative justice, community service now [are] part of Latvian CJS.

Another aspect was teambuilding among people involved in justice reform at different levels in Latvia. Meeting for the first time in some cases, this group would continue to work together in the years ahead. As one official suggested, the study tour:

> ...created Latvian networks of people and promoted agency cooperation ... and common strategy for reform...it showed [Latvians] need to work all together...the study tour didn't just alter [my] attitude, but changed the attitude of all that participated.

Another important aspect of the trip that was consistently identified by the participants was the involvement of Latvian-Canadians. They organized meetings with the Latvian Embassy, and held a number of social events including dinners and parties at private homes. On one occasion the Latvian Peace Church hosted the entire delegation to an evening focused on developments in Latvia. More than fifty older Latvians living in Canada attended, asked numerous questions, and listen intently as the delegation described the project and their roles in the justice system. The evening ended with the singing of Latvian songs, tears, and embraces. Many Latvians suggested it had been one of the "...most powerful moments in Canada." In general, many participants noted the value and contributions made by the Latvian-Canadians who participated in the project. According to one Latvian participant, the Latvian-Canadians were seen as "role models" and central to the success of the project. She stated:

> These people [Latvian-Canadians] were easy to communicate with and brought many experiences and expertise...they helped us to see and understand using Latvian language.

However, not all reports were positive. Some reports suggested that Canadian trainers and project staff saw the Latvian-Canadian advisers as "pushy," "arrogant," and driven in a way that was sometimes viewed as detrimental to the project. Some members of the Baltic diaspora advisory team reported feeling that the reform process was too slow, officials too corrupt, and the general public too unwilling to support real change. For example Jānis Gobiņš (2006) points out:

> ...in the Soviet Union a generation has grown up who have a completely different concept about honesty... a totally different concept about integrity and ethics. That is a basic barrier why Western Latvians have difficulty interacting and integrating with Latvians in Latvia.

The complexity between Latvian-Latvians and those who returned has not been well documented. There is some evidence, however, of a certain resentment of "foreign expertise". Some suggest those of Latvian descent who returned to advise Latvia and Latvians were manipulated for political advantage (Muižnieks & Viņķelis, 2008). Nevertheless, among the Latvians involved in this project the overall role of Latvian-Canadians was uniformely praised. They were seen as "...less formal than some of the other trainers" and offered "...unique insight." Many Latvian participants suggested they have remained in touch with the Latvian-Canadians after the project ended in 2004 and that these individuals have visited Latvia, both professionally and socially. These relationships provided a mean to overcome the inter-governmental challenges that emerged.

4.3.2 Overcoming Legislative Challenges

The establishment of probation is perhaps best seen as the latest development in a series of legal amendments beginning in 1994 designed to reform the application and execution of punishments in Latvia. Early reforms focused on introducing a more progressive system to challenge the reliance on incarceration, and to ease prisoner transfer policies to better match offenders with existing prison security levels (Zeibote, 2008). In 1997 the Criminal Code was amended to impose additional conditions, including therapeutic interventions that have to be satisfied before prisoners who had been sentenced for substance abuse could qualify for early release (Lakes & Engesbak, 1998). Since that time a complete set of new legislation has been introduced. A new Execution of Punishment Code in 1998, and new Criminal (Penal) Code and Criminal (Penal) Procedural Code came into force in 1999 all of them designed to modernize legislation and bring it closer in line with European and international norms and standards.

Through the LLRP, Mr. Berzins was central to a number of legislative amendments, and a committed voice for alternatives to punishment, mediation programs between victims and offenders, and ways to combat the widespread punishment based focus of the existent justice system (Berzins, 2002). Over the course of the project, Berzins developed a number of papers, consulted with Ministry of Justice, and was involved in the design of study tours to Canada and the identification of additional Canadian justice experts and practitioners (AUCC, 2005). He also offered direct assistance to the Probation Working Group who developed the legal framework for probation. His efforts have continued and he has offered advice and assistance on a number of questions and subsequent legislative challenges. Key recommendations made by Mr. Berzins are outlined in Figure 4.4.

Figure 4.4 Key LLRP Legislative Recommendation

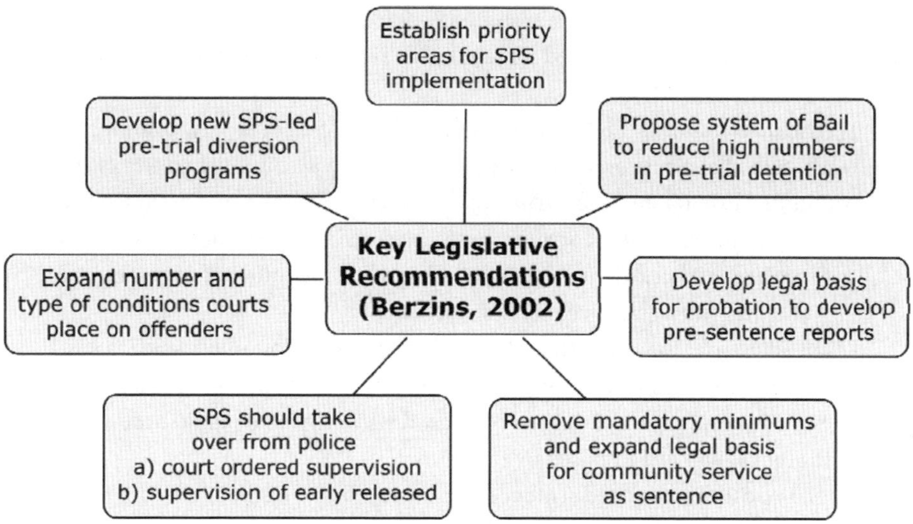

Of specific interest are suggestions taken up by the Probation Working Group. These included the concept of probation, the legal basis of probation functions, and the ways in which courts could impose conditions a new probation service might supervise. Berzins (2002) suggested:

> The current definition of "probation" in the concept document is linked to the notion that "probation services will be provided in accordance with court judgments". However, the concept includes functions which are not based on court judgments, namely "helping offenders who have been released from imprisonment (at the expiration of their sentences)" (postpenitenciara palidziba), and the function of conducting victim-offender mediation (izligums).

Berzins noted that Crime Prevention initiatives and Diversion (nosacita atbrivosana no kriminalatbildibas) are other functions that may involve the probation service and are also not based on court judgments. This challenge was a result of the formalities of the civil law tradition in Latvia, as introduced above. In Latvia courts had limited authority to sentence an offender to a term of imprisonment followed by a specified period of community supervision.

For example in the past, the only probation related provision was court ordered "Police Control" in addition to a prison sentence. By law this was available for a very limited number of offences and was rarely imposed. Moreover, in cases where it had been imposed the police carried out very minimal supervision of the offender. Berzins (2002) suggested a number of amendments to allow probation to play a central role in the supervision of those conditionally sentenced. As a result of a series of amendments in 2007, probation can be served as part of a suspended sentence. The relevant provision now reads:

> 1) If, in determining sentence in the form of deprivation of liberty, community work, custodial arrest or a fine, a court, taking into account the nature of the committed offence and the harm caused, the personality of the offender and other circumstances of the matter, becomes convinced that the offender, not serving the sentence, will not commit violations in the future, it may sentence the offender with a sentence that is suspended;
> (2) In such case, the court shall decide that the execution of sentence is suspended if, within the term of probation adjudicated by it, the convicted person does not commit a new criminal offence, does not violate public order, and fulfils the obligations imposed by the court;
> (3) In imposing suspended sentence, the court shall prescribe a term of probation of not less than six months and not exceeding three years.

Immediate sentencing for those found guilty under section 300 of the Criminal Procedure Code presented a significant challenge for justice reform. As noted by Perry and Barrows (2009), this requirement limits a core function of most probation services to provide courts with pre-sentence reports in order that they have as much information as possible about an offender before deciding what sentence to impose. The preparation of complete pre-sentence reports is time consuming and judges would have to be given the authority to delay sentencing after rendering a verdict of guilt to allow the SPS to develop such a report. Another challenge was based on Latvia's civil law tradition related to who could require clients to participate in probation programs. Initially only the court could impose treatment for a convicted person who has committed a criminal offence due to alcoholism, drug dependency including psychotropic or other addictions. Berzins (2002) advocated expanding the list of conditions a court could impose. He stated:

> The type of conditions that currently may be imposed is quite limited and the laws should be amended to expand the list. A greater variety of optional conditions would provide more flexibility to take into account individual needs and would allow probation officers to have greater impact on the people under their supervision.

Berzins (2002) argued the above expansion should apply to: Conditional sentences (nosacita notiesasana), section 55 of the Criminal Law, Police control (policijas kontrole), section

45 of the Criminal Law, and section 123 of the Sentence Enforcement Code (Latvijas Sodu Izpildes Kodekss). Early release from imprisonment (nosacitu pirmsterminu atbrivosanu) is based on section 61 of the Criminal Law and section 115 of the Sentence Enforcement Code and Bail (ar brivibas atnemsanu nesaistitie drosibas lidzekli) is discussed in sections 68-75.2 of the Criminal Procedure Code, while other forms of Diversion (nosacita atbrivosana no kriminalatbildibas) are presented in section 58.1 of the Criminal Law. Through several additional amendments to the Criminal Law, clients are now required to register with local Probation offices and participate in programs as directed by the Probation service, not local judges. In addition, based on amendments to the CPL in 2007, section 55 of the criminal law now reads:

> (6) In imposing a suspended sentence, the court may place upon the convicted person the following obligations:
> 1) to allay the harm caused, within a specified term;
> 2) not to change his or her place of residence without the consent of the State Probation Service;
> 3) to register periodically at the State Probation Service and to participate in probation programs according to *directions of the State Probation Service* (my emphasis);
> 4) not to frequent specified places; and
> 5) to be present at his or her place of residence at the time specified.

As is clear from the discussion of the legal basis for probation in Chapter 2, the recommendations by Mr. Berzins were adopted in some cases, and adapted in others. Discussed in more detail in Chapter 5, this process was based on the practices in the pilot regions and on the administrative needs of the nascent SPS. While the legislative challenges based on the existing legal framework were significant, other social, cultural, and linguistic challenges were also a product of occupation. One issue not often discussed is Latvia's "Russian problem."

4.3.3 Russian Speakers and Latvian Probation

In his 1996 classic *Latvia in Transition*, Juris Dreifelds identified the large number of Russian non-citizens as one of the largest challenges for Latvian attempts at state building in the post independence era. Located in large numbers in the capital city Riga, and southeastern Latvia, Russian speakers outnumber Latvians and in the past tensions have emerged. Some, like a mayor in Eastern Latvia who refused to speak Latvian at official functions, made headlines but were quickly forgotten. Other challenges were more complex.

As discussed in the first intermission, the underlying power dynamics between Latvian and Russian speakers remain less clear. Since the mid 1990s a number of policies designed to naturalize Russian-speaking residents have been implemented and Latvian language lessons have been provided, and if they wish, those who identify themselves as Russians, Ukrainians, or with other countries of the FSU have been given the opportunity to obtain citizenship in these countries, even while remaining in Latvia. According to the Latvian Ministry of Foreign Affairs about one-half of all Russians in Latvia are citizens of Latvia, through inheritance or naturalization and less than one-half are non-citizens – permanent residents without the right to vote who have not yet naturalized. According to official Latvian data, close to 20,000 are citizens of a foreign country, most commonly Russia.

This is an issue that forms part of the cultural fabric of Latvia and was addressed in the implementation strategy designed by the SPS through the expansion process. To address the "Russian Question" head on, two cities with large Russian speaking residents were selected as among the first of the six pilot officers established in 2003. In addition to offices in Tukums, Saldus, Valmiera, Bauska, the majority Russian speaking cities of Rezeknes and Daugavpils were also established. Until the SPS took over the funding and delivery of various programs and services, two individuals were hired in each municipality to negotiate with local municipalities to buy existing municipal social service programs (AUCC, 2005). The selection of officers in each region was key and success required the appropriate education, experience, and contacts within the city – and also an ability and willingness to speak both Latvian and Russian. Early reports suggested identifying volunteers to work with the probation service proved difficult in Rezeknes and Daugavpils, but today there is no significant difference between volunteer participation in majority Russian or majority Latvian cities and towns (Jurevičius, 2010).

It is folly to suggest the issues between Latvians and Russians have now been addressed. Ethnicity remains a complicated issue in contemporary Latvia. The party system is structured around the Latvian-Russian speaker divide, with the majority Latvian parties refusing to consider a governing coalition with the Russian-speaking parties. After the 2002 parliamentary elections, the new government created the post of Special Assignment Minister for Social Integration and appointed Nils Muiznieks, an American-Latvian who is also a fluent Russian speaker. Focusing initially on language and ethnicity as core issues of social integration, in recent years there has been a focus on addressing intolerance, particularly towards homosexuals. Ironically, the anti-gay demonstrations in recent years have uniquely managed to bring together Russian and Latvian extremists in a common cause.

Nevertheless, and despite common intolerance among these groups, language issues persist, and the so-called plight of ethnic Russians is an issue that remains part of the strained relationship between Moscow and Riga. Yet, there are reasons to be hopeful. The younger generation of Russians appears to be integrating much more easily into Latvian society. The majority has Latvian citizenship, speak Latvian proficiently, and hold values similar to their Latvian peers. However, West European experience suggests that second generation immigrants can be more assertive than their parents. This has occurred in Latvia among young Russian-speakers with regard to the ongoing reform of minority education, which has evoked considerable ethnic mobilization. A recent study suggests differences between competing narratives of statehood and nationhood are shaped by political and social factors outside the school, such as power relations among groups (Golubeva & Austers, 2011). No doubt future research into client demographics, program participation, and treatment outcomes will better address this question (Jurevičius, 2011). At present there is no evidence that this long-standing issue is relevant to the operation of probation in Latvia.

4.4 Understanding the Role of Diasporas in Development

A key finding in past research is the role of the Latvian-Canadian diaspora. Interest in the role of diasporas in the politics of their homelands is not new (Sheffer, 1986; Shain, 2002) and a recent and comprehensive effort Sheffer (2003) have traced the roots of 'diasporism' back as far as prehistoric times. A useful starting place is the experience of classical diasporas, such as the Jews in medieval Europe or the Greeks and Armenians in the Ottoman Empire. These groups were part of a feudal political arrangement, filled specific niches, and were confined to specific occupations. By contrast, modern diasporas are understood as distinct trans-state social and political entities that result from the voluntary or forced movement of a people from a homeland to a new region. One of the central characteristics of such a movement is the generational continuity of identification with the former "homeland" and the maintenance of discernible cultural, social, political, and economic interactions (Lyons, 2004).

Useful discourses exploring these interactions are emerging (Turner, 2008). One view focuses on the enormous annual rise and role of monetary remittances by diaspora communities to their 'homeland' (Sørenson, 2005). Recognized as a key tool in economic development (Davies, 2007), these funds can assist families and communities to afford basic needs and provide a crucial safety net in the absence of a social welfare system (Koser, 2007). In this role diaspora networks have played a central function in supporting refugee populations such as Liberian refugees in Ghana (Savage & Harvey, 2007) and Somali refugees in Europe and the Gulf States (Radtke, 2005). Yet, these financial flows may also have more negative outcomes (Anderson, 1998). There is convincing evidence that financial remittances often contribute to the destabilization of regions and can support recurrent cycles of violence (Collier & Hoeffler, 2001). The role of diasporas in conflicts zones including Croatia and Bosnia-Herzegovina (Skrbis, 2007), Palestine (Bamyeh, 2007), Sri Lanka (Gunaratna, 2003), and Turkey (Østergaard-Nielsen, 2006) is not in doubt. As a result of these competing visions of diasporas, an emergent view acknowledges that diaspora networks can serve as both 'peace-makers' and 'peace-wreckers' (Smith & Stares, 2007).

While economic remittances are no doubt important, less has been written on the role of diaspora communities through other sorts of interactions. These may include the sharing of technical assistance, advice, and expertise with their homelands. One example is the recruitment of individuals from diaspora communities to assist in drafting new constitutions, advising political parties, and even taking key political positions (Koser, 2007). North American diaspora communities have played a role in African nation building (Clegg, 2004), Armenian policy making (Ohanyan, 2007), and peace brokering in Northern Ireland (Cochrane, 2007). Most recently the Middle Eastern Diaspora has been tapped to play important roles in the opposition talks, and the formation of new governments. Another approach offers a middle ground between viewing diaspora communities as financiers on the one hand, or as a pool of potential political appointments on the other. By using what has been described as a distinct 'third level' of interaction connecting interstate and domestic politics (Shain, 2002), diaspora networks can enable exchanges of technical expertise and experience through international development initiatives. This view stresses the heterogeneity and diversity of the technical, managerial, or creative talents of expatriate professionals who make up diaspora networks (Kuznetsov, 2006), and harnesses the 'moral economy' (Turner, 2008) of diaspora communities in more practical ways.

Despite the general interest in the role of diaspora communities in international engagement, recent treatments appear to discount the role of diasporas in countries of the FSU (Smith & Stares, 2007). Yet, the shape of the post-1989 international political scene may have allowed diasporas an enhanced opportunity to interact with those in their homeland states (Cohn, 2008). By helping to uncover how informal structures impact the implementation of formal 'rules' on the ground (Chodosh, 2005), the narratives of these individuals can usefully complement existing governance indices, which are often too numerically driven (Kaufman *et al.* 2005). By making the most of their displaced expertise to assist and contribute to public policy reforms, the North American and European diaspora communities should been seen as valuable resources for justice reform programming.

4.5 Counter Views and Contrarian Considerations

In this section, more critical views on contextual considerations are presented. A number of concerns can be traced to ways in which the recent financial crisis challenged the institutional gains made by SPS. In 2009 Latvia was identified as the European Union's most troubled economy. This has resulted in short term budget reductions for the State Probation Service and longer term musings about whether Probation should be subsumed under

Prison Administration, an organization with very different goals, philosophies, and approaches to crime, justice, and rehabilitation. This reflects that the broader societal views about punishment and probation remain. Before the mid 1990s, the concept of probation was completely unknown in Latvia. Even in academia there was little knowledge about probation and the underlying justification for its operation. This lack of understanding has sometimes resulted in the adoption of policies from other countries without the adjustments required to make them relevant in Latvia. These contextual challenges are hardly unique.

All around the world criminal justice is increasingly delivered in ways that attempt to minimize risk and resources and downplay or outsource rehabilitation (Garland, 2001). In both Estonia and Lithuania, probation services are part of correction and prison administrations and in Latvia there are those who seek to make probation itself a client of the correctional system as opposed to a stand-alone agency. Even after many years of Latvian-Canadian interaction and an acceptance of more rehabilitative approaches to justice, some within the SPS remain pessimistic about translating this understanding to the broader society. However, it should not go unremarked that the advent of sex offender programming in Latvia includes the restorative justice program known as Circles of Support and Accountability (COSA). It remains to be seen to what extent this volunteer-dependent program can be successful, but the interest and willingness to pilot this approach is impressive. For those interested in social rehabilitation, community involvement, and crime prevention the Latvian experience here will be instructive.

In addition, there are a few possible objections to the picture presented in this chapter about how project activities tackled some of the pervasive and macro-level contextual constraints in Latvia. One assumption of this book is that Latvian-Canadian cooperation was a collaborative endeavor based on international and regional pressures, and combined with the inspired inclusion of Latvian-Canadians. Two lingering concerns remain. Conceptually it might be argued that the development of probation was not the result of an equal partnership. Despite the fact that the EC did not prescribe a particular system or model:

> ...the lack of direct pressure does not rule out the possible role of interdependence, where 'soft' recommendations by international organizations coupled with looking for the approval of the West in general, may make reforms in new democracies dependent on exogenous factors (Randma-Liiv & Kruusenberg, 2010, p. 12).

While international pressures created the conditions for legal reform in Latvia, an important distinction should be drawn between legal reform through occupation, and projects that are voluntary, cooperative, and participatory. While some may see the expansion of the

EU as simply another sort of occupation, it is difficult to compare the humiliations suffered under militaristic occupation with Progress Reports – no matter how strongly they may be worded. A central assumption in this book is that at least nominal support for justice reform through legal technical assistance was a precondition for sustainable reform in Latvia. Whether this support may be a function of international pressure or criticism ought to be considered carefully. Provided external influences identify problems, challenges, and issues while refraining from forcing one model over another, partnerships can be designed to promote exchange and not adoption. Certainly other countries may define standards upon which membership in regional organizations depend. Latvia's re-emergence as an independent country requires that it be treated as every other sovereign nation, whose citizens may choose to accept or reject international standards as they see fit.

Another issue surrounds study tours. Despite their utility in this project, their use is not uncontroversial. Critics frame study tours as a perk for would-be reformers and as tourism dressed up as international education (Dandurand *et al.* 2008) and some suggest they are often poorly designed with little connection between sites visited in one country and the conditions faced at home (Griffiths *et al.* 2005). When study tours seek to promote imitation and adaptation, critical views about the value of study tours may have more merit. While critics do raise important issues about the design of tours and how they fit within other aspects of project delivery they sometimes miss the intangible benefits. When designed as part of a larger strategy to develop and support community leaders to be local reform champions, study tours can play an integral role in developing the relations, networks, and personal ties required on the front line of any reform movement. Thus, while tours are indeed informational, they also appear to serve an integral relational function as well.

Finally there may be a question about the role of Latvian-Canadians. While their cooperation was invaluable, one might reasonably wonder if other areas of aid were missed because those involved did not suggest them (Calder, 2005). In addition, some Canadians reported working with some within this group was not always easy. It may be that the tension between the potential for diaspora communities to assist justice reform and the challenges posed by the very personal frustrations they face provide yet another window into the process of development and its associated complexities. The experience in Latvia is by no means unique. As discussed above, the role of diasporas in development is an area of emergent interest and deserves an additional focus by developmental researchers. Whether the involvement of those with a more personal stake in the project is always a good thing is debatable. In Latvia, no one denies the contribution of Latvian-Canadians, even if the negatives made the positives more difficult at times to discern. If nothing else, the role of the diaspora community offers an important consideration for future justice reform programming.

4.6 Concluding Remarks

Latvia's history of occupation throughout the 20th century remains significant in understanding the environmental realties that have influenced the social and psychological fabric of the country. The contextual challenges are broad and include the overall political and economic stability, the existing legal framework, and the psychology and normative understandings of the relationships between individuals, communities, and the state. Where once laws were intended to facilitate a transition to a Socialist utopia, independence and societal restructuring changed how the role of law in society was viewed. This evolution in thinking was shaped in part by regional and international views of Latvia's criminal justice system. Efforts to reform that system were complicated by cultural differences in East-West exchanges and world views.

Independence has forced Latvia to adjust to new circumstances, challenges, and regional relationships. As a result, previously unknown pressures have necessitated new and interculturally interesting relationships with international trainers and explored new ways to understand the relationships between individuals, communities, and the state. As new laws have been introduced and accepted, democratic structures and practices have had to be revived, created, or revised. While progress has been made since independence, significant challenges remain. Latvia's re-emergence as an independent sovereign state and its history of occupation has influenced both its institutions and identity.

While the recognition of the problems within the justice system and new regional political realities forced new sorts of interactions, it appears as if Latvian-Canadian cooperation was facilitated by the Latvian Diaspora residing in Canada. The role of diasporas in development is complex and their influence can be both positive and negative. In Canada, the legal expertise, linguistic facility, and cultural understanding, allowed the Latvian diaspora proved vital in overcoming complex cultural differences, and creating a sense of common purpose. It is clear the program successes in Latvia were at least in part a product of the relationships forged between Canadians of Latvian descent who returned to Latvia to share their expertise and experience. Other aspects of the project are also relevant.

Chapter 4 Bibliography

G. Abols. *Contribution of history to Latvia's identity*. Cesis, LV: National Library of Latvia, 2002.

B. Anderson. *The Spectre of Comparisons: Nationalism, Southeast Asia and the World*. London, UK: Verso, 1998.

S. Asquith. *Report on alternatives measures for dealing with young offenders in Latvia*. Riga: Latvia: United Nations Development Project, 2002.

Association of Universities and Colleges of Canada. *Latvian legal reform program: Report to CIDA*, 2005.

M. Bamyeh. The Palestinian Diaspora. In H. Smith, and P. Stares (Eds.), *Diasporas in conflict: Peace-makers or peace-wreckers?* Tokyo: UN University Press, 2007, pp. 90-105.

B. Berberoglu. Globalization and the Contradictions of Development in Eastern Europe and the Former Soviet Union: Prospects for Post-Soviet Development in the Age of Globalization. *Canadian Journal of Development Studies*, Vol. 26, No. 4, 2005, pp. 867-887.

A. Berzins. *Report to The Working Group on Probation in Latvia*. The Legal Reform Capacity Program in Latvia, Ottawa, ON: Association of Universities and Colleges of Canada, 2002.

A. Bilmanis. (1951). *A history of Latvia*. Princeton, NJ: Princeton University Press, 1951.

E. Botchkova, C. Tittle & O. Antonaccio. General Strain Theory: Additional Evidence Using Cross-National Data. *Criminology*, Vol. 47, No. 1, 2009, pp. 131-176.

W. Bowring. Russia and Human Rights: Incompatible Opposites? *Göttingen Journal of International Law*, No. 2, 2009, pp. 257-278.

W.E. Butler. Crime in the Soviet Union: Early Glimpses of the True Story. *British Journal of Criminology*, No. 32, 1992, pp. 144-159.

J.M. Brinkerhoff. Digital diasporas and conflict prevention: the case of Somalinet.com, *Review of International Studies*, No. 32, 2006, pp. 25-47.

S. Caldwell. *Evaluating the evaluation: Review of CIDA'S work in the Baltics*. Toronto, ON: University of Toronto, 2005.

C. Cartledge, P. Tak, & M. Tomic-Malic. *Probation in/en Europe*. Hertogenbosch, NE: European Assembly for Probation and After Care, 1981.

F.G. Castles. Introduction. In F.G. Castles (Ed.), *Families of Nations. Patterns of Public Policy in Western Democracies*. Dartmouth: Aldershot, 1993, pp. xii-xxii.

S. Chesterman. *You the People: the United Nations, Transitional Administration, and State-Building*. Oxford, UK: Oxford University Press, 2004.

H. Chodosh. *Global justice reform: A comparative methodology*. New York: New York University Press, 2005.

Canadian International Development Agency. *Canada and the Baltics: Partners in Transition*. Gatineau, PQ: Canadian International Development Agency, 2004.

C. Clegg. *The Price of Liberty: African Americans and the Making of Liberia*. Chapel Hill, NC: University of North Carolina Press, 2004.

W.C. Clemens. *The Baltic Transformed: Complexity Theory and European Security*. Landham, MD: Rowman & Littlefield Publishers, 2001.

F. Cochrane. Civil Society Beyond the State: The Impact of Diaspora Communities on Peace Building. *Global Media Journal Mediterranean Edition*, Vol. 2, No. 2, 2007 pp. 19-29.

P. Collier & A. Hoeffler. *Greed and Grievance in Civil War*. Available at: <http://ideas.repec.org/p/wbk/wbrwps/2355.html>. Retrieved March 10, 2009.

A. Dallin. *German Rule in Russia 1941-1945*, Macmillan: London and New York, 1957.

D. Dallin & B. Nicolaevsky. *Forced labour in Soviet Russia*. London, UK: Hollis and Carter, 1948.

Y. Dandurand, C. Griffiths & V. Chin. *Justice and security reform and development: Discussion note*. Gatineau, PQ: CIDA Americas Branch, 2004.

Y. Dandurand, C. Griffiths & V. Chin. Training and effective support of comprehensive justice and security reforms: Outcomes to date and lessons learned. In K. Aromaa & S. Redo (Eds.), *For the rule of law: Criminal justice teaching and training @cross the world*. Helsinki: Fi: European Institute for Crime Prevention and Control, 2008, pp. 53-67.

R. Davies. Reconceptualising the Migration-Development Nexus: Diasporas, Globalisation and the Politics of Exclusion, *Third World Quarterly*, Vol. 28, No. 1, 2007, pp. 59-76.

V.V. Davydov. Problems of developmental teaching: the experience of theoretical and experimental psychological research. *Soviet Education*, Vol. 30, No. 9, pp. 3-47.

J. Dreifelds. *Latvia in transition*. Cambridge, UK: Cambridge University Press, 1996.

European Commission. Regular Reports from the Commission on Latvia's Progress Towards Accession (1998-2002), 1998.

European Commission. Regular Reports from the Commission on Latvia's Progress Towards Accession (1998-2002), 2000.

European Commission. Regular Reports from the Commission on Latvia's Progress Towards Accession (1998-2002), 2001.

European Commission. Regular Reports from the Commission on Latvia's Progress Towards Accession (1998-2002), 2002.

A. Ezergailis. *The holocaust in Latvia 1941-1944*. Riga, LV: The Historical Institute of Latvia, 1996.

A. Fatic. *Crime and social control in Central-Eastern Europe*. Aldershot, UK: Ashgate, 1997.

T. Foglesong & P. Solomon. *Crime, Criminal Justice, and Criminology in Post-Soviet Ukraine*. National Institute of Justice: Washington, DC, 2001.

K. Gerner & S. Hedlund. *The Baltic states and the end of the soviet empire*. London: UK: Routledge, 1993.

Z. Gestautaite. *Penal and policy reform in Lithuania and the involvement of Canadian expertise*. Unpublished Masters Thesis, Carleton University, Ottawa, ON, 2001.

M. Gimbutas. *The Balts*. London, UK: Thames and Hudson, 1963.

J. Gobins. Interview. In M. Hinkle. Latvian-Americans in the Post-Soviet Era: Cultural Factors on Return Migration. In *Oral History Interviews*. Rockville, MD: American Latvian Association (ALA), 2006.

M. Golubeva & I. Austers. *Alternative Civil Enculturation Political Disenchantment and Civic Attitudes in Minority Schools in Estonia, Latvia, and Slovakia*. Riga, LV: Providus, 2011.

F. Gordon. *Latvians and Jews Between Germany and Russia*. Stockholm: Memento Press, 1990

R. Gunaratna. Sri Lanka: Feeding the Tamil Tigers. In K. Ballentine and J. Sherman (Eds.), *The Political Economy of Armed Conflict*, Boulder, CO: Lynne Rienner, 2003, pp. 197-223.

K. Hamai, R. Harris, M. Hough, R. Ville & U. Zvekic (Eds.). *Probation Around the World: A Comparative Study*. London, UK: Routledge Press, 1995.

R. Harris. Probation Around the World: Origins and Development. In K. Hamai, R. Harris, M. Hough, R. Ville & U. Zvekic (Eds.), *Probation Around the World: A Comparative Study*. London, UK: Routledge Press, 1995, pp. 25-70.

B. Hebenton & J. Spencer. *Assessing international assistance in law enforcement: Themes, findings and recommendations from a case study in the republic of Estonia*. Helsinki, FI: HEUNI – European Institute for Crime Prevention and Control, 2001.

E. Herring & G. Rangwala. *Iraq in Fragments: The Occupation and Its Legacy*. London, UK: Hurst, 2006.

M. Hinkle. *Latvian-Americans in the Post-Soviet Era: Cultural Factors on Return Migration, in Oral History Interviews*. Rockville, MD: American Latvian Association (ALA), 2006.

M. Joutsen. Managing international technical assistance projects in criminal justice: Experiences with assistance in the reform of crime prevention and criminal justice in central and eastern europe. United Nations European Institute for Crime Prevention and Control (HEUNI) Paper No. 8, 1996.

T. Judt. *Postwar : A history of Europe since 1945*. New York: Penguin Press, 2005.

I. Jurevičius. Implementing Probation programs in Latvia. Presented at STARR conference What Works in Reducing Re-offending? April 28-30, 2010. Downing College, University of Cambridge, UK.

I. Jurevičius. Recruitment and training of probation officers in Latvia. Presented May 26, 2011, Center for European Probation, Utrecht, Netherlands.

I. Jurevičius. *Creation of the State Probation Service.* (Unpublished Masters Thesis) University of Latvia: Riga, 2008.

A.M. van Kalmthout & I. Durnescu. *Probation in Europe.* Nijmegen: Wolf Legal Publishers, 2008.

A. Kamenska. *Par piespiedu sabiedrisko darbu kā sodu Latvijā.* Cietumu un policijas reformu programmas apkārtraksts Alternatīva, Nr.1, 2000a.

A. Kamenska. *Probācijas dienests Lielbritānijā.* Cietumu un policijas reformu programmas apkārtraksts Alternatīva, Nr.1, 2000b.

A. Kamenska. Latvia. In A. van Kalmthout, J. Roberts and S. Vinding (Eds.), *Probation and Probation Services in the EU Accession Countries.* Netherlands: Wolf Legal Publishers, 2003.

K. Kārlis. Life in the Post Soviert Era. In M. Hinkle (Ed.), *Latvian-Americans in the Post-Soviet Era: Cultural Factors on Return Migration in Oral History Interviews.* Rockville, MD: American Latvian Association (ALA), 2006.

I. Kavass & A. Sprudzs (Eds.). *Baltic States: A study of their origin and national development.* Buffalo: NY: William S. Hein, 1972.

D. Kaufman, A, Kraary & M. Mastruzzi. *Governance matters IV: Governance indicators for 1996-2004.* World Bank, Washington, DC, 2005.

D. Kealey, D. Protheroe, D. MacDonald & T. Vulpe. Re-examining the role of training in contributing to international project success: A literature review and an outline of a new model training program. *International Journal of Intercultural Relations*, No. 29, 2005, pp. 289-316.

S.W. Kim & W.A. Pridemore. Social change, institutional anomie, and serious property crime in transitional Russia. *British Journal of Criminology*, No. 45, 2005, pp. 81-97.

D. Kirby. *The Baltic world 1772-1993.* London, UK: Longman, 1995.

I. Klavin, A. Briedea, V. Rodinovb, I. Kokoritea, E. Pareleb & I. Klavinaa. *Heavy metals in rivers of Latvia.* Riga: Latvia: University of Latvia, 2000.

R. Kleinfeld. Competing definitions of the rule of law. In T. Carothers (Ed.), *Promoting the rule of law abroad: The problem of knowledge.* Washington, D.C.: Carnegie Endowment for International Peace, 2003, pp. 31-74.

H. Klingemann, D. Fuchs & J. Zielonka. *Democracy and Political Culture in Eastern Europe.* New York: Routledge, 2006.

K. Knapp & A. Knapp-Potthoff. The Man (or Woman) in the Middle – Discoursal Aspects of Non-professional Interpreting. In K. Knapp, W. Enninger, A. Knapp-Potthoff (Eds.), *Analyzing Intercultural Communication.* Berlin: Mouton de Gruyter, 1987, pp. 181-211.

K. Koser. From Refugees to Transnational Communities. In Nadje Al-Ali and Koser, *New Approaches to Migration: Transnational Communities and the Transformation of Home.* London, UK: Routledge, 2002.

K. Koser. African diasporas and post-conflict reconstruction: an Eritrean case study. In H. Smith & P. Stares (Eds.), *Diasporas in Conflict: Peace-makers or Peace-wreckers?* Tokyo, JP: UN University Press, 2007, pp. 239-252.

A.L. Kroeber & C. Kluckhohn. *Culture: A critical review of concepts and definitions.* New York, NY: Random House, 1952.

Y. Kuznetsov (Ed.), *Diaspora Networks and the International Migration of Skills How Countries Can Draw on Their Talent Abroad.* Washington, DC: World Bank Development Studies, 2006.

G. Lakes & P. Engesbak. The Lakes/Engesbak Report of Council of Europe Expert Mission to the Latvian prison system. NordBalt: Oslo, Norway, 1998.

Lavent v. Latvia, no. 58442/00 2551 (ECHR, 2002). Retrieved from <www.echr.coe.int/ECHR/EN/Header/Case-Law/Case-law+information/Lists+of+judgments/>

M. Lauristin Contexts of transition. In M. Lauristin (Ed.), *Return to the western world: Cultural and political perspectives on the Estonian post-communist transition,* Tartu: Estonia: Tartu University Press, 1997, pp. 25-40.

A. Lieven. *The Baltic revolution: Estonia, Latvia, Lithuania and the path to independence.* New Haven, CONN: Yale University Press, 1993.

G. Liepiņş. Cultural Exchange between Latvia and North America 1967-1990, paper presented at Konference "Trimda, kultūra, nacionālā identitāte" referātu krājums, October 1-3, 2004, Nordik.

R. Linton. *The Cultural Background of Personality.* New York: Appleton-Century-Crofts, 1945.

M. Los. *Communist ideology, law and crime. A comparative view of the USSR and Poland.* New York: St. Martins Press, 1988.

M. Los. Crime in transition: The post-communist state, markets and crime. *Crime, Law & Social Change*, No. 40, 2003, pp. 145-169.

B. Luksenaite. Evaluation of CIDA programming in the Baltic states, 1990-2003. A Review. Toronto, ON: University of Toronto, 2005.

T. Lyons. *Engaging Diasporas to Promote Conflict Resolution: Transforming Hawks into Doves.* Institute for Conflict Analysis and Resolution, George Mason University. Available at: <www.tamilnation.org/conflictresolution/lyons.htm> retrieved March 15, 2009.

C. Manning. Political Elites and Democratic State-building Efforts in Bosnia and Iraq. *Democratization*, Vol. 13, No. 5, 2006, pp. 724-738.

I. Markovits. The Death of Socialist Law? *Annual Review of Law and Social Science*, No. 3, 2007, pp. 233-253.

S. Marx. Russia's withdrawal from the baltics. *Jane's Intelligence Review*, Vol. 6, No. 12, 1994, p. 565.

R.J. Misiunas & R. Taagepera. *The Baltic states: Years of dependence, 1940-1990.* Berkley, CA: University of California, 1983.

A.A. Mohamoud. *African Diaspora and Post-Conflict Reconstruction in Africa.* Copenhagen, DN: Danish Institute for International Studies (DANIDA), 2006.

A. Ohanyan. On money and memory: Political economy of cross-border engagement on the politically divided Armenia-Turkey frontier. *Conflict, Security & Development*, Vol. 7, No.4, 2007, pp. 579-604.

E. Østergaard-Nielsen. *Diasporas and Conflict Resolution – Part of the Problem or Part of the Solution?* Paper presented at seminar on Diaspora and Conflict, Peace Builders or Peace Wreckers? Copenhagen, DN: Danish Institute for International Studies (DANIDA), 2006.

R. Paris. International Peacebuilding and the 'Mission Civilisatrice'. *Review of International Studies*, Vol. 28, No. 4, 2002, pp. 637-656.

D. Perry & R. Barrows. The Interpretation of Dreams. *Eurovista*,Vol. 1, No. 2, 2009, pp. 72-78.

L. Piacentini. Researching Russian Prisons: a consideration of new and established methodologies in prison research. In Y. Jewkes, *Handbook on Prisons.* Cullompton: Willan, 2007, pp. 152-173.

A. Plakans. *The Latvians. A short history.* Stanford, CA: Hoover Institution Press, 1995.

K. Radtke. *From Gifts to Taxes: The mobilisation of Tamil and Eritrean diaspora in intrastate warfare.* Working Papers Micropolitics No. 2, Humboldt-University, Berlin, 2005.

T. Randma-Liiv & R. Kruusenberg. West-East policy transfer: motives, scope, role models and agents. Paper presented at IRSPM Conference held April 2-9, 2010, Berne, SW.

G. von Rauch. *The Baltic States: The Years of Independence, 1917-1940.* Berkeley, CA: University of California Press, 1974.

R. Rose. *Learning from Comparative Public Policy: A practical guide.* London, New York: Routledge, 2005.

S. Rosso. Border Crossing and Boundary Breaking: Reflections on the Baltics and a Rewarding Association with the Baltic American Partnership Fund, BAPF Closing Report, 2008.

J. Rutkis. *Latvia: Country and people.* Stockholm, Sweden: Latvian National Foundation, 1967.

K. Savage & P. Harvey. Remittances During Crisis: Implications for Humanitarian Response. Humanitarian Practice Group, Report No. 25. London, UK: Overseas Development Institute, 2007.

Y. Shain. The Role of Diasporas in Conflict Perpetuation or Resolution, *SAIS Review*, Vol. 22, No. 2, 2002, pp. 115-144.

Y. Shain & A. Barth. Diasporas and International Relations Theory. *International Organization*, No. 57, 2003, pp. 449-479.

M. Shaw & Y. Dandurand (Eds.). Effective Technical Assistance in Crime Prevention and Criminal Justice: Maximizing the Effectiveness of the Technical Assistance Provided in the Fields of Crime Prevention and Criminal Justice, Working Paper 49 (Helsinki, HEUNI), 2006.

C. Shaw & H. McKay. *Juvenile delinquency in urban areas*. Chicage: Il: University of Chicago Press, 1969.

G. Sheffer. The Jewish Diaspora and the Arab-Palestinian-Israeli Conflict. In H. Smith & P. Stares (Eds.), *Diasporas in Conflict: Peace-makers or Peace-wreckers?* Tokyo, JP: UN University Press, 2007, pp. 65-89.

G. Sheffer. *Diaspora Politics: At Home Abroad.* Cambridge, UK: Cambridge University Press, 2003.

G. Sheffer. *Modern Diasporas in International Politics.* London, UK: Croom Helm, 1986.

L. Shelley. The sources of soviet policing. *Police Studies*, Vol. 17, No. 2, 1994, pp. 49-66.

L. Shelley. *Policing soviet society: The evolution of state control.* London, UK: Routledge, 1996.

L. Shelley. Post-socialist policing: Limitations on institutional change. In R.I. Mawby (Ed.), *Policing across the world: Issues for the twenty-first century*. London, UK: UCL Press, 1999.

D. Shichor. Penal Policies at the Threshold of the Twenty-First Century. *Criminal Justice Review*, Vol. 25, No. 1, 2000, pp. 1-30.

J. Shklar. Political theory and the rule of law. In P. Hutchinson, & P. Monahan (Eds.), *The rule of law: Ideal or ideology*. Toronto, ON: Carswell Publishing, 1987, pp. 1-16.

R. Simmons, P. Fajans & L. Ghiron. *Scaling up health service delivery: From pilot innovations to policies and programmes*. Geneva, Sw: World Health Organization, 2007.

D.D. Simpson. A conceptual framework for transferring research to practice. *Journal of Substance Abuse Treatment*, Vol. 22, No. 4, 2002, pp. 171-182.

Z. Skrbis. The mobilized Croatian diaspora: its role in homeland politics and war in H. Smith & P. Stares (Eds.), *Diasporas in conflict: Peace-makers or peace-wreckers?* Tokyo, JP: UN University Press, 2007, pp. 218-238.

B.D. Slife & R.N. Williams. *What's behind the research? Discovering hidden assumptions in the behavioral sciences*. Thousand Oaks, CA: Sage Publications, 1995.

H. Smith & P. Stares (Eds.), *Diasporas in conflict: Peace-makers or peace-wreckers?* Tokyo, JP: UN University Press, 2007.

H. Smith. Diasporas in international conflict. In H. Smith & P. Stares (Eds.), *Diasporas in Conflict: Peace-makers or Peace-wreckers?* Tokyo, JP: UN University Press, 2007, pp. 3-16.

N.N. Sørenson. *Opportunities and Pitfalls in the Migration-Development Nexus: Somaliland and Beyond* (Working Paper 2004/21). Copenhagen, DN: Danish Institute for International Studies (DANIDA), 2004.

N.N. Sørenson. *Migrant Remittances, Gender and Development*. Brief, Copenhagen, DN: Danish Institute for International Studies (DANIDA), 2005.

A. Spekke. *History of Latvia: An outline*. Stockholm, Sweden: M. Goppers Publishing, 1957.

S. Ting-Toomey. *Communicating Across Cultures*. New York: The Guilford Press, 1999.

M Turner. *Three Discourses on Diasporas and Peace building*. Paper for WISC 2008, Ljubljana, Slovenia July 23-26, 2008.

V. Vardys & R.J. Misiunas (Eds.). *The Baltic States in Peace arid War 1917-1945*, University Park and London, 1978.

V. Vike-Freiberga. A structural analysis of lexical and contextual Semantics – Latvian balts 'white' in sun-songs. *Journal of Baltic Studies*, Vol. 11, No. 3, 1980, pp. 215-230.

V. Vike-Freiberga (Ed.). *Linguistics and poetics of Latvian folk songs: Essays in honour of the sesquicentennial of the birth of kr. barons.* Kingston: ON: McGill-Queen's University Press, 1989.

V. Vike-Freiberga. *Latvia's place in a new Europe.* London: UK: Federal Trust for Education and Research, 2000.

J. Wheeldon. *Mapping Knowledge Transfer: Latvian-Canadian Cooperation and Justice Reform* (Unpublished PhD Dissertation). Burnaby, BC: School of Criminology, Simon Fraser University, 2009.

M. Wyman. *Europe's Displaced Persons, 1945-1951.* London, Cornell University Press, 1998.

L. Zeibote. Probation in Latvia. In A.M. van Kalmthout & I. Durnescu. *Probation in Europe.* Nijmegen: Wolf Legal Publishers, 2008.

5 Organizational Constraints: Pilot Projects, Coordination, and Trialability

Latvian-Canadians offered a means for project activities to overcome some of the contextual challenges to justice reform discussed in Chapter 4. Yet a number of additional challenges were a function of these macro level realities. These constraints required an understanding of how historical, political and socio-economic pressures inhibited the early years of Latvia's national re-birth and resulted in a number of organizational and institutional constraints. Often the most complex aspect of reform, in Latvia the ways in which past occupation influenced governing institutions also had an impact on the role of civil society and community groups. Specifically, these constraints included initial governmental inaction, the challenges of agency coordination, and the problem of community buy-in.

One successful approach used to address these challenges was the development of local pilot projects. Based on a National pilot project competition, the pilots were funded in communities throughout Latvia and were designed to respond to municipal needs, promote regional coordination, and develop local expertise. Using pilot projects in this way may suggest a means to connect a common development approach with emergent calls for participatory development programming based on trialability. In Latvia, the early pilots are credited with creating the conditions under which greater criminal justice reform could occur. In this way, once the right political conditions existed, local services, partnership models, experts, and reform leaders ensured Latvia's nascent State Probation Service (SPS) could begin to operate almost immediately.

5.1 Latvia's Initial Steps Toward Justice Reform

Although Latvia eventually implemented large-scale justice reforms, this process was slow. The Latvian government's first foray into substantive criminal justice reform can be traced to 1994 and amendments to the Sentence Execution Code of Latvia. Designed to address prison overcrowding and speak to regional and international pressures, it established – for the first time – a progressive system of imprisonment (Jurevičius, 2008). Throughout the 1990s the Latvian Ministry of Justice embarked on a number of initiatives in partnership with various local, regional, and international actors. When the Latvian Prison Administration hosted a delegation from Norway and Sweden in October 1996, they developed an initiative based on cooperation among prisons through The Nord Balt Prison Project (NBPP).

Funded by the Council of Europe to improve the operation of Latvian prisons, the NBPP project supported new programs and services related to education, industrial training, and the development of employment skills for prisoners. Cooperation among prisons in Latvia, Sweden, and Norway resulted in the development of institutional capacity within the Latvian Prison Administration. This provided invaluable knowledge about the experience of other countries allowed reformers to challenge well-established Latvian views about the functions and role of prisons. Vitolds Zahars, who was Head of Prison Administration from 1997 until 2002, suggests that the NBPP was an "…inflow of fresh air into the Latvian prison system", and resulted in significant improvements in the prisons' operation (Jurevičius, 2008).

In 1997, a conference organised by the Soros Foundation-Latvia debated capital punishment. Experts from different fields discussed not only the abolishment of capital punishment but also about the liberalisation of the whole penal policy in Latvia. A group of enthusiastic reformers emerged and continued to press for both legislative and operational reforms (Kamenska, 2000b). As discussed in Chapter 2 this led to the introduction of "Community Work" for less serious offences. While judges retained the ability to impose custodial sentences for more serious offences, this alternative sanction had the potential to reduce prison numbers. Unfortunately, within a few months it became clear that neither municipalities nor judges understood the meaning of "Community Work", and inadequate funding existed for municipalities to administer this new punishment (Jurevicius, 2008). In 1999 Soros Foundation-Latvia filled this gap and undertook the implementation of this alternative sanction in partnership with selected local municipalities.

Later that year another conference was organised to explore models of community service. It included experts from Finland, Sweden, and Zimbabwe. Despite cultural, geographic, and historical differences, many at the conference identified the Zimbabwean model as most appropriate for Latvia based on the fact that it required fewer financial resources (Kamenska, 2000a). As a result of training workshops and salaries for regional coordinators funded by the British Embassy in Riga, Soros Foundation-Latvia provided information to popularize this new sentence. By 2002 more than a thousand individuals have been supervised in the community by municipal staff (Kamenska, 2000b). While these developments were positive and usefully built on existing concept papers concerning the Social Rehabilitation of Ex-Prisoners (1998), additional amendments to establish a new probation service with specific tasks such as maintaining regular contact with prisons, assisting post-prison reintegration including accommodation and obtaining required documentation, and engaging in broader crime prevention did not result in a clear action plan or funding.

Despite the local challenges and modest political support for reform, the energy and enthusiasm of the Latvian diaspora in Canada convinced CIDA to fund a project in Latvia focused on juvenile justice. As discussed in Chapter 4, in 1999 Canada began working in

Latvia through the CIDA-funded *Latvian Criminal Justice Reform Project* (LCJRP) to assist communities to develop pilot projects in their regions through cooperative interagency ventures. Between 2000 and 2001 these programs had become models and CIDA agreed to fund a one-year extension through the *Legal Reform Capacity Project* (LRCP). This project, based on upon the LCJRP's pilot project experience, sought to promote the transfer of community expertise to National institutions, and specifically the Latvian Ministry of Justice (AUCC, 2005). Yet challenges existed including, most notably, the lack of political will at the national level.

5.1.1 Explaining Governmental Inaction

In Latvia, the lack of political will required to implement large scale reform might be explained by the host of other financial and political priorities facing the Ministry of Justice.[1] Government action was also undermined by frequent changes of governments and Ministers of Justice during the 1990s and a lack of coordination between the National government who made laws, and local municipalities who were tasked with implementing them. For example, Latvia's new Criminal Law came into force in April 1999 and introduced community service as a possible punishment.[2] Despite the fact that municipalities would now be obliged to create separate institutions or appoint persons to be responsible for community works, municipalities were not consulted or provided with funding or additional support during the development of this new criminal punishment. By the summer of 1999 it became clear that neither municipalities nor regional judges understood the meaning of this sanction, and no funding had been assigned to administer it (Jurevičius, 2008). The challenges faced by Soros-Latvia are similar to those faced by other civil society organizations in the FSU (Batt, 1996). While justice reform initiatives were often discussed, authorities rarely pursued the kind of coordinated approaches required to make localized reforms sustainable. One explanation for this inaction is the strong resistance to the involvement of civil society groups in policy making (Norgaard *et al.* 1999). This reality is common in transition and post authoritarian countries. It represents a core challenge for attempts at participatory development.

1 Ministry of Justice priorities at that time can be found in Latvia's Contribution to the Regular Report from the Commission on Latvia's Progress towards Accession (National Progress Report 1999-2001). See <www.mfa.gov.lv/data/file/l/LNPR-2001.pdf> retrieved April 14, 2008.

2 LR Saeimā 1998.gada 17.jūnijā pieņemtais Criminal Law, stājās spēkā 1999.gada 1.aprīll.

5.1.2 *Social Disorder and Community Cooperation*

While governmental will and donor coordination are two important aspects of an international project's organizational success, scholarship has emerged which suggests that the adoption of sustainable reforms in CEE requires new forms of interactions among individuals and communities (Jacoby, 2006). Justice reform projects may do best when they empower the populace in developing countries by focusing on civil society and communities (Golub, 2003). Democratically expanding the incorporation of international norms of legal regulation can add layers of complexity (MacDonald, 2002). One way to consider this cultural challenge in Latvia is to connect Durkheim's view (1893) of the value of social order, stability, and integration with the situation countries in the FSU faced during the post independence period. The dire economic situation faced by many Latvians made volunteering one's time difficult to justify. In addition, the historic focus on more communal approaches to social interaction identified by Lauristin (1997:39) had, during occupation, been manipulated for political ends.

Cooperation in occupied Latvia was not a free choice but a requirement of socialist ideology. Community members throughout the FSU were required to partake in new forms of community supervision and youth, co-workers, and neighbors were enlisted to observe, monitor, and report to the state (Harris *et al.* 2005). As a result social disorganization is a useful way to understand how the socio-cultural challenges in the FSU resulted in low levels of participation in community organizations and the weakening of social bonds in the post-independence environment (Kim & Pridemore, 2005). Given the history of occupation, different expectations of identity, and types of interaction (Lauristin, 1997), international project activities needed to be designed to consider organizational and institutional impediments to reform. This meant supporting institutions and agencies to foster broad-based cooperation, try new things, and learn from both limited successes and partial failures.

5.2 Organizational Constraints and Latvian Agencies

Organizational constraints most frequently identified in international development include partner selection, clarity of objectives, management structures and responsibilities, and the cultural fit among collaborating organizations (Kealey *et al.* 2005). These general factors are relevant for building strong partnerships, local ownership, and positive and sustainable outcomes (Kealey & Protheroe, 2002). They may also be related to the ability of project managers to implement the proposed reforms with stakeholders' approval, based on the compatibility of norms (Sundstrom, 2006:169). For probation programs, a number of elements may be specifically relevant. These include: inter and intra agency cooperation, the administration and operation of the legal system, role of judges, and relationships between the government, civil society, and the community (Canton, 2009).

Significant scholarship suggests that reforming justice systems requires focusing on organizational challenges between and among agencies (Klockars *et al.* 2000). The combined challenges of the job, the exercise of individual discretion, and assumptions about the integrity of the justice system complicate the role of those working within the system and require flexible and responsive organizational structures. Lyman (2002) suggests a variety of factors influence how justice professionals adapt to their agency, adhere to ethical codes of conduct, and interact with their clients and the public. One of these factors involves the ways in which unwritten codes of conduct within criminal justice agencies operate, and how norms of secrecy and loyalty undermine or complicate ethical actions by justice actors (Williams & Arrigo, 2008). In law enforcement, this code is often referred to as the "blue wall of silence" (Westmarland, 2005), but this is by no means limited to policing. The "us" versus "them" attitude has been documented in prisons (McCarthy, 1998) as well as in other areas of public service (Johnston, 1982).

In Latvia, by 1994, the government had begun to take initial steps toward reform by supporting legislative amendments and community based programming. It was not until 2002 that the Ministry of Justice put in place a clear plan to build on existing initiatives, establish a new National service, and fully fund the development of a headquarters, trained staff, and offices throughout Latvia. This gap can be explained in part by the organizational constraints faced by reformers in Latvia and international partners. These constraints included an initial lack of governmental action, local expertise and reform examples, along with limited community buy. Together these issues are central to ensuring sustainability in many types of legal reform. These are presented in Figure 5.1.

Figure 5.1 Key Aspects of Organizational Constraints in Probation Programming

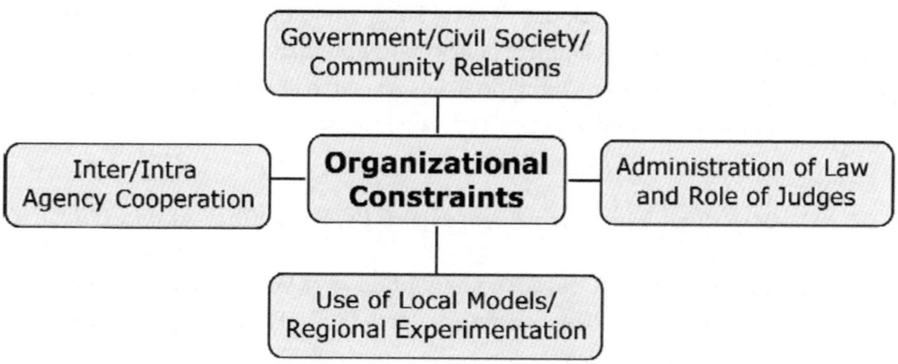

5.2.1 *Understanding Organizational Development*

Historically, organizational elements have been favored when framing knowledge transfer (Lewin, 1951; Rogers 1962; Simpson, 2002). Organizational understanding is also an important challenge to international project success (Kealey *et al.* 2005) given the significant institutional constraints inherent in attempting more systemic reform (Jiao *et al.* 2005). Overcoming this barrier requires a foundation of mutual commitment and a shared understanding among development partners and stakeholders. It demands an understanding of how historical, political and socio-economic impediments to reform have influenced governing institutions. A variety of tools have been consistently used to assist the reform of criminal justice systems (Carothers, 2003). Related to legal technical assistance, organizational training tools are defined as manuals, handbooks, and toolkits (Dandurand *et al.* 2008, p. 63) and are widely used in training and technical assistance to enhance overall organizational ability (Griffths *et al.* 2005). As Dandurand (2006) suggests this requires effective needs assessments that consider not only legislative or human resource gaps or weaknesses but also acknowledge the organizational context in which they will operate.

Another observation that is organizationally relevant is the difficulty of trying to root reform within an agency. There is an emerging understanding that instead of pursuing national reform strategies, incremental approaches and processes that cultivate understanding over time should be favored. In this way, legal technical assistance can support bottom-up, community based reform efforts (Chodosh, 2005). As Carothers notes, the process of national trial and error through pilot projects can be an "...essential contributor to the realization of a legitimate democratic and legal order" (2003, p. 43).

As discussed in Chapter 3, this approach is of interest to developmental economists (Banerjee & Duflo, 2008) and experiments are emerging as a powerful tool for testing development theories (Karlan & Zinman, 2005). Yet to be valuable, those who engage in these experiments must take seriously the multiple challenges to reform and design reforms that are rooted in theory (Heckman, 1992). Thus, while the focus on evidence-based approaches alone to guide development policy may be premature, specific elements within these approaches are attractive. One approach is related to how projects can engage communities in reform while modeling new programs and services.

5.2.2 *Modeling Community Engagement: Experimentation and Civil Society*

In 1999, two projects sought to engage communities, work with local municipalities, and develop alternative programs. Based on the work of the Soros Foundation-Latvia, a number of Latvian municipalities participated in study tours and conferences about alternatives to imprisonment. To assist municipalities in implementing community service projects,

Soros-Latvia provided information, training workshops, and salaries for regional coordinators (Kamenska, 2000a). With support from the British Embassy in Riga, Soros-Latvia published the newsletter "Alternatīva" to provide information, support information exchange, and popularize community service as a sentence in Latvia (Kamenska, 2000b). Despite the increase in its use as a form of punishment from 183 sentences in 1999 to 1216 in 2002,[3] the Latvian government would not fund community service in the same way as Soros-Latvia had. As a result municipalities reduced their support for community service (Jurevičius, 2008).

During the same period, as introduced in Chapter 1, the Canadian International Development Agency (CIDA) began working with the Latvian Ministry of Justice and the Association of Universities and Colleges of Canada (AUCC) to develop alternatives to incarceration as a part of broader juvenile justice reform (AUCC, 2002). In development since 1993 (CIDA, 1997), project documents benefitted from scholarly exchanges with Eastern Europe and the Former Soviet Union, organized by Doris Bradbury. Canadian programming began in earnest in the fall of 1999 and through the LCJRP project a group of Latvian judges and prosecutors, including several Supreme Court judges and the Prosecutor General travelled to Canada. This was followed by a conference, in May 2000, in which Latvian police, social workers, psychologists, and legal officials met to study the Canadian legal process, including prevention strategies, the court system, correctional facilities, and post-custody programs.

Through the LCJRP, a Latvia-wide pilot project competition was launched in 2001 to develop alternative approaches for the juvenile justice system. Conceived by Tawnia Sanford, these projects required interagency cooperation between two or more organizations or municipal departments, a detailed list of in kind contributions from local businesses, the involvement of NGOs, and a commitment to identify community volunteers. The competition resulted in a variety of projects that ranged from after-school prevention programs, community service programs, drop-in centers, and supervision programs in Brocentu, Cesis, Saldus, Valmiera and Tukums. Pilot project directors were supported during the project through training and capacity building, but direct funding was limited. Unlike Soros-Latvia funding, however, by 2002 local governments in Saldus, Cesis, Tukums, and Valmiera had adopted the pilots as municipal services and hired the pilot project directors to run them.

A challenge in justice reform as well as other sorts of development programming is the failure of different development actors to work together. This is an issue the *Paris Declaration* is meant to address and the situation in Latvia in the early 2000s provides some insight into the importance of more coordinated approaches. Despite having the same clients in

3 Retrieved from <www.sodi.lv/index.php?id=246&sadala=141&PHPSESSID=85e4f2b8c1ea9b> on March 18, 2009.

host countries, different development agencies rarely compared notes and often appeared to be in competition for recognition and prestige. The failure to seek donor cooperation in the early days of justice programming also extended to international organizations working in Latvia to promote reform. While the UNDP was most active in providing funding for research, workshops, and conferences, AUCC and Soros-Latvia focused on the development of pilot projects in local communities. Soros-Latvia often took a hands-on role by chairing meetings, sitting on advisory committees and panels, and funding salaried positions in various communities. Based on a strong presence in Latvia, this direct approach often complicated governmental cooperation. Some officials found cooperation with Soros-Latvia difficult as staff, based on an advocacy-based approach to participation, pushed for hard targets and clear deadlines (Wheeldon, 2009).

Despite, or because of, this strong role, the importance of Soros-Latvia to justice reform in Latvia and throughout the region cannot be doubted. Yet, in Latvia, on more than one occasion what began as Government-Soros co-funded initiatives, ended in either project cancellation or a failure on the governmental side to re-approve funding. Canadian programming took a different approach. Although refusing to fund individual salaries, initial programming was based on pilot projects that required the support of local governments, and multi-agency cooperation. In this way, AUCC was able to support municipalities to integrate these new projects into their social services systems themselves (Bell *et al.* 2002). Another important feature of Canadian programming was the focus on establishing coordination councils comprised of a number of justice professionals working in one region. This resulted not only in shared information about alternative approaches in use by those working in the field, but also furthered the development of informal networks among these professionals who, in some cases, formed during study tours to Canada (Wheeldon, 2009).

These networks proved invaluable when at long last the Ministry of Justice demonstrated renewed interest in the coordination of a probation system and supported additional alternatives to imprisonment. In 2002, AUCC expanded this approach through a Memorandum of Understanding (MOU) with Soros-Latvia and the UNDP. In this agreement, the organizations pledged to inform each other of upcoming projects and initiatives and to work toward cooperation and co-financing wherever possible. Yet, between 1999 and 2001, the competition and variance in approaches between and among donors complicated the identification of local examples and community best practice in Latvia (Wheeldon & Sanford, 2002).

5.3 PROJECT PROGRAMMING: PARTNERSHIP, PROGRAMS AND PILOTS

The delivery of international aid occurs through a wide variety of means, methods, and practices (Parpart & Veltmeyer, 2004). Two modes of immediate interest are projects and programs. Projects are temporary and transient entities to which resources can be assigned. They are designed to bring about strategic change or innovation (Turner & Muller, 1998) through a specific set of activities in a particular location. By contrast, programs are larger endeavors consisting of several sub-projects supported by an agency within the same sector, theme or geographical area. Through programs multiple projects provide a means for more coordinated approaches (Gosling, 2003, pp. 339-340).

To deliver both projects and programs, partnerships are a common strategy in international development. As discussed in Chapter 1, partnership is an attractive term because it offers a more equitable basis for initiatives that are based in one country but funded by another. To increase access to human, financial, technical, and intellectual resources, calls to improve partnership are common (Fowler, 1998; Hoksbergen, 2005). While the underlying principles of equal participation, mutual respect, transparency, and mutual accountability within these relationships are laudable, they are rarely matched on the ground. This may be because partnerships can be seen as simply a product of funder requests, which, while often sound in theory, may miss the practical implications that result. Short time frames for development agencies to respond to Requests for Proposals (RFPs) complicate local partner selection, and favor some firms over others. As a result, early assessments may be inexact and incomplete, based on partnerships with local organizations who meet funder criteria but who may not have the capacity or contacts required to engage meaningfully with the identified issue (Hatton & Schroeder, 2007, p. 168).

Despite the constraints and inherent limitations of true partnerships within the development sphere, collaborating with institutions in the host country is a common feature of development programming. The partnership model is designed to encourage local governments to engage in more consultative mechanisms to draw out local preferences. It is assumed that by engaging with more stakeholders, international best practice can better inform local examples, and that these examples can be used to channel local lessons into the policy process. Yet too often these arrangements are only vaguely outlined, difficult to maintain over the life of a project, and lack critical analysis or assessment (Kapoor, 2005; Lister, 2002; Vincent & Byrne, 2006). Indeed it is this lack of analysis that makes research on knowledge transfer and cross-national learning a contentious issue (Chodosh, 2005). There are three aspects of Canadian programming of immediate interest.

5.3.1 *Pilot Projects and Local Experimentation*

While pilot projects are widely used in international development, little time or energy has been devoted to exploring their use, utility, and function. Pilot projects can help model new kinds of policies, processes, and approaches and demonstrate how envisaged reforms actually operate. As part of larger initiatives, pilot projects can be used to gather data to facilitate subsequent project choices. Decisions and pilot studies can help to demonstrate the technical feasibility of options under consideration. Recent explorations consider pilot studies and usefully compile what has been written about their role in facilitating reform (Turner, 2005). One means has been to better define the role of pilot studies in social science research generally and development more specifically. The term pilot study is used in two different ways in social science research. It can refer to so-called feasibility studies that are small-scale versions of a larger study (Polit, Beck & Hungler, 2001, p. 467). It can also be the pre-testing or 'trying out' of a particular research instrument to identify potential challenges, limitations, or risks associated with one methodology or another (Baker, 1994, pp. 182-183). Some argue that the findings of pilot studies have not been widely explored because of the type of data they produce. Often based on pre-selected locales or otherwise limited by other kinds of selection bias, these studies are shunned by quantitatively focused research journals and donor aligned development scholars (Van Teilingen & Hundley, 2003).

In the international development context, pilot projects can be seen as a combination of a 'feasibility of change' study, and a means to test certain kinds of reforms on a smaller scale. Part of a larger initiative, they are often used to improve the understanding of the potential challenges and impediments by modeling examples of larger innovations or changes on a smaller scale. One way to see the value of pilot projects is to connect them to the identification and mitigation of risks within project management (Chapman & Ward, 2003). Because change of any kind inevitably entails uncertainty, there may be doubt about what the project will deliver, whether it will achieve stated objectives, or how the processes adopted will affect existent processes and approaches (Turner, 1999). Pilot projects and pilot studies can reduce the uncertainty associated with the change by identifying potential risks, testing different mitigation strategies, and providing valuable data about how reforms may operate within a particular context (Turner, 2005). This information, if properly catalogued, can in turn usefully contribute to the learning of the organization itself (Ayas, 1998).

Pilot projects can also showcase how external expertise is operationalized in local towns, cities, and regions within a country. This data can then be used to develop subsequent initiatives and plan additional activities (Wheeldon, 2009). Pilot projects were often used in the past when aid orthodoxy was primarily project focused and less integrated through broader based programs. While it was hoped that they would provide local lessons and experience to inform larger scale programs, using projects in this way has not been common (Mikkelson, 2009). Instead, too often pilots languish and lessons go unlearned. This may be a result of at least three factors. The first is the recognition that as trial balloons, not all funded pilots projects are based on sound principles or address the needs of those they originally purport to serve. While there is not enough empirical research into why pilots fail, it should be no surprise that not all interventions work. What may appear to be connected causal factors at the outset, may after some study, be better understood as complex and multiple channels of causality not easily disrupted. It may also be that the pilots were developed under special circumstances and in ways that could not easily be transferred to national policy for practical reasons (Simmons *et al.* 2007).

The second is based on more political calculations by governing institutions. The phrase 'death by pilot project,' (Foureur, 2008) refers to decisions to discontinue broader reforms despite initial support, funding, and even success at the local level. As project-funding dries up, so does the pilot project. As a result the individuals trained or services designed often cease to exist. When this occurs those involved become cynical about the reform process and their role in it. The third factor occurs when successful local pilot projects and nascent reforms are continued, but revised in their implementation to bear no resemblance to the design upon which the successes were based. While these challenges should not be underestimated, there is evidence that pilot projects and the consultative and innovative mechanisms that result can lead to changes in the thinking and behavior of government actors. This can spur the transition from governance regimes that previously relied on coercion and intimidation to those that employ more inclusive decision-making models (Manor, 2007).

In Latvia, these projects created local experts, mobilized volunteers, and developed the local organizational capacity to deliver alternative programming. Some Latvian participants from communities viewed this is in more practical terms:

> Pilots provided practical models, could convince people that they could work, and through pilot professionals had more info about [local] services and what could be done.

According to others, the impact of the pilots was important institutionally for the development of probation. Pilots provided policy makers with "…new information, [allowed people] to try different programs and innovations, and created communities and networks of Latvians in justice system to support probation…" This capacity, it was suggested, could be demonstrated through the project based on the indicators provided in Table 5.2.

Table 5.2 Pilot Projects and Local Communities in Latvia (AUCC, 2003)

Indicators of Community Capacity
1. Increased support from local governments evidenced by new budgets that provide administrative costs and salaries for pilot initiatives.
2. Developed local committees on youth justice consisting of relevant youth justice officials, who while initially tasked with specific project co-ordination, have adopted broader mandates to oversee other youth justice initiatives locally.
3. Mobilized volunteer support from various segments of the community including churches, the student community, and various professional groups from police to social workers.
4. Received financial support from private business including corporate sponsorship for project activities and donations of materials, labour and services.

5.3.2 *Scaling Up Reform and National Working Groups*

The delivery of Canadian programming overcame organizational challenges in a number of important ways. While the Latvian Ministry of Justice had officially supported Canadian programming since 1999, AUCC began working on a number of different initiatives simultaneously. Some included national conferences, workshops, and events; others focused on developing community resources in a variety of municipalities. While the political will at the national level was initially inconsistent, AUCC maintained a national presence in Riga while supporting a cadre of young enthusiastic pilot project directors throughout the country. An integral means of support was the pilot project competition that was held in 1999. Based on the success of the first, a second competition took place in 2001. This community-up model for developing and extending justice reform allowed for programs and services to be designed by community members. Local municipalities decided which programs worked best for each community (Bell *et al.* 2002).

In this way local experiments could be used to 'scale up' successful reforms to the national level. Cooperation between agencies modeled in the regions through pilot projects became the basis for national working groups composed of a variety of officials from communities, regions, and the Ministry of Justice. Echoing the views of community participants, a senior official stated unequivocally:

> Pilot projects were basis of probation. They gave practical examples, created networks in the regions and local experts who were hired as Latvia's first probation officers…without [the] pilots, probation would have taken much longer to develop.

An important part of strengthening local capacity was the mobilization of volunteer support from different segments of society. In other countries, including Canada, volunteers play an integral role in probation systems. Although varying by province, volunteers from an offender's community can offer advice and support and can play an important informal supervisory function (Hamai & Ville, 1995). In Latvia, this aspect of probation developed slowly. Volunteerism is suggestive of broader community support for reintegration through an emphasis on inclusion, relationship development, and the humanization of offenders. This was recognized by Latvian project participants who pointed to the need to bring different segments of the community together and "...consider societal challenges and acceptance that they [offenders] needed." As presented in Chapter 2, volunteers play an increasingly important role in Latvian probation. As discussed later this role has both strengths and weaknesses.

Another means to establish community capacity was the support provided to coordination between local innovation and national reform efforts. While the LLRP supported a variety of activities, a core focus by AUCC in Latvia was developing partnerships in Latvia among government officials, community leaders, and NGOs. This was attempted in a variety of ways. As discussed in Chapter 4 regional coordination councils allowed those working within the justice system to share information and work together. Through these meetings local Latvians began to explore "...available services and what could be done through linkages" and "...new blood through innovations and ideas." The coordination councils gave important support, insight and strategies, and modeled new kinds of cooperation, which were picked up at the national level.

The National Probation Working Group took some time to meet and agree on priorities. Once led by Ilona Kronberga, it developed a number of key documents, draft amendments, and secured high-level cooperation. Latvian participants identified its establishment and key legislative reforms as "...leading directly to the Probation Draft Law," passed by the Council of Ministers in October of 2003. For the first time in Latvia, inter-governmental cooperation was based on regional coordination models. This early cooperation among different segments of the justice system in Latvian communities was identified as essential to reform (Bell *et al.* 2002). Ministry of Justice officials noted that the National Probation Working Group was composed of a variety of officials from communities, regions, and the Ministry of Justice. Through it local experience was highlighted and the discussions and debates within the group became the basis for the National Probation Service.

5.3.3 *Operational and Administrative Challenges*

After the 2003 establishment of the SPS, a number of operational and administrative challenges emerged. One such challenge was inter-governmental. While the SPS was to begin coordinating a number of services for individuals conditionally released, there was a lack of a clear dividing line between the tasks of local municipalities and probation service for the co-ordination of community work service. Initiated by CIDA, some local municipalities began paying for services modeled on the pilot projects in 2002. These local leaders reported their decision was based in part on the reduction in crime observed and improved outcomes of the clients working with trained pilot project staff. While the probation law provided for a role for the probation service to serve as an adviser to the local municipalities, the majority of these municipalities had a limited understanding about how the new sentences would expand the services expected of them. With limited financing from the state government and an uneven system of implementation, courts in some non-pilot regions of the country did not apply community work service or applied it only in few cases (Kamenska, 2003).

As part of early programming, the establishment of regional coordination councils was later identified by senior Latvian officials as playing an important role in the discussions and negotiations with local municipalities. Intergovernmental questions concerned how and which services funded by local municipalities should be overtaken and funded by the SPS, and which should remain with the municipalities. The structure and experience within the regional coordination councils provided a useful mechanism for these discussions. In 2005 SPS overtook organization of community work service in 9 regions and by 2006 was organizing community work service throughout the country (Zeibote, 2008). Participants suggested this kind of inter-governmental cooperation had first been modeled in local regions through the project. One useful observation was that:

> Coordination councils provided model for state level… for first [time] in Tukums this kind of cooperation had been tried with a social rehabilitation goal…now prosecutors, judges, police, and probation meets and discuss problems…councils allow for info sharing, legislative solutions, and now greater cooperation between state and municipalities.

While the coordination councils could provide a means for high-level cooperation and future planning, other challenges while more mundane, were no less important. To develop a new service capable of managing offenders in the community, a new set of practical management skills were required. These included general skills such as understanding management information systems and information collection practices, as well as managerial skill sets such as file management, case notes, policy documents, and quality control. According to one participant, Canadian training on how to "…run an office and manage staff" was very important. In fact some suggested that they wished they had personally "…paid more attention to the training provided on administrative requirements."

An important part of the project was support for the development of hiring, training, evaluation, and monitoring policies based on identified needs by the Ministry of Justice and the Probation Working Group. These included the need for a human resources strategy to attract good candidates with relevant qualifications. The Working Group decided these qualifications should include: relevant educational background, work experience, demonstrable ability to work within local communities and/or state agencies, training on relevant tasks of Probation officers, and international exposure to Probation as a component of overall rehabilitative criminal justice system. This, of course, privileged Latvian participants who had been part of the international programming, most notably the early Canadian-led training sessions. These sessions had addressed a number of practical work related matters but also began with the concept of discretion, authority, and professionalism. This was a central concern in the early years to ensure confidentiality in terms of what info can be released/disclosed to the public and to other institutions (AUCC, 2005). In addition, subsequent training underlined the need to acknowledge staff wellness including the provision of counseling for probation officers in recognition of the difficulty of their positions and their work.

Perhaps the most important operational concern was how probation officers should organize their work once their caseloads increased. The SPS has adopted the Risk/Needs Responsivity (RNR) model to guide supervision. Since its first presentation, the RNR model has been elaborated upon and contextualized within a general personality and cognitive social learning theory of criminal conduct (Andrews & Bonta, 2006). It has emerged as perhaps the most influential model for the assessment and treatment of offenders (Blanchette & Brown, 2006; Ward, Mesler & Yates, 2007). While the use of these assessments is not uncontroversial (Brennan *et al.* 2009; Cole, 2007), a number of principles have been added to the core theoretical outline to enhance and strengthen the design and implementation of effective interventions. These additional principles describe, for example, the importance of staff establishing collaborative and respectful working relationships with clients, and the role of correctional agencies and managers providing policies and leadership that facilitate and enable effective interventions (Andrews, 2011).

A key Canadian on this aspect of probation training was Mr. Robert Watts. Watts, who was then the Provincial Director, British Columbia Community Corrections has, worked in a variety of capacities as a probation officer, trainer, and manager and built on the existing the knowledge base by pulling a number of different training elements together. One important aspect was the use of risk-based instruments. Since 2000, juvenile probation officers had been using a variant of the pre-sentence report from the Province of Ontario, provided by Gail Steeds, to assist judges to make determinations about which youth could be supervised under the municipal probation program and which could not. Subsequent Canadian training went further to outline how risk assessments can be used to organize supervision. Juvenile probation offices in Cesis and Tukums used a variant of the Levels of Supervision Instrument (LSI), an early forerunner to the RNR, and early training focused on how to use information about client age, maturity, character, behaviour, attitude and willingness to make amends to structure a supervision plan.

Later operational training by Watts built on training by Steeds and Linda Alexander and focused in more detail on the aspects of case management as a philosophy and operational tool and focused on more recent developments within RNR – perhaps the most popular risk assessment instrument in the world. In general effective case management strategies seek to bring about a change in a client's criminal behaviour and a client's criminogenic needs while effectively protecting the public. They have been shown to reduce the offender's recidivism (Tonry, 1998), and have led to a variety of refinements and improvements. Training sessions in 2003 by Watts focused on the tenets of case management, and how to manage the risk/needs presented by the offender in a manner that is consistent with service wide approach to promote change in an offender's behavior. As discussed briefly in Chapter 2, this is an area in which the SPS has been pro-active. Canadian training introduced three principles of the case management system including: the idea that the level of supervision offenders receive should correspond to their risk level; service to offenders must correspond to their criminogenic needs that are emperically linked to criminal conduct; and resources ought to be focused on higher risk/needs cases.

Based on these principles the higher the overall risk/needs level presented by an offender, the more supervision, surveillance, intervention and program services the offender requires. On the other hand, the lower the risk/needs level, the less the offender requires and receives. To succeed, the appropriate levels of supervision, surveillance, intervention and program services must be provided and supervision should decrease over time and/or be adjusted in accordance with the offender's performance in the community. Other aspects of Watts's training focused on managerial concerns and the need for strategic planning, a clear vision for the role of the service, and continuing education, data collection and dissemination, and the establishment of professional standards to guide the future of the service. The use of the RNR has continued in Latvia and Watts has been involved in supporting subsequent training, the provision of additional documents, and facilitated site visits to Canada. Watts suggests:

> The ability of the SPS to manage "change" is impressive. They have progressed from a "foreign concept" to a forward thinking evidence based Latvian organization in less than a decade. In doing so The SPS have constantly had to focus on ensuring that the organization did not "get ahead" of its staff, its minister or the Latvian people. As the evolving demands and expectations placed its SPS services continue to mount however; care will be needed to ensure that past successes are consolidated and the resilience of the organization is sustained.

While the value of specific hands-on training to improve operational and administrative functions cannot be doubted, Watts usefully built on past training provided by AUCC. By highlighting local programs, service delivery models developed and the experiences of those working in Latvian communities since 1999, the training was located first in the Latvian experiences. The value of this approach to participatory legal technical assistance is hardly a new observation (Chambers, 1984; Korten, 1986). Yet the Latvian experience may offer a useful way to see various participatory elements within a clear and well-designed framework. The role of trialability in international development is essential.

5.4 UNDERSTANDING TRIALABILITY AND 'EVIDENCE' IN DEVELOPMENT

Trialability refers to the degree to which a localized innovation may be tested (Rogers, 2005, p. 16). In international development settings this may be implicitly linked to more participatory processes, especially given the failure of past top-down process, as discussed in detail in Chapter 3. People who experiment with an innovation understand the strengths and weaknesses of the new practice and this experience often benefits subsequent adoption (VeneKlasen & Miller, 2007). Participatory models can allow participants to determine the end goals of development, and provide a means to engage people in how broader goals can be achieved through local reform. Developed in response to early development practices, Latin American scholars of the 1970s sought to replace models in which the "subjects" of development were assumed to require changes in their values, work habits, and lifestyles. In the place of the imposition of views by powerful donor nations, participatory development claimed to have a greater concern for the "people," and a desire for the "people" to gain power and improve their conditions (Huesca, 2002, p. 499).

One of the major tensions running through participatory development is the debate over whether the participatory model serves as an end in itself, rather than simply a means to a predefined end. For some, participatory development serves as a process based on the assumption that it functions as a "utopian panacea for development" (Huesca, 2002, p. 504). For example, building on the renewed interest in participatory development VeneKlasen and Miller define participation using a framework that appears to be drawn from an activist and advocacy-based frame. For them participation is:

> ...an organized political process that involves the coordinated efforts of people to change policies, practices, ideas and values that perpetuate inequality, prejudice and exclusion. (2007, p. 6)

This view of participation prioritizes context (Mody, 2002, p. 428), and stands in stark contrast to what is seen as the traditional development paradigm, where donors seek to apply universal principles to all people, without consideration of their specific context, needs, and concerns (Huesca, 2002, p. 504). For those working under this assumption the suggestion that development initiatives "go local" is unprofessional (Chambers, 1984; Korten, 1986) and defies the vaulted role of "expertise" that has dominated in the past. One solution may be to combine the need for practical outcomes within participatory processes. Trialability within justice reform allows local communities to determine needs, develop pilot projects, and then "test" their implementation by examining not only specified outputs but also the ways in which social practices help, hinder, or otherwise complicate the goals of the project (Chodosh, 2005).

To understand the value of the Latvian experience for participatory models of knowledge transfer in legal technical assistance, it is useful to consider two models of criminal justice policy-making (Knepper, 2005). The Campbell Collaboration promotes a collaborative review process that involves broad networks of academics that undertake to review the research on a particular topic. Based on the public health model to combat disease, reducing risk factors first requires their identification. This approach to crime prevention is advanced by the Campbell Collaboration. By systematically reviewing evaluation studies from around the world, the Campbell Collaboration this approach seeks to determine "what works, what doesn't and what's promising." Patterned after the use of clinical trial research in medicine, this approach, according to Knepper (2005), can result in neglecting to incorporate the sort of regional variances that may remain invisible through the broad brushes required to derive meaning from large scale systematic reviews.

Another model, envisioned by the Open Society Institute (OSI), is the reflexive model. This model pursues change without a blueprint based on the findings of social science research and rejects attempts to map strategies from natural science onto social science. Because of the unique position of people as subject and object and cause, deriving universalistic notions of knowledge will always be limited and more attention should be paid to Karl Popper's emphasis on the social situation and social tinkering as the means to making reforms (Knepper, 2005, p. 71). This model provides a useful theory of how and why engagement that emphasizes community participation through social interaction can facilitate social tinkering and local innovation to promote reform. One contribution is the work by Robert Sampson that explores the value of collective efficacy and social capital within communities. Sampson (2004) argues that a community must first have social capital, developed through informal networks, in order to have collective efficacy.

Pilot projects in Latvia provided a means to develop local capital, overcome initial organizational constraints to reform, and offer evidence of local service delivery that can be taken up by other municipalities and the national government itself. By supporting creative experimentation at the community level, development initiatives can "...midwife the process of policy discovery" (Banerjee & Duflo, 2008, p. 30) and support National reforms based on the successes and failures of past approaches. While a sea change from the development policies of the past, this approach is of increasing interest to a development community seeking to challenge past approaches based on modernization, dependency, and neoliberal theories (Mikkelsen, 2006). It may offer a means to address the complications inherent in implementing cross-national justice reforms. The problem is that it is:

> ...much more difficult to carry out a useful intervention on an international scale. The difficulty comes in trying to incorporate the sociology of accidents. The difference between utopian and piecemeal social engineering has to do with reformers' preparedness for unavoidable surprises. Confident of their success, utopian reformers seek to legislate bold and broad changes. If research findings suggest that an intervention will work on a national scale, then projecting it on an international scale will work even better. The result is unplanned planning...Piecemeal social engineers are sure they have overlooked something; they expect mistakes and intend to learn from them. They avoid wide-scale interventions because of the difficulty in sorting out what happened. From this point of view, national projects might follow from local projects and international projects from national projects...(Knepper, 2005, p. 68)

On this view, the dichotomy presented above between evidence based and reflexive development is a false one. Justice reform need not follow an either/or approach, but instead be cognizant that different approaches are of utility depending on the area of reform one chooses to focus on. Indeed, the Latvia project demonstrates how both models can work together. The reflexive model offers an initial means for more participatory approaches and the identification of bottom up strategies of local relevance and utility. As these projects become institutionalized as part of local municipalities, they can provide evidence for how reforms can overcome both structural or cultural impediments to reform, and the social resistance to change (Chodosh, 2005, pp. 79-82). In theory and through more detailed and systematic review, one could identify better and worse ways to deliver pilot projects, or more and less useful development outcomes for specific types of projects (Fisman & Miguel, 2007).

Systematic review may offer the best way to establish the utility of pilot projects, multi-agency participation, and locally identified solutions. But just as reflexive models need to account for the desire to promote more generalizable development delivery norms, evidence based researchers need to better appreciate how context defies 'universalizing' motivations within social science research. The failure to acknowledge the importance of local politics, personalities, and predispositions undermines the ultimate utility of evidence-based models. By triangulating multiple measures and giving voice to the experiences of those working on these projects, the types of contextual, social, and local impediments can be identified and better understood. This mixed model, as discussed in some detail in Chapter 3, offers a means to rely upon reflexive models to generate theories, explanations, and approaches, while evidence based practices provides a means to test, refine, and validate them (Wheeldon & Ahlberg, 2012).

Also discussed in Chapter 3, the importance of acknowledging the need for mixed models is a specific issue for research attempting to understand probation practices around the world. All research is based on assumptions of one sort or another and experimental designs may not easily fit within the actual work required by professional officers. At issue is the attempt to generalize about different treatment options or supervision strategies by treating the individuals who do this work as essentially inter-changeable. Imported from medicine, laboratory experiments, and drug trials these methodologies may not be well suited to the "...intricate work of individual professionals working with individual offenders" (Harris, 1995, p. 6). All supervision and all offender types are not the same, and simplistic models may not be able to adequately address the nuances of this inherently social endeavor. Evidence-based aid practices must be combined with practice-based evidence, if meaningful international lessons are to be learned.

5.5 Counter Views and Contrarian Considerations

This chapter has argued that a key feature of Latvian programming was local adaptation, as distinct from adoption. Not everyone concurs. Based on interviews with a very few Latvian probation officials, Randma-Liiv & Kruusenberg (2010) suggest several aspects of the probation system were simply copied from the Canadian system. They point to programs for group work with offenders that were translated from English and put into practice with only minor modifications. While this may have been the case in the early days of the project, this critique belies a lack of understanding about probation in Canada and suggests limited access to key project documents and personnel. In the first place there is no such things as a "Canadian system" since probation is organized at the provincial level. While some similarities exist across Canada, each province varies in how they organize probation – with the differences between the Quebec and Ontario approach being an obvious example. In Latvia models from Nova Scotia, Ontario, Quebec, Manitoba, and British Columbia were all presented – Latvians chose aspects to adopt, and then adapted them as required (Wheeldon, 2011).

Secondly, even a cursory review of project documents suggests how Latvian officials picked from a variety of programs in designing their system. For example, in the place of models of restorative justice provided through the project, the SPS adopted more formal approaches based on Czech and Norwegian models. Canadian programming had also focused on a separate national youth justice strategy, which was more or less ignored, as was Mr. Berzins' focus on bail. While the training on post prison reintegration based on a unique program from Manitoba did influence how the SPS approached the needs of those releasing from Latvian prisons, as discussed in Chapter 2, most aftercare functions in Latvia have been suspended. A particular limitation of this more critical analysis is the failure to understand the role of the pilot project approach in Latvia. In addition to the benefits discussed above, it also appears to have challenged a common occurrence in development whereby a lack of domestic expertise results in too much influence assigned to foreign expertise. Instead of simply importing various aspects of the Canadian system, by the time national initiatives were underway, local experts all ready had some experience and had developed and modified Canadian practices to address the specific needs of their town, city, region, and country (Zeibote, 2008).

A more penetrating critique might be related to the risk/needs frameworks drawn initially from Ontario and later from British Columbia. Introduced in Chapter 2 and discussed in more detail in Chapter 7, this critique is connected to the concern that simply exporting risk/needs models without validating them in the local context can have the effect of formalizing assumptions and practices that while relevant in one context, is inappropriate for another (Kemshall *et al*, 1998). There are signs that Latvian officials are taking a more scholarly and rigorous approach to reviewing their own operations and outcomes, yet it may be the case that suggesting that probation's function is to manage crime, rather than trying to understand it has had longer term impacts. The implications of the model and the approach to probation that was adapted are discussed in more detail in Chapter 7. While certainly worthy of discussion and perhaps critique, it must be based on an informed understanding of the actual practices on the ground. For some Latvians, it is the case that the SPS has become:

> ...too focused on paper not people. Canadians warned against this...but administrative functions have increased and reduced amount of time for client visits.

This comment may be related to another challenge. While this chapter argues that pilot projects, were found to be very useful in Latvia (Bell *et al.* 2003), one senior probation official also identified an inherent drawback to this approach. While pilot project directors have played an integral role in the development of probation their experience and their resultant 'feelings of ownership,' according to one senior official, have created management challenges. Although more participatory and power sharing arrangements led to its establishment, probation now exists as an institution of criminal justice, fully entrenched in the Latvian bureaucracy. While shared power approaches may have produced more sustainable organizational change at the outset, continued power sharing arrangements are more complex. It is perhaps inevitable that organizational strains will emerge. In Latvia individual probation offices, once free to design, develop, and deliver local programming as they see fit must now implement less popular, less relevant, or less inclusively developed mandates from probation headquarters.

In recent years, the SPS has been forced to confront a number of challenges related to program development. In addition to risk assessment tools and reports, another component of the LLRP was developing programs such as cognitive behaviourial programming, anger management, and substance abuse programs. Yet, as reported by Imants Jurevičius (2010), while the LLRP was successful in introducing these tools and programs, their operation on the ground has been uneven. Before 2005 no established experience of using group work programs existed within the Latvian criminal justice system. Since the establishment of Probation, the role and value of probation programs has not been widely accepted. Even staff in local probation offices were at times resistant to the idea of probation programs. According to a Latvian project participant:

> ...a group work program for correction of behaviour was a concept hard to understand for [Latvian] society and many people view this as waste of resources...ok for rich countries, but something Latvia cannot afford.

In part this was a result of the a decision by the central office to train only certain "specialist" staff in these programs which undermined program delivery when staff left their positions and there was no one within the local offices who could effectively deliver these programs. The approach to programs has evolved as the service has grown. There is a strong incentive for clients to participate in programming, as failing to fulfill obligations could result in the re-instatement of the original sentence. Yet, the reliance on volunteers has resulted in some missteps. For example, as reported by Jurevičius (2010):

> Once [an] angry mother of a juvenile offender phoned headquarters. She was very worried about what we are doing with her son. After sessions of a substance abuse probation program, he often came home drunk. Previously her son had no problems with alcohol or abuse of other substances.

This example points to two challenges. The first is a reminder of the ways in which judges and probation interacted in the past. The second is the importance of how programs are delivered. Specifically, the substance abuse programming by the SPS has had to contend with participants who were drunk and/or under the influence of drugs, complicating the efficacy of group work. As a result of being placed in a program that was not based on his risks or needs, this juvenile offender was now going to drink with his new friends from the program. While this is hardly a successful outcome for a program with such laudable goals, as a result of an open acknowledgment there has been a new focus on volunteer training, peer reviews between probation offices, and a new focus on training for all probation officers on the role, value, and challenges of probation programming in their communities (Jurevičius, 2011).

Of some interest will be the extent to which future SPS training considers the so-called Good Lives Model (GLM) proposed by Ward and Maruna (2007). Discussed in more detail in Chapter 7, GLM seeks to offer an alternative to some assumptions about motivation inherent in the Risk/Needs Responsivity (RNR) model. This model focuses much more on an understanding of the motivation, engagement, and autonomy related not only to a reduction in criminality but also to the acquisition of a new self-narrative. It may have benefits for staff as much as for clients.

5.6 Concluding Remarks

Organizational constraints to change are complex and deeply rooted. In the context of probation programming they can include agency cooperation and the operation of the legal system. A significant challenge is establishing a shared approach among collaborating organizations and stakeholders at the individual, community, and national levels. One approach employed in Latvia to explicitly involve communities in reform was pilot projects. These projects designed, tested, and evaluated programs and services to address community needs by supporting local people to decide which programs work best for them.

An important result of this model has been the clear identification of dedicated, committed, and enthusiastic community leaders in Latvia. Willing to try new things and learn from mistakes through participatory processes, they developed local capacity, involved volunteers in their projects, and established new local services in their communities. While basing developmental policy solely on methodologies drawn from developmental economists may be problematic, using pilot projects as one part of a broader approach to legal technical assistance may be an important contribution to sustainable justice reform programming. It may also provide a means to consider how evidence-based aid can be applied in criminal justice reform settings.

This approach appears to be of specific relevance to countries emerging from authoritarian rule where governments have been reluctant to yield to local preferences. Pilot projects have considerable potential for the establishment of trust, flexibility, and accommodation. In Latvia, they provided a means to allow for community involvement while delaying the widespread implementation of these reforms until they have been shown to be of utility. While no guarantee or panacea, they often result in creative solutions and the kind of local ownership required to support sustainable efforts at political reconciliation and perhaps even democratic reform. When larger scale reforms are implemented based on micro successes, they can facilitate changes in the thinking and behavior of government actors and produce reforms that have been shown to be useful in context and among local populations.

Chapter 5 Bibliography

D.A. Andrews. The impact of nonprogrammatic factors on criminal-justice interventions. *Legal and Criminological Psychology*, Vol. 16, 2011, pp. 1-23.

D.A. Andrews & J. Bonta. *The psychology of criminal conduct* (4th ed.). Newark, NJ: LexisNexis/Matthew Bender, 2006.

Association of Universities and Colleges of Canada. *Legal reform capacity project: Report to CIDA*. Ottawa, ON: AUCC, 2003.

Association of Universities and Colleges of Canada. *Latvian legal reform program: Report to CIDA*. Ottawa, ON: AUCC, 2005.

K. Ayas. Learning through projects: meeting the implementation challenge. In R.A. Lundin & C. Middler (Eds.), *Projects as arenas for renewal and learning processes*. Boston, MA: Kluwer Academic Publishers, 1998, pp. 89-98.

T.L. Baker. *Doing Social research* (2nd Ed.). New York, NY: McGraw-Hill, 1994.

A. Banerjee & E. Duflo. *The Experimental Approach to Development Economics*. Abdul Latif Jameel Poverty Action Lab, Department of Economics, Cambridge, MA: Massachusetts Institute of Technology, 2008.

J. Batt. *The New Slovakia: National Identity, Political Integration and the Return to Europe*. London, UK: Royal Institute of International Affairs, 1996.

S. Bell, R. Corrado, Y. Dandurand & C. Griffiths. *Report of the LRCP advisory panel*. Ottawa, ON: Association of Universities and Colleges Canada, 2002.

K. Blanchette & S.L. Brown. *The assessment and treatment of women offenders: An integrative perspective*. Wiley Series – Forensic Clinical Psychology, 2006.

T. Brennan, W. Dieterich & B. Ehret. Evaluating the Predictive Validity of the Compas Risk and Needs Assessment System. *Criminal Justice and Behavior*, Vol. 36, No. 1, 2009, pp. 21-40.

R. Canton. Taking Probation Abroad. *European Journal of Probation*, Vol. 1, No. 1, 2009, pp. 66-78.

Canadian International Development Agency. Regional Framework: Canada's Cooperation Program with CEE/NIS Countries in Transition. CIDA, PQ: Gatineau, 1997.

T. Carothers. Promoting the rule of law abroad: The problem of knowledge (Working Paper No. 34). Washington, DC: Carnegie Endowment for International Peace, 2003.

R. Chambers. Participatory rural appraisal (PRA): Analysis of experience. *World Development*, Vol. 22, No. 9, 1994, pp. 1253-1268.

C.B. Chapman & S.C. Ward. *Managing project risk and uncertainty*. Chichester, UK: Wiley Publishers, 2003.

H. Chodosh. *Global justice reform: A comparative methodology*. New York, NY: New York University Press, 2005.

D. Cole. The Umpires Strike Back: Canadian Judicial Experience with Risk-Assessment Instruments. *Canadian Journal of Criminology and Criminal Justice*, Vol. 49, No. 4, 2007, pp. 493-517.

Y. Dandurand. Effective technical assistance in crime prevention and criminal justice. *Maximizing the Effectiveness of the Technical Assistance Provided in the Fields of Crime Prevention and Criminal Justice,* Vienna, Austria. No. 49, 2006.

Y. Dandurand, C. Griffiths & V. Chin. Training and effective support of comprehensive justice and security reforms: Outcomes to date and lessons learned. In K. Aromaa, & S. Redo (Eds.), *For the rule of law: Criminal justice teaching and training @cross the world.* Helsinki: European Institute for Crime Prevention and Control, 2008.

E. Durkheim. *The division of labor in society*. New York, NY: Free Press, 1893/1997.

R. Fisman & E. Miguel. *Economic Gangsters: Corruption, Violence and the Poverty of Nations*. Princeton University Press, Newark: NJ, 2008.

T. Foglesong & P. Solomon. *Crime, Criminal Justice, and Criminology in Post-Soviet Ukraine*. National Institute of Justice: Washington, DC, 2001.

M. Foureur. Creating Birth Space to Enable Undisturbed Birth. In K. Fahy, M. Foureur, C. Hastie (Eds.), *Birth Territory and Midwifery Guardianship*, Elsevier, Oxford, UK, 2008, pp. 57-78.

A.F. Fowler. Authentic NGDO Partnerships in the New Policy Agenda for International Aid: Dead End or Light Ahead? *Development and Change*, Vol. 29, No. 1, 1998, pp. 137-159.

S. Golub. The legal empowerment alternative. In T. Carothers (Ed.), *Promoting the rule of law abroad: The problem of knowledge*. Washington, D.C.: Carnegie Endowment for International Peace, 2003, pp. 161-190.

L. Gosling. *Toolkits:A Practical Guide to Planning, Monitoring, Evaluation and Impact Assessment*. London, UK: Save the Children, 2003.

C. Griffiths, Y. Dandurand & V. Chin. Development assistance and police reform: Programming opportunities and lessons learned. *The Canadian Review of Policing Research*, Vol. 2, 2005, pp. 101-113.

K. Hamai & R. Ville. Origins and Purposes of Probation. In K. Hamai, R. Harris, M. Hough, R. Ville & U. Zvekic (Eds.), *Probation Around the World: A Comparative Study*. London, UK: Routledge Press, 1995, pp. 71-110.

R. Harris. Probation Around the World: Origins and Development. In K. Hamai, R. Harris, M. Hough, R. Ville & U. Zvekic (Eds.), *Probation Around the World: A Comparative Study*. London, UK: Routledge Press, 1995, pp. 25-70.

M. Hatton & K. Schroeder. Partnership Theory and Practice: Time for a New Paradigm. *Canadian Journal of Development Studies*, Vol. 28, No.1, 2007, pp. 157-162.

B. Hebenton & J. Spencer. *Assessing international assistance in law enforcement: Themes, findings and recommendations from a case study in the republic of Estonia*. Helsinki, FI: HEUNI – European Institute for Crime Prevention and Control, 2001.

J. Heckman. Randomization and social policy evaluation. In C. Manski & I. Garfinkel (Eds.), *Evaluating Welfare and Training Programs*. Cambridge, MA: Harvard University Press, 1992, pp. 201-230.

R. Hoksbergen. Building Civil Society through Partnership: Lessons from a Case Study of the Christian Reformed World Relief Committee. *Development in Practice*, Vol. 15, No. 1, 2005, pp. 1-27.

R. Huesca. Participatory approaches to communication for development. In B. Mody & W. Gudykunst (Eds.), *Handbook of international and intercultural communication*. Thousand Oaks, Calif: Sage, 2002 pp. 499-512.

W. Jacoby. Tutors and pupils: international organizations, central European elites, and western models. *Governance*, Vol. 14, No. 2, 2001, pp. 169-200.

M. Johnston. *Political Corruption and Public Policy in America*. Monterey, CA: Brooks/Cole Press, 1982.

A.Y. Jiao, R. Lau, W.K. Raymond & P. Lui. An institutional analysis of organizational change: The case of the Hong Kong police. *International Criminal Justice Review*, Vol. 15, No. 1, 2005, pp. 38-57.

I. Jurevičius. Implementing Probation programs in Latvia. Presented at STARR conference What Works in Reducing Re-offending? April 28-30, 2010. Downing College, University of Cambridge, UK.

I. Jurevičius. Recruitment and training of probation officers in Latvia. Presented May 26, 2011, Center for European Probation, Utrecht, Netherlands.

I. Jurevičius. *Creation of the State Probation Service*. Unpublished Masters Thesis. University of Latvia: Riga, 2008.

A. Kamenska. *Par piespiedu sabiedrisko darbu kā sodu Latvijā*. Cietumu un policijas reformu programmas apkārtraksts Alternatīva, Nr.1, 2000a.

A. Kamenska. *Probācijas dienests Lielbritānijā*. Cietumu un policijas reformu programmas apkārtraksts Alternatīva, Nr.1, 2000b.

A. Kamenska. Latvia. In A. van Kalmthout, J. Roberts and S.Vinding (Eds.), *Probation and Probation Services in the EU Accession Countries.* Netherlands: Wolf Legal Publishers, 2003.

D. Kapoor. NGO Partnerships and the Training of the Grassroots in India. *Development in Practice* Vol, 15, No. 2, 2005, pp. 210-215.

D. Karlan & J. Zinman. *Expanding Credit Access: Using Randomized Supply Decisions to Estimate the Impacts*, MIMEO, Yale University, 2007.

D. Kealey. A study of cross-cultural effectiveness: Theoretical issues, practical applications. *International Journal of Intercultural Relations*, Vol. 13, 1989, pp. 387-428.

D. Kealey. *Cross-cultural effectiveness, A study of Canadian technical advisors overseas.* Gatineau, PQ: CIDA Briefing Centre, 1990.

D. Kealey. The challenge of international personnel selection. In D. Landis, & R.S. Bhakat (Eds.), *Handbook of intercultural training* (2nd ed.). Thousand Oaks, CA: Sage Publications, 1996, pp. 81-105.

D. Kealey. *Cross-cultural effectiveness – A study of Canadian technical advisors overseas.* Gatineau, PQ: Centre for Intercultural Learning, Canadian Foreign Service Institute, 2001.

D.J. Kealey & D.R. Protheroe. *Cross-cultural collaborations: Making north-south cooperation more effective.* Hull, Québec: Centre for Intercultural Learning, Canadian Foreign Service Institute, 1995.

D. Kealey, D.Protheroe, D. MacDonald & T. Vulpe. Re-examining the role of training in contributing to international project success: A literature review and an outline of a new model training program. *International Journal of Intercultural Relations*, Vol. 29, 2005 pp. 289-316.

H. Kemshall, P. Holt, R. Bailey & G. Boswell. Beyond programmes: organisational and cultural issues in the implementation of What Works. In G. Mair (Ed.), *What Matters in Probation* Cullompton, UK: Willan, 2004, pp. 170-186.

S.W. Kim & W.A. Pridemore. Social change, institutional anomie, and serious property crime in transitional Russia. *British Journal of Criminology*, Vol. 45, 2005, pp. 81-97.

C.B. Klockars, S.K. Ivkovich, W.E. Harver, & M.R. Haberfeld. *The measurement of police integrity* (No. 181465). Washington, DC: National Institute of Justice, 2000.

P. Knepper. Crime prevention in a multinational open society. *International Criminal Justice Review*, Vol. 15, No. 1, 2005, pp. 58-74.

D. Korten. *Community Organizations and Rural Development: A Learning Process Approach.* Ford Foundation, New York, 1986.

M. Lauristin. Contexts of transition. In M. Lauristin (Ed.). *Return to the western world: Cultural and political perspectives on the Estonian post-communist transition.* Tartu: Estonia: Tartu University Press, 1997, pp. 25-40.

K. Lewin. *Field theory in social science.* New York, NY: Harper and Row, 1951.

S. Lister. Power in Partnerships? An Analysis of an NGO's Relationships with its Partners. *Journal of International Development*, Vol. 12, No. 2, 2002, pp. 227-239.

M.D. Lyman. *The police: An introduction.* Englewood Cliffs, NJ: Prentice Hall, 2002.

R. MacDonald (Ed.). *(Book review) The tools of government: A guide to the new governance by Salamon, Lester.* London, UK: Oxford University Press, 2002.

J. Manor. *Aid that Works: Successful Development in Fragile States.* Washington: The World Bank, 2007.

B. McCarthy. Keeping an eye on the Keeper: Prison Corruption and its Control. In M. Braswell, B. McCarthy & B. McCarthy (Eds.), *Justice, Crime and Ethics* (2nd Edition). Cincinnati: Anderson, 1996, pp. 229-242.

B. Mikkelson. *Methods for Development Work and Research: A New Guide for Practitioners.* New Delhi: Sage Publications, 2005.

B. Mody. Introduction. In W.B. Gudykunst & B. Mody (Eds.), *The Handbook of Intercultural Communication.* Thousand Oaks, CA: Sage, 2002, pp. 415-435.

O. Norgaard, D. Hindsgaul, L. Johannsen, H. Willumsen & E. Helgar. *The Baltic States after Independence* Cheltenham, UK: Edward Elgar, 1999.

J.L. Parpart & H. Veltmeyer. The Development Project in Theory and Practice: A Review of its Shifting Dynamics. *Canadian Journal of Development Studies,* Vol. 25, No. 1, 2004, pp. 39-60.

D.F. Polit, C.T. Beck & B.P. Hungler, *Essentials of Nursing Research: Methods, Appraisal and Utilization* (5th Ed.). Philadelphia: Lippincott Williams & Wilkins, 2001.

T. Randma-Liiv & R. Kruusenberg. West-East policy transfer: motives, scope, role models and agents. Paper presented at IRSPM Conference held April 2-9, 2010, Berne, SW.

E.M. Rogers. *Diffusion of knowledge* (1st ed.). New York, NY: Free Press, 1962.

R. Sampson. Neighborhood and community: Collective efficacy and community safety. *New Economy,* Vol. 11, 2004, pp. 106-113.

R. Simmons, P. Fajans & L. Ghiron. *Scaling up health service delivery: From pilot innovations to policies and programmes.* Geneva, Sw: World Health Organization, 2007.

D.D. Simpson. A conceptual framework for transferring research to practice. *Journal of Substance Abuse Treatment*, Vol. 22, No. 4, 2002, pp. 171-182.

L.M. Sundstrom. *Funding civil society: Foreign assistance and NGO development in Russia.* Paulo Alto, Ca: Stanford University Press, 2006.

M. Tonry. Evaluating Intermediate Sanctions Programs. In J. Petersilia (Ed.), *Community Corrections: Probation, Parole, and Intermediate Sanctions.* Oxford: Oxford University Press, 1998, pp. 79-96.

J. R. Turner. *The handbook of project based management.* (2nd ed.) London, UK: McGraw-Hill, 1999.

J. R. Turner. The role of pilot studies in reducing risk on projects and programmes. (Editorial). *International Journal of Project Management,* Vol. 23, No. 1, 2005, pp. 1-6.

J.R. Turner & R. Muller. On the nature of the project as a temporary organization. *International Journal of Project Management,* Vol. 21, No. 8, 2003, pp. 1-8.

E.R. Van Teilingen & V. Hundley. The importance of pilot studies. *Social Science Research Update*, Issue No. 35, 2003.

L. VeneKlasen & V.L. Miller. *A New Weave of Power, People, and Politics: The Action Guide for Advocacy and Citizen Participation*. Bourton-on-Dunsmore: Practical Action, 2007.

R. Vincent & A. Byrne. Enhancing Learning in Development Partnerships. *Development in Practice*, Vol. 16, No. 5, 2006, pp. 385-399.

T. Ward & S. Maruna. *Rehabilitation: Beyond the risk paradigm*. New York, NY: Routledge, 2007.

T. Ward, J. Melser & P.M. Yates. Reconstructing the risk-need-responsivity model: A theoretical elaboration and evaluation. *Aggression and Violent Behavior*, Vol. 12, 2007, pp. 208-228.

R. Watts. Personal Communication October, 2011.

L. Westmarland. Police Ethics and Integrity: Breaking the Blue Code of Silence. *Policing and Society*, Vol. 15, No. 2, 2005 pp. 145-165.

J. Wheeldon. *Bringing British Columbia to Latvia: Canadians reflect on expert designation in an international criminal justice project*. Burnaby, BC: School of Criminology, Simon Fraser University, 2007.

J. Wheeldon. *Mapping Knowledge Transfer: Latvian-Canadian Cooperation and Justice Reform*. Unpublished PhD Dissertation. Burnaby, BC: School of Criminology, Simon Fraser University, 2009.

J. Wheeldon & M. Ahlberg. *Visualizing Social Science Research: Maps, Methods, and Meaning*. Thousand Oaks, CA: Sage Publications, 2012.

J. Wheeldon & T. Sanford. Toward Integrated Community Justice in Latvia. *Law and Justice*, Vol. 9, No. 37, 2002, pp. 258-260.

J. Wheeldon & J. Heidt. Contesting 'Evidence': Challenging Criminal Justice Reform in an Era of Evidence-Based Practices. Paper presented at Western Society of Criminology, February 4-6, 2010 Honolulu, HI.

J. Wheeldon. To Guide or Provoke? Maps, Pedagogy, and the Value(s) of Teaching Criminal Justice Ethics. *The Journal of Criminal Justice Education*, Vol. 22, No. 4, 2011, pp. 1-25.

C.R. Williams & B.A. Arrigo. *Ethics, Crime, and Criminal Justice.* Upper Saddle Rover, NJ: Prentice Hall, 2007.

L. Zeibote. Probation in Latvia. In A.M. van Kalmthout & I. Durnescu. *Probation in Europe.* Nijmegen: Wolf Legal Publishers, 2008.

6 Individual Constraints: Communication, Connection, and Interactive Training

As discussed in Chapter 5, Canadian programming between 2001-2002 worked to transfer pilot project expertise from local communities to larger National institutions. Central to this process was the establishment of the Probation Working Group. This group included both pilot project directors from local communities and senior Ministry of Justice personnel – police, prison officials, and legislative experts. Headed by Ilona Kronberga, the working group developed new policies and interim agency approaches, drafted the Probation Act, and advocated for legislative amendments to give probation practical effect. In Canada, the success of the Latvia program was recognized by CIDA and in late 2002 AUCC's proposed *Latvian Legal Reform Program* (LLRP) was approved and co-signed by the Latvian Ministry of Justice. It was implemented between 2002-2004.

This chapter presents some of the individual challenges to project success. In the context of international development, individual challenges to project success include the need for basic cross-cultural skills such as the capacity to succeed in unfamiliar cultures, communication, and a willingness to learn how social structures influence inter group relationships. Through the project, training models were developed using problem-based and interactive approaches and exercises based on restorative principles and participatory education models. Although there is a growing recognition of the importance of the above factors, there is less information about which specific training and technical approaches can usefully be employed to promote change. In Latvia these challenges included the linguistic issues associated with communication, perceived differences between government and community participants, and cultural variations about the proper role of punishment among participants with different levels of education, job experience, and assumptions about the role of the criminal justice system.

6.1 Building on Past Programming: The Latvian Legal Reform Project

While Canadian programming up to 2002 had been broadly defined, in late 2002 developments in Latvia led CIDA to fund a targeted two-year project entitled the *Latvian Legal Reform Program* (LLRP). Designed to support the Latvian Ministry of Justice's establishment of the State Probation Service (SPS), the project provided training, technical assistance, and capacity development to ensure the probation service was based in law and in line with international standards of human rights and justice. The LLRP responded to and further supported a number of additional developments within the field of criminal justice, including bail supervision, victim-offender mediation, and alternative dispute resolution (AUCC, 2005). It represented the most targeted programming in the region to date.

The choice by the Ministry of Justice to focus on probation was perhaps logical. External pressure require some sort of action and in the Baltics, a court-based system of supervision had been in place in Estonia since 1998 (Berzins, 2002). Probation offered a means to reduce prison populations while ensuring a continued role for supervision. The choice to work with Canada, based on the years of existing cooperation, perhaps made some philosophic sense as well. Probation services exist on a continuum between a focus on rehabilitation and treatment on the one hand, and supervision and control on the other. While the Canadian model is more supervision focused, rehabilitation remains a core element and probation officers serve as case managers for offenders within the criminal justice system. As service brokers, they act as a bridge between the assessment of probationer needs and the allocation of available and appropriate community resources.

The LLRP operated through four (4) components and assisted to establish the State Probation Service (SPS) by developing new laws, amending existing laws, training staff, and providing support to leading officials within the Latvian Ministry of Justice. The Legislative component was designed as an advisory component in which Canadian expertise was used to advise Ministry of Justice staff on the Canadian experience of drafting and implementing proposed legislative reforms (AUCC, 2005). This included support to the development of the probation draft. In addition legal and policy reform provided mechanisms for more formal cooperation with agencies such as the police. Canadian expertise supported existing efforts to promote legislative reform in Latvia and to ensure probation was securely based in law. This involved ongoing consultation from Canada related to efforts to reform the Latvian Criminal Procedure Code and elements of the Criminal Law.

The Communications component was designed to contribute to building public confidence in the State Probation Service and to developing resources that could be used in future awareness campaigns. It included the development of a public awareness commercial, training video, pamphlets, and the SPS website located at: <www.probatija.lv>. The Partnership component also sought to sustain past partnerships in Latvia among international legal reform programming and local organizations to promote more coherent and coordinated approaches in the field of justice reform. Based on approaches used since 2001, such as pilot projects, coordination councils, and working groups, these programs, services, and personnel in 2002 became the basis for the probation service.

Of specific interest in this chapter is the Training Development component. Designed to support the development of a comprehensive training program for central office staff, probation officers, and a corps of probation officer trainers in Latvia, it involved another more specifically designed study tour, and in-country training. The training through the

LLRP was provided over ten (10) months, between February 2003 and November 2004, and was delivered by a variety of trainers drawn from Probation and Justice agencies in Nova Scotia, Ontario, Manitoba, and British Columbia. Training modules included: roles and responsibility of probation officers, administrative procedures, risk assessments and plans of care (psychological problems, violence and substance abuse), case management of adult criminal justice process, case management of juvenile justice process, supervision of male, female, and special needs offenders.

In addition, the program included training on coordination between SPS and Prison Administration, supervision of conditional orders and post-prison supervision, restorative justice models, and community development. As the training program neared completion, technical assistance efforts targeted identifying and addressing key institutional challenges within the nascent service. This included the formalization and implementation of a training program for newly hired probation officers.

6.2 Individual Constraints and Latvian Participants

While Chapter 5 presented literature that focuses on the role of organizations and the structural constraints to ethical behavior, agencies are made up of individuals whose values also influence workplace practices (Betz, O'Connell & Shepard, 1989; Conser & Russell, 2000). As Black and Mendenhall (1990) suggest, increased internationalization in the economic, political, and social arenas has resulted in the acknowledgment that cross-cultural training is a means of facilitating more effective interactions. Recently, scholars have rediscovered the importance of individual and interpersonal programming elements (Beeson & Davis, 2000; Rogers, 2005). This literature has focused on the importance of understanding local informal and interactional processes (Helmke & Levitsky, 2004). Some is critical of the role of Western-based expertise (Dezalay & Garth, 2000) for continuing to export failed professional models to developing countries even after the negative consequences were well known (Brillon, 1980; Mandal, 1989; Rotimi & Oloruntimehin, 1992). In the post-Cold War, era some argue that a wide range of new economic and social processes are influencing the mechanisms of policy decision-making itself.

Those less critical of the role of experts in development policy point to some successes in reforming policing (Griffiths *et al.* 2005) and the judiciary (Hammegren, 2007). They challenge the simplistic expert/learner dichotomies that often characterize critical treatments of development initiatives. Instead of focusing on nefarious Western experts, these outsiders may be far less important to understanding legal processes than how the day-to-day practices between individuals and groups impact law and regulation (Valverde, 2003). In North America, one idea is that a few individuals who self-select into the profession hold the very values that may lead to unethical behavior (Kleinig, 1996). Through detailed and useful empirical research, a limited test of this so-called importation hypothesis has found that those drawn to criminal justice careers do not possess certain values that were distinct or uniquely different from those of the general population (Bjerregaard & Lord, 2004). While these findings appeared to challenge previous explorations (Dantzker, 2000; Goldstein, 1977; Skolnick, 1991; Walker, 1983), there seems little doubt that how an individual's beliefs and values develop influences how he or she makes decisions (Conser & Russell, 2000; Rokeach, 1973).

Individual and interpersonal elements to project success have been studied for more than two decades. In general they are connected to the personal characteristics of those involved in the project. These include basic cross-culture skills, the capacity for adjusting to the new environment, communicating, creating networks, taking part in social life, and getting along in unfamiliar cultures (Kealey *et al.* 2005). A number of studies have focused predominantly on the skills required among those who deliver assistance through training and technical assistance abroad (Abramson & Ai, 1999; Chatterjee, 2001; Hawes & Kealey, 1981; Kealey, 1990; Luo, 1997). For example, Kealey's early work considered the role of communicative competency in cross-cultural adaptation and the importance of the selection of technical assistance personnel to lead international technical assistance (Hawes & Kealey, 1981).

Individual challenges thus can also be connected to how well those working on international projects understand the culture in which they are to live and work including its historical, political and socio-economic features and social models, and the ways in which individuals operate alone and in groups (Kealey *et al.* 2005). For probation programming, specific individual challenges include the use of the language of human rights and a belief in rehabilitation, the relative influence of traditionalists versus reformers, and the relationships between managers, staff, and trainers. Training activities can transfer knowledge, build skills, and provide an entry point to facilitate greater inter-institutional cooperation and collaboration in criminal justice (Protic, 2005). Yet, there is a view that training is limited and often unsustainable when based on expert-driven seminars delivered by members of the 'development jet set' (Griffiths *et al.* 2005; Wedel, 1998). Too often experts are unaware of cultural issues and thus are under-prepared to deliver more context specific training (Channell, 2005).

In addition, technical assistance projects tend to focus on senior officials instead of engaging front line officers and civil society (Dandurand *et al.* 2008). To build trust among participants, experts must be seen as modest, be willing to continuously learn, and avoid employing old notions about what worked in other countries. A significant contribution to how one understands individual challenges is the notion that successful technical assistance requires more than technical knowledge. These challenges, outlined in Figure 6.1, include: the use of the language of rights and a belief in rehabilitation, the relative influence of traditionalists versus reformers, past learning styles and open to new approaches, and manager, officer, and trainer relations.

Figure 6.1 Key Aspects of Individual Impediments in Probation

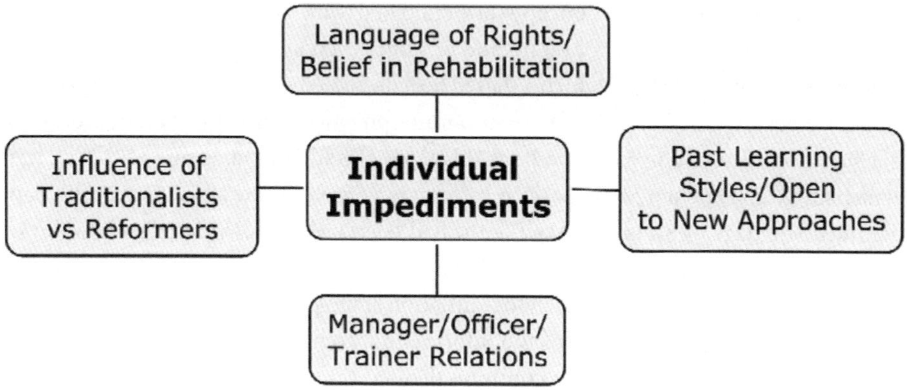

In addition, effectiveness requires that trainers understand the importance of professional modesty, encourage local experts to share their experiences, and consider cultural dimensions to create positive learning environments (Kealey & Protheroe, 1995). By relying on intercultural competence, trainers must develop adaptive capacity (Berg, 1993) to effectively understand and accommodate the demands of the host culture (Taylor, 1994). Of immediate interest are two aspects of overarching import: communication and the differences between Latvian training participants.

6.2.1 *The Challenge of Communication*

As introduced in Chapter 3, there may be no more important set of related issues for understanding the means and mechanisms of individual knowledge transfer than that of translation and interpretation. A relevant distinction should be made between translation – transferring from one language to another ideas expressed in writing – and interpretation, which consists of transferring ideas expressed orally. Although interpretation requires different skills than translation, similar challenges exist as a result of trying to transfer concepts in one language, based on concepts drawn from another (Spencer-Oatey & Xing, 2007). Because interpreters are not always able to provide a firmly defined one-to-one correlation between the words and phrases of different languages, the focus is on developing phrases that carry similar scope and shades of meaning as the original (Kelly, 1979). It has been suggested that policy transfer often takes place between countries sharing a common language and the role of language in policy transfer has been investigated in some detail (Castles, 1993; Evans, 2004).

Within the criminal justice training environment this challenge is especially complex. For Canadian trainers, concepts like human rights, civil liberties, supervision, due process, rehabilitation and reintegration all come with a historical context born of North American experience. Given that these concepts are endowed with specific meaning in Canada through the Canadian Charter of Rights and Freedoms, it may not be reasonable to assume a common starting place from which a shared lexicon could be established. All respondents in both studies identified the role of translation/interpretation within the training workshops as a significant issue. For the Canadians this issue was identified as one of the "…most challenging." The Latvian participants were less concerned. While all Latvian participants identified language as an issue, many felt it had been well handled, especially when the training materials were translated and provided before the sessions. According to one Canadian trainer, while this approach to translation could provide the specific terminology and vocabulary at the beginning of the information exchange, it was often not enough. One Canadian trainer articulated a common theme:

> …the nodding of heads could be misleading. To be sure we [Canadian trainers] were being understood, we needed to find practical ways to communicate certain concepts.

6.2.2 *Variance in Governmental and Community Actors*

Another important dynamic identified by the Canadian trainers was the variance in styles and approach between Latvian participants drawn from communities and those from the government and formal institutions of the Latvian criminal justice system. Differences emerged based on education and experience, and the Canadian trainers observed variance in people's willingness to engage in participatory training exercise, turn off cell phones, and work in teams to solve group based training problems. This suggests support for emergent views in Canada that challenge traditional assumptions about the role of external legal expertise (Valverde, 2003). Instead, informal interactions between and among those working on the ground may be a significant impediment to broader efforts (Helmke & Levitsky, 2004).

The existence of these informal impediments suggest broader problems in encouraging the sorts of open-ended interactions required to pursue deliberative discussions about the place of law in society. To overcome these challenges, and instead of relying upon assumptions that a common view exists, space may need to be created for the variation that exists in the understanding of law among training participants. Many Canadians suggested the nature of the social interactions was more positive among the community practitioners. While regional differences were noted by some others pointed to age as a more significant factor. According to one Canadian trainer:

> ...the younger representatives from the government side have lots of energy and enthusiasm and appeared more able to adapt than older participants. The younger ones seem to have a foot in both worlds.

This generational challenge appeared to also be connected to cultural differences within the groups about the role and utility of punishment. Based on broader societal and cultural beliefs, many believed in the value of punitive approaches to social problems. Finding ways to challenge these sorts of ingrained attitudes in ways that do not impose more moderate and less punitive views may be the most complex challenge facing those who support international exchanges of justice related experience. The punishment-based mentality of many Latvians was noted both by Latvian and Canadian participants. While this cultural factor exists as a broader societal phenomenon, it also exists as a specific issue among individuals working within the justice system.

One Canadian trainer recalled one of the early training sessions when a senior official during an exercise suggested loudly that the best thing to do with criminals was "... to line them up against a wall and shoot them." This was not an uncommon view and presented a challenge to Canadians. While probation in Canada may not be as treatment focused as in other countries, there appeared to an assumption among the Canadian trainers that probation provided a means for clients to engage and participate in their own rehabilitation and that collective security required a respect for individual rights. Some Latvians reported that this view was naïve. While some Latvian participants drawn from the community saw the limitations in a punitive justice policy, a common theme from a number of these participants can be summed up by one quote from a community-based probation officer:

> Look, we [Latvians] see things differently than these Canadians...we don't like change...we believe you must punish, not these things like programs and this rehabilitation. Latvia is not like this...

Based on their own experiences through the pilot projects, some participants argued this mentality could not be changed through laws and policies but instead had to address personal, and even larger societal factors. While these impediments were identified as significant challenge for public acceptance of reform, Latvian participants expressed optimism that they could be overcome as younger, more open individuals replace older generations. For example, when asked about the biggest barrier to justice reform in Latvia, one younger participant from the Ministry of Justice who had been recently promoted suggested it was "...old, stupid Latvians."

6.3 PROJECT PROGRAMMING: INTERPRETERS, LOCAL EXPERTS, AND RELATIONSHIPS

Although there is a growing recognition of the importance of the above individual factors, there is less information about which specific training and technical approaches can usefully be employed to promote change. Some literature is critical of study tours, training modules, and the approach taken by Canadian experts overseas (Griffiths *et al.* 2005). Other literature is skeptical of the focus on universal absorption over the acknowledgment of local distortions and modifications inherent in international knowledge transfer (Sundstrom, 2006, p. 172). Despite these challenges, Canadian programming in Latvia addressed the above constraints in three important ways. Interactive training session involved interpreters in the training to help provide locally appropriate context to the specific terminology used (Knapp-Potthoff & Knapp, 1987). In addition, Canadian trainers used a variety of experiential exercises based on restorative principles. A key aspect in both strategies was the role of relationships. An integral aspect within these sessions than the relationships that are forged between and among participants, trainers, and local experts.

Another aspect was the challenge of communication. Some Latvian participants who had served as informal interpreters suggested that a word-to-word translation was insufficient. Instead trainers needed to establish "... the meaning of what was said [by] providing examples that would make sense in the Latvian context." Others, while acknowledging the challenge of the language barrier, suggested that understanding could be achieved through connections and relations with trainers during non-formal activities such as dinners, saunas, and parties. For the Canadians, successfully presenting concepts meant "...reshaping and reworking training plans so they could be of some value to those involved." This was seen as very challenging. One answer was the use of more participatory and interactive approaches. According to one Canadian trainer, when trying to communicate key concepts, of importance was:

> ...establishing a relationship ahead of time, reviewing the terms that may be new or unique, and seeking regular confirmation throughout the workshop. You have to make room for some give and take... You can translate language, but without a common frame of reference it is easy to miss the nuances. The meaning of what you are saying can be easily lost.

While communication barriers are a significant individual challenge to knowledge transfer and project success, another is related to differences between community leaders and government officials. In hindsight, it appears the project was able to break down these barriers in a variety of ways. As discussed in Chapter 4 one aspect of the project was study tours to Canada. In addition, throughout the training modules, specific efforts were made to include local Latvian expertise including the sharing of locally developed probation tools such as presentence reports and risk/needs assessments. While based on the translation of these tools during past pilot projects, through the training seminars, senior officials and community leaders worked to develop new formats and substantive reporting guidelines to meet the needs of the nascent service. A wide variety of styles were utilized throughout the training sessions including: lectures, problem-based learning scenarios, work groups, role-plays, and experiential exercises drawn from restorative justice principles and practices.

6.3.1 *Interactive Training and Skill Development*

A significant Canadian contribution to knowledge transfer is that effectiveness in technical assistance requires more than technical expertise. Kealey and Protheroe (1995) argued that to be effective Canadian trainers had to understand the importance of curiosity, respect, the involvement of local experts and mutual learning. It was not always easy for trainers to work as part of a long distance team. One trainer suggested:

> Joining the project in its later stages came with its own challenges. I was concerned I could cause confusion if I appeared to contradict preceding advisors or indeed lose my audience altogether if I insensitively presented information that had already been considered and rejected by our Latvian hosts. To that end I vividly remember pulling "all nighters" preceding virtually every session in an attempt to incorporate local knowledge/context into the content of my presentations. While I have had the privilege to continue my involvement with the SPS, the lessons learned from these initial experiences have continued to guide all subsequent interactions with my Latvia colleagues.

One way to address the challenges of language and communication, and regional variances between and among participants was to focus on developing relationships amongst project participants and designing learning opportunities through interactive training techniques. In the Latvian project, training groups considered how to develop pre-sentence reports and create plans for clients under supervision and put themselves in the place of their future clients. To understand the value of each of these theories to a more interactive approach, it is important to understand that participants in the training had grown up and been educated under the Soviet model of education. Teaching in the former Soviet Union was based on a highly prescriptive pedagogy and a uniform curriculum. Slogans placed above classroom blackboards stated "What is good for the country is good for you," and teachers and students were closely monitored. In terms of pedagogy, the emphasis was on passive knowledge, rote learning, and the memorization of facts (Davydov, 1988). Few teachers let students express their own ideas or opinions and there was little self-directed learning. As a result students acquired few critical thinking skills, and had little experience with student-centric models of participatory education and experiential learning (Dundua, 2003).

Many participants spoke of the utility of the seminars that provided practical exercises and drew comparisons between learning styles: "...the shift in learning styles from authoritarian to interactive and participatory [through the project] was initially difficult." These participants identified "...role-plays, interactive exercises...client focused small group work sessions" as the most important elements within the training seminars. A number of participants spoke about activities in which groups were given facts and constructed treatment options for clients. In these sessions, role-plays were used to help future probation officers practice developing "...presentence reports, assess risks and client needs, and also for working with difficult clients." These tools were part of what participants saw as the "...sharing of the case management approach," and the report and assessment exercises and the tools that resulted were seen as the most useful aspect of Canadian training. Participants specifically identified the adaptation of the presentence forms by Latvians in the training sessions as important in the "...development of a Latvian supervision model" and a "...change in mentality about justice."

Other participants identified the interviewing exercises as very useful in assisting them to be able "...to start a conversation" and "work with difficult clients." Of some interest was the different ways the participants viewed the various exercises and tools that were delivered trough the training. In the process of thinking through how best to adapt things like pre-sentence reports and risk assessments for use in the Latvian context, arguments within the group took place about the amount of discretion that should be relied upon during their use. Community members who had been involved in the pilot projects argued for the need to consider numerous factors in the development of presentence reports and remain flexible in their use of risk/needs assessments. Government officials and participants drawn from police and prison administration favoured far more formulistic approaches, arguing that one standard should be applied equally to each offender.

This points to an inherent challenge within international technical assistance. While training activities can transfer knowledge, build skills and provide an entry point to facilitate greater inter-institutional cooperation and collaboration in criminal justice (Protic, 2005), it often fails to properly engage with civil society and focuses on senior officials instead of front line officers. Through these more experiential-based training activities, participants considered how their personal experiences had shaped their assumptions, expectations and even the way they interacted with others. By individualizing general and abstract concepts such as punishment, shame, fear, and second chances, those within the group were encouraged to discuss, debate, and consider the role of law in society.

6.3.2 *Experiential Learning and Participation*

Another aspect to international training concerns the importance of mentoring, job shadowing, and performance evaluation along with other alternative approaches to training (Dandurand *et al.* 2008, pp. 64-65). A recurrent theme among all those involved in the training in Latvia was the acknowledgement that significant differences existed even at the most basic level about how Canadians and Latvians thought about crime, punishment, rehabilitation and reintegration. This acknowledgement required that adjustments be made in the delivery of core concepts related to Probation. Both Latvian and Canadian participants identified the training as successful when it went beyond the presentation of facts and figures and used participatory training approaches to engage participants through group activities. These included role-plays, group based scenarios, and the participation of local experts who presented on the reform experiences of their communities. For some Canadian trainers, these exercises "...allow[ed] trust to be built amongst participants" and provided valuable insight into some of the "...informal impediments" to justice reform.

A striking number of participants later recalled with some specificity experiential exercises drawn from the restorative justice movement. This suggests these exercises may have served as an important means considering more profoundly the challenges associated with the concept of discretion. Delivered by Liz Elliott, Lana Maloney, Michelle Joubert, Jane Lutes and Julian Hermida these sessions focused on three common themes presented in Figure 6.2.

Figure 6.2 Common themes in RJ training

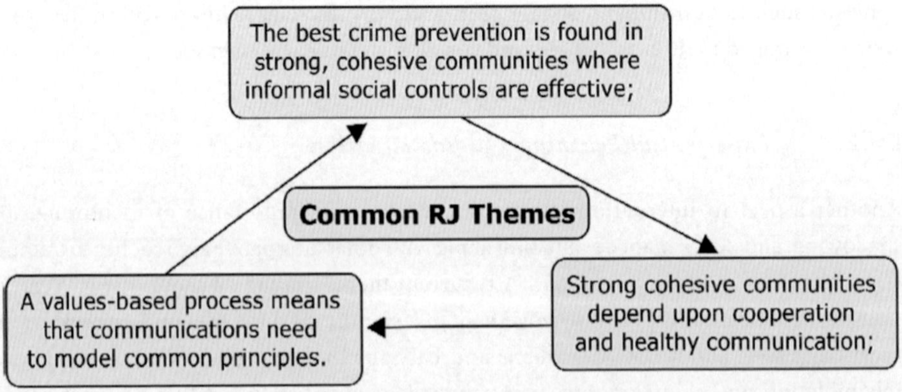

While more general interactive exercises were used as introductions and ice-breakers, exercises based on elements drawn from restorative practices, such as dialogue circles, were also used to promote participatory debriefs following different group activities. In these debriefs and wrap ups, everyone took a turn to speak through the use of a mutually agreed-upon "talking piece." Some Latvian participants spoke about the initial difficulty of "staying quiet" when listening to a speaker with whom they did not agree. Some of these discussions were spurred by the focus in the RJ sessions on how laws reflect values. These sessions introduced the concepts of *probity,* or the sense of empathy for others' moral right to maintain ownership of their belongings without concern of theft, and *pity* which refers to empathy for others' moral right to be physically safe and healthy. An integral series of conversations explored the extent to which the process of law is also premised on these values.

Other exercises focused on value-based interviewing designed to provide an experience of interviewing one and another and beginning to understand the importance of the stories people tell, and putting oneself in the shoes of another. Participants were asked to reflect on what was it like to have people listen to their stories, whether they felt safe to tell their stories, and how probation clients might feel in similar situations. Following the exercise the group worked together to develop common values that should guide the interviewing process. During the final debrief participants were asked to reflect upon the idea that unless people come to peace with themselves they may find the very personally challenging work of the justice system far more difficult.

In several sessions, restorative justice based exercises were used to highlight how difficult, emotional, or stress-related environments or situations can alter one's actions or responses. While a new concept for many participants, many recounted the experiential nature of the exercises in great detail. The ways in which the Latvian participants interacted through the group exercises, came to consensus or did not, often provided important what were called "...clarifying moments" for Canadian trainers. Moments of disagreement during group exercises, usually around what new concepts meant, often led to more meaningful discussion about the similarities and differences in how participants understood a given concept. Many Latvian participants also noted the training approach as useful. Some specifically identified the seminars that provided practical and participatory exercises as the most important element within the training seminars. These included interactive exercises and client-focused small group sessions in which facts were provided and participants constructed treatment options for clients. Some exercises had a very practical impact. According to a senior SPS Headquarters official:

> ...mediation is now a part of SPS functions and we use some examples from Canada, although most from Czech and Norway experience. Some exercises are being used in mediation training sessions in prison and schools, led by probation officers.

The Latvians acknowledged the adaptive ability of Canadian trainers, whom they described as having an ability to "change [the] training program" as required, and address emergent questions and concerns as they arose. Attempts to encourage more critical and self reflective examinations of their experiences, beliefs, and expectations also encouraged participants to become more involved in the training sessions. The idea that people could participate through a process of developing justice reforms and revisiting the rules within the legal system become more acceptable. The RJ sessions specifically focused on the idea that the reform process was an opportunity to be attentive to the values espoused by society at large and the participants in the room. These kinds of approaches may be valuable when attempting to uncover some of the more informal impediments to reform including the underestimation of the role of powerful interests in developing countries and the mischaracterization of the interrelation of legal and social challenges to reform (Chodosh, 2005, pp. 79-82). For Canadian trainers, these participatory training exercises assisted in developing a "human connection" among Canadians and Latvians and tested the "personal dynamics" at play among the agencies in the room. Indeed, all respondents made clear statements about the role of relationships within the project.

6.3.3 *The Role of Relationships*

A core aspect of relationship development for Canadian trainers was related to social interactions framed around Latvian cultural events. These included evenings in the sauna, the frequent singing and playing of music at gatherings, visits to historic sites, and meeting the friends and families of the Latvian participants. These interactions also seemed to include an attempt to understand the complexity of life in Latvia. Canadian participants identified the stark poverty in the streets of Riga and were cognizant of the relative poverty of the Latvian participants. Many identified conversations with Latvian participants about the differences between life today and life during 'Soviet times' as a useful mechanism to begin to appreciate some of the social processes that operate outside the formal legal rules. Common reflections focused on the relationships that formed both through the formal delivery of project activities and through the social exchanges and events that were part of Latvian culture. For many Canadian trainers: "...without relationships no knowledge transfer was possible. They can make or break training sessions."

Often overlooked, it is these relationships that provided a basis for difficult discussions about crime, justice, and the purpose and goals of Latvian probation. For the Latvians, the role of the Canadian trainers was almost universally expressed as positive. Identified as "friends and colleagues," trainers provided background information about approaches taken in Canada and shared both successes and failures. Latvians identified the Canadians as "...open, friendly and humble." The trainers "...presented without forcing ideas" and it was up to Latvians to "take what they wanted." Some spoke of Canada as their "second country" and suggested Latvians and Canadians were "...somehow soul relatives." As one senior official suggested:

> ...unlike trainers from other countries they [Canadians] took time to learn about Latvia. You know, sometimes we feel like trainers from outside Latvia are telling us what to do...Canadians only asked, how can we help?

Others were more critical and suggested that the Canadian trainers were sometimes "...too naïve" and suggested that for Latvians more "...formal, hierarchical and 'get tough' approaches were required to get through to [us]." Various constraints were also identified. These included the limited time spent in country, the cultural and linguistic differences, and the difficulty in avoiding traditional and hierarchical expert/learner roles. Yet the "...special feeling" many of the Latvian participants had for Canada and Canadians seemed to help overcome these challenges and allowed participants to trust, ask for clarification when needed, and participate in exercises that were for many a new experience. As one Latvian participants stated "...we trusted them [Canadians] and this made working easier...we had to participate in sometimes strange exercises...but it was ok...it was good."

For the Canadians, being a trainer in Latvia was associated with some sort of personal or professional growth, and three trainers suggested it was one of the most "...rewarding times of their professional career." They were uncomfortable with identifying themselves as "experts" and preferred to see their role as presenting information, based on a "serve yourself buffet" style of operational models, approaches, and programs. For many, participation in the project was a chance to share "information" and the experience gained through a "lifelong learning" in the field of criminal justice in Canada. Working in Latvia appeared to foster both the recognition of the assumptions that informed their understanding of justice and an appreciation for the Canadian system.

While some Canadians remained involved in post project programming funded by the Latvian Ministry of Justice, others have remained informally in touch through material donations of time and equipment. Many saw the opportunity to share their thoughts and experiences with a group so eager to make changes as a "privilege and honor" and extremely "humbling," especially when compared to the more "...complacent and cynical attitude to justice reform sometimes found in Canada." Those who continued to work with the SPS beyond the completion of the project in 2005, are perhaps better able to assess the role of Canada and Canadians in a new light. Some spoke about being able to "...re-evaluate and reconsider principles, policies, and desired outcomes of the project in the light of Latvian experience developing the SPS." This additional insight into the achievements in Latvia included the view that, as one Canadian stated:

> ...the Latvians have, with little money or experience, made great strides in reforming their system by relying upon community examples and taking best practice from around the world. In some ways, I think Canada has a lot to learn from them.

During a November 2003 trip to British Columbia, two SPS senior staff visited a number of probation offices, community based programs and training institutes in British Columbia. Organized by Robert Watts these visits included meetings with representatives from the Provincial government, including the Community Corrections Branch, trainers from the Justice Institute of British Columbia, and more social visits with former project staff. Long after the project was completed, the SPS visited British Columbia and found funds to connect key staff from the Justice Institute and others who have worked with British Columbian government to the SPS. Most recently, through a grant from the Norwegian government, the SPS has begun a process to revamp and upgrade the way in which it assesses, treats, and manages sexual offenders.

Perhaps unsurprisingly given the personal relationships established with Canada going back more than a decade, when the SPS sought additional training, they approached the Justice Institute of British Columbia on the use of the RNR model, and specifically how it can be applied to community supervision, and new risk assessments on sex offending. As discussed earlier, a recent development has been the provision of training from specialists from Victoria, BC on a restorative supervision model called Circles of Support & Accountability (COSA). COSA is a prisoner reentry program that works with high-risk sex offenders for individuals who struggle with inappropriate sexual attraction to vulnerable populations, including children. It involves trained volunteers from the community who gather around an ex-offender to monitor, support, and reduce the potential for sexual re-offending. The approach used in COSA represents perhaps the most unique and intensive programming that relies upon community participation. Despite its potential and perhaps because of the political nature of sex crimes, it is not a program widely used around the world. Once again Latvia is leading the way in the Baltics and is one of a few services in Europe seeking to involve communities in emergent and specialized models of supervision. It may be that the restorative approach by some of the Canadians has had broader impacts than is often associated with traditional training models.

6.4 Understanding Learning in International Development

There may be no such thing as a neutral education process. Education either functions as an instrument to facilitate conformity among individuals or promotes the integration of individual experience into the present system (Mayo, 1999). This presents challenges for international training missions that seek to share ideas rather than instill a singular view of what are complex problems. Based on the work of Swedish cognitive scientist Peter Gärdenfors (2010), there are four main perspectives on learning. Each can be connected to the kind of learning that occurs and the pedagogical method that often results. Table 6.3 below has been adapted, but retains the essential meaning of the original.

Table 6.3 Basic Perspectives in Learning (Gärdenfors, 2010, p. 121)

Perspective	Form of Knowledge	Learning Method
Learners who do	Know how	Imitation
Learners who know	Know that	Acquire Facts
Learners who think	Know why	Construct new knowledge
Learners who research	Know how to know	Manage their own learning

Using this framework, in early stages of development, learners understand how to do something by imitating others around them. Later, they begin to know things about the world by acquiring facts and comparing and contrasting existing knowledge presented to them. Through the construction of new knowledge learners' cognitive abilities grow and they begin to think for themselves and understand why the world operates as it does. Finally, learners who begin manage their own learning, apply and challenge existing knowledge and their own past beliefs. By thinking critically about the ways in which our past experience informs our current way of thinking, new kinds of personal connections can be made.

As Canada's national representative of Canadian universities, the Association of Universities and Colleges of Canada technical cooperation division made a lot of use of Canadian educators to share knowledge abroad. One attempt to identify best practice through University based partnerships is through the University Partnership and Cooperation in Development (UPCD) program. Since its launch in 1994, the UPCD program has funded a number of projects throughout the developing world in an array of disciplines – including education, natural sciences and the humanities – through University based partnerships. As part of its management of the University Partnerships in Cooperation and Development (UPCD) program, AUCC developed a number of resources to identify best practice and to support team members in the design and implementation of technical assistance projects. A number of lessons emerged through this international experience.

One lesson relates to problem-based learning (PBL). Based on a constructivist account of how people learn, this approach is based on understanding how interactions shape learning when the goals of the learner are central to the learning process. PBL advocates a system of learning which situates education within authentic activities in which students learn by solving problems and reflecting upon their experiences. These approaches are popular in courses at medical and business schools (Barrows, 1985; Williams, 1993) and research suggests that students participating in these kinds of learning activities are more motivated to learn, and see what they learn as more useful and easier to apply (Blumenfeld, *et al.*, 1991; Hmelo, 1995). Placing the learner front and center and using practical education models requires a focus on learning styles.

Experiential learning techniques include a rich variety of interactive practices whereby participants, as actively and personally engaged in the process, have opportunities to learn from their own and each others' experiences. For Kolb (1984), Experiential Learning Theory (ELT) provides a model of the learning process that emphasizes the central role that experience plays in learning. ELT argues for an integration of cognitive and behaviourial learning theories, with other approaches that recognize the formative role of affect, context, and subjective experience within the learning process. Combining Dewey's philosophical pragmatism, Lewin's social psychology, and Piaget's cognitive-developmental genetic epistemology, ELT begins with a central premise that:

> Simple perception of experience alone is not sufficient for learning; something must be done with it. Similarly, transformation alone cannot represent learning, for there must be something to be transformed, some state or experience that is being acted upon (Kolb, 1984, p. 42).

Through ELT, learning is seen as a process of resolving conflicts between two opposed dimensions. The *prehension* dimension is how an individual grasps experience and includes two ways to approach the question of knowledge, ranging from unconscious, intuitive experience based on tacit knowledge to a more conscious and acknowledged comprehension of the experience. The *transformation dimension* entails the conversion of this experience through reflective observation and active experimentation and is either based on an active orientation possessed by those willing to take risks and to learn from errors or failure, and those with a more reflective orientation, preferring to transform experiences through reflective observation. Taken together these dimensions to learning are part of a complex process and differ according to which end of the two dimensions learners inhabit.

Based on these dimensions, Kolb has identified four learning styles (Kolb, 1984; Kolb, 1999). Some prefer to work in groups and integrate differing opinions into a coherent structure; others prefer readings, lectures, exploring analytical models and theories to interacting with others. Some prefer to experiment with new ideas, simulations, laboratory assignments, and practical applications, rather than learn from people; others prefer to work with others to get assignments done, to set goals, to do field work, and to test out different approaches to completing a project. Once recognized, these learning styles cannot be ignored because different types of learners do better with different types of educational approaches. As depicted in Figure 6.4, immediate or concrete experiences are the basis for observations and reflections. These reflections are assimilated and distilled into abstract concepts from which new implications for action can be drawn (Kolb, 1984: 141). Meaningful learning involves engaging both concrete and abstract knowing.

Figure 6.4 Mapping Experiential Learning

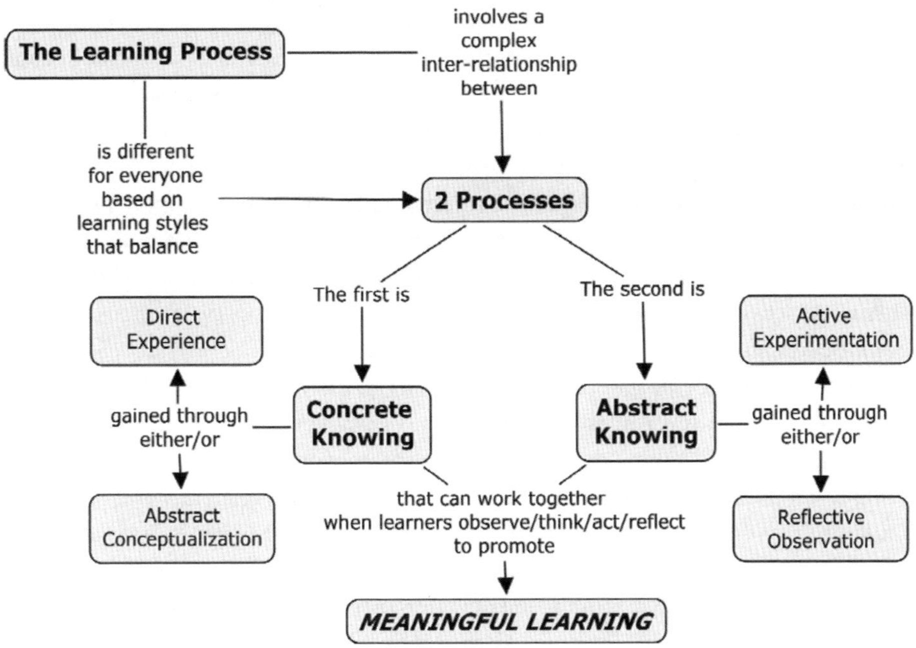

The recognition that differing styles of learning exists requires more than relying on the prescriptive pedagogies of the past. In the place of traditional trainer-directed approaches that rely on structured lessons or lecture formats and the passive learning that often results, is the need to consider deeper individual questions that arise through the training. Tony Hobbs provides a useful example of the problem.

> If student nurses or doctors are taught about how to encounter dying patients or their relatives and the information is imparted to them in a teacher-directed mode, they do not have the necessary opportunity to reflect on their own thoughts and possible fears of death and examine such deep feelings together with their peers in the first place. In such cases they do not learn how their own fears of death might affect the quality of their work with such people (Hobbs, 1992, p. 14).

The need to examine one's own thoughts and feelings in medical care settings is no less important for front line justice practitioners. Of importance here is that integrated learning occurs best when learners move through the learning cycle based on their individual style and engage in the complementary modes of knowing as described above. Sheckley, Allen

& Keeton argue "what learners 'know' influences what they 'experience' and conversely what they 'experience' influences what they 'know'" (1994, pp. 60-61).

For international legal technical assistance projects, this may be relevant to understand how training sessions may be about more than simple skill acquisition. By exposing people to different experiences through role-plays and other kinds of interactive training activities, participants can identify and perhaps challenge their own preconceptions, beliefs, and assumptions. The purpose of training, then, becomes an educative process that provides individuals with the tools to engage in a project of reflection, and evaluation. By creating the conditions under which people can be exposed to new ideas that make the once familiar appear different or even strange, cognitive dissonance for those participating within interactive and experiential exercises can occur. When properly facilitated, this can provide participants with new and unexpected insights. Experience provides context and reflection can provide insight. While Kolb points to Dewey, Lewin, and Piaget, other approaches drawn from criminology may also be relevant (Wheeldon, 2009).

Social learning is learning that occurs as a function of observing, retaining, and replicating behaviour observed in others. In social learning, one's reference group plays an integral role in the way in which one learns social norms (Einstadter & Henry, 1995, p. 179). These social structures affect social psychological processes in individuals and the role of positive and negative reinforcement within social structures plays a formative role in the development of social learning (Akers, 2004). Social learning theory may be useful because it so clearly provides a basis for the view that learning is principally a social endeavor. Applied to cross-cultural training approaches (Black & Mendenhall, 1990), through modeling, interaction and positive reinforcement training and education take on a new dimension.

In addition, the contributions of moral development provide a key insight into what areas training should target and how it might be practically delivered. Moral development, first described by Kohlberg (1974) and later reformulated by Gibbs (1979) explores how people develop internal moral and ethical standards. Palmer (2003) has identified various attempts to promote moral development through specific programming. While tested in prison environments (Arbuthnot & Gordon, 1988; Bonta & Andrews, 2003), moral development exercises can also include role-playing and dialogue for other groups, outside the prison walls (Ross *et al.* 1988). Restorative practices might also be seen in the light of moral development and experiential learning. Minor and Morrison (1996) have also argued along these lines suggesting that restorative justice practices may be able to further moral development by emphasizing mutual problem-solving, communication, negotiation, compromise and responsibility. In Canada, Liz Elliott (2011) has argued meaningful change requires that we participate in the processes that affect our lives. She suggests, this is:

> …more likely to invigorate the sense of civic responsibility in people that helps build community. The potential of this aspect of restorative justice has been under-explored, having been shadowed by the general absorption of restorative justice programs under the criminal justice imperatives (pp. 204-205).

If moral stage advancement emerges as individuals are confronted with real dilemmas, then it is not simply a matter of maturation or socialization. Instead 'social experiences can promote development…when they stimulate our mental processes' (Crain, 1985, p. 126). One reading of Kohlberg suggests that as we are challenged, we develop through an increased competence in balancing conflicting value-claims. By exposing individuals to morally significant questions, trainers can support discussions designed to allow the parties to understand and clarify those norms and values that are shared, disputed, or confusing (Van Ness & Strong, 1997). By questioning one's own views and being challenged to justify these views, individuals are motivated to come up with new, more comprehensive positions through reflexive thinking exercises (Ross *et al.* 1988). The point is not to resolve all issues in which moral divergence operates, but instead to allow differences to emerge and model a process by which these disagreements can remain respectful.

Another way to understand how these theories might work together is to consider the work of Paulo Freire. Identifying with more critical approaches to education and participatory models of development, Freire (1970) argued that education should encourage individuals to take responsibility for their own potential. By thinking critically about the ways in which past experience informs our current way of thinking, one can forge new sorts of personal connections. Because people can act as oppressors or as liberators, Freire emphasized that the purpose of education is to create autonomous persons who engage with a project of emancipation. By creating environments where individuals can reflect on their own behaviour in social situations and consider real life scenarios, education becomes a cycle of engaging a theory, applying it, and reflecting on it to augment the original theoretical starting point.

This iterative approach to learning may flatten traditional expert/learner dichotomies used through traditional training programs and education and has been used in a variety of international settings. In the health sectors in Brazil, Bolivia, and Chile this approach to training has enabled individuals to be active participants in the learning process and to become dedicated agents of change. Díaz & Cabral (2007, p. 162) state this approach:

> …takes into account the life experience, knowledge, expectations and self-esteem of learners and addresses cognitive, cultural and affective aspects including the feelings that emerge during the training process. Participants are expected to develop a greater sense of self-awareness and autonomy as well as a common sense of solidarity.

Together these theories may provide justification for the training model employed in Latvia. While more study is necessary in order to understand the value and applicability of this approach, the need to build relationships through participatory processes is integral to the development of a core team of reformers from a variety of justice sectors within the host country. If indeed learning occurs through social interaction it may require that deliberation and debate be supported because:

> ...change is produced not by simply changing management systems and structures, but involves meaningful and value laden interaction of complex individual human beings. (Schuck, 2000, p. 181)

In the Latvia project, there is evidence that, through common experiences, study tours, social gatherings, and inclusive project coordination, a small group of reformers can have a large impact.

6.5 Counter Views and Contrarian Considerations

There are a number of possible objections to the suggestion that the training models in Latvia are useful for future justice programming. One is connected to the discussion in Chapter 4 and based on the view that the selection of Canada as a foreign partner was based on the role of Baltic diaspora, and past Canadian programming. Thus, Latvia did not choose the best country as a role model, but made a selection based on a limited number of informal contacts and the initiative of AUCC and CIDA. Randma-Liiv & Kruusenberg (2010) argue that these factors limited the choice to existing contacts and resulted in insufficient consideration of potential role models.

This might be attributed to the role of relationships developed through the project. Unlike other projects, Canadian staff and some trainers lived in Latvia for months and even years. They established personal relationships with officials from the Ministry of Justice, and were embedded within the Latvian communities in ways that perhaps are not feasible in other projects or countries. The role of relationships was also relevant when one considers the small number of government officials were involved in making major decisions concerning the models, training, and policies to be transferred. According to Randma-Liiv & Kruusenberg (2010, p. 15):

> This represents a broader problem in new democracies – insufficient institutionalization of policy-making allows individuals (most often individual civil servants or influential policy middlemen) to assume a significant role and creates considerable risks in the policy-making process, including policy transfer. In

several cases, personal contacts of actors from the importer jurisdiction determined the circle of countries considered as role models.

Yet, viewed another way, this may simply require that far more attention be paid to the ways in which relationships between trainers, participants, experts, and learners collectively shape subsequent reforms. While there must always be a role for critical, searching and broad-based theoretical debates, the simplistic dichotomy between expert and learner in international development is outdated. More in depth, academic, and inclusive empirical study is needed about the role of these interactions. There is no doubt Latvian-Canadian relationships were important in the success of the project, but it may be useful to ask, if not Canada, what country *should* have worked with Latvia? How can one say with certainty that the factors that led Latvia to cooperate with Canada to develop their probation service were not positive in the end?

Another problem, perhaps the opposite of the one above, is that in the rush to leave the Baltics, opportunities for longer term collaboration was missed. In 2004, CIDA appeared eager to wrap up project activities in time for what was called 'Baltic graduation' – a pejorative term borrowed from the American programming in the region (Wedel, 1998). Latvian and Canadian Participants, and senior probation officials felt the project had ended too quickly and were surprised when an expressed desire to continue to partner with Canada was not continued. Many suggested that the Canadians should have "...stayed on and assisted as mentors." One approach might have been to focus more on establishing a culture of research within the project. The need for detailed, credible, and peer reviewed research in Latvia is three-fold. One area of importance is the validation of existing tools including risk and needs assessments, pre-sentence reports, probation programs, and supervision models. While there is growing concern about their use in other countries (Kemshall, 2004), local studies are needed to assess the use of these tools in the Latvian context.

Another issue is the growing concern about the role of western-based expertise in developing local legitimacy (Dezalay & Garth, 2010). These critiques suggest expert knowledge has played an integral role in the formation of the transition states and pushed a neoliberal agenda of decentralization, privatization, and individualization (Phillips & Ilcan, 2004). Rarely neutral or unbiased, external actors use their expertise and influence to order social relations and may continue to shape domestic political and economic power relations based on long held assumptions from colonial times (Mitchell, 2002). The line between facilitation and imposition is a fine one.Cultural superiority and arrogance must be resisted when finding ways to promote more critical reflections about the role of punitive approaches in Latvia.

Finally, supporting a culture of research would be especially valuable to understanding the use of exercises drawn from restorative principles and practices. Within Canada, the use of restorative principles that have influenced that nation's legislation, programs, and services (Roach, 1997), represents a trend of trying to restore a greater sense of democracy at the community level (Burtch, 1992). Although many in the Latvia project recalled these activities as central to the training program, it can be dangerous to open up discussions and dialogue, to flatten traditional hierarchies based on cultural norms, and to promote the democratization of education and training. Peeling back the lid of societies historically living under certain forms of control can lead to unexpected and sometimes ugly outcomes.

One reply may be that this ugliness is a necessary part of reform, and that to continue to keep unpopular views under wraps is more dangerous than allowing them to surface and facilitate a conversation about the implications that may result. This is a good answer in some ways but requires a certain level of skill and ability around facilitating such a dialogue. These skills are not easily acquired and there is danger when amateurs attempt to guide these processes. An unsuccessful example concerns an early mediation effort organized by a Canadian volunteer. In 2000, a young person had committed a property crime, and the juvenile probation service had negotiated with the police to hold a mediation in a circle, with relevant community members participating. Typically, restorative processes require a great deal of attention be paid to setting the space, ensuring participants understand the goals, the rules, and the process. These include the idea that while an individual should be held accountable and hear from the people he or she has harmed, the ultimate goal is to allow this person to come to their own conclusions about their actions and what they might do to make amends. The space should never be hijacked to shame or demean.

Unfortunately, in this one case, this is what happened. Participants around the circle each took turns telling the young man how bad he was, how bad his actions were, and threatening worse outcomes if he did not change his behavior. While this occurred in the early years of the pilot projects on youth probation, it had a profound effect in the community, and undermined efforts for years. Restorative justice has a unique power to allow people to recognize how their actions impacted others. Its power must be respected. When the process is not properly facilitated, it can have the effect of substituting formal punishment with informal judgment. In a small community, this may do far more harm than many expect.

6.6 Concluding Remarks

The LLRP represented the most targeted and specific justice programming to date by CIDA in the Baltic States. The project consolidated partnerships in Latvia and assisted to draft and reform existing laws, support the development of probation, and train a corps of Latvia's first probation officers. Identified by Kealey *et al.* (2005) as the most important element of international project success, significant individual challenges exist for successful knowledge transfer and training in legal technical assistance projects. In Latvia, these included the challenge of communication, differences within training groups, and cultural differences about the role of punishment. Just as pilot projects have the potential to model more inclusive and community based reform models at the organizational level, this chapter argued that more interactive approaches to training and technical assistance assisted to overcome individual and personal impediments to reform. Well-designed training activities can create specific opportunities for selected individuals to become more involved in criminal justice reform process.

By considering how to develop pre-sentence reports and create plans for clients under supervision, Latvian probation officers had to put themselves in the place of their future clients. In addition the use of experiential exercises drawn from the restorative justice movement allowed participants to consider more deeply the influence of one's past on one's future and challenged simplistic conceptions of right and wrong. Associated with the concept of discretion, this approach led some participants to consider other viewpoints. Through multiple interactions with others, participants in these sessions explored how to evaluate their own views more carefully. These activities may have additional benefits.

Social learning and moral development theories suggest another way to understand why training courses that included interactive and relevant group-based exercises were useful. Through group work, role-taking, and role-playing, problem-solving strategies were considered, accepted and rejected. In addition, participants appeared to value the use of exercises drawn from the restorative justice movement including the use of circles in the openings and debriefs of each training day and ceremonial closings at the end of training modules. Through specifically planned social events based on Latvian culture trainers were given a first-hand and often uncensored experience of both the challenges and potential within the group. This sort of personal interaction is not without risks. It may be that without taking these risks the broader debates that are required to develop and sustain reform are made more difficult or perhaps become not possible.

Chapter 6 Bibliography

N.R. Abramson & J.X. Ai. Canadian companies doing business in china: Key success factors. *Management International Review*, Vol. 39, No. 1, 1999, pp. 17-27.

R.L. Akers. *Criminological theories.* Los Angeles, CA: Roxbury Publishers, 2004.

Association of Universities and Colleges of Canada. *Latvian legal reform program: Report to CIDA*, 2005.

J. Arbuthnot & D.A. Gordon. Crime and cognition: Community applications of sociomoral reasoning development. *Criminal Justice and Behaviour*, Vol. 15, 1988, pp. 379-393.

I. Beeson & C. Davis. Emergence and accomplishment in organizational change. *Journal of Organizational Change Management*, Vol. 13, No. 2, 2000, pp. 178-189.

E. Berg. *Rethinking technical assistance cooperation: Reforms for the capacity building in Africa.* New York: United Nations Development Program, 1993.

A. Berzins. *Report to The Working Group on Probation in Latvia.* The Legal Reform Capacity Program in Latvia, Ottawa, ON: Association of Universities and Colleges of Canada, 2002.

M. Betz, L. O'Connell & J.M. Shepard. Gender differences in proclivity for unethical behavior. *Journal of Business Ethics*, Vol. 8, 1989, pp. 321-324.

B. Bjerregaard & V.B. Lord. An Examination of the Ethical and Value Orientation of Criminal Justice Students. *Police Quarterly*, Vol. 7, No. 2, 2004, pp. 262-284.

S. Black & M. Mendenhall. Cross-cultural training effectiveness: A review and a theoretical framework for future research. *The Academy of Management Review*, Vol. 15, No. 1, 1990, pp. 113-136.

J. Bonta & D.A. Andrews. A commentary on Ward and Stewart's model of human needs. *Psychology, Crime & Law*, Vol. 9, 2003, pp. 215-218.

Y. Brillon. *Ethnocriminology of Black Africa.* Montreal, PQ: University of Montreal Press, 1980.

B. E. Burtch. *The sociology of law: Critical approaches to social control.* Toronto, ON: Harcourt Brace Canada, 1992.

F.G. Castles. Introduction. In F.G. Castles (Ed.), *Families of Nations. Patterns of Public Policy in Western Democracies*, Dartmouth: Aldershot, 1993, pp. xii-xxii.

W. Channell. *Lessons not learned: Problems with western aid for law reform in postcommunist countries.* Washington, DC: Carnegie Endowment for Peace Paper No. 57, 2007.

S.R. Chatterjee. Relevance of traditional value frameworks in contemporary Chinese organizations: Implications for managerial transitions. *Journal of Human Values*, Vol. 7, No. 1, 2001, pp. 21-32.

H. Chodosh. *Global justice reform: A comparative methodology*. New York: New York University Press, 2005.

J.A Conser & G.D. Russell. *Law enforcement in the United States*. Gaithersburg, MD: Aspen, 2000.

W.C. Crain. *Theories of development*. New York: NY: Prentice Hall, 1985.

Y. Dandurand, C.T. Griffiths & V. Chin. Training and effective support of comprehensive justice and security reforms: Outcomes to date and lessons learned. In K. Aromaa, & S. Redo (Eds.), *For the rule of law: Criminal justice teaching and training @cross the world*. Helsinki: Fi: European Institute for Crime Prevention and Control, 2008.

M.L. Dantzker. *Understanding today's police*. Englewood Cliffs, NJ: Prentice Hall, 2000.

V.V. Davydov. Problems of developmental teaching: the experience of theoretical and experimental psychological research, *Soviet Education*, Vol. 30, No. 9, 1988, pp. 1-81.

Y. Dezalay & B. Garth. Marketing and Selling Transnational 'Judges' and Global 'Experts': Building the Credibility of (Quasi) Judicial Regulation. *Socio-Economic Review*. Vol. 8 No. 1, 2010, pp. 113-130.

Y. Dezalay & G. Bryant. Dollarizing state and professional expertise: transnational processes and questions of legitimation in state transformation, 1960-2000. *Revista Brasileira de Ciências Sociais*, Vol. 15 No. 43, 2000, pp. 163-176.

M. Díaz & M.F. Cabral. An innovative educational approach to capacity building and scaling up reproductive health services in Latin America. In R. Simmons, P. Fajans & L. Ghiron. *Scaling up health service delivery: From pilot innovations to policies and programmes*. Geneva, Sw: World Health Organization, 2007.

S. Dundua. The legacy of the Soviet Education System and attempts to introduce new methodologies of teaching in Georgia. *Child Education*, Vol. 79, No. 6, 2003, pp. 347-359.

W. Einstadter & S. Henry. *Theoretical criminology: An analysis of its underlying assumptions* (2nd ed.). London, UK: Rowman & Littlefield Publishers, 2006.

E. Elliot. *Security, With Care: Restorative Justice and Healthy Societies.* Halifax, NS: Fernwoord Publishing, 2011.

M. Evans. Understanding Policy Transfer. In M. Evans (Ed.), *Policy Transfer in Global Perspective.* Ashgate: Aldershot, 2004, pp. 10-42.

P. Freire. *Pedagogy of the Oppressed.* New York, NY: Continuum International Publishing Group, 2000.

P. Gärdenfors. *Lusten att förstå: Om lärande på människans villkor (in Swedish).* (The desire to understand: On learning in a human way). Stockholm: Natur & Kultur, 2010.

Goldstein, H. *Policing a free society.* Philadelphia, PA: J.B. Lippincott, 1977.

C. Griffiths, Y. Dandurand & V. Chin. Development assistance and police reform: Programming opportunities and lessons learned. *The Canadian Review of Policing Research,* Vol. 2, 2005, pp. 101-113.

G.R. Gibbs, S. Friese & W.C. Mangabeira. The use of new technology in qualitative research. *Forum Qualitative Social Research,* Vol. 3, No. 2, 2002, pp. 1-3.

L. Hammergren. *Envisioning Reform Improving Judicial Performance in Latin America.* Penn State Press: University Park, PA, 2007.

F. Hawes & D. Kealey. An empirical study of Canadian technical assistance: Adaptation and effectiveness on overseas assignments. *International Journal of Intercultural Relations,* Vol. 1, No. 5, 1981, pp. 239-258.

G. Helmke & S. Levitsky. Informal Institutions and Comparative Politics: A Research Agenda. *Perspectives on Politics.* Vol. 2, No. 4, 2004, pp. 725-740.

T. Hobbs. *Experiential Training: Practical Guidelines.* Routledge, London: UK, 1992.

D. Kealey, D. Protheroe, D. MacDonald & T. Vulpe. Re-examining the role of training in contributing to international project success: A literature review and an outline of a new model training program. *International Journal of Intercultural Relations*, Vol. 29, 2005, pp. 289-316.

D. Kealey. A study of cross-cultural effectiveness: Theoretical issues, practical applications. *International Journal of Intercultural Relations*, Vol. 13, 1989, pp. 387-428.

D. Kealey. *Cross-cultural effectiveness, A study of Canadian technical advisors overseas.* Gatineau, PQ: CIDA Briefing Centre, 1990.

D. Kealey. The challenge of international personnel selection. In D. Landis, & R.S. Bhakat (Eds.), *Handbook of intercultural training* (2nd ed.). Thousand Oaks, CA: Sage Publications, 1996, pp. 81-105.

Kealey, D. (2001). *Cross-cultural effectiveness – A study of Canadian technical advisors overseas.* Gatineau, PQ: Centre for Intercultural Learning, Canadian Foreign Service Institute, 2001.

D.J. Kealey & D.R. Protheroe. *Cross-cultural collaborations: Making north-south cooperation more effective.* Hull, Québec: Centre for Intercultural Learning, Canadian Foreign Service Institute, 1995.

D.J. Kealey & D.R. Protheroe. *Getting International Projects Right: A Challenge for the 21st Century.* Hull, Québec: Centre for Intercultural Learning, Canadian Foreign Service Institute, 2002.

H. Kemshall, P. Holt, R. Bailey & G. Boswell. Beyond programmes: organisational and cultural issues in the implementation of What Works. In G. Mair (Ed.), *What Matters in Probation.* Cullompton, UK: Willan, 2004, pp. 170-186.

H. Kemshall. *Risk in Probation Practice.* Hampshire, England: Ashgate, 1998.

L.G. Kelly. *The true interpreter: A history of translation theory and practice in the west.* New York: St. Martins Press, 1979.

J. Kleinig. *The Ethics of Policing.* New York: Cambridge University Press, 1976.

K. Knapp & A. Knapp-Potthoff. The Man (or Woman) in the Middle – Discoursal Aspects of Non-professional Interpreting. In K. Knapp, W. Enninger & A. Knapp-Potthoff (Eds.), *Analyzing Intercultural Communication.* Berlin: Mouton de Gruyter, 1987, pp. 181-211.

D.A. Kolb. *Experiential Learning*, Englewood Cliffs, NJ.: Prentice Hall, 1984.

A. Kolb & D.A. Kolb. Bibliography of Research on ELT and the Learning Style Inventory. Department of Organisational Behaviour, Weatherhead of School of Management. Cleveland, Ohio: Case Western Reserve University, 1999

L. Kohlberg. *Essays on moral development, vol. I: The philosophy of moral development.* London, UK: Harper and Row, 1981.

M. Lauristin. Contexts of transition. In M. Lauristin (Ed.), *Return to the western world: Cultural and political perspectives on the Estonian post-communist transition.* Tartu: Estonia: Tartu University Press, 1997, pp. 25-40.

Y.D. Luo & M. Chen. Does guanxi influence firm performance? *Asia Pacific Journal of Management*, Vol. 14, 1997, pp. 1-16.

K. Mandal. American Influence on Social Work Education in India and its Impact. *International Social Work*, Vol. 32, 1989, pp. 303-309.

P. Mayo. *Gramsci, Freire, and Adult Education: Possibilities for Transformative Action.* London, UK: Macmillan Press, 1999.

T. Mitchell. *Rule of experts: the techno-politics of modernization in Egypt.* New York: NY University Press, 2002.

K. Minor & J.T. Morrison. A theoretical study and critique of restorative justice. In B. Galaway & J. Hudson (Eds.), *Restorative justice: International perspectives.* Monsey, NY: Criminal Justice Press, 1996, pp. 117-133.

E.J. Palmer. *Offending Behaviour: Moral reasoning, Criminal Conduct and the Rehabilitation of Offenders.* Cullompton, UK: Willan Publishing, 2003.

L. Phillips & S. Ilcan. Capacity-Building: The Neoliberal Governance of Development. *Canadian Journal of Development Studies*, Vol. 25, No. 3, 2004, pp. 393-409.

D. Protic. Judicial reform in Serbia: Enhancing judicial performance through training. In EBRC (Ed.), *EBRC in transition 2005 courts and judges.* London: UK: European Bank of Reconstruction and Development, 2005, pp. 75-79.

T. Randma-Liiv & R. Kruusenberg. West-East policy transfer: motives, scope, role models and agents. Paper presented at IRSPM Conference held April 2-9, 2010, Berne, SW.

K. Roach. What's new and old about the legal process? *University of Toronto Law Journal*, Vol. 47, pp. 363-394.

E.M. Rogers. *Diffusion of innovations* (5th ed.). New York, NY: Free Press, 2005.

M. Rokeach. *The nature of human values.* New York: Free Press, 1973.

R.R. Ross, E.A. Fabiano & C.D. Ewles. Reasoning and Rehabilitation. *International Journal of Offender Therapy and Comparative Criminology*, Vol. 32, pp. 29-35.

A. Rotimi & S. Oloruntimehin. Teaching and Research Network in Africa in the field of Criminology. In M. Mushanga (Ed)., *Criminology in Africa.* Rome: UNICRI, 1992, pp. 243-255.

B. Sheckeley, G. Allen & M. Keeton. Adult learning as a recursive process. *Journal of Cooperative Education*, Vol. 28, No. 2, 1994, pp. 56-67.

P. Schuck. *The limits of law: Essays on democratic governance.* Boulder, CO: Westview Publishing, 2000.

J.H. Skolnick. Deception by police. In M.C. Braswell, B.R. McCarthy, & B.J. McCarthy (Eds.), *Justice, crime and ethics.* Cincinnati, OH: Anderson, 1999, pp. 57-82.

H. Spencer-Oatey & J. Xing. The impact of culture on interpreter behaviour. In H. Kotthoff & H. Spencer-Oatey (Eds.), *Handbook of Applied Linguistics* (HAL) Vol. 7. Intercultural Communication. Berlin: Mouton de Gruyter, 2007, pp. 219-236.

L.M. Sundstrom. Foreign assistance, international norms, and civil society development: Lessons from the Russian campaign. *International Organization*, Vol. 59, No. 2, 2005, pp. 419-449.

E.W. Taylor. A learning model for becoming interculturally competent. *International Journal of Intercultural Relations*, Vol. 18, No. 3, 1994, pp. 398-408.

M. Valverde. *Law's dream of a common knowledge.* Princeton: Princeton University Press, 2003.

D. Van Ness & K.H. Strong. *Restoring justice*. Cincinnati, OH: Anderson Publishing, 1997.

S. Walker. *The police in America: An introduction*. New York: McGraw-Hill, 1983.

J.R. Wedel. *Collision and collusion: The strange case of Western aid to Eastern Europe 1989-1998*. New York, NY: St. Martin's Press, 1998.

J. Wheeldon. *Mapping Knowledge Transfer: Latvian-Canadian Cooperation and Justice Reform*. Unpublished PhD Dissertation. Burnaby, BC: School of Criminology, Simon Fraser University, 2009.

C.R. Williams & B.A. Arrigo. *Ethics, Crime, and Criminal Justice*. Upper Saddle Rover, NJ: Prentice Hall, 2007.

Intermission 2: Looking Back and Moving Forward

As discussed in Chapter 3, one of the most important contributions to social science research in the last few decades has been the growing acceptance that all research is limited in one way or another. To address this concern, qualitative researchers study the experiences, influences, and activities of research participants, while explicitly considering personal and epistemological reflexivity to acknowledge their own biases. By exploring my own role in research, I must acknowledge that my conclusions and reflections are in many ways tentative – only educated guesses perhaps. There are many possible interpretations of the Latvia story. I can only do my best to present as much credible information as possible and situate my experience honestly. As I have shown, while sometimes the data confirm my theories, in other cases they appear to challenge it. Readers may not be convinced by my conclusions; hopefully, however, they will find the path I took to get there credible. Reflexive research requires an awareness of the researcher's contribution to the construction of meaning. While not comprehensive, in the first intermission I described how I became involved in this project as a young, inexperienced, and perhaps naïve post graduate.

In this section, I would like to consider some of the limitations of my research, of which there are a number. Of specific interest was how the Latvian participants viewed different training approaches and how they characterized the role and value of elements within the project. It may be that the research participants focused more on their positive experiences of the training. Rather than providing a practical outline of the most useful aspects of the legal technical assistance provided – from pilots to probation – my studies in this area are simply recording the Latvian's most memorable moments, alongside the aspirations of the Canadian participants. While it may be that memorable experiences and positive associations are inexorably linked to successful learning, without further study, this remains a supposition. Yet, the findings of this book suggest that the process of knowledge transfer in legal technical assistance appears more nuanced and complex than previously detailed. Few would doubt that positive learning environments result in better learning outcomes. It remains to be seen to what extent the experience in Latvia might be useful for countries emerging from conflict or attempting to democratize institutions twisted by authoritarian regimes.

As part of this narrative, I also presented some of the maps gathered through my research over the years. The maps served as a key mechanism to guide my interviews with Canadian trainers and Latvian participants, and perhaps provided some insight into how my colleagues and friends saw the project. They also might be seen as an important limitation. While the data from this book was based on interviews with more than fifty individuals, my interview questions were guided by and designed based on the visual maps collected from four Canadians and nineteen Latvians to design subsequent interviews. As a relatively new data collection tool, maps have both strengths and weaknesses that are still being assessed. While there is evidence that concept maps provide a useful and novel way to conceptualize knowledge and assist in the details and depth of responses of participants, they may not be perceived as acceptable methods of data collection among certain populations. While the graphic representation of experience may be useful for certain populations and individuals, it may alienate others. Although a majority appreciated the way the maps made them "think about all that had happened… and organize key events," some participants suggested completing a map was "…difficult, strange, and counterproductive." While the utility of the maps may have overcome their novelty for these participants, the potential for their broader application remains unclear.

A major limitation of this book is the extent to which the development of probation in Latvia can be applied to the Middle East. This is an important question and cannot be answered without data. As I discuss in some detail in the final chapter, the challenges and constraints in the countries of MENA are very different from those in the Baltics. There are, however, at least some similarities. If the question is how to develop civil society groups, promote inclusion, and engage in dialogue on questions of law and justice, probation offers an entry point. Although flexibility of probation provides reform results based on the needs, values, and approach of countries in which it is established, there is no guarantee that probation is a panacea or that even after millions of dollars and years in the region, reformers in Beirut can overcome the challenges observed elsewhere. David Perry and Randal Barrows speak about instituting probation through collaborative processes as a dream, a hope, and an aspiration. Probation programming, while a leap of faith, is one that Sweden, the United Kingdom, and the European Union are willing to make. I hope this book makes a small contribution to the important work these countries and individuals are undertaking.

A final and significant limitation relates to my role on the Latvia project. As discussed previously, I was centrally involved in all aspects of the project and my former role may have impacted the collection of data for this project in two important ways. The first relates to my relationship with the research participants. As discussed, it may be that certain participants, based on their relationship with me, sought to share only their more 'positive retrospections.' While questions were included which were designed to provoke more critical reflections, a key feature of my findings is the high level of satisfaction with the project amongst the project participants. A second relates to the possibility that my experience on the project influenced the themes identified in this book. While there is growing evidence about the need to consider country context, organizational constraints, and individual challenges to development assistance, some of my findings challenge existing orthodoxy within this field.

There may be no way to adequately address critics who charge that my role on the project stains the utility of the conclusions I have drawn – in some ways I agree. Yet my experience in Latvia and with project participants and Canadian trainers did suggest something more was happening than the translation of forms, manuals, and institutional policies. What was less clear was the interaction between the need for practical tools that could be used by future probation officers and the more personal aspects of training, learning, and interacting. The potential for this challenge to bias my view of the project is a serious one. Ideally, those involved with project delivery should never undertake evaluations of that same project. The potential for a conflict of interest and self-serving findings is too great. While it is likely that the LLRP would not have been otherwise studied, projects of this kind should be the exception and not the rule.

Ironically, if I am too close to events in Latvia, I am nowhere near close enough to the Middle East. Having never travelled or lived there, it is hard to understand the many complexities of the region as anything more than an academic exercise. In this case, I have attempted to defer to those with hands-on experience in the region. Through writing this book, I have met and corresponded with a number of trainers, consultants, and local groups working in the Middle East and North Africa. As someone who knows something the complications and difficulties they face, I wish them the very best of luck. When asked I have offered a few suggestions. The most important is to begin to engage communities from the outset. In training sessions, be sure to allow participants to provide feedback on the material, and what is happening in the room. Use these comments as a jumping off point. Do not assume what is being presented by trainers is the same as what is being understood by participants. Do not be afraid to throw out that day's lesson plan if an opportunity for a deeper and needed conservation emerges. Within institutions, it is important to define measure, work toward goals, and create a culture of research and learning. While the statistics year over year must be compared and analyzed, the people who do this work can offer other important insights. Narrative reflections matter too. One place to begin is the gathering of the visual and verbal experiences of those who worked collaboratively on justice projects. Limited, partial, and far from complete, these narratives and maps are an important starting places for the more complex analyses required to fully consider the potential for evidence based aid.

In addition to the detailed limitations provided above, there is another issue lurking behind the successes and failures of this project. Latvia has a long and sometimes proudly declared history of alcoholism. Learning about this legacy and its complicated place within Latvian society was perhaps one of the most challenging aspects about my time there. From quick nips in the Ministry of Justice as part of meetings to hosting dinners and parties that got out of hand, I was never more out of my element than trying to understand what was culturally appropriate and what was ignorant, arrogant, or abusive. Personal liaisons became complicated in some cases, and I did not always use good judgment in project affairs or my own relationships. Some consultants would leer and make inappropriate comments after a few drinks and others would not partake in the party at all. Both could complicate interactions. While I valued going for a drink or two with some of the consultants involved in the project as an easy way to debrief, I left Latvia with some mixed feelings. It is trite to say that alcohol abuse is a serious public health concern – but its ramifications have a ripple effect on projects, families and societies. It also can destroy individual lives.

Looking back, one event that might challenge the positive reports contained within this book occurred on the last day of the 2003 study tour to Canada. Two Latvian participants – one male, one female, one from the government, one from the community – started the day with a bottle of wine and by the time we gathered in the hotel lobby to check out and depart for the airport were drunk. I do not recall them making a scene, and I was either too exhausted after coordinating a two-week tour or not properly informed. I was sad to see them go but happy in the way only those who organize international study tours may understand. I put everyone on the plane, got in a cab and headed home. I had not made it to my door when I received a call from the embassy. The two individuals had been taken off the plane, despite their efforts to drop the names of some of the Canadians they had met during the tour. The caller informed me that they were with embassy staff. I panicked. Only that day, and after a lot of work, a story had appeared in the *Ottawa Citizen* about the tour, the project, and AUCC. It is only luck that no one at the airport put the story and the noisy Latvians, being escorted off the plane by security, together. I met with them later than night, and I was incredibly angry. One of them told me, "Now you know us, really. Now you know Latvia." It was an awful feeling.

Alcohol was also relevant in the loss of two very important individuals. One founded the first community service organization in Latvia and worked with former offenders in his small community for years before adequate funding and support was forthcoming. In 2003 he died of liver failure, months before probation was formally established. Another individual is still alive, for now. Having started the first wilderness therapy camps for juvenile offenders in Latvia, this individual worked long and hard to raise funds to bring Canadians to Latvia. He launched the first camp and trained a new generation of youth case-workers, to identify youth in the Cesis correctional facility and support them to succeed in various programs. Youth who complete the program on the inside got the opportunity to attend a wilderness therapy camp. The camp combined team work, trust exercises, reflection, and even elements of Latvian pagan spirituality.

A former offender himself, this individual sometimes struggled to complete the proper paperwork and file appropriate taxes. He also enjoyed a drink. This had caused problems with the Ministry of Justice before and these problems were reportedly increasing. During my last visit to Latvia, I travelled to meet him. Staggering and far too skinny, he immediately demanded a drink and promised to tell me whatever I wanted to hear. While it was clear I could not include him in my study, the most immediate concern to me was his wife and five children. When I mentioned this to former colleagues and friends in Latvia, the response was a shrug. This was common in Latvia, they suggested, and there was nothing to be done. This is a useful reminder that no matter the money, the design, or quality of technical assistance that is provided, there are structural, societal, cultural, and historic forces at work, which constrain all development initiatives. Yet, while some may suggest this is an example of why we ought to be reticent to support international endeavors, I do not subscribe to this sort of intellectual defeatism. While challenges exist, there is too much at stake to simply throw our hands in the air and give up.

Whatever the challenges in the local countries, it is clear that projects require meaningful cooperation and collaboration between two parties who respect one another. For this reason, neither Canada nor the United States may be well placed to attempt to coordinate probation programming in the countries of the Middle East and North Africa (MENA). Whatever the existing intentions of the United States, there is too much history, collusion, ongoing military entanglements, and charges and counter charges to truly facilitate open dialogue and constructive reform. The US should consider funding and offering expertise where requested but leaving the organization and coordination to countries with a better record in the region. The excellent work of the National Center for State Courts (NCSC) should continue and there are many foundations, think tanks, endowments, and other organizations that are doing important work in the region and beyond. The problem for more detailed involvement in probation is that US incarceration rates remain too high for anyone to take seriously the idea that American justice models should be emulated. While true leadership would fund "learn from our mistakes" tours, the price of foreign misadventures have limited the kind of development in the region that may have the most promise. While the US is on a path to reconcile their passion for punishment with the costs of these policies – economic, social, and philosophical – developments are slow and continue to frustrate efforts to connect evidence and policy-making. Many are discovering that "change" is far more difficult to implement that many had "hoped" and it is important that America find a more humble role for itself. The Middle East is a good place to start.

In Canada, there is a depressing irony in the notion that just as CIDA has developed the international experience and expertise to preach and teach the values of community corrections, the Federal Government of Canada is poised to undertake the huge expansion of prisons and importation of punitive and failed American-style justice polices. By embracing the nonsensical "get tough" on crime approach of the US, Canada's Conservative government will now implement a series of measures designed to increase the length of sentences and expand prisons at a time when the crime rate in Canada is at an all time low. If the US example is any indication, prison expansion will require a significant reduction in funding for community corrections. Canada may not be in the same position to offer advice and expertise on how to avoid the costly over-reliance on prisons. Perhaps instead of international efforts to address the justice failings of other development countries, Canadians ought to take a long hard look at the policies they are about to adopt. Maybe Canada ought to ask for some international advice from countries with which it once collaborated.

After a decade of playing a rather important role in the Baltics and the FSU, the idiosyncrasies of Canada's development, and the US policy toward the Middle East may limit future involvement in the region. This is not to say that individual consultants should not be involved in future programming, or that Canada or the US should not remain a site for study tours and training workshops. They should. North American experts should find ways to share their experience with their European colleagues who are better funded, better organized, and more committed to learning from the past. As Europe emerges as an increasingly important player in the region, the diversity of its population, diaspora networks, and commitment to human rights bode well for its role in the region's political evolution. Proximity, diplomatic ties, commercial connections, and economic and political frameworks have given Europe influence, and yet a multitude of challenges to meaningful democratic reform and human rights protection exist. Frameworks alone rarely succeed, as they must be matched by motivation on the ground to be sustainable.

The new energy for democracy in the Middle East represents an enormous opportunity for Europe. Just as the EU played an invaluable role in helping influence the political direction of Central and Eastern Europe after 1989, it may be possible to do something similar in MENA. Incentives on trade and aid for states that respect democratic principles, protect human rights, and begin the long process of reform, may provide the best means to consolidate the few and fragile gains to date. Probation programming, especially as presented in this book, may also be a good starting point. By modeling reforms in local communities and slowly building toward large-scale reform, probation programs can reverse brutal penal policies, promote social inclusiveness, and model the sorts of processes required for other democratic reforms to succeed.

In the next chapter, I acknowledge in great detail some of the challenges for the countries of MENA. It is important to remain realistic and recognize that some cynicism in this area is just good common sense. It is useful to remember the story of Hugh Everett. While a PhD student at Princeton in 1957, Everett first proposed the controversial *Many Worlds Theory*, a startling interpretation of quantum mechanics. Although ignored at the time by Nobel laureate Niels Bohr and other physicists, decades later it was rediscovered and has influenced a generation of physicists, science fiction writers, and inspired many films, television series, and books. Should the three-tier model be seen as such a development? Will visual maps become to the new Likert-scale survey? Are the modest lessons from a small Baltic country likely to influence the next generation of development practitioners around the world? This is perhaps unlikely (!). Nevertheless, to contribute to the slow process of knowledge accretion, of testing, revising, and re-testing ideas, this book has offered a number of theories to consider, and rooted the three-tier model in both the literature and empirical data drawn from project participants. The voices of those on the ground ought not be ignored.

7 Probation and Justice Reform from the Baltics to Beirut

The countries of the FSU have undergone incredible changes since 1989 and generations of occupation have influenced the justice system and the professionals who work within it. Previous chapters have argued that it is the development of probation services that can offer a means to reduce the sole reliance on incarceration, develop community-based alternatives to punishments, and promote greater participation of society in the justice system. Probation's flexibility is perhaps its greatest strength. This chapter explores the potential of probation by considering some of the challenges facing the countries of the Middle East and North Africa (MENA). In a region where a new generation is demanding dignity, freedom, and economic opportunities, now may be the moment to engage in meaningful justice reform. Probation programming may be an essential component.

As this book has presented, the development initiatives of the past have been motivated both by economic interests and assumptions, and humanistic goals and values. It has argued that it is the justice system that is the site in which these objectives converge and collide. Probation has some distinct advantages when promoting cross-national collaborations in justice reform. Based on the three-tier model of project delivery, this chapter provides a principled and pragmatic area of reform on which to focus in some of the countries of the Middle East and North Africa (MENA). The debates that emerge through justice reform programming of this nature can be seen alongside the broader goals of democratization. Law and justice, punishment and leniency, and the line between the state and the individual are central cleavages within all states. How these issues are debated and resolved is really a question about if and how different voices and agendas can be reconciled.

7.1 From the Baltics to Beirut

The protests that sparked a generational revolution in Tunisia and Egypt have spread far and wide. While there is a tendency to see this as the first real wave of democratization, as Kazziha (2010) points out, democratic expansion in the region has been the subject of debate and discussion since 1967. On this view, the most recent developments are simply the latest in a long process in many countries in the region to more fully embrace reforms designed to replace authoritarian regimes with democratic norms and standards. Many have pointed to the similarities between the events of 1989 in what was then the USSR and those in MENA in 2011. Yet, as Thomas Carothers (2011) has pointed out comparing the

Arab Spring with the end of the Soviet Union is awkward. While the communist governments in the FSU had been externally imposed and maintained with limited local involvement, Arab autocracies survived by cleverly mastering the internal dynamics of their countries and playing international superpowers against one another (Crystal, 2001). In some cases, like Jordan, monarchical legitimacy has ensured stability. More often it has been the craven use of national military and/or paramilitary police forces that kept the peace by disappearing those who challenged the established and politically convenient orthodoxy of oil and Islam.

In addition, while the failure to account for the differences in histories and political orientations among countries of the FSU has long been an issue, successful reform has varied depending on the type of regime that emerged post occupation (Avineri, 2010). The two-dozen countries of MENA are vastly more economically, culturally, and socially distinct. However, as a general matter, the use of internal security forces to quell dissent and preserve the interests and values of undemocratic regimes does appear similar to the approach taken during Soviet times (Los, 2003). It cannot continue if democratic reforms are ever to take root in MENA. A further concern is the potential for future reform efforts in the region to be co-opted as they were in the early days of programming in the FSU. The apparent desire to embrace democratic norms and reform governance institutions must contend with both the practical machinery of the justice system developed in the late colonial era, and the postwar period of independent state formation. In the countries of MENA it is the ways in which each country's regime has suppressed civil society and used the coercive power of the state, including torture, for their own political and/or religious ends that must be confronted.

The existing approach by many donors working in justice reform in the region is to focus on the "hardware" – courts and court administration, including digitizing records and streamlining administrative processes (Carothers, 2003). Unless projects begin to target the "software" including the people, personalities, and informal practices, the evidence suggests meaningful reform will not occur (Jones & Newburn, 2007). The ideas and options, and the ways in which society talks and thinks about crime and punishment are other crucial dimensions. Yet, such a focus is limited by the lack of experience of citizens in these countries of true independence, meaningful political participation, or the protection a constitutionally limited state affords those who dissent. Developmental investments designed to promote and/or reform economic governance structures will go nowhere unless future policy is at least nominally guided by the experiences of the past. It is clear the role of abusive police, corrupt officials, and inefficient justice systems cannot be ignored (Power, 2009). Just as in the Baltic States, criminal justice systems in countries throughout MENA will continue to be central sites of reform and dialogue. This book has argued it is the flexibility of probation services that make them an attractive means to begin a longer-term engagement. A critical question might be: what is the problem probation purports to solve in the region?

On one view, prison rates are relatively low in MENA as compared with the United States, Russia, and even the Baltic countries despite reductions over the last decade. While exceptions exist, such as Tunisia, Iran, and the UAE, if one ignores the high prison rates in Israel, the median rate of incarceration is 1/6 that of the US. In the past, this has been ascribed to strict adherence to Islam and the reliance on intentional bodily harm of offenders (Sanad, 1991). Others suggest it is the strict application of Shari'a law that has a cleansing influence, promotes collective morality, and fosters a non-criminogenic environment (Souryal, 1987). Despite lower rates of incarceration, the conditions for those who are imprisoned are often brutal. Support for politicized police states in the ongoing global 'war on terror' have served to justify shocking human rights violations in the name of partnership, prevention, and peace. Arbitrary detention, ill treatment, unfair trials, torture, and extra judicial murder have characterized the region's efforts to tackle terrorism and disrupt those accused of supporting it. Indeed the language of terror has been used to restrict the freedom of expression and association, and the detention of prisoners of conscience. The physical and corporal component to punishment is designed to both instill fear and consolidate political power and control. The challenges are immense. However, it may be that it is the practical potential to promote human rights through a renewed focus on rehabilitation and social inclusion that offers the most compelling argument for citizens and states in the region. Justice reform projects promote inclusion and engage a broader cross-section of the populace in a conversation about the role of law in society.

Recently states in the region have pointed to the effectiveness of front-end diversion and rehabilitation programs for youth (CRC, 2011). It is these developments that may provide the most secure basis for the expansion of community-based corrections that promote inclusion and engage a broader cross-section of the populace in a conversation about the role of law in society. While it is no doubt premature to promote large-scale development initiatives to develop probation services throughout the region, there are lessons that should not be ignored. To date, international engagement in each of these countries and regions has faced a variety of significant challenges. Just as the Latvian experience cannot be simply applied to other countries of the FSU, neither should anyone harbor illusions that what worked in one place will be appropriate in another. With this proviso firmly in mind, there is no reason in principle that the three-tier model presented in Chapter 3 could not serve a useful starting place to consider how future engagement might occur. It may be that Arab states, like so many others, begin to recognize that one's approach to democracy rests on where one draws the line between individual liberty and collective security. As this book has asked: who should be involved in that conversation?

7.1.1 Exploring the Three-Tier Model in MENA

Presented in Chapter 3, there are a variety of elements within a region, country, and project to consider. Beyond the purview of this chapter is a country-by-country analysis of the various contextual, organizational, and individual challenges to the establishment of probation in the more than two dozen countries throughout MENA. While distinct challenges will exist in each individual country, there are a number of common crosscutting challenges that might usefully be considered first. As in the past, the potential success of probation practices as a new approach to the administration of justice will depend on how it is framed and to what extent it balances care and control through the right mix of supervision and encouragement, sanction and inclusion. The three-tier model offers one way to conceive of the challenges.

Figure 7.1 Three-Tier Model of Probation Programming

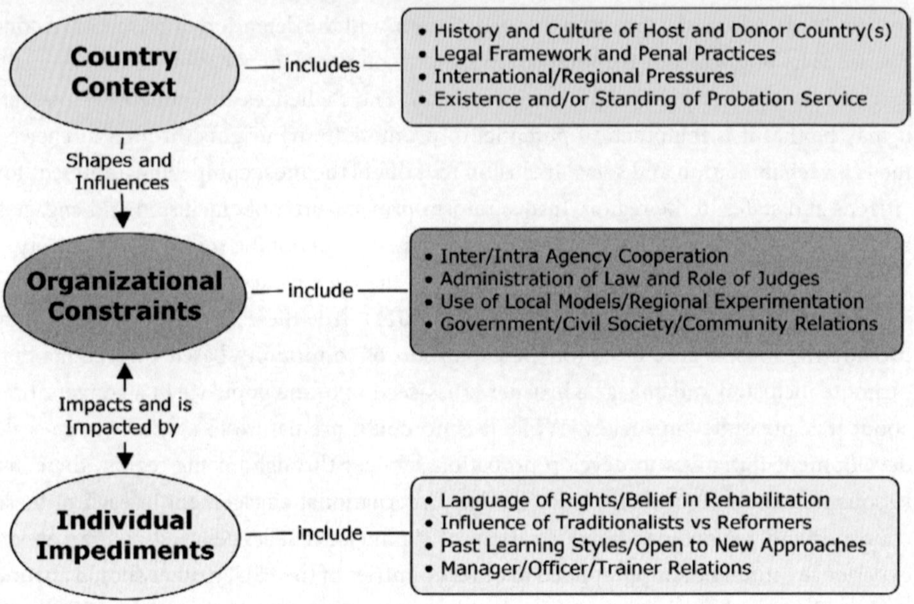

7.1.1.1 Country Context

Broad contextual aspects of immediate interest are related to the socio-political role of Islam in Arab societies, the punitive and physically coercive justice orientation, and the entrenched and persistent power of the security apparatus. In political terms the importance of Islam in much of MENA must be seen against a background of the autocratic regimes that Islamic groups opposed. Most moderate Islamic political organizations have assumed the role once played by national liberation movements and advocate for democratic reform as the only means by which to influence policy. As Brown *et al.* (2006) points out in countries that allowed the formation of legal Islamic parties such as Morocco and Jordan, these parties have established a presence in each country's parliament. In countries, such as Egypt under Mubarak, Islamists were banned or forced them into exile, like in Tunisia and Syria. Ironic to some, it is the Islamist opposition movements that have emerged as strong voices advocating democracy and political participation from outside the formal political system.

As a result, many fear true democracy in the region will mean a renewed role for those who advocate a return to a fundamentalist view of Islam. Carothers (2011) argues this fear is overblown. There is little evidence that almost a billion people have any desire to return to a seventh-century lifestyle and a recent and extensive study of Islamist political participation suggests most Islamist parties are far less popular than many assume (Kurzman & Naqvi, 2010). Perhaps more challenging for true reform is the Islamic establishment that exists in many countries, described as "the complex of Islamic organizations, clerics, and institutions close to the government" (Brown *et al.* 2006, p. 5). While differences exist within the region, the influence of this establishment cannot be ignored. Just like elites all over the world, their reach is difficult to untangle. What cannot be doubted is that some in this establishment favor the use of "Islamic" criminal law. This involves ordering the proscribed punishment for criminal prohibitions found in the Qu'ran, such as theft and adultery. While in the past simplistic scholarly treatments have had the effect of "...conjuring up images of severed hands and religious police" (Crystal, 2001, p. 469), it is the case that under Islamic law, once the offence is established and conditions for applying the punishment satisfied, a court is divested of any discretion in the matter (Lawan, Sada & Ali, 2008). In many countries, amputation and stoning remain part of judicially sanctioned penal policy.

Yet the inflexibility sometimes ascribed to the Qu'ran and the role of Shari'ah law in Saudi Arabia, Iran and the Sudan (not to mention Oklahoma) often obscures rather than enlightens. In the majority of Middle Eastern states it is Islamists who have suffered numerous injustices and brutality by the police, indifference by the courts, and torturous treatment in prisons and detention centers. The potential that a more modern approach to Islam could humanize the existing structures is difficult, but certainly not impossible, to imagine. Islamic law is not a single, well-defined legal code contained between two covers of a book. Instead it is a complex body of rules and interpretations that spans many centuries and follows different schools. As such, many suggest it may be time to begin a legal reform process in earnest. Tariq Ramadan (2008) urges reform based on the Qu'ran itself and the sayings of the Prophet (Hadith). In addition, he suggests that a more in-depth consideration of the history of this scholarship would benefit existing reform efforts by highlighting how pioneers of the major Islamic schools of law (Madhab) developed their approach to Islamic jurisprudence. He proposes a new approach to defining the sources of law that seeks reform in the name of coherence.

> One should know what one wants. If we aim to return to scriptural sources and extract higher objectives and ethical goals, we should then equip ourselves with the means to respect them across history and the diversity of societies. In a time of complex globalization where all the fields of human activity interact and have multidimensional consequences, there can be no question of having an isolated, partial or formalist approach. (Ramadan, 2008, p. 252)

One impediment to reform of the justice system based on Western notions of rule of law is that neither the Qu'ran nor existing jurisprudence in MENA sets out a system of criminal procedure or the rules that govern criminal investigations and prosecutions. There are few if any limitations on state power and often no procedural protections guaranteed for the accused. One promising approach has been to identify rules and principles drawn from Islamic legal literature to bring the modern practice of Islamic criminal law into closer conformity with both international standards of criminal due process and Islamic notions of justice (Reza, 2006). Given the time it took for individual rights in the Anglo-American tradition to emerge, this approach may be more promising over the longer term. Yet, it is useful to recall that in both the UK and the US, justice reform grew from concerns about the treatment of prisoners and in some cases was motivated explicitly by religious beliefs.

In addition to the formal judicial system, another complication is the power and influence of the internal security forces and paramilitary police. These forces are a product of the historical and political realities in the region, a legacy of the colonial period that left serious and systemic problems in the region. This legacy undermined the process of state-making in the region including developing constitutions, establishing territorial borders, and accepting the relationship between religion and identity (Zubaida, 1989). The weaknesses and vulnerabilities of states in this region may assist to explain the obsession of their elites with the concept of security. Too often demands for political participation, economic redistribution, and social justice added new pressures at an early stage in the state-building process. This did not change following World War II and the rise of Arab nationalism. Based on colonial notions of the nation-state, state-building in this region required overcoming conflicting views about national identities, including separatist insurgencies, and attempting to establish the legitimacy of state boundaries and national institutions (Ayoob, 1995, p. 28). Yet, whatever the role of colonialism in the perceived need for the strong internal security services, their persistence since independence has been based on their ability to disrupt and destroy political opposition (Crystal, 2001). By using force to suppress dissent and maintain the fragile support of ruling coalitions, security services have grown ever more powerful, staging coups in some cases while consistently thwarting prospects for social, economic, and political change.

There have, of course, been exceptions. The democratic revival in the 1970s and 80s overcame attempted coups in Morocco and Jordan, and in some cases like Egypt, Sudan, Tunisia, and Algeria the political system began to open up (Owen, 1993). However, with the exception of Jordan, whose reforms of the 1980s and 90s resulted in fairly free legislative elections, developments elsewhere have not been as promising (Brown & Shahin, 2010). Until recently the West had little problem with one party rule and the use of the state apparatus to control dissent throughout the region (Youngs, 2010). This was perhaps most pronounced in oil producing states where Crystal (2001) notes Western advisors to the military and police often ensure that the interests of the former colonial powers and of the US were reinforced through the institutions of criminal justice.

The result was that crime prevention and policing by consent took a back seat to attempting to control the political realities on the ground. Heavily armed security forces were trained to root out political opposition and deal with dissent by force. Regime maintenance in the region has involved threats, overt torturous acts of depraved indifference, assassination, and extra judicial murder. Reforming governance structures in MENA cannot occur without addressing the existence of multiple security agencies and external advisers that have in the past served only the political needs of the regime. It will not be easy. In Egypt, following Mubarak's arrest, the security service was disbanded – although apparently re-constituted with many of the same personnel under a new name. In other regions real reform will require bringing other services under civilian control and transparent oversight. Throughout MENA, agencies empowered to employ even nominal policing functions must enforce the rule of law equally and equitably, if meaningful reform is to be sustained.

The Latvia experience suggests one way to address the complexity of country context in the countries of MENA. The inclusion of Diaspora networks in the countries in which these projects are implemented is certainly one strategy. More study is needed, however, to understand the complexity inherent in representing both the land in which you or your parents were born and the country you identify as your home. In some cases Diaspora groups have been able to promote human rights and democratic ideals (Brinkerhoff, 2006; Mohamoud, 2006). In others, the recruitment of 'political elites' and individuals from Diaspora communities abroad has caused friction with local stakeholders (Manning, 2006). In Afghanistan and Iraq, relying upon this approach (Krause & Jütersonke, 2005; Paris, 2004) has undermined broader efforts at more sustainable governance outcomes (Chesterman, 2004; Herring & Rangwala, 2006). Diaspora networks in MENA may be as fragmented as the Latvian Diaspora. As discussed in Chapter 4, people hold on to old prejudices for all kinds of reasons and these biases may not be easy to dislodge. While the views among Diaspora networks should not be the sole basis for setting development priorities, their role can be a useful complement to local efforts on the ground.

Perry and Barrows (2009), based on their experience working with the Czech Probation and Mediation service, have identified another lesson. While probationary functions require a concrete understanding of the existing legal frameworks in individual countries, it cannot be divorced from the broader strategy that provides actors within the system guidance about how to use legislation. They suggest:

> Our view is that a strategy, which needs to include vision, purpose and values, should be developed first. Legislation, which needs to incorporate the purpose and values, is part of the implementation of that strategy and in all the elements of the legislative process the strategic goals need to be retained. Other elements of implementation are institution building (including enabling legislation concerning structure, staff, and funding), followed by implementation and practice development. This has not been widely appreciated, and ironically many projects include strategy development as an activity after legislation has been passed and institutions created. (Perry & Barrows, 2009, p. 74)

This provides one explanation of why laws on the books may not reflect actual practice on the ground. In Latvia, while laws gave effect to Probation as early as 2004, the ways in which the system could become operational required new laws to allow additional roles and functions. Ironically, it might be said that making the law effective *required* a service to push for a new relationship between judges and agencies and officers. This might suggest that countries where laws giving effect to probation functions exist or where services have been established may not necessarily be favored over others that do not. It is the people involved that matter more than laws. Laws will be ignored unless they are part of the larger socio-cultural fabric. As such, probation cannot exist as a meaningful means of justice reform unless it considers how the broader contextual challenges shape and influence organizational constraints.

Organizational Constraints

At the organizational level, a number of practical constraints exist. In MENA, these include the role of judges, the power of the police, and the influence of civil society. Of specific interest are existing attempts to experiment and model potential justice reforms. In the Baltics, convincing judges to use new or amended laws was a significant institutional challenge. In the countries of MENA, judges are perhaps even more constrained by the broader contextual challenges described above. One observation is that in many countries in MENA there is an inadequate separation of powers between government and the judiciary. This compromises the effectiveness of criminal justice systems and complicates the relationships between the three major types of courts that exist in the region. These include Shari'ah courts, which most often are used for personal and family matters, and Civil Law courts that apply code law, based on European and indigenous sources. In addition, an extrajudicial system of military, security courts, and ad hoc tribunals exist. These courts issue executive orders and summary justice, often in secret. As discussed in Chapter 4, in practice this means there is often even less room for judicial discretion than is normally the case in Civil law systems.

In addition to the role of internal security forces in the region, another legacy of the colonial era is the overt politicization of the police. During the colonial period in the Middle East, police who operated in urban areas focused on suppressing dissent and maintaining civil order. Too often it led to methods that were violent and unaccountable. As a result, police forces in many regions in the Middle East are detested (Crystal, 2001). The specific problem for the development of probation practices is that while legislation exists to allow supervision as an alternative punishment, it is too reliant on the police to do it. For example in Egypt, while not available as a "primary" punishment (*'uqubat asliyyah*), "ancillary" punishments (*'uqubat tab'iyyah*) can include deprivation of certain rights and privileges, and probationary supervision by the police (Reza, 2011).

Police supervision, it should be recalled, was also available throughout the FSU. It was rarely used, however, and it did not include the social rehabilitation function that is generally a part of probation practices. An issue in the FSU post independence was that many citizens distrusted the police based on their past practices. There is no doubt this is also the case in many countries of the MENA. The potential for the police to take on meaningful supervision as part of any rehabilitative and reentry program seems limited. Just as hiring former prison guards undermined meaningful correctional reform in Lithuania, it seems doubtful that the public would accept attempts to reform policing in such a way as to include supervision. The distrust of police is not exclusive to Lebanon. It exists throughout the region. It may be useful to recall the 2010 murder of Khaled Said by two plain-clothes policemen in Alexandria, Egypt. The beating that led to his death was in response to a video he shot of these same individuals sharing the spoils of a drug bust. The murder incited mass outrage. Even if the Egyptian transitional government is able to completely overhaul police laws and regulations and invest in new education and training methods – no small feat – overcoming past policing in which torture, abuse, and humiliation were commonplace will not be easy.

Another challenge is the role of civil society. Despite recent uprisings in the name of democracy, economic freedom, and basic human rights, democratic institutions in the region are often weak. In the past, few participated in the formal political process. While the willingness to risk life and limb in pursuit of democratic rights seems an obvious precursor to larger governance reforms, the slow process of building or reforming institutions that are able to secure and protect these rights is a different skill set. It may be particularly difficult in cases where there is little history, tradition, or understanding of what political participation means. It may be that promoting community members and civil society organizations to work together through local processes on issues of common concern – such as who should be incarcerated, and who should be supervised – can offer a practical means to engage with one another on a central question faced by all states.

In Latvia, a key lesson is the role of pilot projects in providing demonstrations and local exemplars of what justice reform looks like on the ground. In addition to the practical benefit of developing a group of committed and enthusiastic reformers, there may be political benefits to the phased implementation of justice reform. As an area fraught with political complications, and intricate social and familial ties and loyalties, proceeding slowly is sensible. By involving local citizens in testing new approaches to the justice system, the development community can become involved in those countries and communities that are open to assistance. In the place of the impatient processes of the past, reform initiatives can proceed deliberately without attempting too much, too quickly. On this point, the distinction between constructive and proscriptive justice reform becomes essential. With this principle in mind, it may be useful to consider some existing models and reform initiatives.

Despite the lack of fully independent and legislatively-based probation service in MENA, there are some useful examples and possible new developments to build upon. Probation services can operate in some form in three stages in the criminal procedure. These include post incarceration, as an alternative sentence, and increasingly as part of pre-charge diversion, especially for youth. In terms of post incarceration and release, developments in Jordan specifically for juveniles suggest one model to build upon. Over the last decade, Jordan has engaged in a number of reforms focused on juvenile justice that involve social and community based foundations and societies. In an exhaustive review of penal practices, Kholood Ahmed Al-Oran (2000) concludes the best way to address crime, as a social problem in the Kingdom, is to develop new institutions to supervise and support offenders returning to their community. Programs have been designed to train social workers on the role and function of probation and supervision and to better identify existing community resources, foundations, aid societies, and community groups to assist youth in conflict with the law (UNDOC, 2008).

The supervision of suspended sentences is another function of most probation services. Introduced in the Middle East during the colonial era, it remains on the books in many countries. As discussed in Chapter 2, in Europe in the 18th century, the focus shifted from corporal punishment to incarceration and surveillance because of societal pressure. The 19th century spurred community-based supervision models often led by religious groups, who sought to be of service to those in conflict with the law. While existing institutions of social control in the Middle East are more explicitly coercive, this is not true everywhere. In Lebanon, the development of probation can be traced to a study visit to the UK in 1951

(Page, 1992). Today, probation is a part of "preventive measures entailing restrictions on liberty" under Article 71 of the Criminal Law. The purpose of probation as defined in Article 84 is "...to ascertain the good behavior of the convicted person and facilitate his reintegration into society."

A person on probation in Lebanon is prohibited from frequenting certain places and must comply with the orders imposed by the Judge. Such orders may be altered while the measure is being enforced. The period of probation can range from one to five years, and a report on the conduct of the convicted person must be submitted to the Judge at least once every three months. Any person on probation who breaches an order or who persistently evades supervision shall be sentenced to imprisonment with labor for a term of three months to three years. Another set of examples are connected to efforts to reform juvenile justice. In Lebanon, juvenile supervision is entrusted to special institutions recognized by the State and in 2011, Lebanon reported to the United Nations Committee on the Rights of the Child (UNCRC) that:

> Lebanese courts are very sensitive to the status and social circumstances of minors who have committed a particular offence and in most cases impose alternative measures to imprisonment even if the law provides for a prison sentence or detention. (UNCRC, 2011, p. 6)

This is in line with recent developments by European probation services that attempt to facilitate front-end diversions from the formal justice system. However the law also provides that in the absence of probation services, the police shall be in charge of supervision. Schmid and Riachy (2003, p. 109) suggest this is because:

> As regards probationary and protective measures, they are only rarely resorted to owing to the lack of personnel with the professional qualifications required and the absence of the necessary structures for application and follow-up.

This points to a challenge that also existed in Latvia. Without credible alternatives prison often becomes the de facto response to crime. Developing these alternatives in practice first required a renewed focus on supporting civil society groups in various regions. Instead of simply targeting justice elites, judges, or policymakers, this approach began a process of community driven reform. However, reform efforts are unlikely to be sustained without local models and examples developed and improved with the explicit involvement of community members, regional leaders, and eventually government officials. The Latvian example suggests reform must come from the ground up and success cannot be externally imposed.

In terms of front-end diversion, developments are few. However one example is Jordan's Juvenile Act No. 52 of 2002 (amended) that includes a variety of special safeguards applicable to the prosecution of juveniles. Among these is the restriction of the power to detain juveniles to the judiciary, and the need to designate juvenile cases as urgent and confidential. A juvenile is tried under the Juvenile Act before a specialized juvenile court unless he/she participates with an adult in the commission of the crime. A project funded by the Penal Reform International (PRI) Middle East and North Africa (MENA) Regional Office, based in Amman, Jordan, in cooperation with the United Nations Children's Fund (UNICEF), has to focus on how to introduce alternative measures for youth. Early activities have attempted to broaden policy debates and improve the dialogue and cooperation among justice agencies. Specifically, programming seeks to:

> ...introduce an effective system for the centralization and the exchange of information among all the active institutions and bodies in the field of juvenile justice; to encourage the dialogue and cooperation among the various stakeholders, particularly the judiciary, the police, the juvenile and his family, the victim, the social experts and members of the civil society; and to establish a body in charge of monitoring and following up the reforms and to report periodically to the relevant governmental authority. (PRI, 2007)

While dialogue among central agencies of the justice system is no doubt important, it is not yet clear what it is these officials are dialoguing about. Without community based programs and services with which to entrust youth in conflict with the law, talk shops and promises to monitor are not enough. Other aspects of the project, however, seek to challenge more ingrained individual attitudes though the provision of training and technical assistance.

7.1.1.2 Individual Impediments

Throughout countries in MENA there are policy documents and legislation that appear progressive, along with a number of justice reform projects well underway. However, it is clear that, just like the FSU in the 1990s, the reality on the ground is not as rosy as the legislation suggests. Prisons remain the de facto punishment for juveniles in the region and the use of probation or other forms of community-based supervision is rare. While this is a function of contextual and organizational constraints and challenges, the biggest hurdle may be changing the views of the general population. The idea that the state should be constrained in its actions and that inalienable rights of individuals are protected requires rethinking the balance between care and control within the justice system. These assumptions may be at odds with some traditions within the countries of MENA. Based on politicized rhetoric that uses Islam as cover for other social and economic interests, religious duty has been used to justify violence against women, the denial of rights of minorities, and freedom of speech. According to Sachedina (2009, p. 8), "…Islam is facing a self-cultivated epistemological crisis brought about by a failure to connect theology, ethics, and law within Islamic traditions." The confusion about the proper role of religion in public life exists throughout the region.

A significant challenge is that human rights are often, although not always, based on secular foundations. Yet, the false choice between human rights on the one hand or Islamic beliefs on the other is both untenable in the short term and not a true reflection of many principles within the Qu'ran. One immediate solution may be to engage in processes like Reza (2011) and Ramadan (2008) have done to root probationary principles in the language of Islam. A longer-term strategy may be to begin a conversation about the role of rights in Islam and the role of religion within the state. Just as human rights can be rooted in more than one religious tradition, so too can space exist for a dialogue on differing views of Islam. Indeed, it is important to recognize that a great disparity in views, approaches, and reverence for Islam exists throughout the region. As Mayer argues attitudes in the Muslim world toward human rights "…run the gambit from total rejection to whole hearted embrace" (2007, p. 6).

Another important impediment is the relative influence of modernists and reformers within MENA countries. In Latvia, variance in the approach to punishment and rehabilitation was based both on region and age. The question of how to bring those who took to the streets throughout the countries of MENA into a process that can result in dialogue, give and take, and accommodation remains unanswered. For Carothers (2011) the ways in which the "deep state" and the entrenched power structures beyond presidents or government officials appear to be holding on do not bode well for the sort of patient, laborious, and step-by-step process required to reform existing regimes. One idea to keep the opposition unified and practically oriented is to make justice reform a central first step in the larger process of democratization and governance reform. In some countries, there are projects that could accommodate such a goal.

In Jordan, Prison Reform International (PRI) has relied on the tried and true method of study tours for senior officials to showcase alternatives to imprisonment for children in conflict with the law. A 2009 trip to Nova Scotia, Canada focused on exposing senior Jordanian policy makers to the Canadian experience with regard to restorative justice for children in conflict with the law. This exchange of experience is based on the view that deprivation of liberty for children should be used rarely, for as brief a time as possible, and as a last resort. In Canada, wide-ranging alternatives based on restorative justice practices exist for youth in contact with the law. As one Jordanian participant noted "…one of the basic points that we learned from this experience is that 'there is no bad child, just sad child."

This sentiment, if sustained, is an important indicator of evolving views. Yet the insight of one official is inadequate in the face of the challenges represented by needed large-scale systemic reforms. To be sustainable, existing projects must be expanded to include more voices and stakeholders, specifically civil society groups. The Latvia example suggests study tours can have important and lasting outcomes, when properly managed. However, the over-reliance on senior officials and other elites is problematic. Unless the civil society community is explicitly included into the reform process as an equal partner, tours risk being becoming shopping trips, dressed up as education. Thankfully, other programmatic elements have more potential to begin to engage in a process of addressing other individual constraints. Key PRI training activities are outlined in Table 7.2.

Table 7.2 Key PRI Project Activities in MENA

Activity	Target
Training to develop and conduct social and educational investigations and coordinate with police, prosecution, and the judiciary	Probation officers Social rehabilitation
Training on use of discretion and value of alternative methods to minimize juvenile detention	Police Juvenile Court Judges Prosecutors
Information sessions on need and value of separate juvenile courts	Judges
Training on need for separate policies and practices for juveniles	Detention personnel

7.2 Understanding the Promise of Probation

As presented in Chapter 2, probation services operate at the intersection of a number of justice actors. They often combine an institutional presence with connections and cooperation between and within communities. In general all probation services exist on a continuum between control and care. As an entry point to international justice reform, probation represents a means to tackle the formal processes of the state, and the informal processes of those who work within it. While common in many countries, probation programming provides a means for participatory approaches to international development that can result in local probation variants based on the histories, cultures, and legal systems in which they are located. Probation, Robert Harris argues:

> …is not a 'thing' to be taken or left but a set of ideas and possibilities to be used creatively and strategically to solve local problems of criminal justice… a

framework into which locally feasible and desirable solutions may be fitted. (Harris, 1995, p. 207)

It is this idea of probation as a framework that is of interest for justice reform in other post conflict and post authoritarian contexts. North American experience in the FSU can inform broader lessons about the complexities of knowledge sharing through legal technical assistance. Sometimes the lessons can be difficult to untangle. As discussed in Chapter 3, the challenges of exporting the Latvian approach to Russia and Ukraine should not be ignored. Indeed learning from the Latvian model, discussed in Chapters 4, 5 and 6, would be incomplete without consideration of the challenges that remain. These include the economic challenges that continue to threaten the further expansion of Latvian probation, organizational deficits related to continuing education and staff recruitment and retention, and both individual and societal views of punishment. As discussed in Chapters 1 and 3, perhaps the greatest concern is the failure to develop a culture of research through legal technical assistance projects (Carothers, 2003). While the Latvian service is improving the kind of practices that can lead to research on rehabilitation and policies based on evidence-based approaches, for North American development agencies, the jury is still out.

7.2.1 *Learning from Latvia: Design and Delivery*

There are a number of lessons from Latvia to be considered. These are not new. Taken together, however, they offer a means to rethink the complexities of legal technical assistance suggested by the three-tier model. While not a recipe for success, the following considerations might usefully guide project design and delivery with partner governments, local executing agencies, and civil society. An emergent trend in international development is a greater reliance on local executing agencies. By giving effect to the watchword of 'partnership,' local agencies with a record of past experience and commitment to achievable results in a realistic time frame should be favored. Ideally these agencies or coordinators can be located within an institution central to the reform initiative. In the early days of a project, staff should establish numerous networks and relationships with host institutional staff to avoid the project becoming overly dependent upon a few key people. Managers can promote sustainability by facilitating project activities rather than micro managing and by relying upon local coordinators with specified responsibilities that increase as the project meets key goals. The relationship with the local coordinator is integral and frequent travel to the region in the initial stages of the project can be extremely useful. Projects can build trust and goodwill by co-funding the local coordinator's salary while requiring in kind institutional contributions at the outset of project delivery.

In terms of project delivery, the contributions of the Baltic Diaspora in Canada, discussed in Chapter 4, has emerged as an important factor in development. This community provided initial information about the state of affairs in Latvia and combined linguistic capacity with personal connections and networks. In the initial stages of project design, efforts should be made to promote positive connections between the host government and others with ties to that country. This may include members of a Diaspora living in the host country or others with intimate knowledge of the region. In Latvia, Canadian project staff better understood the challenges and opportunities in the region as a result of the Diaspora network, which helped to build trust, confidence, and durable partnerships. Weiner echoes the importance of this finding for the MENA region by pointing to the South Asian experience:

> …to foster the kind of identity transformation necessary for liberalizing state modernization, it is essential to support and develop international ties with Muslim professional associations in law, medicine, the professoriate, and other fields, as lawyers from Western nations did in offering their solidarity to the Pakistani bar in its confrontation with President Pervez Musharraf in 2007. (2011, p. 44)

The role of civil society in creating and sustaining the impetus for reform should not be ignored. Civil society exists at local, national, and international levels. Locally, projects should establish networks among existent organizations, involve civil society in project activities, and facilitate their introductions to other national and international donors. While cooperation with other donor agencies is not always possible or practical, information sharing, co-planning, and funding of relevant activities can be a useful way to maximize development funding and build networks that connected different stakeholders working in different reform areas. Although projects must always retain their independence, inviting other donors to relevant meetings and workshops and developing more formal relationships can bring greater harmonization to development actors who for too long have operated through more competitive means.

An important aspect of civil society engagement is the potential for project activities to build capacity and allow local communities to participate. While national reform is the ultimate goal, much can be achieved by funding community pilot projects that are based on locally identified needs. By relying upon competitive processes requiring multi agency cooperation, in kind contributions, and the support of local governments, pilots can experiment and innovate with new kinds of programming in a microcosm of the country. Not every project will work. Understanding how local successes resulted in the achievement of agreed results can assist in the identification of key community and reform leaders. The emergence of these leaders can be combined with study tours to share international best practice, build multi agency networks of reform champions, and provide an important means to change mindsets among those who participate.

In Latvia this is connected to what might be called a community-centric pilot project approach (Wheeldon, 2007). This approach relies upon local community members to work together to design their own community justice initiatives within a broader framework. This approach allows for 'trialability' and exploring different approaches to broader reform goals by testing new programs and services in the local context. In the short term, this approach serves as a valuable means to develop community-based programs and create an environment in which local reform champions can emerge. Historically, of course, a focus on large institutional elements was favored when framing reform and organizational development (Lewin, 1951; Rogers, 1962). More recent explorations of how innovations are adopted focus on 'early adopters' as central to creating broader organizational change (Simpson, 2002; Rogers, 2005). By trying new approaches, institutional and contextual constraints inherent in any attempt to promote systematic reform can be identified and overcome (Manor, 2007). As discussed in Chapter 5, in Latvia, the pilot projects provided examples of more participatory processes that included "community-up" rather than "national-government-down" models to extend justice reform (Bell *et al.* 2002). This approach may also be relevant to those who call for 'evidence-based aid.' By combining robust data collection about how new, localized approaches can guide national reform efforts, more sustainable development assistance policies can result (Banerjee, 2007).

Finally, as the capacity of these local champions grows, specific training workshops can be designed to build on their success, and their inclusion as local experts on national policy working groups can be supported. Working groups that have an official mandate, agreed tasks, clear deliverables, and specific timelines can facilitate useful inter-institutional interactions. While perhaps overly broad and still incomplete, these lessons from Latvia offer practical suggestions to project managers and funders. While learning from success is important, perhaps more important is recognizing what went wrong, and how continuing challenges hamper the sustainability of project initiatives. This requires a commitment to data collection, transparency, and a willingness to learn from the past.

The importance of what might be called an interactive training model is perhaps the most important outcome of the Latvian project. Supporters of this model maintain that the need to build relationships through participatory processes is integral to the development of a team of reform champions drawn from a variety of justice sectors. Through multiple interactions, common misunderstandings between those working on reform initiatives and about structural or cultural impediments to reform can be identified. These may include underestimating the role of powerful interests in developing countries and mischaracterizing the interrelation and associated constraints of legal challenges on the one hand and the social resistance to change among those within the justice community on the other (Chodosh, 2005, pp. 79-82). As Beeson and Davis (2000, p. 180) suggest:

> ...change process often overestimates the role of management and the central place of systems and structures without engaging the numerous actors whose behaviour is not only adaptive but also creative and contentious.

One approach may be to explicitly connect training with multiple social interactions and more participatory models of engagement, adequate question and debrief sessions, and the encouragement of teambuilding. Hawes and Kealey (1979) have demonstrated that knowledge and expertise is not enough to ensure project success and that, without interpersonal and intercultural skill sets, technical assistance may be not effective at all (Vulpe *et al.* 2001, p. 54). If indeed learning occurs through social interaction and requires deliberation and debate, the processes used through legal technical assistance must move away from an exclusive focus on technical skills. In Latvia, the focus on encouraging different groups to train together and then following up by applying the cooperative results of that learning within and among institutions was invaluable. As discussed in Chapter 6, training and capacity development must become education in the classical sense of calling forth and inviting participants to be authors of their own transformation (Freire, 1970). At the same time, this training must model strategies that empower providers, program managers, and community leaders to become agents of change (Simmons *et al.* 2007). This presents a central challenge in how probation is conceived and how best to approach the role of probation officers.

7.2.2 The Future of Probation: Rethinking Control (RNR) and Care (GLM)

A specific tension that emerges from the Latvian example is related to how probation has been instituted. A major component of the LLRP was the focus on developing risk/need assessment tools as well as assessment reports for pre-sentence and parole reports. One important theme among line officers in the regions outside Riga was that Probation had become too formal, too institutionalized, and too hierarchical, with a focus on reporting at the expense of clients. Some probation officers in the regions outside Riga suggested that, as Probation had grown, the focus had shifted to "...paper over people." Latvian participants acknowledged that Canadian trainers identified this challenge and a community based probation officer pointed to a 2002 report by Andrejs Berzins in which he stated:

> A major problem in the Latvian criminal justice system, which virtually everyone acknowledges, is the enormous amount of paperwork officials are required to do in order to comply with formal requirements at each stage in the process. Unless this problem is seriously addressed when designing the new

> probation service there is a great risk that this tradition will continue and severely limit the effectiveness of probation officers in their work with offenders.

Nevertheless, despite the warnings and the broader recognition, more formulistic approaches have been instituted by the SPS in the years since the project ceased. This challenge is connected to broader developments in public sector administration based on the adoption of approaches drawn from the natural sciences. It has resulted in more evaluative, managerial approaches to governance (Henkel, 1991) and the rendering of what has been called statistical justice (Reichman, 1986). When organized correctly to guide practice through the case management system, it is also the best approach we know about to date.

As discussed in Chapter 2, over the last century probation has been an integral part of the criminal justice system in the common law countries of Canada, the US, and the UK. Combining supervision with therapy, it represents an example of the social welfare model of justice. Since the 1970s, probation has been viewed as soft on crime and an inadequate punishment and has undergone a radical transformation. In moving away from the social welfare model (Haggerty, 2004), its operation is now often characterized by strict procedures and intensive supervision. A far cry from the traditional goals of treatment and rehabilitation, in some cases probation has become "…the management of risks and resources" (Garland, 2001, p. 177).

In Latvia probation is an order issued through the court, based on the written pre-sentence reports of probation officers. Through various risk assessment instruments (Andrews *et al.* 1990), offenders are assigned to different levels and kinds of supervision. By categorizing offenders, and by identifying and assessing risk factors and criminogenic needs, one can use models to predict which offenders are likely to reoffend and who may benefit most from rehabilitative efforts (Hannah-Moffat & Maurutto, 2003). Programming such as cognitive-behavior treatment programs for substance abuse, domestic violence, and sexual offending have shown promise (Ross & Fabiano, 1985; Robinson *et al.* 1991). Although the list of principles has been expanded beyond the original ones described in 1990 (Andrews *et al.*, 1990), as discussed in Chapter 2, the principles of risk, need, and responsivity remain at the core. The RNR model is outlined in figure 7.3.

Figure 7.3 RNR Principles

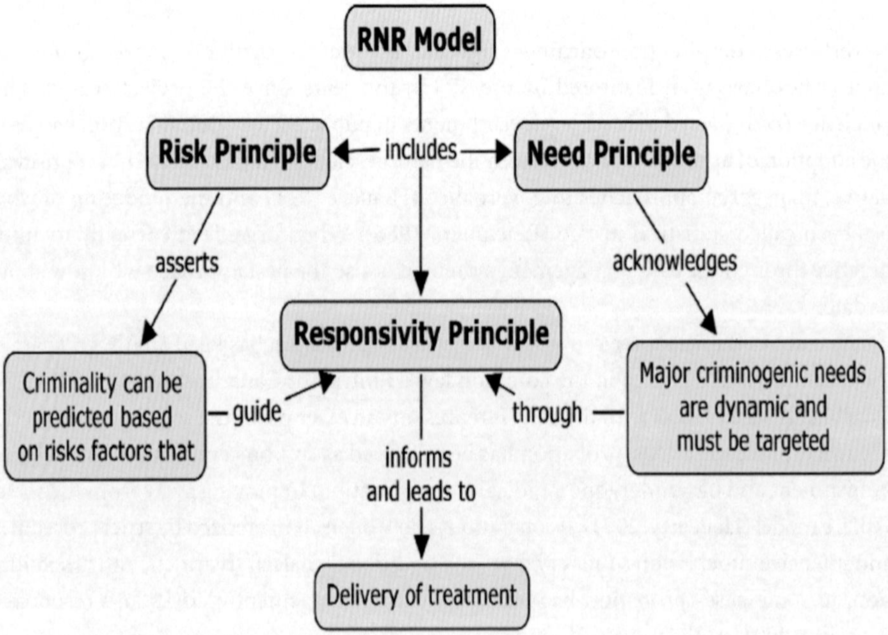

The risk-need-responsivity (RNR) model has been widely regarded as the premier model for guiding offender assessment and treatment and has exerted a considerable influence on correctional theory, practice, and policy (Ogloff & Davis, 2004; Ward, Melser, & Yates, 2007). For those interested in evidence-based policy, the RNR model is the only theoretical model, based on existing systematic reviews of the research literature, that has consistently demonstrated the value of its precepts (Andrews, 2011).

However, critics argue this approach formalizes subjective moral assumptions (Kemshall, 1995) and leads to a false sense of certainty. They are no doubt right that this can occur when these tools are used without specific training to establish a common approach to interpreting risk information, and local testing to ensure the instrument is valid in the context in which it is being employed. Without clear guidelines and validated instruments, probation can amount to placing complex individuals into categories that, while administratively useful, may not be exact (Hacking, 1991). In North America this has led to judicial concern about the over-reliance on risk assessment (Cole, 2007). The chief problem for critics is that interventions that adhere to the RNR principles are associated with significant reductions in recidivism, a fact that most critics concede (Andrews & Bonta, 2010).

There may be a socio-political element to the criticism, however. Relying on the RNR to guide one's professional interactions does seem to alter the early probation principles of 'advise, assist and befriend.' Indeed some have argued that the explicit reliance on criminogenic risks ignores more basic human needs that underlie optimal personal fulfillment. Instead, some argue, one should focus on how "friendship, enjoyable work, loving relationships, creative pursuits, sexual satisfaction, positive self-regard, and an intellectually challenging environment" (Ward & Stewart, 2003, p. 142) can better address criminality. The Good Lives Model (GLM) is based on the idea that all people fundamentally seek autonomy, connectedness, and self-respect (Ward & Gannon, 2008). As a result programming must be designed to acknowledge that for many offenders conventional routes are blocked (Ward, 2010; Ward, Melzer, & Yates, 2007). At the root of this criticism may be the idea that a reliance on the RNR model results in an approach to probation that embraces the idea that the community should impose probation activities *on* an offender, rather than viewing programs as an opportunity to develop and implement a plan *with* a client. As Davies observes, part of the concern is that:

> The effects of defining needs from a community safety perspective as opposed to a welfare perspective (that is, what needs to be changed in this person to achieve public protection) for the relationship between supervisor and for supervisee and for the motivation of the individual to participate in rehabilitative efforts are high-lighted. (Davies, 2008, p. 96)

While the RNR model can, when employed responsibly, overcome this concern (Andrews et. al. 2011), GLM might usefully be seen as complimentary to RNR in the particular areas of offender motivation and personal identity (Ward, Melzer, & Yates, 2007). In the place of a focus on avoidance associated with the identification of dynamic risk factors in RNR, GLM invites practitioners to rely upon positive reinforcement around engagement and autonomy and employ more collaborative approaches to rehabilitative interventions (Ward & Maruna, 2007). One of the most interesting aspects of the GLM is the suggestion that understanding the personal narratives of clients can best guide rehabilitative efforts. Since the stories we tell ourselves about our experience, our relationships, and the world around us can themselves be favorable to crime, the idea that understanding these narratives and how they inform behavior cannot be dismissed. There are, however, important questions about research designs that adequately measure what GLM asserts, and operationalize what appear to be qualitative and constructivist epistemological underpinnings.

It should be no surprise that these two distinct approaches to changing the behavior of those in conflict with the law should be opposed and yet in some way connected to one another. As discussed in Chapter 2, Probation has historically been understood as existing on a continuum between two competing principles of care and control. Therefore, it might be that the RNR model is as popular as it is, given its focus on quantitative construction and organization as a means to assist officers to organize case loads. Yet, few with any understanding of the swinging pendulum of policy pronouncements could be surprised at the backlash of what are seen as increasingly managerial approaches to supervision (Hedderman & Hough, 2004). The expansion of state control through probation can undermine the more practical kinds of support to assist offenders reintegrating into their communities. Access to health care, employment, and housing delivered by community members, charity groups, and public service organizations are examples of this kind of practical assistance (Kemshall *et al.* 2004). From one viewpoint, RNR simply represents the latest incarnation of the focus on the culture of control (Garland, 2001), while the GLM can be seen as a model that returns to the roots of probation. The idea that a role for personal relationships exists in the rehabilitation of those in conflict with the law (UN, 1954) perhaps requires that officers use the power of empathy and understanding to reach clients and facilitate change.

This may be too simplistic however. The care/control distinction may be a tactically unpromising way of conceiving probation. According to Rob Canton (2007: xxxiii), if these are in opposition, governments may reject care because they cannot face giving up control.

> The history of probation has ... been characterised as a journey from 'advise, assist and befriend' to 'enforcement, rehabilitation and public protection'...there is now a weight of evidence and argument to show that the way to get the best from people is to treat them well – with fairness, respect, encouragement and personal interest. This is not only ethically valuable, but also conduces to probation's objectives. In each of its phases, probation has sooner or later made this discovery. Perhaps the best way to enforce, rehabilitate and protect the public is by advising, assisting and befriending.

Another interpretation is that these models may guide different elements within probation services themselves. One distinction might be to understand which model can guide "hardware," and which might be used to influence "software" (Jones & Newburn, 2007). There can be no doubt of the utility of the RNR model to guide specific programmatic elements for courts and case management. However, the focus on relationships in the GLM may go beyond offenders and may offer a way for staff to see their clients and their role as agents of change. Working in the criminal justice system is more difficult personally and professionally than many imagine. Rob Watts (2011) observes:

> At the end of the day the value-add of any probation service is firmly linked to the integrity of its case management process. Supervision unto itself has limited usefulness, other than to enforce the court order or provide structure to other interventions. The glue that should bring all this together are case management

> practices. This can only be achieved by increasing the skill level of probation officers to better understand behavioural change approaches. There is no single recipe to move in this direction thought there are a number of options that will all contribute to this objective. I have evolved to a point where I believe that there must be some form of ongoing clinical support for the Officers. This again can take many forms but it speaks to the need for an environment of continuous learning and methods to ensure practical quality assurance.

The future of probation will involve understanding not only how these models can co-exist but also which of these two approaches is more appropriate for which type of individual, service, country, or region. Indeed, future research in this area might usefully be organized on how these models can be combined, integrated, or otherwise connected. Efforts must be made to resist simply relying on "common sense" as a basis for reform efforts (Carothers, 2003). Unless various models can be assessed and validated both quantitatively and qualitatively, they cannot benefit probation officers, clients, services, and the broader communities. This cannot occur without recognizing the role of professionals, volunteers, and the complexity associated with emergent developments within probation services.

7.2.3 Professionals, Volunteers, and Developing Probation

In some ways the philosophic debates about which complex model of probation should be employed and their associated theoretical and philosophic underpinnings is premature for the initial stages of probationary programming. Certainly there are those who have the ability and understanding to employ RNR, GLM, or some combination of the two within a newly constituted probation service. However until there is some practical experience on the ground, instituting one approach or the other is not in line with the idea that to be sustainable, collaborative probation programming must reflect the practices of the country in which it operates. While the consideration of which model is best suited to which country need not be definitively answered immediately, the question of how to develop local pilots, experiments, and models that involve communities must be considered.

Nearly all probation services around the world make use of volunteers in one way or another (Hamai & Ville, 1995). In North America, and increasingly in Europe, probation services are seen as more effective when they are based in the communities in which offenders reside, and when they rely upon volunteers to assist, support, and in some nominal sense, supervise those in conflict with the law. While asking law abiding citizens to volunteer to spend time with offenders may appear strange, programs in North America have shown the potential for approaches like these to reduce crime through greater societal involvement (Hinzman, 2000). This has been true even within programs that include offenders whose crimes shock our collective conscience (Prinzo *et al.* 2007). In countries emerging from authoritarian regimes, involving volunteers, and communities may be challenging. In the FSU the history of spying on one's family, neighbors, and co-workers during Soviet occupation provides a worrying literal meaning to community supervision. It may also be a clear example of what has been called the covert expansion of social control (Cohen, 1985). Ironically, this has not been a concern in Latvia. The SPS has increased volunteer participation and attempted to support individuals, communities, and governments to cooperate in new ways.

As discussed in Chapter 5, in 1999 in Latvia, community volunteers developed new programs and services, were hired by municipalities on a trial basis, and then secured their positions as the probation service was established nationally. By 2006, these locally developed services were being funded by the SPS, and some in the community who had previously volunteered their time were now involved in paid community-based probation and social rehabilitation efforts. It was the process of growing capacity from the ground-up that mattered in Latvia. It may be that without a focus on civil society partnerships, few probationary practices organized by the state will be able to achieve the same results. While the professionalization of probation is an integral step in the development of a sustainable service, it can have the effect of separating the administration of justice from the places in which the harms occurred (Elliott, 2011). Just as prisons keep those on the inside from getting out, they likewise keep those on the outside from getting in. The promise of probation is that communities can participate, a little or a lot, in rehabilitative efforts as part of the administration of justice. By offering a means for control when necessary, it is the focus on care that can better re-connect those who have committed harm with the communities to which they are most likely to return.

Whatever the potential for probation in MENA or beyond, the sole reliance on state-centric approaches is problematic. To facilitate the debates and deliberations, the conversations and contestation, community members must be active participants and must be supported to develop programs and services that can cooperate with the agencies of the state to support, assist, and ultimately reintegrate an offender with his or her community. Harris (1995, p. 207) notes:

> If probation is to prosper in developing countries it must build on existing structures of social support by working to enhance what is all ready there and repairing any fractures to the social fabric brought about by rapid social change…it is advisable to involve members of the community, not necessarily only on the individualistic basis of western volunteerism but possibly drawing too on the former Eastern European tradition of which sees supervision as by and in the community.

It is the active development and integration of civil society community, the reform of state agencies, and ways in which identity and community are understood in the region that requires more detailed discussion. To date, while justice reform efforts have begun to lay the groundwork for future programs, questions around how best to identify, work with, and involve the civil society sector has not been properly conceived or considered. Future programming must do a better job.

7.3 Legal Technical Assistance as Democratic Practice: Rule of Law or Rule of the Clan?

A central question that pulls at one premise of this book is: to what extent can justice reform initiatives – and specifically international probation programming – create a space to question, consider, and contest larger socio-cultural values and assumptions? While avoiding the historic arrogance and universalism of development initiatives is not easy, one observation is that when existing structures have a negative outcome for the least powerful in a society, the ways in which these structures are justified by those who benefit from them is relevant (Manor, 2007). Focusing on the quality of the justification provided may provide an answer to critics – whose views have proven prophetic – and who continue to argue that existing legal technical assistance projects exist simply as a means to continue the exportation of western economic interests. A central question for future scholars in this region concerns how rule of law programming can operate alongside clan-based governance in the countries of MENA.

Ethical universalism implies there are at least some values and principles that apply equally to everyone without exception. Often associated with Immanuel Kant, the human rights movement is one in which individual basic rights not only exist but obligate protection. While the protection of at least some rights is inherent within many conceptions of the rule of law, the role of rights has several implications. At least one cleavage as presented in Chapter 1 concerns formal and substantive rights protections and expectations.

Figure 7.4 Rule of Law: Formal and Substantive Considerations

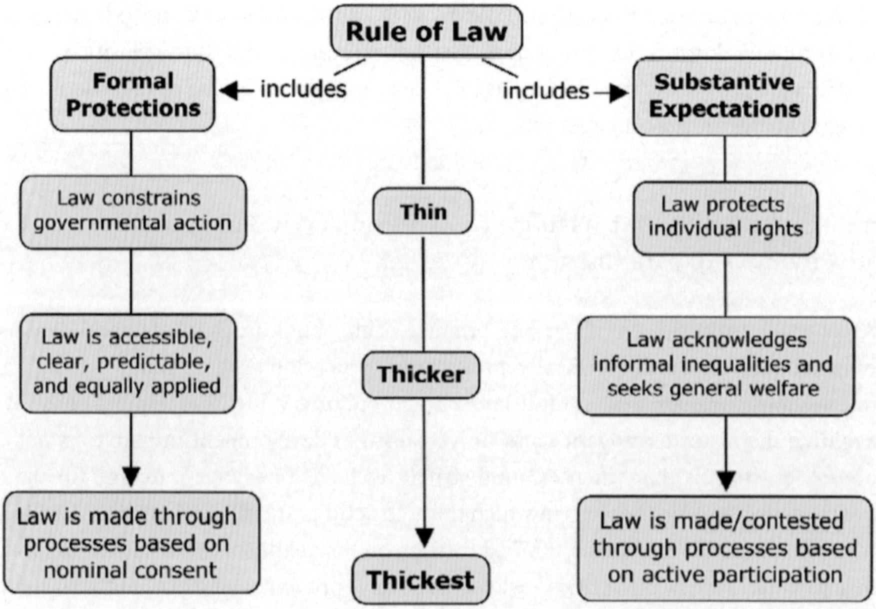

In the West of course, law is seen through the prism of liberalism and thus international engagements naturally focus on the importance of individual rights first. This is a product not of divine right, nor, despite the rumors, the end of history. Western understanding is a product of the experiences, cultural interactions, and societal pressures that have shaped Western societies. As Ruth Benedict points out:

> No man ever looks at the world with pristine eyes. He sees it edited by a definite set of customs and institutions and ways of thinking. Even in his philosophical probings he cannot go behind these stereotypes ... The life-history of the individual is first and foremost an accommodation to the patterns and standards traditionally handed down in his community. From the moment of his birth the customs into which he is born shape his experience and behaviour. By the time he can talk, he is the little creature of his culture, and by the time he is grown and able to take part in its activities, its habits are his habits, its beliefs his beliefs, its impossibilities his impossibilities. Every child that is born into his group will share them with him, and no child born into one on the opposite side of the globe can ever achieve the thousandth part. (1934, pp. 2-3)

In the past the variety of meanings, assumptions, and conceptions regarding the rule of law have been seen as perhaps a weakness, or a means to muddy the waters of definitional certainty. However the contrary may be true. Like probation, the flexibility that it implies might also be its greatest strength. Instead of presuming that the rule of law must naturally proceed along a predefined path from the formal protection of individual rights to more substantive expectations of equal opportunity and participation, in many countries of MENA the rule of law is conceived in communal terms. Development programming might then consider on what basis this collective character of law and legal development can serve the broader interests as articulated by the community itself.

In the place of a focus on secularized universal ethical principles and preferred developed outcomes, a more practical (yet inherently messy) approach may be required which involves compromise between those who fund and those who are funded. Discarding normative assumptions and empirical evidence about the role of gender, inclusion, and equity in reform may not always be possible for external reformers and donors (Ecevit, 1993). Likewise convincing internal elites in host countries that real reform requires re-balancing the longstanding authority of tribes and clans with local, regional and ultimately national reform initiatives will not be easy (Weiner, 2011). This is where the rubber meets the road. There may be no more important challenge to democratic reform in the region than the question of how to encourage clans to participate in and become stakeholders of emerging democracies.

To understand the challenges posed by clans to attempts to broaden inclusion through dialogue and deliberation, it may be useful to understand the role of clans using the three-tier model. Weiner (2011, p. 40) defines clans as:

> …corporate units of social organization based on descent from a real or fictional common ancestor. Clans provide their members with a range of social, economic, and cultural goods, including a fundamental sense of personal identity, while also defining their members' legal rights and obligations. Naturally, clan structures exist in different forms…

The role that clans play may be difficult for those outside the culture to appreciate. In terms of country context, members of clans are united by powerful cultural feelings of solidarity that limit overarching national identity, commonly assumed to be essential for democratic citizenship. Organizationally, clans often function as basic units of social associations and claim to hold legitimate authority to administer justice for their members by using their own force. When clans exert legal powers that are independent from those of the state and outside public control, they can create the potential for violence and instability. Individually, clans pose a challenge for the role and language of human rights in justice reform. In collectivist societies, ruled by clans, people are afforded protection not as individuals but as members of the ancestral groups to which they belong.

To address the challenges to democratic reform represented by the role of clans in the countries of MENA, Farmer & Weiner (2011) argue for three considerations to inform future programming:

> First, history teaches that in this aspect of state-building, as in most others, development must not be imposed from without, which invariably freezes the process of democratic bargaining among interest groups, but rather must arise from within. Ground-level knowledge and long-term political relationships are essential – a fact powerfully illustrated by the story of Muhammad, whose deep familiarity with Arabian clans, gained through his early years as a trader and trusted mediator of tribal disputes, was critical in building the early Islamic state. Second, contrary to current rule of law initiatives, which have tended to ignore or compete with the clans, exiling them to the margins of state-building, clans should be encouraged to participate in and become stakeholders of emerging democracies. They must be afforded national incentives to cede local authority. Finally, in addition to encouraging trade and economic development, the United States should do what it can to help reformers in the region strengthen the identity and power of the intellectual and professional classes, among whom personal identity is most powerfully peeled away from the social core of kinship.

These considerations are no doubt important, and may be connected to Kazziha's (2010) suggestion that the best means to expand democratic practice in the region is for external actors to promote the expansion of political constituencies. However, practical suggestions about how to operationalize these theoretical ideas are needed. This book has presented probation as a means to fill this gap while serving consistent political, practical, and philosophical tenets. In Latvia, developing ground level relationships among individuals, civil society groups, and local governments was achieved through pilot project competitions designed to meet local needs. In the countries of MENA this will necessitate the explicit support of local clans, tribes, and power brokers. How can these groups who have held power through informal social arrangements be convinced to cede local control and participate as equals with those of other ethnicities, cultures, genders, and religious views? What are needed are models of dialogue in the region and examples of what ceding clan-based control looks like. Lebanon, at a political crossroad, may be the country to lead.

7.3.1 *Juvenile Justice Reform and the Importance of Lebanon*

Whatever the challenges on the ground discussed above, all member states of the Arab League (with the exception of Somalia) have signed and ratified the UN Convention on the Rights of the Child (CRC). Most of them have tried, to varying degrees of success, to bring their national legislation to comply with their obligations under the CRC. Probation as part of broader juvenile justice reform in the region is already underway. Juvenile Justice projects funded by the Swedish International Development Agency (SIDA) and implemented by Prison Reform International (PRI) have been in progress since 2004 in Algeria, Egypt, Jordan, Morocco, and Yemen. Efforts have been made to strike a balance between security needs and penal and prison reforms that uphold the rule of law and international human rights standards. While PRI reports successes at the policy level, real change on the ground remains elusive. In addition to the lack of basic security for the population, governments have been slow to focus on international commitments on human rights and engage in meaningful reform agendas.

There are a variety of reasons juvenile justice probation programming in Lebanon should be considered. Lebanon is a country of 18 communities grouped into two large religious entities – Christian and Muslim – each one enjoying some legislative and judiciary autonomy. It has made great strides since 2002 when a number of legislative reforms (Schmid & Riachy, 2003) were passed to support justice reform throughout the country and the withdrawal of Syrian troops in 2005 has led many to hope democracy can prevail over the narrow interests promoted by the sectarian system (Salloukh, 2010). While developments have been uneven, the American Bar Association (ABA) has recently recognized these strides in its World Justice Report's 2011 Rule of Law Index. For the 5 countries surveyed in MENA, the rank, in order, was as follows: United Arab Emirates, Jordan, Iran, Lebanon, and Morocco. Within the report, however, there are useful indicators of the developments in Lebanon. For example:

> Lebanon stands out in the region due to its efforts to guarantee civil rights and freedoms amongst its people (ranking 1st in the region and 26th globally)....Of particular concern is the case of the administration of justice, mainly because of corruption and political interference within the civil courts, delays, discrimination against marginalized groups, and absence of guarantees of due process of law in criminal cases. (WJP, 2011, p. 34)

Despite existing challenges, the report goes on to state that Lebanon outperforms other countries surveyed specifically related to the right to life and security of person, freedom of opinion and expression, freedom of belief and religion, arbitrary interference of privacy, and freedom of assembly and association. In addition to these encouraging developments toward an adherence with certain aspects of rule of law, Lebanon has been the site of a number of past reform initiatives. As such those on the ground have a significant base of knowledge, and positive and negative experiences to assist future programming. Of course, challenges remain. Lebanon often appears to be an open arena in which competition and compromise between regional and international powers play out. Iran, Syria, Saudi Arabia, France and the United States all have interests and local allies. While Iran and Syria are accused of using assassinations and supplying local groups with weapons, support for the western-leaning camp is mostly political and financial. This support has recently been complicated by indictments by the Special Tribunal for Lebanon and accompanying arrest warrants relating to the murder of former Prime Minister Rafik Hariri and more than twenty others. It is not yet clear if Lebanon will comply with the Tribunal.

During the upheavals of recent months the citizens of the Middle East have made it clear to the world that the rule of law and accountability are among the pillars upon which people in the region want to re-build their societies. Although a founding member of the United Nations, Lebanon's system of justice operates within a political environment that has in the past resorted to the traditional focus on stability through fear. The divide and conquer strategy to 'manage' various sectarian groups of the past is not easy to dislodge. This undermines the longer-term potential for justice as a foundation for lasting peace and stability. For Cassese (2011), the indictments of the special tribunal represent an opportunity for a re-awakening in Lebanon and the region – this is a chance that must not be missed. To embrace the true potential of these developments, dialogue must be used to lead to compromise, and compromise must be seen as the basis for legitimate and credible governance structures.

Reforming the justice system in a multi-ethnic society remains a key challenge. The experiences gained in Lebanon, albeit limited to date, can be of great value to others making similar efforts (Schmid & Riachy, 2003, p. 116). So can future reform efforts if they embrace the notion that rule-of-law promotion activities must respect the importance of dialogue, deliberation, and debate within processes designed to allow legitimate legal orders to emerge. Juvenile justice reform may be the best short-term hope given the interest throughout the Arab World in juvenile justice reform in the field of child protection and juvenile justice. While challenges exist, it should be recalled that this was also the case in the Baltics even years after independence. By engaging communities and starting alternative programs for youth, projects soon expanded and resulted in a service that managed both youth and adult clients. In the place of impatient initiatives seeking instant gratification, future programming might consider how to apply other more specific elements of project design and delivery as discussed above. While Lebanon is not the only country in which reforms may succeed, nor even the best example of sustainable change, it is incredibly important for the region. To date sectarian calculations and external influences have undermined efforts to build a democratic Lebanon based on dialogue and mutual accommodation (Salloukh, 2010). As an ethnic and cultural mosaic, Lebanon can serve as a model for the adaptability of probation and the difficult conversations associated with the democratization of the state and the reform of an outdated and ill-adapted system of juvenile justice. How that conversation unfolds, however, matters.

7.4 DIALOGUE, DELIBERATION, AND DEBATE: RIGHTS AND RESPONSIBILITIES

What if meaningful justice reform is connected to the *process* of learning to disagree without being disagreeable? While there may be no universal principles, there may be universal constraints that any practice relying upon dialogue and deliberation must respect. It is a question that requires further extrapolation, analysis, and testing, of course. Yet conceptually, when it comes to matters related to justice, rights, and reform disagreements are inevitable. The process of accommodation based on a commitment to peaceful and non-coercive relationships, even with people with whom we vehemently disagree, becomes central (Wong, 2006). One constraint in this process must be that when debating the value of structures that have long privileged some people and groups over others, it is the quality of the justification for these social practices that must be considered. Just because governance systems in North America have failed to instill confidence, or demonstrate anything like quality as a political virtue, those failures need not be determinative for others seeking to learn from these experiences. Perhaps it is the fact that our system mocks the values which most of us espouse that has created this era of cognitive dissonance. Perhaps we have more to learn than to teach.

This book has argued in addition to the practical benefits of promoting human rights protection within justice reform, legal technical assistance projects can also be seen as part of international efforts to promote democracy and good governance. Specifically, probation provides a means to focus on legal outcomes, while engaging the personalities who give effect to legal rules. By expanding the number of actors and the use of discretion, justice reform can support a shift away from the concentration of power and model more inclusive decision-making. It should be seen as a central milestone toward further democratic reforms to the extent that it results in systems or services that mimic ours. Instead, justice reform should be seen as part of a larger process of democratization. While it was a precursor to the accession of many post-communist countries in Central and Eastern Europe to the European Union, reforms relating to democracy, human rights and the rule of law have continued (Czarnota, 2006). In Latvia at least, justice reform has had a profound effect on those previously incarcerated, their families, and their communities.

Whatever the challenges that remain in Latvia, and whatever the limitations of applying this model elsewhere, the space created through a collaborative process to reform the justice system opens a deeper and more inclusive conversation about the role of law, justice, punishment, and rehabilitation. In North Africa and the Middle East, the situation is both more complex and has, perhaps, even more potential. Political and social instability continue to pervade the region and past armed conflicts in Iraq, Lebanon, Israel and Palestine have expanded to Libya, Syria, and Yemen. Too many have resulted in civilian deaths and casualties leading, until recently, to a pervasive pessimism. Yet it is risky to attempt to be categorical about the impediments for democracy in the Middle East (Ecevit, 1993). Justice reform may provide a means to continue the conversation.

Despite the complexities that exist there is a renewed interest in role of the justice system. In 2010, United Nations Office of Drug Control (UNDOC) announced a five-year program to improve drug and crime control and criminal justice reform in the Middle East and North Africa. The program focuses on combating organized crime and terrorism, strengthening integrity and justice, and preventing drug abuse in the region. While the focus on drug control and terrorism may lead skeptics to discount the program as a whole, the program has the potential to create a new momentum for promoting the rule of law and human development in the region. Indeed the explicit recognition that criminal justice systems are under-resourced and prison conditions need to be improved may serve as an important opening for more detailed discussions.

Recently in Jordan, a new three-year joint United Kingdom and European Union program will focus on adult probation programming and correctional reform. Designed to complement past youth programming, one focus includes improving access to alternative sanctions to imprisonment. While existing in law, there are largely absent in practice. This absence creates both challenges and opportunities. For McInerney (2005), projects like these provide a means for more deliberative models of development. Building on Jurgen Habermas he suggests:

> Problems of knowledge, politics, social practice, and incentives challenge the effectiveness of hierarchical and centralized approaches to law and development. To the extent that law-making priorities are set through negotiation and bargaining between states and donors, state institutions and democratic impulses fail to grow organically... The deliberative democratic legal-reform model avoids stretching the cognitive limits of such a top-down approach and imposing an artificial separation between development of democracy and the rule of law. The deliberative process simultaneously cultivates democracy and the rule of law not through great leaps in tension with democratic values, but through actual democratic practice. (McInerney, 2005, p. 969)

It would be a mistake, however, to attempt to replace one development orthodoxy with another. Instead broader participation must be itself cultivated through local reforms that meet the real and practical needs of people on the ground. As the experience in Latvia suggests, probation can do this. Properly conceived, a community corrections model can lead to the development of local services that encourage citizens to take more responsibility and become more involved in the justice system as a whole. For Canton (2009, p. 74), the aspiration should be to:

> ...enable each country to introduce and develop probation practices that they can recognise and value as their own, even if modeled on the organisation, policies and practices of others.

This view is no doubt right. The more participation, dialogue, and deliberation that is possible, the more sustainable the eventual result. Yet just as probation operates at the intersection of the justice system, it also exists on a conceptual continuum. Its practices often reflect the values of the society in which it exists and it is this feature that allows for fundamental questions – both philosophic and practical – to emerge. It may not always be pretty; flexibility is needed for host countries and donor countries alike. Perry and Barrows (2009, p. 77) suggest that host countries consider that the process of international cooperation is not what many expect. They suggest: "...help will always come at a price, and the outcome will almost certainly be different to your dream" and they warn ".... Sometimes we will party, sometimes we will shake our heads in despair at our partners."

In line with the discussions in this book and the three-tier model it has presented, they warn against the arrogance that has characterized past development relationships. They urge countries that provide expertise and advice to:

> Understand the beneficiary country; understand the political and resource realities and expect to be humbled by how much can be achieved at the beginning with enthusiasm and commitment. Do not assume that systems, methods and tools that have been used in your own jurisdiction can be simply exported. Not only do they need to be adapted legally and technically but they also need to be 'owned' by the beneficiary: this means understanding the local political, economic and cultural drivers and helping managers and professionals find their own solutions to their strategic goals. Be ready for the second wave, when professional management approaches must follow the initial enthusiasm if the changes are to be sustained and developed further. (Perry & Barrows, 2009, p. 77)

In conclusion, the value of probation to the region may be three-fold. Politically, it offers an issue that can keep the opposition unified. While debates must continue, this book has argued that justice reform is a central first step in the larger process of democratization. Practically, it offers a means to engage in justice reforms designed to better protect and promote human rights through a renewed focus on rehabilitation and social inclusion. Philosophically, based on the lessons from Latvia, probation programming can offer a means to model the sort of step-by-step democratic approaches that can allow civil society to confront the underlying systemic dysfunction within an existing state's governance systems. Without promoting inclusion and engaging a broader cross-section of the populace in a conversation about the role of law in society, the potential for the renewal of Spring will turn instead into the retrenchment of a cold Winter.

Chapter 7 Bibliography

K. Al-Oran. *Correctional System in the Hashmite Kingdom of Jordan*. Unpublished Masters Thesis. Department of Criminal Justice, Ohio: Youngstown State University, 2000.

D.A. Andrews. The impact of nonprogrammatic factors on criminal-justice interventions. *Legal and Criminological Psychology*, Vol. 16, 2011, pp. 1-23.

D.A. Andrews, I. Zinger, R.D. Hoge, J. Bonta, J P. Gendreau & F.T. Cullen. Does correctional treatment work? A clinically relevant and psychologically informed meta-analysis. *Criminology* Vol. 28, No.3, 1990 pp. 369-404.

D.A. Andrews & J. Bonta. Rehabilitating Criminal Justice Policy And Practice. *Psychology, Public Policy, and Law* Vol. 16, No. 1, 2010, pp. 39-55.

D.A. Andrews & J. Bonta. *The psychology of criminal conduct* (4th ed.). Newark, NJ: LexisNexis/Matthew Bender, 2006.

S. Avineri. Transformations in Eastern Europe and lesson for the Middle East. In N. Brown & E. El-Din Shahin (Eds.), *Introduction in The Struggle over Democracy in the Middle East: Regional Politics and External Policies*. London, Routledge, 2010, pp. 87-101.

M Ayoob. *The Third World Security Predicament*. Boulder, CO: Lynne Rienner Publishers, Inc., 1995.

A. Banerjee. *Making Aid Work*. MIT Press: Cambridge, MA, 2007.

I. Beeson & C. Davis. Emergence and accomplishment in organizational change. *Journal of Organizational Change Management*, Vol. 13, No. 2, 2000, pp. 178-189.

S. Bell, R. Corrado, Y. Dandurand & C. Griffiths. *Report of the LRCP advisory panel.* Ottawa, ON: Association of Universities and Colleges Canada, 2002.

R. Benedict. *Patterns of Culture.* New York: Houghton Mifflin, 1934.

A. Berzins. *Report to The Working Group on Probation in Latvia.* The Legal Reform Capacity Program in Latvia, Ottawa, ON: Association of Universities and Colleges of Canada, 2002.

J.M. Brinkerhoff. Digital Diasporas and conflict prevention: the case of Somalinet.com. *Review of International Studies*, Vol. 32, 2006, pp. 25-47.

N. Brown & E. El-Din Shahin. *Introduction in The Struggle over Democracy in the Middle East: Regional Politics and External Policies.* London, Routledge, 2010, pp. 1-10.

N. Brown, A. Hamzawy & M. Ottaway. *Islamist movements and the democratic Process in the Arab World: Exploring the Gray Zones.* Washington DC: Carnegie Endowment for International Peace and the Herbert-Quandt-Stiftung, 2006.

R. Canton. Taking Probation Abroad. *European Journal of Probation*, Vol. 1, No. 1, 2009, pp. 66-78.

R. Canton. Introduction. In R. Canton and D. Hancock (eds.). *Dictionary of Probation and Offender Management.* Collompten; UK: Willan, 2009.

T. Carothers. Promoting the rule of law abroad: The problem of knowledge (Working Paper No. 34.) Washington, DC: Carnegie Endowment for International Peace, 2003.

T. Carothers. *Think Again: Arab Democracy.* Washington, DC: Carnegie Endowment for International Peace, 2011.

A. Cassesse. *A Decisive Movement for Lebanon.* Op/Ed *New York Times*, July 12, 2011.

S. Chesterman. *You the People: the United Nations, Transitional Administration, and State-Building.* Oxford, UK: Oxford University Press, 2004.

H. Chodosh. *Global justice reform: A comparative methodology.* New York: New York University Press, 2005.

S. Cohen. *Visions of Social Control: Crime, Punishment and Classification*. London, UK: Polity Press, 1985.

D. Cole. The Umpires Strike Back: Canadian Judicial Experience with Risk-Assessment Instruments. *Canadian Journal of Criminology and Criminal Justice*, Vol. 49, No. 4, 2007, pp. 493-517.

CRC. Annual Report United Nations Committee for the Rights of the Child. New York: UN Publications, 2011.

J. Crystal. Criminal Justice in the Middle East. *Journal of Criminal Justice*, Vol. 29, No. 6, 2001, pp. 469-482.

A. Czarnota. Barbarians ante portas or the Post-Communist Rule of Law in Post-Democratic European Union. In W. Sadurski & A. Czarnota, M. Krygier (Eds.), *Spreading Democracy and the Rule of Law? The Impact of EU Enlargement for the Rule of Law, Democracy and Constitutionalism in Post-Communist Legal Orders*. Springer, 2006, pp. 283-297.

K. Davies. Book Review: Ward, T. & Maruna, S. Rehabilitation. *Probation Journal* Vol. 55, 2008, pp. 95-99.

B. Ecevit. Prospects and Difficulties of Democratization in the Middle East. In E. Goldberg, R. Kasaba & J. Migdal (Eds.), *Rules and Rights in the Middle East: Democracy, Law, and Society*. Seattle, WA: University of Washington Press, 1993, pp. 141-163.

E. Elliott. *Security, With Care: Restorative Justice and Healthy Societies*. Halifax, NS: Fernwood Publishing, 2011.

J.F. Farmer & M. Weiner. Rule of the clan a challenge to Middle East North Africa. *New Jersey Voices*, July, 17, 2011.

P. Freire. *Pedagogy of the Oppressed*. New York, NY: Continuum International Publishing Group, 1970/2000.

D. Garland. *The Culture of Control: Crime and Social Order in Contemporary Society*. Chicago, Il: University of Chicago Press, 2001.

I. Hacking. *The Taming of Chance*. Cambridge: Cambridge University Press, 1990.

K.D. Haggerty. Displaced expertise: Three constraints on the policy-relevance of criminological thought. *Theoretical Criminology*, Vol. 8, No. 2, 2004, pp. 211-231.

K. Hamai & R. Ville. Origins and Purposes of Probation. In K. Hamai, R. Harris, M. Hough, R. Ville, & U. Zvekic (Eds.), *Probation Around the World: A Comparative Study*. London, UK: Routledge Press, 1995, pp. 71-110.

K. Hannah-Moffatt & P. Maurutto. *Youth Risk/Need Assessment: An Overview of Issues and Practices*. Ottawa, ON: Department of Justice Canada, 2003.

R. Harris. Probation Around the World: Origins and Development. In K. Hamai, R. Harris, M. Hough, R. Ville, & U. Zvekic (Eds.), *Probation Around the World: A Comparative Study*. London, UK: Routledge Press, 1995, pp. 25-70.

F. Hawes & D. Kealey. An empirical study of Canadian technical assistance: Adaptation and effectiveness on overseas assignments. *International Journal of Intercultural Relations*, Vol. 1, No. 5, 1981, pp. 239-258.

C. Hedderman & M. Hough. Getting tough or being effective: what matters? In G. Mair (Ed.), *What Matters in Probation* Cullompton, UK: Willan, 2004, pp. 146-169.

M. Henkel. *Government, Evaluation & Change*. London, UK: Jessica Kingsley Publishers, 1991.

E. Herring & G. Rangwala. *Iraq in Fragments: The Occupation and Its Legacy*. London, UK: Hurst, 2006.

G.R. Hinzman. Broken Windows, Broken Buckets: Solutions for Safer Communities. *Corrections Management Quarterly*, Vol. 4, No. 2, 2000, pp. 23-33.

T. Jones & T. Newburn. *Policy Transfer and Criminal Justice*. Maidenhead: Open University Press, 2007.

W. Kazziha. The fantasy of Arab democracy without a constituency. In N. Brown & E. El-Din Shahin (Eds.), *Introduction in The Struggle over Democracy in the Middle East: Regional Politics and External Policies*. London, Routledge, 2010, pp. 42-59.

H. Kemshall. *Risk in Probation Practice*. Hampshire, England: Ashgate, 1998.

H. Kemshall, P. Holt, R. Bailey & G. Boswell. Beyond programmes: organisational and cultural issues in the implementation of What Works. In G. Mair (Ed.), *What Matters in Probation* Cullompton, UK: Willan, 2004, pp. 170-186.

K. Krause & O Jütersonke. Peace, Security and Development in Post- Conflict Environments. *Security Dialogue*, Vol. 36, No. 4, 2005, pp. 447-462.

C. Kurzman & I. Naqvi. Do Muslims vote Islamic? *Journal of Democracy*, Vol. 21, No. 2, 2010, pp. 50-63.

M.A. Lawan, I. Sada & S. Ali. *An Introduction to Islamic Criminal Justice: A Teaching and Learning Manual, with Dr. Ibrahim Sada, Prof. Shaheen Ali*, UK Centre for Legal Education, 2008.

K. Lewin. *Field theory in social science*. New York, NY: Harper and Row, 1951.

M. Los. Crime in transition: The post-communist state, markets and crime. *Crime, Law & Social Change*, Vol. 40, 2003, pp. 145-169.

W. Mahmoud. Civil and Criminal Justice. In N. Bernard-Maugiron & B. Dupret. *Egypt and Its Laws*. London: Kluwer Law International, 2002, pp. 136-180.

A.E. Mayer. *Islam and Human Rights*, Westview Press, 2007.

C. Manning. Political Elites and Democratic State-building Efforts in Bosnia and Iraq, *Democratization*, Vol. 13, No. 5, 2006, pp. 724-738.

J. Manor. *Aid that Works: Successful Development in Fragile States*. Washington: The World Bank, 2007.

T.F. McInerney. Law and Development as Democratic Practice. *Vanderbilt Journal of Transnational Law*, Vol. 37, 2005, pp. 935-975.

J.R.P. Ogloff & M.R. Davis. Advances in offender assessment and rehabilitation: Contributions of the risk-needs-responsivity approach. *Psychology, Crime and Law*, Vol. 10, No. 2, 2004, pp. 229-242.

R. Owen. The Practice of Electoral Democracy in the Arab East and North Africa. In E. Goldberg, R. Kasaba & J. Migdal (Eds.), *Rules and Rights in the Middle East: Democracy, Law, and Society*. Seattle, WA: University of Washington Press, 2003, pp. 17-40.

M. Page. *Crime fighters of London: A History of the Origins and Development of the London Probation Service 1876-1965*. London: Inner London Probation Service Benevolent and Educational Trust, 1992.

R. Paris. International Peacebuilding and the 'Mission Civilisatrice'. *Review of International Studies*, Vol. 28, No. 4, 2002, pp. 637-656.

D. Perry & R. Barrows. The Interpretation of Dreams. *Eurovista*, Vol. 1, No. 2, 2009, pp. 72-78.

S. Power. The Enforcer. *The New Yorker*, January 19, 2009, pp. 52-58.

M. Prinzo, A. McWhinnie, R. Wilson, J. Picheca & F. Cortoni. Circles of Support and Accountability: Engaging Community Volunteers in the Management of High-Risk Sexual Offenders. *Howard Journal of Criminal Justice*, Vol. 46, No. 1, 2007, pp. 1-15.

T. Ramadan. *Radical Reform: Islamic Ethics and Liberation*. Oxford University Press, 2008.

N. Reichman. Managing Crime Risks: Towards an Insurance Based Model of Social Control. *Research In Law Deviance and Social Control*, Vol. 8, 1986, pp. 151-172.

S. Reza. Egypt. In C.M. Bradley (Ed.), *Criminal Procedure: A Worldwide Study*, Durham: Carolina University Press, 2007, pp. 107-147.

S. Reza. Egypt. In K. Heller & M. Dubber (Eds.), *Handbook of Comparative Criminal Law* Stanford: Stanford University Press, 2011, pp. 179-208.

D. Robinson, M. Grossman, & F. Porporino. *Effectiveness of the Cognitive Skills Training Program: From Pilot to National Implementation*, Ottawa, ON: Correctional Service of Canada, 1991.

E.M. Rogers. *Diffusion of innovations* (5th ed.). New York, NY: Free Press, 2005.

E.M. Rogers. *Diffusion of knowledge* (1st ed.). New York, NY: Free Press, 1962.

R. Ross & E. Fabiano. *Time to Think: A Cognitive Model of Delinquency Prevention and Offender Rehabilitation.* Johnson City, Tennessee: Institute of Social Sciences and Arts, 1985.

A. Sachedina. *Islam and The Challenges of Human Rights.* Oxford University Press, 2009.

B. Salloukh. Democracy in Lebanon: The primacy of the Sectarian System. In N. Brown & E. El-Din Shahin (Eds.), *Introduction in The Struggle over Democracy in the Middle East: Regional Politics and External Policies.* London, Routledge 2010, pp. 135-150.

N. Sanad. *The Theory of Crime and Criminal responsibility in Islamic Law: Shari'a.* University of Illinois: Chicago, 1991.

A. Schmid & R. Riady. Juvenile Justice Initiatives in Lebanon. *Forum on Crime and Society,* Vol. 3, No. 1/2, 2003, pp. 105-116.

R. Simmons, P. Fajans & L. Ghiron. *Scaling up health service delivery: From pilot innovations to policies and programmes.* Geneva, Sw: World Health Organization, 2007.

D.D. Simpson. A conceptual framework for transferring research to practice. *Journal of Substance Abuse Treatment,* Vol. 22, No. 4, 2002, pp. 171-182.

S.S. Souryal. The Religionization of a Society: The Continuing application of Shari'a law in Saudi Arabia. *Journal for the Scientific Study of Religion.* Vol. 24, No. 4, 1987, pp. 429-449.

United Nations. Proceedings of European Seminar on Probation, London, 20-30 October, 1952. United Nations. Secretariat Technical Assistance Administration. ST/TAA/Ser.C/11 New York, 1954.

T. Vulpe, D. Kealey, D. Protheroe & D. MacDonald. *A profile of the interculturally effective person.* Gatineau, PQ: Department of Foreign Affairs and International Trade, 2000.

T. Ward & S. Maruna. *Rehabilitation: Beyond the risk paradigm.* New York, NY: Routledge, 2007.

T. Ward & C.A. Stewart. Criminogenic needs and human needs: A theoretical model. *Psychology, Crime, and Law.* Vol. 9, 2003, pp. 125-143.

T. Ward, & T. Gannon. Rehabilitation, etiology, and self-regulation: The Good Lives Model of rehabilitation for sexual offenders. *Aggression and Violent Behavior.* Vol. 11, 2006, pp. 77-94.

T. Ward, J. Melser & P. Yates. Reconstructing the risk-need-responsivity model: A theoretical elaboration and evaluation. *Aggression and Violent Behavior,* Vol. 12: 2007, pp. 208-228.

R. Watts. Personal Communication. October, 2011.

M.S. Weiner. Religious Freedom and the Rule of the Clan in Muslim Societies. *The Review of Faith & International Affairs,* Vol. 9, No. 2011, pp. 39-45.

J. Wheeldon. *Bringing British Columbia to Latvia: Canadians reflect on expert designation in an international criminal justice project.* Burnaby, BC: School of Criminology, Simon Fraser University, 2007.

D.B Wong. *Natural Moralities: A Defense of Pluralistic Relativism.* New York: Oxford University Press, 2006.

World Justice Project. Rule of Law Index. American Bar Association, Washington DC, 2011.

R. Youngs. Democracy and security in the Middle East. In N. Brown & E. El-Din Shahin (Eds.), *Introduction in The Struggle over Democracy in the Middle East: Regional Politics and External Policies.* London, Routledge, 2010, pp. 29-41.

S. Zubaida. *Islam: The People and the State.* London: Routledge, 1989.

Epilogue: Incarceration, Community, and Control

This book presented international development projects as important sites of cross-cultural interaction. In the Baltic country of Latvia, cooperation between Latvians and Canadians occurred at a time and place shaped by the past, while looking toward the future. For those interested in the important work of promoting justice reform through international technical assistance, there are lessons to be learned from this experience. Whether these lessons are valid for other countries emerging from post-authoritarian regimes around the world is an open question. The model presented in these pages offers a way to both conceive and perhaps begin to address the systemic contextual, organizational, and individual impediments to reform. Of course, more research is needed that puts the voices of those involved in reform front and center. This effort must be seen as but one attempt – not yet the definitive account. Justice reform is infinitely more difficult than many imagine.

This difficulty arises in part because these reform projects represent an intersection point. As competing interests approach these sites of collision and/or cooperation, they may arrive at the same time while moving at very different speeds. However, probation practices can serve as a central intermediary between incarceration and rehabilitation and offer a means for communities to moderate the social control exercised by formal justice and governance institutions. Latvian-Canadian programming had to confront questions about law, justice, and punishment through the lens of a national identity shaped in part by fifty years of occupation. The international community cannot ignore these realities elsewhere, and especially as it looks to overcome the legacy of colonialism and build on the potential of the "Arab Spring" in the countries of MENA.

Three stories have formed the basis of this book. The first explored some of the difficulties, confusion, and failures associated with the provision of international assistance. Despite pressures from the international community, national strategic and economic interests, and bureaucratic demands, this book has argued that those working legal technical assistance must reconsider the role of research in developing a strategic vision for its delivery. This call is hardly new, yet the perils of failing to develop a culture of research within development are becoming increasingly evident. While funding to countries of the FSU will be reduced over the next decade, the abrupt transition from hierarchical to more participatory forms of governance offers important lessons for researchers and policy makers. While every country is unique and there is no sustainable one size fits all approach, experiences in one region can assist us to understand other, perhaps more subtle and gradual traditions that are being attempted in others. Probation may be a key institution in the transition underway in many countries within the Middle East and North Africa.

The second story described Latvia's struggle to overcome the legacies of occupation, including the psychological impacts of political, cultural, and social domination, resulting – this book has argued – in significant impediments to reform. The book has described how Latvians themselves engaged in various kinds of reforms to bring their own justice system in line with European standards and international norms. This included a number of collaborative legal technical assistance efforts, including initiatives since 1999 funded in partnership with CIDA. While Canada's Latvian Diaspora assisted to bridge the cultural divide, they also identified some specific programming choices and contributed to the process of discovering a more sustainable means for community partnership and participation. One lesson is that legal technical assistance requires that reform be pursued through local innovation and the provision of practical and adaptable tools. To do this, interactive, participatory, and experiential training methods should be used to promote group-based problem solving. Through this process a broader debate about the place of law in society can be facilitated among those working to reform justice systems. This is responsibility cannot be taken lightly. The promotion of simple and singular views cannot support meaningful and sustainable reform. Yet, projects can serve as a meaningful site for debate and deliberation and as such they are worthy of more attention. While more research is needed to understand the promise of probation, the three-tier model presented in this book offers a framework to do so.

The third and final story revolved around the process of interaction among those on the project. Creating a pro-reform environment grounded in respect for democratic values and human rights may be the most difficult task faced by those who engage in legal technical assistance. Of course, any institutional reform is by its nature, a political exercise requiring new sorts of negotiations between communities and governments to promote more participatory interaction. One impediment to meaningful reform is the pursuit of institutionally focused democratic development initiatives that omit value considerations, and compete rather than cooperate with existing structures. In the countries of MENA this will involve engaging the tribes and clans that play an important role in the social organization of the region.

It is easy to forget the feelings of euphoria among so many when the Berlin Wall fell. Many on both sides of the East/West divide held hopes for a quick re-unification and supported assistance based on the presupposition that it was the "West" who offers models, while the "East" adopts them. In the Middle East, the role of the West in building democratic institutions has been tied to other geo-political calculations and in too many cases lacked credibility. Reframing support for this region must be combined with new understandings that simplistic donor/recipient models of development and reform are not only pejorative but also demonstrably unconvincing as the basis for sustainable and meaningful reform.

Nevertheless, there is a real risk that the arrogance of past approaches will continue as the international community begins to re-engage countries in North Africa and the Middle East following the events of 2011.

This book has argued there is no silver bullet, no universal remedy except the old ones – dialogue, deliberation, disagreement – and slow and eventual accommodation and reconciliation. Probation can be a practical and specific element of programming that as part of broader justice reform initiatives can serve the interests not only of authoritarian elites, but also those of the citizens who live in these countries and regions. A central question remains how to effectively use the lessons of the past to extrapolate future practice. To move past failed development models we must recognize the expertise and the elegance of those with hands-on experience. With a deepening respect for the differences within and between countries, an honest accounting of successes and failures can be integrated into current practice. Yet acknowledging in-country differences does not obviate the need to compile various sources of empirical data about existent development projects. This information can provide complementary data to inform governance indicators of both formal and informal impediments to reform. Together these facts can pragmatically present, reflect, and support the challenges faced by those working on the ground.

Based on the experiences described in this book, probation should be seen as an example of legal technical assistance that requires an understanding about how common values and social networks cause people to use, revise and reinterpret legal reforms. As a result, training and technical assistance might usefully be seen as a means not only to transfer knowledge, but also to model inclusive and more democratic interactions. While explicitly connecting values to any aspect of foreign policy is fraught with controversy, norms promoted by Western donors may have the most dramatic influence on the success of development projects abroad. One norm worth pursuing is that, at the core of democracy, participatory mechanisms can balance conflicting value-claims and find ways of disagreeing without being disagreeable. Reform is unlikely without a commitment to this sentiment, and a fidelity to the resulting practices and outcomes.

Probation when viewed as a set of ideas and strategies can be used creatively to solve local problems of criminal justice. Yet to be successful, concepts such as partnership, stakeholder participation, increased local ownership, and sustainability must not simply exist as boxes to tick on a results-based management report to funders. Instead, these concepts and a commitment to research developmental outcomes must shape both the design and the delivery of legal technical assistance projects in real and meaningful ways. As one Latvian participant put it, the LLRP was "...the right project, with the right people, at the right time." While this combination of right time, right place and right people may be rare, funding for projects of this kind around the world is likely to continue. As such, the three-tier model presented in this book can be used to guide project design and delivery and to detail the empirical exploration of successes and failures. Through a more inclusive academic approach to international legal technical assistance, quantified measures can be combined with the narratives of those who worked on these projects. These interactions can shape specific policy outcomes and should inform how cross-national learning can guide future international justice reform and democratic development. While the value and applicability of the Latvian model should not be presumed, neither should the lessons learned there be ignored. If human rights, rehabilitation, and social inclusion are indeed the basis for democracy, then the Latvian experience can tell us something. As described on the SPS website:

> The creation of the State Probation Service is the proof that the sentencing system in our country does not have retaliation characteristics, that the offender is not lost for the society, and that the state takes responsibility for the members of its society.

Appendix A: Participants Interviewed and Specialists Consulted

Mr. A. Aksenoks, Former Latvian Minister of Justice, Riga, Latvia
Ms. L. Alexander, Justice Institute of British Columbia, New Westminster, NB
Dr. C. Alkon, Appalachian School of Law, Grundy, VA
Ms. I. Audescone, Prosecutor, Cesis, Latvia
Dr. S. Asquith, University of Glasgow, Glasgow, UK
Mr. J. Bams, Tukums Police, Tukums, Latvia
Dr. M. C. Bassiouni, International Human Rights Law Institute, Chicago, IL
Dr. S. Bell, Saint Mary's University, Halifax, NS
Mr. E. Bergman, Project Officer, VBTAC, Riga, Latvia
Mr. A. Berzins, Former Crown Prosecutor, Ottawa, ON
Mr. J. Botero, World Justice Project, ABA, Washington DC
Ms. I. Brieze, United Nations Development Program, Riga, Latvia
Ms. I. Briteniece, Training Coordinator, SPS, Saldus, Latvia
Dr. N. Brown, George Washington University, Washington, DC
Dr. R. Canton, University of Durham, UK
Ms. L. Castets-Poupart, International Development Research Council, Ottawa, ON
Dr. M. Conley, Acadia University, Wolfville, NS
Dr. R Corrado, Simon Fraser University, Burnaby, BC
Dr. J. Crystal, Auburn University, Montgomery, AL
Mr. Y. Dandurand, University of the Fraser Valley, Abbotsford, BC
Mr. A. Dementievs, Director, SPS, Riga, Latvia
Dr. P. Dutkiewicz, Carleton University, Ottawa, ON
Ms. V. Dzarkane, Latvian Anti-Corruption Bureau, Riga, Latvia
Dr. L. Elliott, Simon Fraser University, Burnaby, BC
Dr. C. Griffiths, Simon Fraser University, Burnaby, BC
Dr. J. Harding, University of Hertfordshire, Hertfordshire, UK
Dr. J. Hermida, Dalhousie University, Halifax, NS
Mr. R. Jabber, Penal Reform International, Amman, Jordan
Ms. J. Jordan, Probation Officer, Ottawa ON
Ms. M. Joubert, Manitoba Department of Justice, Winnipeg, MN
Mr. I. Jurevicius, Probation Manager, SPS, Riga Latvia
Ms. E. Jurkane, Prosecutor, Riga, Latvia
Ms. A. Kamenska, Project Officer, Soros Foundation, Riga, Latvia

Mr. M. Kersten, London School of Economics, London, UK
Mr. K. Koberidze, Deputy Minister for Penal Reform, Tbilisi, Georgia
Ms. I. Kronberga, Deputy Director, Prison Administration, Riga, Latvia
Mr. G. Kutris, Deputy Minster of Justice, Riga, Latvia
Mr. I. Lankshear, Justice Reform Project Manager, Monmouth, UK
Dr. M. Los, University of Ottawa, Ottawa, ON
Mr. R. Lutes, Crown Prosecutor (retired), Wolfville, NS,
Ms. J. Lutes, Restorative Justice Specialist, Wolfville, NS
Ms. B. Maculska, Translator, Riga, Latvia
Mr. W. Madhoun, International Development Specialist, Ottawa, ON
Ms. L. Maloney, John Howard Society, Winnipeg, MN
Ms. M. Marley, President, YWCA, Vancouver, BC
Dr. B. Mikkelsen, Development Specialist, Lyngby, Denmark
Dr. M. Nellis, University of Strathclyde, Glasgow, UK
Ms. M. Nikoula, Canadian Bureau of International Education, Ottawa, ON
Ms. P. Ochandarena, Director of Evaluation, Chemonics, Washington, DC
Ms. G. Ozolina, Youth Worker, Cesis, Latvia
Mr. D. Perry, Director, PointFive Consulting, Cumbria, UK
Ms. I. Purite, Probation Officer, Riga, Latvia
Ms. A. Reinfelde, VBTAC, Riga, Latvia
Ms. A. Revina, Probation Officer, SPS, Tukums, Latvia
Dr. S. Reza, New York Law School, New York, NY
Ms. T. Sanford-Ammar, Agri-team Canada, Kiev, Ukraine
Ms. V. Simanis, Project Manager, Correctional Services Canada, Ottawa, ON
Ms. I. Spure, Deputy Director, Prison Administration, Riga, Latvia
Ms. G. Steeds, Probation Officer, Ottawa, ON
Ms. S. Svike, Education Program Specialist, Cesis Juvenile Prison, Latvia
Mr. D. Taylor, Probation Manager (Retired), Ottawa, ON
Ms. K. Thompson, National Center for State Courts, Washington, DC
Ms. D. Valerio, Justice Reform Project Manager, Brussels, Belgium
Ms. M. Viatere, Probation Officer, SPS, Valmiera, Latvia
Mr. V. Zahars, Former Director Prison Administration, Riga, Latvia
Mr. J. Zardins, Probation Officer, SPS, Cesis, Latvia
Mr. K. Zehr, Project DARE, South River, ON
Ms. L. Zeibote, Deputy Director, SPS, Riga, Latvia
Ms. I. Zuchova, Deputy Director, SPS, Riga, Latvia
Mr. A. Zutin, Probation Officer, SPS, Rezekne, Latvia
Mr. R. Zvantijas, Director of Riga City Mission, Riga, Latvia

Index

M

R

S

T

U